The Douglas AD Skyraider

LAUNCH A SKYRAIDER!

WHERE IS THE ENEMY,
Admiral wants to see!
What will the order be?
'Launch a Skyraider!'

Deck pitching out of sight,
Seahawks are sitting tight,
Venoms won't fly tonight;
'Launch a Skyraider!'

Oft comes the plaintive wail,
'How can we get the mail?'
Press on through ice and hail –
'Launch a Skyraider!'

Ship gets herself a clout –
how will they sort it out?
You bet your life they'll shout
'Launch a Skyraider!'

What keeps them on the boil?
Hard work and skilful toil;
Takes a lot of midnight oil to –
'Launch a Skyraider!'

Off when it's foul or fine, pitch-
black or bright sunshine;
Three cheers for 849, when they –
'Launch a Skyraider.'

*(By kind permission of
Lt Cdr P.G.W. Morris, RN,
'D' Flight, HMS Bulwark, 1958)*

Douglas AD
Skyraider

Peter C. Smith

The Crowood Press

First published in 1999 by
The Crowood Press Ltd
Ramsbury, Marlborough
Wiltshire SN8 2HR

British Library Cataloguing-in-Publication Data
A catalogue record for this book is available from
the British Library.

ISBN 1 86126 249 3

Photograph previous page: displaying her unique
'barn door' side-opening, fuselage-mounted dive
brakes, a Skyraider, coded 410 R, tips over into its
dive. US Navy official.

Typefaces used: Goudy (*text*),
Cheltenham (*headings*).

Typeset and designed by
D & N Publishing
Membury Business Park, Lambourn Woodlands
Hungerford, Berkshire.

Printed and bound by Bookcraft, Bath.

Dedication
To the memory of Arthur Pearcy – aviation historian and friend.

Contents

Introduction and Acknowledgements

This is the story of a very famous aircraft, certainly one of the longest serving and best loved of its kind. Like many famous dive bombers, the Douglas AD Skyraider was considered an anachronism by critics who, in an age of screaming jets, could not see beyond its homely features and propeller-driven propulsion. What those critics failed to see, in the Skyraider as well as in other aircraft of its type, was that its inherent accuracy, its ability to loiter over the battlefield and its ease of maintenance,

British Royal Navy, the Vietnamese Air Force, the French *Armée de l'Air*, the US Air Force, and the air forces of Cambodia, Gabon and Chad), but almost from job to job. In addition, the Skyraider earned more than its fair share of nicknames over the years: the 'Dauntless-II', in deference to its famous predecessor from the same stable; the 'Able-Dog' from its first designation – AD; the 'Spad', because it was so old; and, less kindly, ignoring its precision and accuracy, the 'Flying Dump Truck'.

An AD-2 carrying torpedoes, two 500lb bombs and twelve 5in rockets in flight over NATC Patuxent River, MD, in September 1950. National Archives, College Park, MD

made it a priceless asset to the troops on the ground in the grim conflicts of Korea and Vietnam. These factors turned the 'obsolescent' Skyraider from something of a joke and an embarrassment into an all-round fighting machine. The dive bomber eventually won over even the USAF, which had been for so long blind to its merits and scornful of its close support role.

Like all long-serving and multi-role military aircraft, the Skyraider went through a bewildering range of designations, which changed not only from operator to operator (the US Navy, the US Marine Corps, the

Some of the nicknames were complimentary, some derogatory, but almost all, finally, reflected a fondness for this aircraft. Despite seeming always to be out of place, the Skyraider won the hearts of most who flew it, or who depended upon it for their safety. GIs in the cold wastes of the Korean trenches, or in the steamy heat of the South-East Asian jungle, may not have known who their enemy was on the ground, but they knew they could rely on that familiar sound and profile in the sky. Similarly, for downed pilots deep in enemy-held territory, the Skyraider meant

salvation. In the light of the way in which the Skyraider was considered by these people, the critics' views on dive bombers can reasonably be dismissed.

My thanks, as always, go first to the men who actually flew the aircraft. Theirs is the real story and their opinions are the ones that count. They are Admiral Sir John Treacher, KCB; Chuck Mullaney, US Navy, Rtd; Charles R. Shuford, US Navy, Rtd; Lieutenant-Commander L. William Dilts, USN, Rtd; Lieutenant-Commander (P) Percy G.W. Morris, RN, Rtd; Frank C. Kleager, USMC; and Ron McMasters, USN.

I would like to express my gratitude for the outstanding help of Commander Stephen J. Riordan IV, USN, at the Pentagon, whose valuable and unreserved assistance was vital to my research. Similarly, I acknowledge the outstanding backing I received from Mark L. Evans, Historian, at the Naval Aviation History Branch, Naval Historical Center, Washington, DC, for his help, and for making available the Ed Heinemann Skyraider Press Release for my use; H.E. Dosker, Jr, Senior Member, Aviation Board of Inspection and Survey at Patuxent River NAS, Maryland, for many valuable documents concerned with the original testing and evaluation of the XBT2D-1 and AD-1 aircraft; Carol A. Keen, FOIA Co-ordinator, Technical Publishing Team, Naval Air Warfare Center Aircraft Division, Patuxent River, Maryland; the Archivist, US Patent and Trademark Office, Washington, DC; Commander, Naval Air Warfare Center Aircraft Division, Patuxent River, Maryland.

Thanks also to Frank Hudson, historian and friend; Martin Bowman, historian and friend; L'Isc (HC) Pierre Dousset, *Chef du Département*, Gestion des Productions, ECPA, Fort d'Ivry, France; Le Lieutenant-Colonel Aussavy, *Directeur de l'Etablissement Cinématographique et Photographique des Armées*, Fort d'Ivry, France; Kevin R. Smith of Fredericksburg, Virginia, for his photographs; Ray C. Sturtivent for

An AD-6 (BuNo 139838) in flight on 7 October 1955. National Archives, College Park, MD

photographs of the Royal Navy AEWs; Audrey Pearcy, widow of my much-missed good friend and fellow author Arthur, for her many kindnesses and hospitality, and for giving me her permission freely to use Arthur's extensive notes and photographs of the Royal Navy AEWs; Keith Ferris, one of the founders, along with R.G. Smith, of the American Society of Aviation Artists; Ray Wagner and Alex J. Lutz, at the San Diego Aerospace Museum, for permission to use photographs from their collection; Kathleen Kienholz, Archivist, American Academy of Arts and Letters, New York, NY; Molly Lloyd, Society of Illustrators, New York, NY; Patricia McGinnis, for helping me so much during my research in the Douglas Archives at Lakewood, Los Angeles, and for granting me permission to use photographs and quote directly from documents held in the archives there; G.A. Smith, Secretary Naval Home Command, *Victory* Building, HM Naval Base, Portsmouth, for kind help and valued assis-

tance in my research into Royal Navy Skyraiders; Robert C. Mikesh, for his expert advice on the South Vietnamese Air Force Skyraiders, and for his permission to reproduce some of his outstanding photographs; Stewart Lanham, for permission to use his special Vietnamese photograph; Tom A. Brown, US Marine Corps Marine Bombers News, Kingston, Ohio, for his great help in locating veterans and documents; and Alan of Frank Smith Aviation, Newcastle-upon-Tyne, for unfailing and unstilted help in tracking down rare references down the years.

My deepest gratitude is also due to Cliff Banyas, Archives Reference Team, Smithsonian Institute, Washington, DC; Gerard Pahl, Education Director of the Kalamazoo Aviation History Museum, for details and photographs of their Skyraider; Troy R. Snead, Public Affairs Officer, Department of the Navy, Naval Air Station Oceana, Virginia Beach, for details and photographs of their Skyraider; William R. Dooner, of

the McClellan Aviation Museum, California, for details and photographs of their Skyraider; Denise Bollinger, and D. Menard of the United States Air Force Museum Wright-Patterson Air Force Base, Ohio, for details and photographs of their Skyraider, and courtesy during my research visit there; Lynda Spalding and Martin Espen of The Fighter Collection, at the Imperial War Museum, Duxford Airfield, Cambridge, for details of their Skyraider, and permission to photograph it; Bob Turner, Curator, Commander David Hobbs, RN, Assistant Curator, and Jerry Shore, Historian, all of The Fleet Air Arm Museum, Yeovilton, Somerset, for their kind hospitality and for details of their Skyraiders at Yeovilton and Culdrose, and permission to take and use photographs of the aircraft; and Hugh V. Morgan, Beaverscreek, Ohio, for his photographic expertise.

Peter C. Smith
Riseley, Bedford

CHAPTER ONE

Wartime Progression of the Dive Bomber

The early years of the Second World War confirmed fully the faith that the United States Navy in their pre-war policy had placed in the dive bomber as a major weapon of war. In Europe, the Royal Navy's Blackburn Skua dive bomber had achieved the sinking of the first major warship, the cruiser *Königsberg*. Between 1939 and 1941, the Luftwaffe's Junkers Ju. 87, in combination with the Panzers, had defeated nation after nation in lightning campaigns that lasted days and weeks rather than years. When the Pacific War erupted in December 1941, it was the Japanese Aichi D3A 'Val' dive bomber that spearheaded the attacks and made its mark at Pearl Harbor, Port Darwin and in the Indian Ocean. When the fight-back came, it was with the carrier-to-carrier duels of the Battles of the Coral Sea and Midway; here, the standard US Navy dive bomber, the much-loved Douglas SBD

Dauntless, had played the major role. As the war in the Pacific continued, the Curtiss SB2C Helldiver had finally taken over the front-line role of the Dauntless, and the Japanese Navy's Yokosuka D4Y Suisei Comet ('Judy') dive bomber had replaced the Val, but their dive-bombing influence remained paramount.[1]

Combining Roles

On land, the dive bombers were most successful when they worked in close co-operation with the Panzers, while, at sea, the Dauntless and the Val achieved most when working in a team with their torpedo-bomber companions, the Grumman TBD Avenger and the Nakajima B5N Kate, respectively. However, as the war continued, questions began to be asked as

to whether these two hitherto separate, but mutually dependent rôles might be combined in one aircraft.

At first, a proposal to merge the two forms of attack in one aircraft seemed absurd, since the methods were totally contrasting. The dive bomber relied for its absolute superiority over other types of bomber on the surprise and accuracy inherent in a steep dive attack from a great height. The torpedo bomber, on the other hand, made its attacks almost feathering the wave-tops, to ensure a smooth drop, so that its highly sensitive torpedo weapon would run and operate correctly. The combination of both methods was considered essential to sink large warships, and especially battleships.

While an accurate dive-bombing attack might cause significant damage to the wooden decks of American and Japanese

The incomparable Douglas SB Dauntless was from the same stable and designer as the Skyraider. This SBD-5 belongs to the Lone Star Flight Museum, and is still flying today. In 1997, it won the Reserve Grand Champion at Oshkosh. T.J. Zalar, Lone Star Flight Museum, Galveston, Texas

carriers (and even to the armoured decks of British carriers, as in the Stuka attacks on the *Illustrious*, *Formidable* and *Indomitable*), it would rarely sink them outright. (The British *Hermes* and the four Japanese carriers at Midway were exceptions.) Heavy cruisers (the British *Suffolk*, *Dorsetshire* and *Cornwall*, and the Japanese *Mikuma*, for example) proved equally vulnerable, while light cruisers and destroyers (such as the German *Königsberg*, and the British *Southampton*, *Gloucester* and *Fiji*) were easy targets for dive bombers. However, it was discovered early on that the

fate of the *Bismarck*, the *Prince of Wales* and the *Repulse*. The flak suppressing bomb hits of the dive bomber allowed the *coup de grace* underwater hits of the otherwise vulnerable torpedo bomber, and in this way the bulk of the Japanese battleships were eventually dealt with.

If one aircraft could be developed to combine both roles, this would be greatly advantageous in relation to the cramped and restricted workings of the aircraft carrier. Three types of aircraft, as well as dive bombers and torpedo bombers (which often doubled up as scouting aircraft and

the arrival of the *Kamikaze* suicide attackers, which had to be shot down to be stopped, the numbers of fighters carried by American carriers greatly increased. This so reduced their offensive capacity that, by late 1944, many seagoing officers were beginning to protest. The influential fighting Admiral, William 'Bull' Halsey, among others, voiced the opinion that the dive- and torpedo-bomber roles should be combined. His view was that the Grumman Avengers of the fleet should be dumped ashore, and the Curtiss Helldiver should be left to do both jobs.

The Curtiss SB2C Helldiver eventually took over the mantle of the Dauntless, and carried the fight right into the Imperial Japanese Navy's backyard in 1945. It continued to be the main strike aircraft of the US Navy until 1947, when it was superseded by the Skyraider. This SB2C-5 was still active with the Reserve Training Squadron at NAS Glenview, Illinois, in 1948. Emil Buehler Library, Pensacola, Florida

armoured decks of battleships made them almost immune to bombing hits alone. The survival of the British *Warspite* off Crete, and of the American *Nevada* at Pearl Harbor, was evidence of this, as was the fact that it proved so difficult to sink the already badly damaged Japanese *Hiei* at Guadalcanal. The battleships' vulnerability to torpedo attack was clear, though, as shown by events at Taranto, and by the

glide bombers), had to be held on board the typical carrier at the time. Squadrons of defending fighters also had to be embarked, both to protect the bombers during their aggressive strikes against the enemy, and to foil the enemy bombers' attacks against their own ships. The aim was always to achieve the right balance between offensive and defensive aircraft embarked, and priorities often changed. For example, with

Role-Combining Aircraft

Halsey's voice may have been the most famous raised in favour of this revolutionary concept, but it was by no means the first. In Great Britain, in the 1930s, the decision had been made to add the rôle of fighter/interceptor to the existing rôle of the new Blackburn Skua monoplane that was then being designed for the fleet. This decision was more a result of the fact that control of Royal Navy aircraft rested with the RAF, who rather neglected it, than anything else. The Air Ministry was totally opposed to dive bombing, which was contrary to their view of long-range heavy bomber laying waste to civilian targets as the best means of winning all future wars. They resisted the Admiralty's repeated requests for an accurate dive-bombing sight, and a suitable aircraft to carry it, and hoped instead to economize by giving a dual rôle to the Skua.

The Royal Navy stressed, both at the time of design and afterwards, that the main rôle of the Skua was dive bombing, but wartime and post-war pundits have repeatedly judged it solely as a fighter. Although it proved very good at dive bombing, its inadequate powerplant meant that it was generally a failure as a fighter[2], and it therefore went into early retirement. As a result, this early experiment in combining rôles was seen as unsuccessful.

There was a similar situation in the US, when the P-51 Mustang fighter was rejected early by the USAAF, because of a disappointing engine that failed to provide sufficient performance at high levels. However, this situation was turned to his advantage by the aircraft's designer, J.H. 'Dutch' Kindelberger, who fitted it with the dive brakes of the Vultee Vengeance and thus created a highly effective dive bomber. Designated the A-36 Apache, it could also act as a fighter and a high-speed reconnaissance aircraft, and was used in these rôles in combat by both the USAAF and the RAF in the Mediterranean Theatre[3]. In this case, opportunistic motives led to a successful combination of rôles, even if the resultant aircraft was subsequently not fully exploited.

For various reasons, other aircraft were adopted in combined rôles, including dive-bombing. The obsolete British naval biplane torpedo bomber types, the Fairey TSR Swordfish and Albacore, had always combined their bomber rôle with that of reconnaissance. Both types were also used as dive bombers, with scant success. The Fairey Barracuda was another design that promised much as a dive bomber but was badly delayed and, finally, proved inadequate. By 1940, the RAF had summarily abandoned the excellent Hawker Henley monoplane dive bomber. When the bankruptcy of their pre-war policies became apparent in the aftermath of Dunkirk,[4] they found themselves using the Westland Lysander artillery spotter and the obsolete

Gloster Gauntlet and Hawker Hector biplanes as makeshift dive bombers.

New Requirements

These examples of dive-bomber use, although an important part of the story, resulted from decisions that were made 'on the hoof', either because of a lack of interest, lack of funds or vital wartime necessity. On the other hand, the US Navy's policy of adding to the rôle of the dive bomber, so that it gradually evolved into the attack bomber, was the result of a more thorough and detailed series of studies that took place during the war years.

The US Navy's Bureau of Aeronautics had paid much attention to the further development of the dive bomber. Basing their decisions on the European war experience (mainly on the British), they introduced 'advances' to the designs that were already under way for the next generation. The dive bombers in production in the USA at the outbreak of the Pacific War were the Curtiss SB2C Helldiver, the Brewster SB2A Buccaneer and the Vultee V-72 Vengeance. Of these, the Helldiver was for the US Navy, with additional urgent orders coming in from the British Royal Navy and the Royal Canadian Navy; the Buccaneer was for the US Navy, but there was also much foreign interest, from the British Royal Air Force (who knew it as the Bermuda), the French *Armée de l'Air* and the Royal Dutch Air Force; the Vengeance was originally a French *Armée de l'Air* order, had been hastily taken over by the British for the Royal Air Force on the fall of

France, and also attracted the attention of the USAAF.[5]

The lessons of air fighting over Europe called for the introduction in all these dive-bomber types of what were considered to be the latest essential features: integral bomb bays instead of externally slung bombs, for greater aerodynamic performance; self-sealing fuel tanks; fully automatic, power-operated gun turrets for defence; fitting of airborne radar sets, which involved an electronics change from the 12-volt to 24-volt system; a change in the offensive gunnery, from machine guns to 20mm cannon; heavy armour protection for the aircrew; and much larger bomb and other ordnance capacity. The last two features increased weights enormously, and a much more powerful engine was therefore required, if the aircraft was to achieve the increased speeds that were now deemed necessary for survival.

These new requirements complicated a design, construction and supply situation that had already been made more complex by the sudden entry of the US into the war. The ever-increasing and ever-changing demands of the contractors always impinged on production lines and designers. The relentless logic of the Mtow[6] formula meant that additions in one area – such as armament, ordnance, speed, range – could only be achieved by concession in another area. The setting up of production lines, which was already complicated by the need to train up tens of thousands of fresh staff and by a shortage of machinery, was hampered by these changes. The varying needs of customers meant that each was ordering aircraft that were very different from the basic dive bomber: the Army Air Force's

The main rival to the Douglas designs was the Martin AM-1 Mauler. A big and powerful strike dive bomber, it was equal to the early Skyraider in terms of the hardware it could tote, as is clear from this 1947 photograph. Eventually, only about 100 were completed; they saw limited post-war service in the US Fleet before being phased out. US Navy official photograph

requirements were not the same as the Navy's, for example, and the various foreign orders were different again. The management was not always equal to the diverse demands made upon it. Eventually, urgent necessity led to the Bureau breaking a cardinal rule, and ordering aircraft straight from the drawing board, before any flight testing had taken place. Predictably, chaos and delay resulted. The Bureau's faith in the integrity of these companies to deliver, despite the rapidly changing specifications and requirements, was to prove a dangerous, if necessary, precedent.[7]

Dive Bombers to Carry Torpedoes

It was the initial shortage of torpedo bombers that first led, in 1942, to the question of dive bombers performing the rôle of both torpedo bomber and dive bomber. The US Navy had 100 semi-obsolete Douglas TBD Devastators on strength at the time of Pearl Harbor; its production had ceased a year earlier. Two replacement designs – the Grumman-built TBF Avenger and the Chance-Vought TBU Sea Wolf – were in hand. Both designs originated in 1939, but, in 1940, the Navy had gone for the Avenger, which appeared to

offer the best package and performance, having a higher speed, longer range and lighter weight than its competitor. This decision was based on the two experimental aircraft, the XBTF-1 and the XBTU-1. However, by 1942, when the situation was clearly desperate – the Devastator's limitations had been cruelly exposed at the Battle of Midway, when it was massacred for no result – it became clear that the Avenger's potential was not to become reality. The Avenger losses were equally dire, but more importantly even than that unpalatable fact, the production aircraft proved to be 1,000lb heavier than predicted. Grumman was forced to modify the aircraft by moving the engine forward 1ft, in order to restore stability.

The need to get torpedo bombers urgently to the fleet led to the resurrection of the Chance-Vought TBU concept. The Navy placed orders, but Chance-Vought was fully committed to producing the new F4U Corsair fighter, and had no spare capacity to reintroduce the Sea Wolf to its production lines. Instead, the aircraft was sub-contracted to Vultee, as the TBY-1. However, that company was also experiencing dire problems with its V-72 dive bombers, due to the enormous growth in RAF, RAAF, Indian, South African and US Army Air Force orders, and could not cope.

The Bureau cast about desperately for a short-term remedy; a possible solution was offered in the idea of making the SBD Dauntless into an interim torpedo bomber.[8] Douglas was one company that was not experiencing difficulties in expanding its already well-automated production facilities. Despite many modifications being made to the SBD, Douglas was managing to produce the aircraft at a steadily increasing rate.

BuAer initiated an urgent study into the problems involved in asking the Dauntless to carry torpedoes, which, according to Parsons, '... reflected both our desperate shortage of torpedo planes and the growing conviction that all dive bombers should be able to carry torpedoes.'[9] Although there is little mention of the fact in Ed Heinemann's memoirs,[10] this aspect of the SBD was studied carefully. Heinemann became a member of an advisory board, at the Navy Torpedo Test Centre, China Lake, and got to know this weapon, which was new to him. Impetus for change also came from the USAAF, which was flying its own version of the SBD in combat as the Douglas A-24 Banshee. Losses had been suffered in the Dutch East Indies, and the biggest gripe Army pilots had with the aircraft was that it was too slow to survive. The Army actively considered asking

Curtiss was also in the field for a new Navy dive bomber, with an improved and modified replacement for the Helldiver. The Curtiss XBT2C carried a special radar compartment in the rear fuselage, and was far ahead of its time. This is one of several prototypes that were tested but, finally, the model was never ordered into production. Stanley I. Vaughn Archive

Douglas for a single-seater version of the Banshee, which tied in with the Navy's torpedo-bomber role, and addressed the aircraft's overweight problem.

It was soon established that, although the faithful little Dauntless could carry a standard US Navy aerial torpedo all right, on a special attachment under the central fuselage, a similarly laden SBD would be unable to take off from a carrier deck with a full, or adequate, fuel load. There was too much weight involved and the Bureau's Lieutenant-Commander J.N. Murphy stated that the special permanent torpedo fixture necessary for the SBD to carry the torpedo weighed some 35lb, which would prove an unacceptable penalty on its primary rôle of dive bomber.

Making the Dauntless into a single-seater might have helped both services, but the Douglas production line was rolling satisfactorily, and any modification might jeopardize this. Problems with the Helldiver and the Buccaneer meant that the life of the Dauntless was being constantly extended, and the Navy could not afford to risk the steady production of its only dive bomber at that stage of the war. The alternative put forward by BuAer was for a more powerful engine to be fitted, to improve take-off ability. However, all such proposals were overtaken by the fact that the Grumman company finally got the Avenger into quantity production, and the immediate problem was thus eased. None the less, the concept of combining both dive- and torpedo-bombing roles had been given an airing, and it would not go away.

As far as Douglas was concerned, the question of a combined dive- and torpedo-bomber came up again in the summer of 1943. At that point, Captain Leslie C. Stevens, the head of the Research and Development Division of the Bureau, returned from the Pacific combat zone with a similar request. Following a discussion at San Diego between Heinemann and his design team, a preliminary order for two prototypes followed that same October. This became the XTB2D-1 Skypirate. It featured a powerful Pratt & Whitney R-4360 engine developing 3,000bhp at take-off, and had a speed of some 300 knots. The powerplant was necessary, for the Skypirate weighed in at 18,000lb; to lift the machine, along with its 2,000lb torpedo, off a carrier deck, it was fitted with an eight-bladed Curtiss Electra counter-rotating propeller and full-span flaps. (During trials in 1945 the XTB2D-1 encountered problems with the propeller controls and, with the unexpectedly early termination of the war, the project was cancelled.)

Meanwhile, the Curtiss SB2C Helldiver was undergoing extensive testing to enable it to carry a torpedo. Curtiss made special adapters for this function and this proved satisfactory after prolonged tests, but the changeover time from dive-bomber to torpedo-carrying configuration was unacceptably long. Finally, Curtiss came up with a remedy by modifying the bomb bay. This meant that the Helldiver could carry a 2,000lb bomb internally, or a torpedo externally, the only necessary modification being the removal of the bomb-bay doors. Again, by the time this solution was achieved, events had moved on; and dive-bomber pilots were less than receptive to the suggestion that they should be part-time torpedo bomber pilots, regarding the latter task as near suicidal![11]

New Techniques

The basic attack mode of the US Navy torpedo bombers had changed during the months of combat. Even before the war, as early as November 1941, Lieutenant J.E. Clarke, the commanding officer of VT-3, had been experimenting with a new technique, which lent itself more readily to the dive-bomber pilot's mode of combat.

Lieutenant Clarke's method, practised and perfected by his unit, abandoned the traditional long, wave-top approach, which, in the face of defending fighters and the increasing numbers of long-range and short-range automatic anti-aircraft guns carried by modern warships, was indeed a hazardous undertaking. Instead, VT-3 introduced a high-altitude approach, which, upon the sighting of the target, changed to a dive approach, followed by a levelling off close to the target, and then the drop. This reduced the approach time by half. Other advantages listed by Clarke were as follows: a much better overview for the torpedo bomber pilots of the evasive manoeuvring of their targets; the extra altitude during the dangerous approach, and the speed involved in the dive to sea level gave much better protection against anti-aircraft fire; in addition, the same defending fighters could protect both the dive bombers and the torpedo bombers during the initial approach, as both would be at a similar altitude.

The US Navy standard airborne torpedo was notoriously unreliable and this fact alone delayed the adoption of Clarke's new technique. With the standard low-level approach, failure rates were enormous, and the dive attack seemed too much for such a temperamental piece of ordnance. However, once improved aerial torpedoes had been developed and perfected, it was deemed appropriate to look at Clarke's method afresh. This decision was hastened by the combined-rôle debate.

The vulnerability and inaccuracy of the horizontal heavy bomber, graphically illustrated by events in Europe, had shattered the pre-war boast that it was possible to 'drop a bomb in a pickle barrel'. This was reinforced for the Americans in the early months of the Pacific War, when the USAAF B-17s had made claim after claim of direct hits on Japanese warships; 100 per cent turned out to be illusory! The USAAF made seven high-level attacks on the Japanese fleet off Midway and failed to score a single hit, and similar attacks off the Philippines and the Dutch East Indies were just as futile. In Europe, the RAF spent months trying to hit the static and stationary German battle-cruisers *Scharnhorst* and *Gneisenau*, which were in dock at Brest, within easy range; they achieved very little, and, indeed, the only real success was scored by a torpedo bomber.

The US Navy, although continuing to fit its aircraft with the Norden bomb sight for possible attacks against land targets, effectively abandoned high-level bombing altogether as useless against ships at sea. Instead, it adopted glide bombing as a much more realistic alternative where dive bombing was not possible. Thus, the Grumman Avenger was used as much in this rôle, by the US Marine Corps as well as the Navy, as in the rôle of torpedo bomber. The British adopted the same policy, using the Barracuda in the glide-bombing rôle against the *Tirpitz*, and again with British Pacific Fleet in 1944–5.

Scouting

As the merger of types was being considered, the rôle of the scout (VSB) came into the equation. US Navy policy was to send out armed SBDs from the Scout Squadrons, each plane tasked to search an allocated sector at a given range, in order to locate the enemy fleet. The SBDs would

A different approach to the dive-bomber concept was the Boeing XF8B-1, which was powered by the 3,000hp Pratt and Whitney Major engine, driving a six-bladed contra-rotating propeller. This gave it an unprecedented top speed for a dive bomber of 432mph (695km/h) during test flights in 1944. It featured an internal bomb bay with a capacity of 1,600lb, with as much ordnance weight again carried under the wings. Despite this, it never went into production. US Navy official photograph

The Kaiser Fleetwing XBTK-1 was a clean, lightweight dive-bomber design, with the Pratt and Whitney R-2800 engine. It was conceived for operations to provide direct close air support to landing forces in the Pacific Campaign from the small 'Jeep' (Escort) carriers, which could not handle the larger dive-bomber types. The abrupt termination of the war in 1945 ended the immediate need for such an aircraft and it never got beyond the prototype stage. This is BuNo 44313, the first such aircraft, at the Patuxent River Naval Air Test Center in August 1945. US Navy official photograph

report the speed, composition and bearing of that enemy, and stay in touch with their home carriers, which would be standing by to launch their main air strikes. There was an inevitable time-lag. Later, armed scouting would enable the aircraft that sighted the enemy actually to deliver preliminary strikes. However, as these were often single-plane attacks, they were never decisive, and often merely served to put the enemy on the alert.

The Americans were always at a disadvantage in long-range scouting, and would remain so throughout the war. The Japanese used float planes launched from the battleships and heavy cruisers for this rôle, and they had much greater range. They also used seaplanes operated from seaplane tenders in the early years. It was almost invariably the case in the carrier-to-carrier battles of the Pacific that the Japanese found the American fleets well before the Americans found the Japanese. The Japanese method also had the added advantage that the main carrier deckloads of bombers could be retained exclusively for hitting the enemy, rather than being wasted in searches. There were hopes that the arrival of airborne radar would reduce the number of aircraft needed for searches, but adding radar sets (and a second crew member for their operation) to aircraft increased weight and, therefore, slowed the aircraft down and made deck take-offs more difficult.

All these factors were being studied as war approached. On 15 December 1941, a week after Pearl Harbor had moved the issue from the academic to the essential, Lieutenant-Commander Murphy, head of VSB design at BuAer, put forward his thoughts on the matter in a letter. His premise was that, given the fact that dive bombers would in any case have to be given fighter escort to the target, it was wasteful to put so much effort and time into weighing them down with power-turrets or flexible guns! According to Murphy, doing this had only led to design complexity and delay, and to additional weight problems, and that, even if the concept were perfected, it would not do away with the need for fighter escorts.

Murphy's argument was that, if the scouting rôle were assigned to torpedo bombers, which could retain the second-seat man and guns, then the dive bomber could be transformed into a speedy single-seater aircraft, able to cruise at the same speed as its escorts. In addition, influenced by VT-3's diving torpedo attacks, Murphy argued that such an aircraft could also act as a speedy torpedo dropper. This was already being suggested for the XSB2D-1 and the XSB3C-1 – carrying the standard aerial torpedo would not be very different from carrying a 1,600lb bomb load to the target. Moreover, the inherent strength built into dive bombers (compared with other types) made such a conversion practical. Lee Parsons sums the situation up as follows:

> Thus, in effect, the scout dive bomber (VSB) would become a dive bomber torpedo plane (VBT). The torpedo plane and horizontal bomber (VTB) with scouting added would become a three-purpose airplane, similar in concept to those that the Navy built between 1921 and 1928. For a time the designation of VTSB was considered for this type, but never put into effect.[12]

Murphy's argument was supported by Lieutenant A.B. Metsger, head of VTB design.

His view was that, with regard to strength and range, if both the dive bomber and the torpedo bomber were to use the diving approach to the attack, then both would require a strong aircraft equipped with dive brakes to do both jobs.

New Designs

On 21 and 22 January 1942, a meeting was held by the eighteen members of the Planning and Engineering Divisions of the Bureau of Aeronautics to thrash out these proposals. As it turned out, there was almost total harmony among the assembled group, and Murphy's proposals were accepted in principle. As a first step, Curtiss Aircraft was instructed to develop a single-seater dive bomber, capable of carrying a 1,000lb bomb for 1,600 miles (2,600km), or two 1,600 pounders as a maximum bomb load over a shorter distance, and with a top speed of 390mph (628km/h). Two designs were to be considered, one built around the R-3350 engine developing 2,300hp (the XBTC-1), the other around the R-4360 engine developing 3,000hp (the XBTC-2). A contract for the former was placed in December 1943.

At the same time, Douglas was asked to design a twin-engined horizontal-attack plane, with scouting and torpedo capability. It was to have a maximum speed of 350mph (560km/h), a ceiling of 33,000ft (10,000m) and the ability to tote either two 1,600lb bombs or a torpedo for 1,500 miles (1,370km), and it was to be radar-equipped. However, Ed Heinemann had his own ideas, involving the R-4360 engine, but in a single-engined, two-seater design. The Navy agreed to this and, on 30 June 1942, issued contract No. 88707, for XTB2D-1. Subsequently, design of the twin-engined aircraft was switched to the Grumman organization, and the aircraft became the XTB2F-1. It had two R-2800-22 engines and would eventually weigh 45,000lb, and prove too heavy to operate even from the *Midway* class carriers that were then being built. In addition, few could be embarked, so their strike capacity was small; a larger number of smaller aircraft was far more cost-effective, and the XTB2D-1 (or XTB2F-1) was therefore stillborn.

One dissenting voice at BuAer was that of Lieutenant-Commander J.G. Crommelin. He argued that Murphy's approach did not go far enough, and suggested that the Douglas XTB2D-1 be made into a single-seater aircraft, and that Murphy be sent to Douglas to help make the changes necessary. Instead of going through the normal chain of command, Crommelin went straight to the Assistant Chief of the Bureau, so, although his argument had much merit, it was not taken up, and the two-seater design was pursued. On 4 February 1942, Rear Admiral J.H. Towers, the Bureau's Chief, approved the original programme and the Navy went on to order 358 SB2D-1s from Douglas.

Eventually, Crommelin was to be proved correct, but only after much heartache and loss of valuable time.

Radar

As the Pacific War rolled on, the influence of radar was found to be increasingly important. Rapid detection of incoming Japanese raids negated their early visual sightings of the Americans and, in theory, enabled the defending fighters to get in place in time to intercept the attackers. At first, the system did not work well; 'clutter' on the screens between circling defending planes and incoming hostile contacts confused operators, communications between ships and fighters was poor, and the Japanese dive and torpedo bombers often managed to break through to inflict heavy damage. Gradually, however, the system improved until, by the time of the Battle of the Philippine Sea, hordes of Grumman Hellcats would intercept the incoming Japanese attacks and almost totally wipe them out before they even saw the American fleet.[13] It was clear that, had the American dive bombers been equipped with airborne radar at the Battle of Midway, they would have found the enemy

Although orders were severely cut back at the end of the Second World War, some Martin TBN Mauler dive bombers did see service in the post-war fleet. Here, a formation from VA-9A, commanded by Captain L.G. Traynor, USN, and based aboard the aircraft carrier *Philippine Sea* **(CV-47), is seen in June 1946.** US Naval Historical Centre photograph

carriers earlier, not wasted valuable time searching visually for them and would probably have sunk them more quickly, thus avoiding the loss of *Yorktown* to a counter-strike.[14] Curtiss was therefore instructed to add radar capability to the SB2C.

Intensive testing was already taking place at Newport, Rhode Island, with regard to the torpedo bomber rôle for this aircraft.[15] In the end, however, the dive bomber never did make torpedo attacks, other than in trials and tests, during the Second World War.

Just as the Grumman type met its end, so did the Curtiss types originated by the Murphy idea – the XSB3C-1 at the end of 1942 and the XBTC-1 six months later. This was mainly due to the problems the company was encountering with the SB2C Helldiver. They continued to develop the XBTC-2 in a limited form, but encountered so many difficulties that, at the end of the war, this project, too, was terminated.

In the meantime, what had happened to the Douglas design?

CHAPTER TWO

False Start

The Douglas Destroyer

On 30 June 1941, Douglas at El Segundo was awarded a contract to build two XSB2D-1s. This seemed to be an assurance for Douglas that the success they had achieved with the much-loved SBD Dauntless would be repeated. The startling victories achieved by the Dauntless during that year gave the company a fund of goodwill, and the Navy had great faith in it. The difficulties being encountered by the rival Curtiss and Brewster companies only served to emphasize the smooth running of Douglas.

The Navy was desperate for a replacement dive bomber and eager to give Douglas every assistance. If ever the Helldiver could be got into service, then it seemed certain that the SB2D would, in turn, replace the Helldiver.

That certainty did *not* become reality. Once again, the Mtow factor came into play. When the first SB2D took to the air in April 1943, it was already 1,400lb over the top weight limit, and it took far too long to get airborne – in fact, its take-off distance precluded it from carrier operations altogether!

Specification

The original order was accompanied by a daunting Navy specification. The engine was specified as the 18 cylinder, twin-row, Curtiss-Wright R-3350-14 Cyclone air-cooled radial engine, developing 2,300bhp (1,715K/w) at sea level, and driving a three-bladed Hamilton propeller of 12ft 7in (3.84m) diameter. Ed Heinemann later stated that he considered this power-plant to be excessive for the design with

Flight tested in 1944, the two-seater XSB2D Destroyer was the original Heinemann design built to the Navy's initial requirement for a new dive bomber. Powered by a single Wright R3350-14 engine, which developed 2,300bhp at sea level, it had a top speed of 255 knots. The XSB2D-1 could carry 4,000lb of mixed ordnance in a large internal bomb bay and had two 20mm wing cannon. It featured the tricycle landing gear first tried out by Heinemann with one experimental BT-1 dive bomber in 1938. Changes in the Navy's requirements led to the cancellation of this design, and a re-work as the single-seater XBTD-1. McDonnell Douglas, Long Beach

which he had hoped to proceed from scratch, but Douglas had to go with it.

The armament was to be revolutionary for its time, consisting of a single 20mm cannon in each wing for forward strafing, with 200 rounds per gun carried. For air defence, not one but two flush-mounted turrets were to be carried, in the dorsal and ventral positions aft the rear cockpit, each mounting a pair of 0.50-calibre machine guns. These were to be remotely controlled from the rear cockpit by a new device, the Farrand telescopic-periscope sight.

If these items were not revolutionary (and heavy) enough, the specification continued. The main landing gear was to be of the tricycle configuration with nose wheel and two wing wheels, all retractable. Although some writers have stated that this feature was not previously found on naval aircraft, Heinemann himself had already fully tested such a design with an experimental BT-1 with nose-wheel configuration in the late 1930s; he had not been favourably impressed. None the less, the Navy decided that this was what it wanted.

The required offensive loading potential was also high for the new dive bomber: a maximum ordnance weight of 4,200lb, or two 1,600lb bombs carried in an internal bomb bay, plus two 500lb bombs on underwing racks, or, alternatively, two 2,100lb torpedoes slung externally below the central fuselage. This enormous increase in combat loading was to be achieved by the adoption of laminar-flow aerofoil, and high-lift slotted flaps fitted below the rear edges of the mid-wing sections.

The internal bomb-bay requirement not only made the aircraft more complicated (as Curtiss were finding to their cost with the SB2C), but forced Douglas to enlarge the wing area, so that the main landing gear could fold back into it instead of the fuselage. This, in turn, led to a redesign of the wings with a negative dihedral, the classical 'inverted gull-wing' shape that typified dive bombers such as the Junkers Ju. 87 Stuka and Vultee V-72 Vengeance, and was later to identify the massive Chance-Vought F4U fighter-bomber. The adoption of this feature enabled the undercarriage to be shorter and thus more easily accommodated in the inner-wing section wheel bay into which the wheels hydraulically retracted.

Limitations of Space

As design work proceeded, the Navy hit Douglas with yet another limitation. The XSB2D-1, unlike the SBD, was to feature fully folding wings, the outer sections folding upwards outboard of the centre section. So far so good, but, with the emergency laying down of the two light fleet carriers Saipan (CVL-48) and Wright (CVL-49), another problem was created. These ships were much smaller than the Essex class fleet carriers for which the XSB2D-1 was originally mainly designed. Although they were not, as Heinemann stated, converted from cruisers, but built as carriers from the keel up, the similar Independence class ships were conversions from Cleveland class light cruisers. The problem remained for both types. They were expected to operate the new dive bombers, but their internal hangar decks were very cramped; maximum breadth in the Saipan was 108ft (32.9m), and only 109ft 2in (33.27m) in the Independence, compared with 147ft 6in (44.96m) in the Essex and 136ft (41.45m) in the Midway. Their funnel trunking also encroached on these limited dimensions. The maximum hangar width came down to about 60ft (18.3m), so, in order for two aircraft to be able to be moved past each other, the maximum wing-folded span had to be specified as 26ft (7.92m). This was to cause Heinemann's team more headaches.

The final wingspan came out at 45ft (13.72m), which reduced to 20ft 4in on folding. Total wing area was 375 sq ft (34.8 sq m). Maximum width of the horizontal tail surfaces was 17ft 9.3in (5.42m). The XSB2D-1's other dimensions were an overall length of 38ft 7in (11.87m), and a height of 16ft 11in (5.16m).

Completion and Testing

It took Douglas a long time to assemble an aircraft to meet this challenging specification and it was not until 17 March 1943 that the first XSB2D-1 (Serial 1207, BuNo 03551) was completed. Another three weeks passed before its maiden flight, on 8 April 1943, some 21 months after the initial order had been placed. Much had happened in that interval, but an order for thirteen SB2D-1s (BuNos 04959-04971 inclusive) was made by BuAer on 9 April 1943, in the expectation that the aircraft would come up to scratch.

Flight testing followed and appeared to go well, even if the XSB2D-1 was not an outstanding performer. During tests, a maximum speed of 289 knots at sea level was reached, and 310 knots was achieved at 14,000ft (4,250m). These figures were respectable – with a speed of 346mph (557km/h), the XSB2D-1 was 65mph (105km/h) faster than the best SB2C-1 Helldiver, with double the bomb load of the latter. It carried 223 gallons of fuel in its internal tanks, giving a maximum range of 960 nautical miles at a height of 10,000ft (3,050m), and a maximum endurance at the same height of 5½ hours. Its stall speed for deck landings was 64 knots, which was not bad for such a heavy machine. Climb rate was 11.3 minutes to 20,000ft (6,100m), with a service ceiling of 27,420ft (8,360m).

These figures were initially respectable enough to persuade the Bureau of Aeronautics to place a further production order for 345 SB2D-1s (BuNos 09048-09392 inclusive), on 31 August 1943.

Weight Problems

In appearance, the XSB2D-1 was unique. The inverted gull-wing was mounted midway up the fuselage, while a dorsal fin extended from the main vertical tail surface and ended in a sharp vertical cut-off to allow the dorsal turret guns room to traverse, making for a very different and readily identifiable profile. The broad, flat base of the fuselage reflected the great capacity of the internal bomb bay and these features, coupled with the tricycle undercarriage, made the XSB2D-1 unmistakable.

If looks alone could decide the fate of an aircraft, the new Douglas dive bomber was well set. However, the overriding concern was that the completed XSB2D-1 was too heavy. This was not entirely Douglas's fault but, none the less, weights came out at 12,458lb (5,651kg) in empty condition, 16.273lb (7,381kg) loaded and 19,140lb (8,682kg) maximum weight, which, as Heinemann himself was to confess, 'was about 2,500 pounds over the specs. We were guilty of the sin I had criticized in other organizations.'[16] This weight penalty translated into a take-off distance from a carrier deck in calm water of 644ft (196m), or, with the carrier at 25 knots into wind, 272ft (83m).

Douglas and the BuAer engineers went into a huddle and various formulae were devised to lighten the aircraft. It was estimated, however, that lightening the structural members would involve a complete redesign of the entire aircraft – at least a year's work. The Navy did not have a year to spare. At the time when this analysis was made, the Helldiver was in deep trouble, and it was uncertain whether it would ever enter service at all. Drastic measures were called for. As with the SB2C, the problem item was considered to be the heavy power turret housing the twin remote-controlled guns. The Emerson 'dumbo' gun turret, which weighed 300lb less, was considered as an alternative, but it proved unsatisfactory in other ways, and was dropped.

Murphy, now promoted to Commander, worked closely with Douglas in an effort to improve the aircraft's take-off performance. A revolutionary solution was to drop the remote-controlled after turret altogether, as well as the second seat. Instead, an auxiliary power unit, in the form of the Westinghouse WE-19Xa turbojet, would be fitted on experimental aircraft in the redesigned after part of the fuselage. This would turn the SB2D into a single-seater dive bomber with jet-assisted take-off and a higher top speed, despite the fact that no weight advantage would result. This was the genus of the BTD-2, but, as the Westinghouse jet was still under development, it could only be a long-term solution.

Two XBTD-2s were modified in this way; they became the first US Navy aircraft to be jet-propelled, as well as breaking new ground for the Douglas company itself. These aircraft (BuNos 04962 and 04964) had the jet's fuel tank emplaced in the bomb bay for trials, and the turbojet itself mounted to the rear of the bay. It was fed by an intake atop the fuselage behind the pilot's cockpit and vented at a 10-degree angle ventrally. The Westinghouse developed some 1,500lb (680kg) of thrust. Great results were expected when testing commenced in March 1944 at the Los Angeles Municipal airport, amid high security. The first flight with this addition to the retained radial took place in May 1944. It was anticipated that a boost of 50mph (80km/h) would result, but the turbojet failed to live up to these expectations, and did not work at speeds of about 200mph (322km/h) or more. With the end of the Pacific War, time ran out for this experiment, among others.

If this idea was initially not immediately practicable, it did at least suggest one way out, and, on 7 August 1943, the Bureau instructed Douglas to remove all the flexible guns and the rear seat from the SB2D, resulting in a net weight loss of 1,000lb. These turrets never worked satisfactorily and were also eventually dropped from the SB2C Helldiver, with no ill effects and much simplification of production. The Farrand rear sight and control apparatus again proved complicated and inefficient in practice, and its loss was of no consequence either. After conversion into single-seater BTD-1s, the take-off problem would be solved. This, in essence, was a return to Murphy's original concept of 1941, and also a vindication of Crommelin's arguments. However, two years had been wasted. This idea was adopted at once, but that was not the end of the difficulties.

Conversions

In the mean time, the second prototype (BuNo 03552) was completed, and flew from Mines Field, but official cancellation followed in June 1944. Douglas now concentrated their efforts on the BTD-1, which were to be modified production SB2D-1s. However, the first on the line (BuNo 04959) was too near to completion to be converted, so it became the second SB2D-1 (BuNo 04960). It was ultimately 'made over' into the first BTD-1, being completed on 15 February 1944.

The conversion was a relatively easy job. The turrets were eliminated completely, along with the rear cockpit, and the original square-cut termination of the tailplane's dorsal stub forward was extended to merge with the reduced-length cockpit and fairing of the single-seater. This gave a smooth and pleasing profile, which should have added to stability.

The removal of so much weight, with the abandonment of the two turrets and the rear-seat man, enabled the BDT-1 to increase its built-in fuel capacity, from 223 gallons to 340 gallons. Extra armour protection for the pilot could also be installed without adversely affecting performance. Most of the other features of the XSB2D-1 were retained in the BTD-1; wingspan and overall length remained unchanged, but the overall height was reduced by 4in and wing area slightly reduced by 2 sq ft. Despite all these reductions, weights actually increased! The Destroyer came out at 12,900lb (5,851kg) empty, and 18,140lb (8,228kg) loaded; maximum weight did come down, to 19,000lb (8,619kg). Wing-loading comparisons were 43.4lb/sq ft (211.9kg/sq m) for the XSB2D-1, compared with 48.6lb/sq ft (237.4kg/sq m). Maximum speed at sea level was reduced by 34 knots, and the new test figures came out at 344mph (554km/h) at 16,000ft (4,905m), while the service ceiling was also reduced, to 23,600ft (7,195m).

The new aircraft, which was given the official name of Douglas Destroyer, made its maiden flight on 5 March 1944. Flight testing, which was already being conducted with the XSB2D-1, continued intensively now with both types. The tests revealed a host of other problems. The XSB2D-1 suffered from poor stability for carrier-deck landings, and, when put into the steep dive, encountered severe buffeting with the dive brakes extended. When the first of the converted BTD-1s was put through its paces, these problems were found to have increased rather than diminished.

Redesign and Further Modifications

Once again, the Douglas team went back to the drawing board, and began another drastic re-working of the design. The dihedral of the aircraft's wing was altered, the control surfaces were redesigned, the control mechanisms were modified, and the original dive brakes were replaced by the picket-fence type used on the Vultee V-72 Vengeance and the North American A-36 Apache. A more radical approach was the fitting of fuselage-mounted instead of wing-mounted dive brakes, located at the sides and underneath of the rear centre of the aircraft. These were composed of six segmented fingers, which opened up; while not a success, they were to re-appear in modified form later. Other ideas tried were parachute braking, and the fitting of a reversible propeller, but these, too, fell by the wayside.

Although claiming that these alterations had cracked the worst problems, Douglas proposed yet further modifications. The wing dive brakes would be abandoned for a new design, with spoiler plates attached to the fuselage; the internal bomb bay would be done away with, with yet more weight saving and design simplification; some of the structural members would be redesigned.

By May 1944, the re-vamped BTD-1 was ready for testing again, and arrived at the Patuxent River proving field for extensive trials. The modifications were not to prove to be the solution to the problems, however.

What should have been the new Douglas replacement for the Dauntless was the BTD-1, a single-seat re-working of the XSB2D-1 Destroyer design. This is the final version, on the ramp at El Segundo, California, on 8 December 1943. It featured the inverted gull-wing form and tricycle undercarriage, but the after part of the cockpit was faired into the fuselage and the angle of the fairing was extended. Although orders were placed for this aircraft by the Navy after testing, the contract was cancelled in July 1944, and only a few machines were finally completed, which never saw active service. McDonnell Douglas, Long Beach

Ed Heinemann's memoirs recall the trials:

It was perfectly understandable, if not frustrating, that some pilots favoured one or more aircraft manufacturers over others. In the aviation business, the companies that succeed produce airplanes that become an extension of the company's character. Some flyers lean toward Grumman, others toward Vought, still others toward Douglas. These aviators based their conviction on experience and careful evaluation. I'm not saying that the BTD did not get fair treatment at Patuxent, but we sure weren't winning.[17]

In fact, in re-testing the Destroyer, the Navy test pilots had found '... the same old deficiencies – too long take-off, marginal stability and buffeting – persisted.'[18] This is in sharp contrast to Heinemann's own view, which was that this plane 'had much better flying characteristics than its predecessor'. This view was endorsed by Commander J.A. Thomas from the BuAer Attack design branch.[19]

These continued problems came at a time when the Curtiss SB2C Helldiver

had finally overcome its shortcomings, and was entering the combat squadrons of the fleet in increasing numbers, and proving itself in combat. There was now no longer such an urgent need for a replacement and the disappointing BTD-1 was no longer seen as the long-term solution either. The Bureau of Aeronautics ordered a sharp cut-back in production.

Some 27 BTD-1 Destroyers (BuNos. 04961-04971, 09048-09062 and 04959) were completed between March 1944 and 8 October 1944. (Serial No. 1891, the number originally allocated to the first production SB2D-1, was now written off.) In October 1944, the Navy finally terminated the contract. The aircraft never saw combat and were used mainly as test machines. At least one of them has survived to the present day.

New Players

Commander Murphy was moved from BuAer, and his place was taken by Com-

mander E.E. Fawkes, who had the added advantage of combat experience in the South Pacific. He backed Murphy's ideas, and under his direction the single-seater combined dive- and torpedo-bomber concept continued to be championed. On 5 January 1944, Fawkes' chief assistant, Lieutenant-Commander J.A. Thomas, further defined the basic requirements of the type – a short take-off, a long range, the capacity to carry a heavy bomb load, a high maximum speed, a good diving speed, and fighter performance at sea level.

Other players entered the scene to try to fulfil these requirements, including the Martin Aircraft Company and the Kaiser Cargo Corporation's Fleetwing Division. The Martin XBTM was the prototype for a heavy dive bomber, capable of hauling two 1,000lb bombs and a whole host of other ordnance, slung externally, but with a take-off distance of 400ft (120m). The company was awarded a contract in May 1944; development work continued steadily with no great problems, and the first flight took place on 26 August 1944.

The BTD-1 assembly line in full swing at El Segundo on 1 January 1944. Despite the Navy's orders and the business of this scene, all but a handful of these aircraft had been cancelled six months later. By then, Heinemann had sold the Bureau of Aeronautics on an entirely new concept. McDonnell Douglas, Long Beach

This is a very rare bird! The Douglas BTD was intended to be Heinemann's successor to the faithful SBD Dauntless. It was conceived in June 1941, two prototypes were ordered (as the XSB2D-1), and the first prototype flew on 8 April 1942. The US Navy's new requirement, for it to combine both dive- and torpedo-bombing capabilities, led to it being re-designated as a single-seater, with bomb capacity increased to 1,451kg, the 2,399bhp Wright R-3350-14 Cyclone 18 engine, and dive brakes taken from the Vultee Vengeance, installed above and below the wings. Orders for 358 aircraft followed by August 1943, and production Destroyers (as they were named) began to leave El Segundo in June 1944. A disappointing performance, and, principally, a long take-off requirement, led to the cancellation of the project after only 28 aircraft had been accepted. Many of the Destroyer's best features, however, re-emerged in the AD Skyraider. This particular survivor, photographed at the Florence Air and Missile Museum, South Carolina in 1992, is in fairly good condition. Peter C. Smith via Stanley Vaughn III

The Fleetwing design was for a smaller, lighter dive bomber, the XBK-1, built specifically to operate from the small escort or 'jeep' carriers in support of amphibious landings. Its main parameters were a 1,000lb bomb capacity and a combat radius of 365 miles (587km). A contract was awarded early in March 1944. The aircraft was supposed to be kept as light as possible but when the prototype (BuNo 44313) eventually flew, in April 1945, powered by a Pratt & Whitney R-2800 engine, it came out at a massive 14,850lb (compared with the 10,700lb of the SBD-5 then operating in this rôle). Testing continued at Patuxent River Naval Air Test Ground, but the end of the war led to the cancellation of this project.

A similar fate befell another contender, the Boeing XF8B-1. This machine was powered by a 3,000hp Pratt & Whitney R-4360 fitted with a unique arrangement featuring the six-bladed, contra-rotating propeller. Otherwise, it was orthodox enough, retaining an internal bomb bay for either a pair of 1,600lb bombs or a torpedo, and also two further 1,600lb bombs on underwing racks. It looked the most promising dive bomber of them all from these figures, especially when it achieved excellent speeds of 432mph under test in 1944. However, it, too, was cancelled at the end of hostilities.

Curtiss tried again, with an improved version of the Helldiver – the Model 84G, XSB2C. A single aircraft, BuNo 65286, was made over and completed in February 1945. Powered by the R-2600-20 engine, with a top speed of only 260mph (418km/h), it was a two-seater at a time when such bombers had gone out of vogue. It was thus doomed.

The Martin Mauler was kept in production, albeit at a reduced level, as the AM-1. Eventually, this brute could carry no less than three aerial torpedoes, in addition to twelve underwing bombs and heavy cannon for strafing attacks.

These other aircraft offered serious competition to the Destroyer, and the writing was clearly on the wall. A series of meetings between the various companies was scheduled with the BuAer in Washington, DC in June 1944. It was very clear that the outcome of these conferences would decide not only the future of the Navy's dive-bomber programme, but also the future of Douglas's participation in any such programme once and for all. Ed Heinemann himself thought, rightly or wrongly, that it was 'make-or-break'.

CHAPTER THREE

Last Chance

A New Concept is Born

Even before the testing of the XSB2D had begun, as early as December 1943, Douglas had begun further in-house design studies relating to dive-bomber design. These continued throughout the first six months of the following year, resulting in an accumulated store of fresh facts, data and information. Later, Ed Heinemann was to draw upon this pool of new knowledge, to good and vital effect.

Conference in June 1944

The company representatives were scheduled to meet with BuAer in Washington, DC that summer; Heinemann was acutely aware that the omens for his company were far from good.

The historic meeting was held on 2 June 1944 in the Bureau of Aeronautics office in Washington, DC. Present on behalf of the Douglas team were Ed Heinemann; his assistant Leo Devlin; Gene Root, Aerodynamics; and Reid Bogart, BTD Project Engineer. Representing the Bureau and the Navy was the Chairman, Assistant Chief of the Bureau, Rear Admiral Lawrence B. Richardson, USN; Leslie C. Stevens, Head, Research and Development Division, BuAer; his deputy; Colonel Charles Fiske, US Marine Corps; Captain Paul H. Ramsey from the Patuxent Naval Test Center; Commander J.A. Thomas, USN; Captain Walter S. Diehl, US Navy; William 'Bill' Frisbie, the civilian engineer who headed the Evaluation Branch of the Bureau; Commander David W. Shumway, USN; Commander Emerson Fawkes, USN; and Lieutenant-Commander John A. Ferguson, a test pilot at Patuxent.

In his memoirs, Heinemann related how, the meeting dragged on throughout the day, with differing viewpoints being expressed on the Douglas Destroyer. The Bureau's own notes on the conference indicate that the main items discussed were the Destroyer's deficiency for carrier use, principally owing to its long take-off at heavy gross weight, and the proposed alternative actions to be taken towards improving the aircraft.[20]

The conference did not, however, have any intention of cancelling the BTD-1, and various reasons for maintaining the project were discussed. These were as follows:

1. Service test of tricycle landing gear for carrier use.
2. Service evaluation of the single-seat dive bomber.
3. Service development of the R-3350 engine.
4. Based on the performance characteristics resulting from flight tests that had been done, the Destroyer, with a redesigned fuselage and other detail improvements, showed promise approaching that of designs then being developed for the future.
5. The required improvements, following redesign, might be attained in production ahead of the new designs.
6. Subject to certain improvements in flight-handling characteristics, and subject to satisfactory completion of other remaining flight-test items, the Destroyer was considered satisfactory for land-based operations in its existing configuration.
7. The only absolutely unsatisfactory characteristic was the take-off distance. Other unsatisfactory flight characteristics were subject to immediate remedy or improvement, to the extent that a reappraisal of the general flight characteristics of the aircraft could indicate that certain remaining deficiencies were not disqualifying. (For details of the take-off distance possibilities for the existing aircraft, based on flight tests that had been conducted, see the table below).

So the Destroyer was not totally written off at the 1944 conference. Ed Heinemann recorded, however, that he felt that discussions were going nowhere, and that he determined to take a radical step. For some months, he had been working on a totally different concept, based on the R-2800 engine; now, out of the blue, he announced to Colonel Fiske that he had an idea he would like to put forward. After a break, he was given the opportunity. He told the conference that he wanted Douglas to be permitted to cancel the existing contract for the BTD, and use what remained of the funds available for the project to develop a new dive-bomber concept. He asked for thirty days to prepare the new design.

Admiral Richardson granted him his chance, but only on the conditions that the design should be ready by 0900 the following day, and that it should be based on the R-3350 engine. Hoist by his own petard, Heinemann could only agree and hope that he could carry out his promise, and, also, that he could carry Douglas with him on such a gamble.

In subsequent telephone conversations, Heinemann convinced both company president Donald Douglas and vice-president

The 2-3 June 1944 BuAer Conference – Choices for the BTD-1

Propeller	Size (ft/in)	hp	rpm	Take-off distance (ft)	Combat radius (miles)
Curtiss 4-blade	12ft 8in	2300	2600	536	337
Curtiss 4-blade	12ft 6in	2500	2700	520	337
Aero prop 4-blade	12ft 2in	2500	2800	470	337
Aero prop 4-blade	12ft 2in	2500	2800	398	212 (Less 120-gallon wing tank)

Art Raymond of the rightness of his proposal. He and his team then worked through the night in his room at the Statler Hotel. By 0300 the next morning, 3 June, they had all the necessary figures, calculations and rough drawings to cover the overall specification changes, general arrangements, aerodynamics, performance, weight and strengths. They had them copied and were able to present them to an astonished BuAer team when the meeting re-convened later that morning.

Representing Douglas at this second meeting, held on 3 June 1944, were Heinemann himself, along with a doubtful Reid Bogart. The BuAer team, under Captain Thomas, comprised Captain C.W. Wiener, Captain D.S. Cornwall, Captain J.S. Russell, Captain W.S. Diehl, Commander D.W. Shumway, Commander J.A. Thomas and Lieutenant W.S. Bagby, all of the BuAer. Commander A. Smith, DCNO (Air), Op-31, Commander P.H. Ramsey, Commander C.T. Booth and Lieutenant-Commander J.A. Ferguson represented the Flight Test Section NAS Patuxent River.[21]

The meeting considered Heinemann's plans without comment and, after further discussion, the following alternative actions were agreed:

1. Accept deliveries as per W-10 schedule of airplane in present configuration for shore-based use only, pending necessary improvement for carrier use.
2. Cut back delivery schedule varying amounts up to complete stoppage until necessary design improvements are incorporated for production.
3. Cancel remainder of airplanes on contract and commence engineering work on complete new design.

The definitive cancellation of the BTD-1 project was a serious step to take, for it would leave the Navy's VSB programme in the near future without any possible successor to the SB2C Helldiver series:

The presently indicated tendency not to issue production contracts prior to flight proof of the experimental article will mean longer than normal expected delay in production of the future superior model aircraft.

Obviously, no immediate decision could be taken until the plans and statistics, which had, after all, been hastily cobbled together, had been more carefully analysed and agreed by more senior representatives.

Commander Thomas's memorandum therefore concluded:

Decisions regarding disposition of the BTD-1 project and related matters of production at Douglas El Segundo were withheld, pending a conference in the presence of the Chief of the Bureau and other interested parties.[22]

The agreement reached in that hot office room in Washington, DC simply gave Douglas breathing space – no more – in which to try to prove themselves again. The legend that the Skyraider was designed overnight in a room at the Statler Hotel is a romantic one, which is given credence by constant repetition in books and magazines. In fact, there was a great deal of hard work, sweat and compromise ahead before the new dive bomber would finally be signed, sealed and settled as a viable aircraft.

The go-ahead for the new dive bomber was, therefore, not given immediately. In July 1944, the Navy finally cancelled the contract for the BTD-1 Destroyer.

Demands and Requirements

The original agreed date to produce a mock-up at El Segundo had been 24 July 1944. At the time, this had seemed optimistic, and it quickly proved to be the case. Almost immediately Douglas had to ask BuAer for an extension. This was granted, and a new, rather more realistic date of 14 August was agreed. The Board of Inspection gave this the thumbs-up, insisting at the same time on a few minor alterations.

On 14 August 1944, following the inspection and approval of the XBT2D-1, the Navy formally approved the provision of 15 prototype and service trials, using the balance of the funds that remained from the aborted XSB2D programme. Fifteen prototype aircraft (BuNos 09085-09099) were ordered.

As soon as the deal was done, the Navy began to make demands based on further studies of combat experience, threatening to compromise what was already a tight specification and schedule. In almost every instance, the demands resulted in increased weight, thus exacerbating the very problem Douglas was trying to solve. A higher rate of climb and a higher maximum speed were demanded. These factors would depend on the success or otherwise of Heinemann's weight-saving efforts, as well as on the new Wright engine. There were high hopes for

this powerplant, but it was delayed in production, late in reaching the production lines, and, ultimately, proved troublesome in service. A large number of engine cutouts were experienced on all types of aircraft utilizing the model.

More demands were made on the hard-pressed team, including a shorter take-off distance, so that the aircraft might be used on escort carriers; extra armour protection, to deal with the increasing scale of AA firepower being met as the Navy Task Forces closed in on Japan's home islands; extended range, after the appalling losses at the Battle of the Philippine Sea, when aircraft ran out of fuel after strikes at the limit of their endurance. The arrival of the *Kamikaze* led to another new requirement – airborne early warning, radar-equipped aircraft, which would give greater protection than the picket destroyers were able to. All these requirements had somehow to be accommodated, and Douglas did their best.

The Powerplant

The Navy had imposed the Wright R-3350 Cyclone 24 engine as its desired powerplant, so, whatever Ed Heinemann might feel about the model, the new Douglas concept would have to fit around it. The size of the engine to some extent dictated the final layout of the XBT2D-1.

The Wright Cyclone R-3350 was a twin-row, supercharged, air-cooled, 18-cylinder engine, with a displacement of 3,350 cubic in. The hp of the various marks varied from 2,200 to 2,800. The first test run for this monster was in May 1937, and, following its general adoption into the US armed services with the beginning of the Second World War, the R-3350 was progressively developed via several increasingly sophisticated marks to the -26WD. This was thought to be one of the most powerful radial aircraft engines ever built in the United States; only the same company's R-4360 was larger. The R-3350-26WD was certainly the largest model to be used on a single-engined aircraft.

The 2,700hp generated by the R-3350 produced some awesome torque at full power. Among the many legends that grew up around the AD was that the right leg of a Skyraider pilot was twice as large as his left leg, because he was constantly having to stomp down on the right rudder pedal, in order to counteract this effect! In later years, pilots with little else but jet engine

The original Skyraider was to have been fitted with exceptionally large spinners, but these featured on just a couple of experimental aircraft, of which this is one. The idea was subsequently abandoned. San Diego Aerospace Museum

experience came to the Skyraider, and this old story went the rounds once more.

The first big contract for this tough and reliable engine was for the Boeing B-29 Superfortress, and subsequent marks were used to power such famous aircraft as the C-119, the C-121, the P2V Neptune and the P-5 Marlin, as well as the BTD-1 Destroyer, the AD Skyraider and numerous commercial aircraft. Despite its reliability, however, the engine later became known for its unstoppable oil leaks, which left their mark on every Skyraider's underbelly.

First-Hand Observations

The enlightened policy of the US Navy at this time was to encourage its aircraft designers to go to sea, to allow them to appreciate first hand the viewpoint of combat pilots, and to gain a feel for real combat operations. Despite domestic problems, Heinemann agreed to partic-ipate, and, in October 1944, he went aboard the carrier USS Ticonderoga (CV-14) at Pearl Harbor; she sailed to the west-ern Pacific War Zone on 19 October.[23]

Heinemann was soon in a position to draw practical conclusions, which were to influence his design. On 24 October, he witnessed a Helldiver skidding across the deck of the carrier after she had turned sharply, with her pilot '… furiously hand-pumping to maintain hydraulic pressure'.

Heinemann did not forget the incident and the effect of power-operated brakes, and this led to his adoption of a direct hydraulic brake system in the BDT2D-1.

Heinemann made many useful personal observations. He saw, for example, that the tail-wheel axle aperture on Curtiss SB2C Helldivers caused deck problems; at seven-sixteenths of an inch in diameter, it was not large enough.

Serving officers made other points directly to Heinemann, and he duly took them on board. Lieutenant-Commander E.L. Anderson of VB-80 gave 70 degrees as the normal dive angle used in combat, with the dives commencing from 10–12,000ft (3,050–3,660m), bomb release at 2,500ft (760m), and pull-out at under 1,000ft (300m), at which they pulled 5G. He thought the trim tabs should be marked with colours to make their lateral move-ment immediately obvious. Other pilots of the same Helldiver squadron suggested a single white recognition light located atop the fuselage abaft the cockpit, to aid ren-dezvous and form-ups; the concentration of all running lights on a single rheostat; a magnetic compass; and hydraulic brakes. Rear-seat men asked for light chart boards on sturdier mountings, while deck crew asked for the cowling formers to be provid-ed with a securing aperture for deck work-ing. For long-endurance flights a 3½in (9cm) thick backpack was required, for comfort.

The contribution of VB-15, which had been operating from the carrier Essex (CV-9), was also very valuable. From them, Heinemann learned that anti-aircraft fire was intense and much more serious a threat to the dive bomber than enemy fighters. The Essex Helldivers had suffered 25 per cent losses, of which 80 per cent in recent operations were due to anti-aircraft fire. Commander Jim Mini described his Helldivers' dive bombing as being made from heights up to 20,000ft (6,100m), but more normally 14,000ft (4,270m), with a long glide at a speed of 200 knots down a 20 mile (32km) slant range. At 10,000ft, making about 240 knots, the final attack dive was entered; again, it was at 70 degrees.

Mini suggested that the cowl-flap switch should be positioned on the port side of the cockpit. This would allow man-ual opening for engine cooling to be made more easily while on full power settings, leaving the right hand free for the control stick. He also recommended concentra-tion on just one type of attack aircraft – a dive bomber with torpedo dropping poten-tial and the range for scouting.

Another point from the Essex Helldiver men was that one of the aircraft's good points was its forward firing 20mm can-non, highly popular as a strafing instru-ment after the main bombing attack. Faults to be programmed out of any replacement included weak tail-hook hold-downs, which caused frequent cable bounces and, therefore, deck-barrier damage, and a less than reliable hydraulic system. It also emerged that the auto-pilot was difficult to maintain and was therefore very infrequently used in operations.

The contributions from VB-11, working from the carrier *Hornet* (CV-12), were made by Air Officer, Commander Roy Johnson, Commander W.E. Gaillard and the squadron's Executive Officer, Lieutenant E.M. Yoder. This third squadron confirmed the optimum angle for dive bombing to be 70 degrees, with the SB2Cs often pulling 10G, although they were officially restricted to 7G pull-outs. Like the other units, they had observed that he aircraft's inherent longitudinal instability difficulties frequently resulted in skin-wrinkling on the wings. The VB-11 men asked for a light indicator in the gun-sight, to help them identify correct bomb release height point while concentrating on their target.

Admiral A.W. Radford, the task force commander, emphasized to Heinemann the need, above all others, for simplicity, both in the new dive bomber's design and in its support maintenance. Keeping the aircraft flying was the important factor, and needless delay caused by too complex a system cut down on combat missions. Captain Frederick Trapnell of VB-80 came up with two requests: an automatic engine-torque compensator and a spring-type bungee for the rudder system.

Next up for interrogation was VB-19, operating from the carrier *Lexington* (CV-16). The contributions of its acting Commanding Officer, Lieutenant Banker, Executive Officer, Commander Southerland, and the Air Officer, Commander Andy Ahroon were similar to those of the previous units, particularly with regard to the 20mm cannon, and to the location of the cowl-flap switch. For them, the effectiveness of enemy anti-aircraft fire had caused 25 per cent casualties in recent combat, so extra armour protection was also one of their priorities.

Other factors raised by VB-19 were adequate range, 250 miles (400km) being rejected as totally insufficient. This ultimately led to the provision of an extra fuel drop tank in the new aircraft. Smaller points were the relocation of the manual bomb-release switch. They also thought provision for rockets was likely to be essential; subsequently, provision of ample hard points for variable ordnance was to become the most significant feature of the

UNITED STATES PATENT OFFICE

146,221

DESIGN FOR AN AIRPLANE

Edward H. Heinemann and Leo J. Devlin, Los Angeles, Calif., assignors to Douglas Aircraft Company, Inc., Santa Monica, Calif.

Application January 30, 1945, Serial No. 117,675

Term of patent 7 years

(Cl. D71—1)

To all whom it may concern:

Be it known that we, Edward H. Heinemann and Leo J. Devlin, both citizens of the United States and residents of Los Angeles, in the county of Los Angeles and State of California, have invented a new, original, and ornamental Design for an Airplane, of which the following is a specification, reference being had to the accompanying drawings, forming a part thereof.

Figure 1 is a top perspective view of an airplane in flight showing our new design.

Figure 2 is a side elevational view of the subject airplane depicted in Figure 1 with the extended landing gear shown in dotted lines.

Figure 3 is a top plan view of the airplane depicted in Figures 1 and 2.

Figure 4 is a front elevational view of the airplane depicted by Figures 1, 2, and 3 with the landing gear thereof being shown in the extended position by dotted lines.

Figure 5 is a bottom plan view of the airplane in flight.

The characteristic features of our design are shown by means of full lines in the drawings.

We claim:

The ornamental design for an airplane, substantially as shown and described.

EDWARD H. HEINEMANN.
LEO J. DEVLIN.

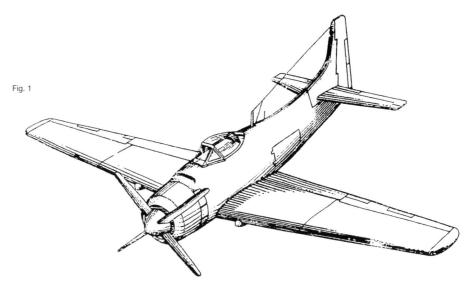

Fig. 1

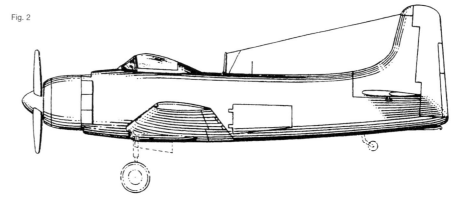

Fig. 2

Fig. 3

Fig. 4

Fig. 5

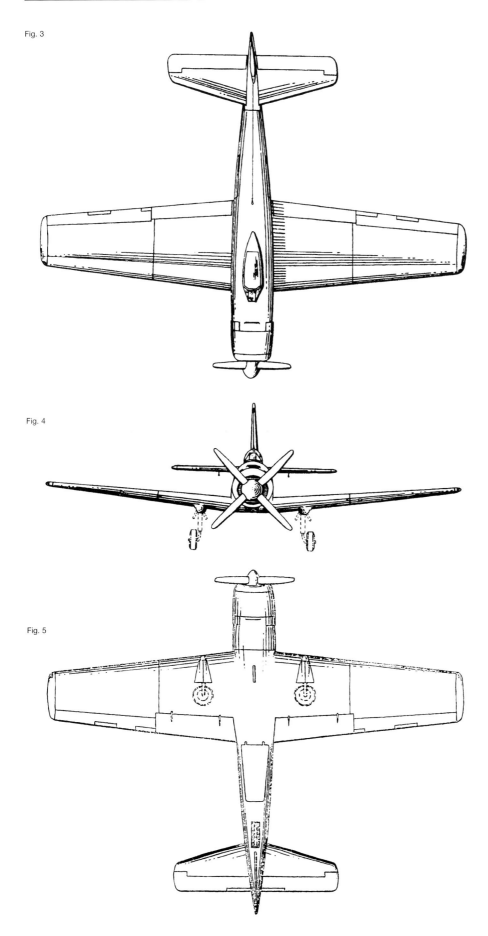

Skyraider. They also asked for accelerometers. However, they warned against too many extra gadgets, which would weigh the aircraft down too much. An increased rate of climb was always a priority.

Visits to shore bases indicated the effect of condensation on aircraft; it became clear that many more drainage holes might alleviate this problem, which was virtually unknown either in the United States or in Europe. Coral dust also led to the need for dust-shield experiments to protect the 20mm guns.

Following the gathering of these practical suggestions, the Navy added further demands following action off the Philippines and Okinawa. In view of what they had come up against there, especially the *Kamikaze* threat, detailed studies were ordered for Douglas to adapt its new dive bomber for other vital rôles, including Airborne Early Warning (to be given a W suffix), Night Attack (N), Electronic Countermeasures (Q), and Photographic (P) variants.

All these lessons and observations were absorbed and taken back to El Segundo for further study and evaluation.

Deadlines and Prototypes

Work continued at high intensity to meet the deadline and the total co-operation of the workforce was enlisted to achieve what was thought by some to be impossible. In March 1945 the team achieved success, with the initial roll-out of the XBT2D-1.

In order to give the already hard-pressed company enough leeway to produce these new types, the Navy authorized that the number of prototype be increased from 15 to 25 (BuNos 09100-09109). This was to result in the prototypes listed in the table on p.26.

At this time, the new dive bomber was provisionally given the name of Dauntless-II.

The next major milestone came on 18 March 1945, when, a fortnight ahead of schedule, the first flight of the XBT2D-1 took place. The aircraft was piloted by Douglas Test Pilot LaVerne Brown. He returned from the hop and reported absolutely no problems or troubles, no drama – just a good, clean flight. It was a wonderful start and this trouble-free initiation continued unabated; over the following three-week period, this aircraft completed no less than 31 successful test flights.

Prototypes and assignments

BuNo	Role	Designation	Powerplant	Notes
09085	Attack	XBT2D-1	R-3359-8	–
09086	Attack	XBT2D-1	R-3350-8	–
09087	Attack	XBT2D-1	R-3350-8	–
09088	Attack	XBT2D-1	R-3350-8	Large spinner
09089	Attack	XBT2D-1	R-3350-24W	–
09090	Attack	XBT2D-1	R-3350-24W	–
09091	Attack	XBT2D-1	R-3350-24W	–
09092	Attack	XBT2D-1	R-3350-24W	–
09093	Attack	XBT2D-1	R-3350-24W	–
09094	Attack	XBT2D-1	R-3350-24W	5in rocket tests
09095	Attack	XBT2D-1	R-3350-24W	–
09096	Photo reconnaissance	XBT2D-1P	R-3350-24W	
09097	Attack	XBT2D-1	R-3350-24W	–
09098	Night attack	XBT2D-1N	R-3350-24W	–
09099	Night attack	XBT2D-1N	R-3350-24W	–
09100	Attack	XBT2D-1	R-3350-24W	–
09101	Attack	XBT2D-1	R-3350-24W	–
09102	Attack	XBT2D-1	R-3350-24W	–
09103	Attack	XBT2D-1	R-3350-24W	–
09104	Attack	XBT2D-1	R-3350-24W	–
09105	Attack	XBT2D-1	R-3350-24W	–
09106	Attack	XBT2D-1	R-3350-24W	–
09107	Early warning	XBT2D-1W	R-3350-24W	XAD-1W
09018	Heavy attack	XBT2D-1	R-3350-26W	XAD-2
09109	ECM	XBT2D-1Q	R-3350-24W	Early warning

Pleased with its achievements, Douglas felt ready for the Navy to give its verdict. On 7 April 1945, the first prototype was duly delivered to the Navy proving ground at Patuxent River. There followed an intensive five-week evaluation programme; this comparatively brief period was something of a record, and was achieved despite various engine problems, which, on one occasion, included even the failure of a master rod.

The Navy's flyers were enthusiastic. Despite Heinemann's earlier doubts as to their bias, there were universally in favour of the new aircraft. Their ratings could be briefly summarized thus:

Flight characteristics – *Very good*
Performance – *Very good*
Wave-off characteristics – *Excellent*
Simplicity of maintenance – *Excellent*
Overall – *The best dive bomber ever tested at
    the centre*

Not everything was perfect, but the alterations called for were minimal. The following changes were recommended:

1. Additional oxygen for the pilot.
2. Additional heating for the pilot.

3. Additional cockpit and after-compartment lighting.

Following the outcome of these first trials, on 5 May 1945, the Navy Department signed a Letter of Intent for Douglas to produce an initial order of 548 BT2D-1 Dauntless-IIs. Heinemann and his team had come up trumps! The order was a fitting reward for an outstanding team effort, and deservedly secured the firm's future.

The End of the War

In June 1945, the first prototypes were accepted into the Navy. However, across the Pacific Ocean, events were unfolding that would thwart any premature expectations of bulging Douglas order books. Most people had expected the war to continue at least into 1946, and probably on to 1947, with the projected invasion of Japan proper. Operation 'Olympic' was being geared up for, and a fanatical and determined resistance by the Japanese of their home islands was expected. However, the dropping of the atomic bombs on the cities of Hiroshima and Nakasaki, the desperate supply position of the Japanese, whose fuel supplies had been cut off by submarine sinkings of their tankers, and the fact that the Soviet Union had ignored its treaty obligations and launched huge land attacks across its Far Eastern borders – all these factors combined to bring about a sudden and unexpected early end to the Pacific War.

On 14 August 1945, the boys started to come home. Welcome as this turn of events was, its effect on military requirements and suppliers was predictable. Almost immediately, the Navy notified Douglas that it was reducing its initial order to 377 aircraft. In a short while, even this requirement went by the board, and the order was further reduced, to a mere 277 aircraft.

The AD-1 and the AD-1Q

With the different priorities of the postwar period there was a slowing down, and the urgency and hard work of Heinemann's team now seemed to have been a wasted effort. It was a time for revaluation and change. As part of that process, in

Early Skyraider XBT2D-1 (BuNo 09109) on the ramp at El Segundo. San Diego Aerospace Museum

February 1946, the Navy announced that the Dauntless-II was to be renamed the BT2D Skyraider. This was another stage in an evolving process; the earlier recommendations and studies finally gelled into acceptance for the combining of the dive- and torpedo-bomber rôles, hastened by the need for economy as much as by war experience. The new designation was 'A' for Attack, in line with the Army Air Force, and thus, in April 1946, the BT2D-1 was redesignated by the Navy Department as the AD-1 and the AD-1Q.

The following month, May 1946, saw a few XBT2D-1s in their new guise beginning intensified service trials at Naval Air Station, Alameda, California, the Pacific Fleet Air Headquarters. The usage was more rugged than at Patuxent River, and this soon showed up the negative as well as the positive aspects of the emphasis on lightness in the Skyraider's design. A whole crop of potentially damaging undercarriage and wing-skin failures were noted.

The first flight of the production model AD-1 Skyraider (c/n 1938, BuNo 09110) took place on 5 November 1946. A further 241 (BuNos 09111-09351) were eventually to follow, with the last being accepted in August 1949. However, the early production aircraft soon showed up faults similar to those seen in the prototypes. Naturally, this caused much consternation. Although the Navy also had the Martin AM-1 Mauler (in very limited production), its hopes had been pinned mainly on the AD-1. Steps to solve these unexpected problems needed to be taken at once.

Three of the test aircraft were fitted out with special instrumentation for detailed tests with Navy pilots at the controls mirroring real-life operations. Analysis of these tests soon showed where the faults lay. In the hands of some pilots it was discovered that the designed landing weight of 14,545lb (6,598kg), and the design limit sinking speed of 14ft/sec (4.27m/sec), were far exceeded in a considerable percentage of the landings. There was only one solution – the AD-1 must be made stronger, hopefully without sacrificing any of its plus points.

Between 1 November 1946 and 8 May 1947, at Patuxent River Naval Air Station, Maryland, there was an investigation of Instrument Flight Techniques and Procedures for Naval Combat Aircraft, to establish standards for use with Ground Control Approach (GCA) using the XBT2D-1.[24A] Veteran dive-bomber pilot Bill Martin was director of the station at the time. The

resultant report stated that, although the testing was conducted throughout with the XBT2D-1 aircraft, it was 'expected that the information contained herein will apply equally to the AD-1 aircraft'.

Some 32 hours of flight testing were involved, including four hours of night flying. From a total of 21 GCA controlled approaches, a number were made under simulated blind-flying conditions, with the pilot under a hood. Pilots with considerable fleet experience in fighters and dive bombers were selected for the project, and the chief project officer was a qualified night-fighter pilot. The main emphasis was placed on noting deficiencies of instrumentation and instrument flight characteristics of the test aircraft.

The XBT2D-1 was provided with a low-frequency range receiver (R-23/ARC-5) and PBX receiver (AN/ARR-23) for radio navigation. VHF-DF, when available to the GCA unit, was found to be the most effective means of directing aircraft into the area of GCA control. The aircraft was found to have no peculiarities requiring any departure from the standard handling pattern by the GCA crew. The recommended approach into GCA control was a speed of 150–160 knots.

The landing cockpit check was given on the down-wind leg one minute prior to the cross leg turn. Speed was gradually reduced after lowering the landing gear and adjusting the power at 2,400rpm and 24in manifold pressure. As the speed decreased below 130 knots, the landing flaps were lowered. It was found that when the attitude of the aircraft was not adjusted simultaneously with the flap lowering, a gain in altitude of 200–300ft (60–90m) resulted. It was deemed advisable to complete the landing cockpit check prior to the cross-wind leg in

order to allow the pilot to devote his attention to flying and executing control directions through the remainder of the approach pattern. Power settings of 2,400rpm and 23in and 26in manifold pressure produced a level flight speed of 100–110 knots with the plane in landing condition. On the cross-wind leg, the pilot concentrated on flying the approach directions accurately and smoothly, and this leg was flown at 1,200ft at 100–110 knots. The standard GCA three-degree glide path was deemed suitable for the XBT2D-1 and the glide path speed of 100 knots with a rate of descent of 540ft/min (145m/min) could be maintained with a power set at 18in to 20in manifold pressure at 2,400rpm. Wave-offs could be safely taken at any time during normal approach. A 500ft/min (150m/min) climb in the landing condition required 26in to 29in manifold pressure at 2,400rpm at airspeed of 100–110 knots.

The addition of a symmetrical loading of 2,000lb of external stores and full machine-gun ammunition was found to have no adverse effect on the instrument flight-handling characteristics of the XBT2D-1. The addition of 3in to 5in manifold pressure over the settings above was sufficient for handling the load, and gave a glide-path speed near 110 knots.

Flying commenced on 1 November 1946 and continued until 8 May 1947. The following conclusions were drawn:

1. That the XBT2D-1 aircraft, with existing instrumentation and handling characteristics, was, 'unsatisfactory for instrument flight, particularly for the instrument flight required for GCA operations'. Except at stalling speeds, aileron control forces were so light that they failed to give the pilot any definite

A. 'landing cockpit check' instructions.
B. landing cockpit check completed – reduce speed to 100 or 110 knots at turn.
C. begin final let down (speed approximately 100 knots)

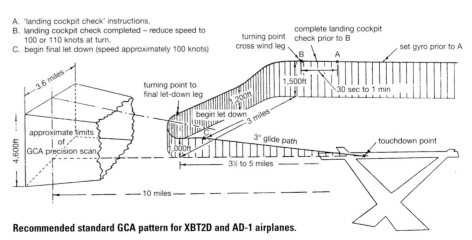

Recommended standard GCA pattern for XBT2D and AD-1 airplanes.

'feel'. The report thought that this deficiency was serious, 'for the plane is extremely sensitive to small aileron movements. The lack of aileron feel makes lateral trimming of the XBT2D-1 a troublesome and continuous task.'

The longitudinal trimming was also found to be 'awkward'. This was accomplished by changing the angle of incidence of the horizontal stabilizer. An electric motor controlled by a three-way switch moved the surface as desired. The trimming motor control was too coarse to permit rapid and accurate trimming of the plane:

During a trimming operation it is necessary to refer constantly to the trim angle indicator, which is poorly located and is not illuminated. At night, pilots were forced to keep a flashlight at hand for illuminating the indicator.

The report felt that the above deficiencies all contributed to pilot fatigue and inefficiency on instrument flights, and that the need for an auto-pilot to be fitted was paramount.

Test flights in the XBT2D-1 proved that effective instrument flying was being hampered by the reverse-pitch presentation of the attitude indicator (R88-I-310) and the small size of the directional gyro (R88-I-1680) or P-3 Master Director Indicator, which had an unusually small dial on which headings could not be read closer than five degrees. 'Since the GCA instrument flight requires flying headings to the nearest degree, this indicator is inadequate for the purpose.'

On the credit side, they stated that the existing instrument panel lighting and instrument arrangement in the XBT2D-1 were 'excellent for instrument flight by day or night'.

2. That the standard GCA pattern (*see* the diagram on page 27) was satisfactory for handling the XBT2D-1.

3. That the deficiencies in the XBT2D-1 instrument flight-handling characteristics would be 'less objectionable if the plane were equipped with an auto-pilot. This device would relieve the burden of routine instrument flying and leave the pilot relatively fresh for the demands of combat, navigation and GCA.'

The conclusion reached was that the XBT2D-1 had undesirable handling characteristics and inadequate instrumentation for instrument flight associated with GCA. It was recommended that the following deficiencies should be corrected:

1. That the standard GCA procedure and pattern described in (b) should be used for the XBT2D-1 aircraft.

2. That instrument deficiencies be remedied thus:
   a) correct inadequate definition of indications of the P-3 Master Director Indicator;
   b) replace attitude indicator R88-I-1310 with an instrument having standard pitch presentation.

3. Improve the instrument-handling characteristics on this aircraft ('particularly the AD-1N version') in the following particulars:

a) steepen aileron control force gradient near the neutral stick position in the cruising speed range (clean condition) and in the approach speed ranges in the landing condition;
b) provide more refinement in control of longitudinal trimming;
c) relocate stabilizer trim angle indicator to main instrument panel, where it can be seen easily by day or night.

4. Furnish operating units with appropriate portions of the report itself.

All the prototypes, along with the first 20 production models that experienced similar problems, were returned to El Segundo for strengthening. Major modifications were made to the fuselage in certain areas, resulting in an increase in weight of 415lb (188kg), to a maximum gross weight of 18,030lb (8,178kg). The modifications continued and over the whole period had the desired effect, resulting in an increased sinking speed, which went from 14ft/sec (4.27m/sec) on the XBT2D-1 to 19ft/sec (5.79m/sec) on the AD-1 and AD-2, to 23ft/sec (7.01m/sec) for the AD-3 and AD-4 and, finally, to 30ft/sec (9.14m/sec) for the AD-5 to AD-7.

The Skyraider now seemed fit for fleet operations and, on 6 December 1946, the first Pacific Fleet squadron, VA-19A, became operational on AD-1 (although still operating from airfields ashore). The next big step in the Spad story was not long delayed, and in June 1947 the first AD units to become carrier-qualified were VA-3B and VA-4B. They undertook their carrier-qualification programme (CARQUALS) in the Pacific, flying aboard the USS *Sicily* (CVE-118), prior to joining their allocated carrier, the brand-new USS *Franklin D. Roosevelt* (CVB-42). The Skyraider was finally afloat.

The second prototype is checked out at the Douglas plant. The Douglas engineer is working on the starboard fuselage dive brake, and this picture gives an indication of the size of this feature. San Diego Aerospace Museum

CHAPTER FOUR

A Stroke of Genius

Development of the Dauntless-II

The Concept

The thinking behind the Dauntless-II, which was later to become the Skyraider, was described at the time by Ed Heinemann in a detailed press release. It is a privilege to be able to understand the designer's thinking and ideas, straight from the horse's mouth, so to speak:[24]

The debut of a new airplane usually results in a shower of inquiries from the aviation public regarding its design arrangement. The BT2D-1 Skyraider was no exception. Immediately after its press release the usual questions were asked. Why no bomb bay? Why fuselage dive brakes, etc?

To start at the beginning, the Skyraider was conceived in June 1944, when it was found necessary to develop a modern single-place, long-range, high-performance dive bomber of much greater striking power as a replacement for the two-place dive bombers then in service that were designed before the war. An earlier model, the Douglas BTD Dive Bomber under development during peace time, first as a two-place, then single-place airplane, was discontinued in favour of the BT2D.

This might be considered a trifle disingenuous, for the bulk of the design period for the BTD actually took place during the war years. However, Heinemann's subsequent comments were certainly most pertinent.

The BTD, like many other peacetime developments, did not contain the many features considered necessary to military requirements as the result of combat experience gained during the first few years of the war.

He listed the new military requirements established for the BT2D as compared with the BTD:

1. Shorter take-off distance.
2. Increased combat radius.
3. Increased rate of climb.
4. Greater load-carrying ability.
5. Greater stability and control.

All of this added up to the fundamental design requirements of more lift and less weight. It had also become obvious from reports, maintenance records and, later, from his own observations at sea with the fleet that the old peacetime-designed aircraft suffered badly due to poor utility and maintenance. For whatever reason, they spent 'too many hours on the ground and not enough in the air'.

The very first off the line. This prototype XBT2D-1 Dauntless-II (BuNo 09085) is seen airborne on early flight tests from El Segundo on 13 June 1945. Note the all-metal finish and the massive hinges on the fuselage dive-brake doors. National Archives, College Park, MD

Heinemann therefore decided that his new and radically different dive bomber would have to show improvements over the ill-fated and apparently doomed BTD. He listed them as the following:

1. Reduce weight from 18,000lb to 16,500lb.
2. Increase maximum lift coefficient from 1.8 to 2.0.
3. Improve utility by reducing fuelling, arming, and maintenance time by 50 per cent.
4. Complete and fly first article in nine months.

How to satisfy all these various requirements occupied the minds of Heinemann and his brilliant team for a number of arduous months. In his discussions with the Bureau of Aeronautics, basing the new design on the elimination of the internal bomb bay and the substitution of a conventional tail wheel in place of the nose wheel of the BTD, an all-up guaranteed weight of 16,500lb (7,490kg) was deemed reasonable. Heinemann deliberately shaved a further 750lb off the target figure and assigned to each engineering group – involved with the design of the wings, fuselage and so on – its 'proportional underweight bogey figure'.

As a result of his own experiences with the BTD, and aware of the problems encountered by Curtiss with the SB2C, which had continually exceeded successive weight limits, despite initial promises, Heinemann was determined to enforce a strict regime on the Douglas team. He later recorded his cardinal rules as follows:

1. No part could be overweight unless an equivalent weight was saved elsewhere.
2. Any indeterminate structure or part that could not be designed to minimum weight requirements would be strength tested rather than add an arbitrary safety factor.

According to Heinemann, 'In other words, the old adage of "A chain is no stronger than its weakest link" was applied and all parts were designed to a uniform positive margin.'

The vital need to reduce weight was emphasized by the putting out of bulletins, which illustrated in the most basic terms just what could be achieved by putting weight reduction above all else. In one example given by Heinemann in his press release, a table stated that, for each 100lb (45kg) of weight saved, the take-off distance from a carrier's deck could be reduced by 8ft (2.43m); this would add an extra 22 nautical miles to the aircraft combat radius. Other advantages given were an increase of 60 statute miles in the aircraft's maximum range; an increase in the sea-level rate of climb of 8ft/min (2.43m/min); and an increase in top speed of about 0.3mph (0.5km/h).

The designers countered with the standard riposte: 'How much additional cost is justified to save a pound in weight?' Heinemann gave them an answer:

A figure of $10·00 per pound was assumed as a reasonable guide, based on tooling for a quantity of 500 airplanes. The assumption proved to be very reasonable for this particular project and, if anything, on the low side. It is now felt a figure of $15.00 or $20.00 per pound might be entirely satisfactory for combat airplanes of this type. The rule would actually vary for other types and in other plants and cannot be applied to all projects.

Although Heinemann was speaking in the mid-1940s, much of this statement was made tongue in cheek, but, importantly, a principle was established. The results were satisfactory for, as he also recorded at that time, the results of this vigorous weight-saving policy were extremely gratifying when the final weighing indicated the weight to be better than 1,000lb (450kg) under the contract guarantee. Thus the normal military bomb load immediately increased and many other items of equipment were able to be added to make the airplane more useful without affecting strength and performance.

Heinemann illustrated these achievements in another table (see below, reproduced here for the first time in its entirety).

Weight savings in BT2D over BTD

Simplified fuel system	270lb
Short carburettor and oil cooler ducts instead of cowl leading-edge type	50lb
Fuselage dive brakes	70lb
3,000 P.S.I. over 1,500 P.S.I. hydraulic system	50lb
Elimination of bomb bay	200lb
Bubble-type cockpit enclosure	40lb
Powder displacing gear instead of mechanical	40lb
Continuous centre wing instead of two-piece	100lb
Continuous horizontal tail instead of two-piece	20lb
Total	**740lb***

In addition there were many indirect savings of secondary structure and equipment.

In an effort to improve the maximum lift, the Douglas design team abandoned the trend at the time – the high-speed 65 series airfoils they had used on the BTD – and went instead for the higher maximum lift section, of the NACA[25] 2400–4400 range.

It soon became apparent that this retrograde step would result in a slight penalty at high speed. Heinemann commented, 'In reality, however, any reduction in maximum velocity due [to] the wing airfoil section amounts to less than gains that were made by improved detail design.' He added, 'It is believed the BT2D lift coefficient of better than 2.0 is attributable to the excellent low-speed flying characteristics which permit realizing the full potentialities of the wing with safety.' (For the overall improvements in lift, see below.)

Summary of lift improvements

Maximum lift coefficient of BTD	nearly 2
Improvement due to change from 65 to 2400–4400 airfoil	nearly .2
Improvement due to improved stability and control	approx. .1
BT2D maximum lift coefficient	better than 2.

Fundamental Simplicity

There was another factor in which the Douglas team took great pride, and which allowed them to make further weight savings. Heinemann termed this 'fundamental simplicity'. He illustrated his point as follows:

By making many layouts and the construction of several mock-ups, an arrangement was finally obtained that permitted carrying all internal fuel in one tank instead of five used in the BTD. This one item alone resulted in reducing the fuel system weight to 270 pounds and at the same time reduced tank replacement time to a small fraction of that of the BTD and SBDs. A single fuel tank, of course, frees the pilot of the responsibility of shifting tanks and according to recent operational statistics will prevent many power failures attributed to tanks running dry. (See the diagram opposite.)

This 'fundamental simplicity' principle extended throughout the entire programme, and Heinemann gave a detailed breakdown (see the table left).

External Bomb Carrying

Heinemann then went on to explain the ordnance lift improvements achieved by abandoning the hitherto sacrosanct internal bomb-bay design. He thus reveals himself to have been well ahead of conventional thinking (indeed, modern combat aircraft today often use underwing ordnance loading).

At the time of the conception of the Skyraider, 1,000lb was considered the normal bomb load. A 2,000lb bomb or torpedo was considered as an alternative or maximum overload. As the result of the Skyraider's underweight, increased lift and improved stability and control at low speed, the normal bomb load is now considered as one 2,000lb bomb or torpedo with a safe alternative overload of 6,000lb, which can be in the form of three 2,000lb bombs, or, if desired, three torpedoes.

He justified his decision fully, claiming that the decision to resort to carrying offensive ordnance externally, instead of in an internal bomb bay, proved 'very desirable'.

The present arrangement of external bomb racks permits carrying bombs, torpedoes and 11in rockets or droppable fuel tanks in most any [sic] combinations,

Extremely simplified fuel system incorporating only one fuel tank for normal load made possible by careful bias considerations of airplane arrangement. Compares with 6 tanks of SBD and 5 of BTD.

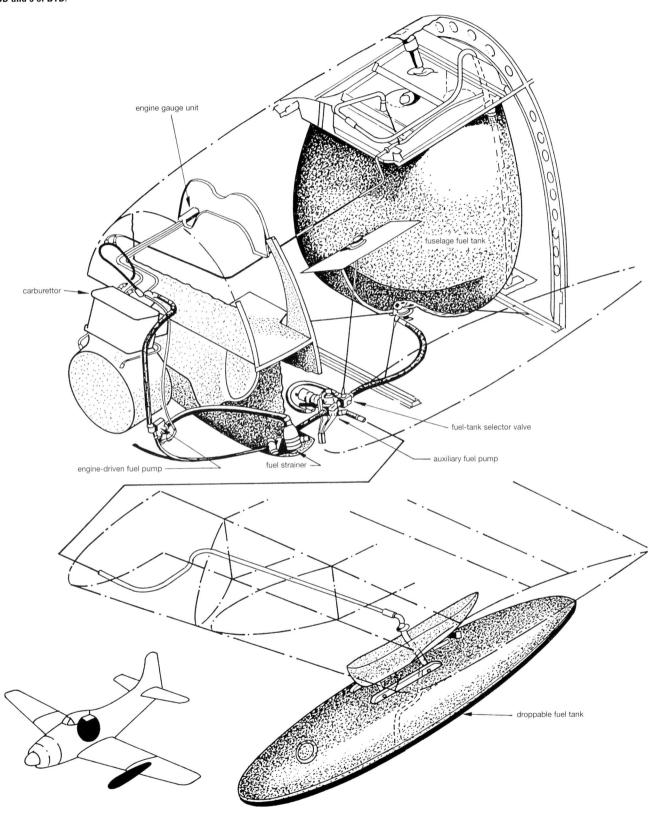

engine gauge unit

fuselage fuel tank

carburettor

fuel-tank selector valve

auxiliary fuel pump

engine-driven fuel pump

fuel strainer

droppable fuel tank

Weight differences in Douglas dive bombers

	SBD	BTD	BT2D
Gross weight (lb)	8,250	18,000	16,500
Airframe weight (lb)	4,387	8,564	6,295
Number of engineering drawings	2,722	5,235	2,381
DIE-FABRICATED PARTS			
Aluminium alloy forgings drawings	59	139	56
Aluminium alloy forging pieces	286	359	56
Steel forging drawings	26	182	82
Steel forging pieces	62	182	82
Aluminium and magnesium sand castings	88	150	67
Aluminium and magnesium sand casting pieces	117	189	74
FUEL SYSTEM			
Number of tanks (bullet-proof)	6	5	1
Tank removal time (man hours)	144	72	2
Fuel system weight (lb/gal)	2.45	1.73	0.93
Filling time (minutes per man)	12	13	5
OIL SYSTEM			
Number of radiators	1	2	1
Length of oil lines (ft)	7	10	5
Oil system weight (lb per gal)	8.64	7.55	4.39
POWERPLANT			
Weight of engine mount and cowling forward of fire wall (lb per hp)	0.154	0.178	0.119
	(1,300hp)	(2,500hp)	(2,500hp)

therefore greatly improving the flexibility and utility of the airplane. In addition to the three main bomb racks, rocket launchers are provided on the outer wings for twelve 5in rockets which further add to the usefulness of the airplane as an attack type for strafing and fighting missions.

It was widely understood that these arguments carried little weight in some circles at the time, and Heinemann knew that there were still many advocates of bomb bays instead of external loading. He was also prepared to admit that, for many types, bomb bays were still the more desirable option. He recorded the following justification, however:

In the case of the Skyraider ... the combat radius would have been no greater with internal bombs assuming bombs are dropped when over the target. A bomb bay would have given slightly greater speed in approaching the target, but the present arrangement without a bomb bay is faster after bombs are dropped, when speed is considered most important.

The German Junkers Ju. 87 Stuka was the classic example of the success of carrying ordnance externally. Progressively developed throughout its long active combat career, this dive bomber proved itself the best ground-attack aircraft of all the European aircraft designed for this rôle, despite a lack of speed. A very strong aircraft, it was designed with external weapon loading, which increased as the years went by, until it was able to carry bombs large enough to sink old battleships. With a redesigned wing, and the addition of underwing slung cannon, it was turned into an ace tank-destroyer. The Skyraider took such wartime developments several stages further.[26]

Aircrew Comfort

Heinemann's fundamental philosophy was also applied to aircrew comfort, which had never been a significant factor with most manufacturers. According to the designer, 'The lack of combat experience during peace time had the bad effect of causing all concerned to take for granted the many inconveniences of military equipment.' Reports came back to Douglas from the Pacific Combat Zone, where long and tiring overwater flights, both before and after intense combat activity, were proving arduous and exhausting to aircrew. During the Skyraider's period of development, strikes against the enemy were becoming longer and longer. (This was due, in part, to the policy of some carrier admirals, concerned more with protecting their carriers than the aircraft they carried. The Japanese had a longer reach, so American tactics at the Battle of the Philippine Sea were to stay out of that reach; as a result, an enormous number of American casualties were caused by aircraft running out of fuel and having to ditch in the sea.)

Anything that could be done to make the aircraft more comfortable would be an important factor in improving the overall efficiency of the aircraft. The Douglas team turned its attentions to the cockpit layout, since this was one place where it was possible to make a difference. They also had to consider the question of survivability in an aircraft that could expect to be damaged frequently by enemy action; carrier-borne aircraft in time of war are prone to such damage more than any other type, with greater demands being made upon them.

In order to ensure operational safety and reduce pilot fatigue, the Douglas team established an especially pilot-friendly design policy. The instrumentation was simplified, laid out more in accordance with the views of Navy and test pilots, and the size of the lettering was enlarged to $\frac{1}{2}$in height, making it more legible. The flap handles and gear handles were designed to resemble the apparatus they worked, which made for less confusion, reducing the risk of error in the heat of battle.

In order to mitigate as far as possible the worst flight situation, including a potential 40G in a crash-landing, a rigid cockpit was designed. This was later to prove its value time and time again. Heinemann added that, to further improve the safety of operation on the ground [by which he really meant the crowded carrier flight deck and hangar decks, with their restricted manoeuvring spaces] as well as safety and sighting vision in combat, a forward and downward vision angle of fifteen degrees, or twice the amount previously considered acceptable, was provided, together with a free-blown cockpit enclosure.

No less than five mock-ups of cockpit designs were constructed and these were subjected to intense ground testing both

SKYRAIDER MEN – Richard Grant Smith

While the AD was, without a doubt, Ed Heinemann's masterpiece, other men helped him to make it the success story that it came to be. One of the main contributors was Richard Grant Smith. Although his chief and most lasting (and deserved) claim to fame rested with his outstanding paintings of Douglas and other aircraft, he was also a highly skilled configuration engineer; it was this expertise that Smith brought to the Skyraider during its most crucial phase.

Born in Oakland, California, Richard Smith graduated from High School in 1931 already determined to become an aircraft designer, inspired by the exploits of his boyhood hero, Charles Lindbergh. He went to the Polytechnic College of Engineering in his home city and gained an engineering degree. He earned money to pay for his tuition by solid hard graft, even working for a time in the northern California gold mines.

With his expertise confirmed, in 1936 he won a job at the burgeoning Douglas Aircraft Company at El Segundo, as a lowly blueprint trimmer, earning the princely sum of either $1 per day, plus room and board, or $18 a week, according to various stories. He worked assiduously, combining the making of detail drawings part time with his main duties. Within six months his skills had come to the attention of Ed Heinemann, who was impressed by his technical drawing and detailed layouts. Within two years, Smith had become part of the Douglas design team, and cut his design teeth on the famous SBD Dauntless. Highly motivated (as were all those on the Heinemann team during the intense war years), Smith worked for long hours to produce detailed and precision drawings accurately, and on time. His reputation grew steadily, as did his interests – in painting, the wildlife and landscape of the Western desert states, and the history of the American Civil War.

'R.G.' married, and fathered a son and a daughter. After the war, he continued his work, but his painting began to occupy more and more of his time. The catalyst that turned him into a full-time artist was a meeting with Commander Arthur Beaumont, USNR, an already famous watercolour artist, who visited the Douglas plant in 1947. This initial contact between two men with the same passion turned gradually into a friendship, and a few years later Smith began to attend weekend art classes taught by Beaumont at Long Beach. He learnt good technique, and good thinking about layout and composition, and combined this with his own outstanding skills of draughtsmanship and attention to detail, to develop one of the most widely acclaimed styles in his field.

Smith continued working at the Lakeside plant for many years, starting early and leaving late, well past his official retirement age. Indeed, he continued to be an honorary designer there, as well as painting official portraits of McDonnell-Douglas aircraft, into the 1980s. In the late 1960s, he went out to the combat zone, where his company's latest products were undergoing one of their most severe tests of fire. As an official US Navy artist, he witnessed the action from helicopters, the rear seats of carrier jets, and from coastal gunboats in the creeks and gullies of South Vietnam. As always, he immersed himself totally in this new duty, often at some risk to his own life, and brought a whole new perspective for his painting.

Smith was inundated with honours from both the art and the aircraft world, but once confessed that his biggest kick was in becoming the tenth Honorary Naval Aviator, a reward for all he had done over the years in his capacity as both artist and designer. His old friend and mentor Ed Heinemann called Smith 'one of our real treasures at El Segundo', and paid tribute to 'his superb intuitive sense of aeronautical design'.

'R.G.' painted more than a thousand beautiful and technically correct pictures of aircraft, ships and other subjects. His works are so animated that they take the breath away; they are exhibited in the United States at the Naval Aviation Museum, Pensacola; the National Air and Space Museum, Washington DC; the Air Force Museum at Wright-Patterson Air Base, Ohio; and the Douglas Offices of Boeing-McDonnell at Lakeside, Los Angeles. Others have been hung in hundreds of other places, including the warships of the fleet, and squadron headquarters the world over. More than a million lithographs of his work have been sold.

It was one of 'R.G.'s paintings, of SBD Dauntless dive bombers at the Battle of Midway, that inspired me to find out more about a neglected but crucial part of military aviation history – dive bombers and dive bombing. 'R.G.' is certainly one of my own inspirational heroes, and deserves the many tributes that have been paid to him.

Skyraider men – R.G. Smith (left) with Ed Heinemann, in a 1952 portrait. McDonnell Douglas, Long Beach

An early example of R. G. Smith's work – From the 1948 Skyraider press release.

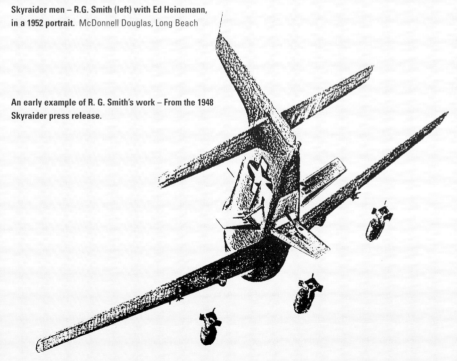

by Douglas test pilots, such as LaVerne Brown, Vance Breese and Bob Rahn, as well as by Navy pilots who had just returned from the Pacific, including Captain Leslie Stevens, to ensure the correct 'feel' was built in. Heinemann admitted at the time that 'five mock-ups sounds expensive, but in the long run it is believed economical as evidenced by the relatively small number of change requests received during demonstration.'

Of the Navy pilots, Commander Tommy Thomas was at the head of a list of favourites. Heinemann later mentioned that he had even built a cigar ashtray into the Skyraider's cockpit especially for him!

Dive Brakes

The vexed question of the dive brakes for the new dive bomber occupied a great deal of time, and conferences between Douglas and the Bureau of Aeronautics were protracted on this issue. According to Lee Parsons:

> Chagrined as they were by the failure of the SB2D-BTD, Douglas engineers were anxious to undertake a new design, the XBTD-1. Meeting with BuAer engineers, they worked out the details, using as a starting point their plans for a modified BTD. The new aircraft, powered by the R-3350 engine, was noteworthy in that it was as much a child of BuAer engineers as of the Douglas Company.[27]

It is doubtful whether Ed Heinemann would have seen it quite like that, although he paid a fulsome tribute to the help given to him by many BuAer officers:

> Most of all, the gentlemen from BuAer deserve a hefty pat on the back. They gave us the chance when it looked as though we didn't have one. They supported us throughout and gave us considerable freedom to innovate.[28]

No less than four different types of dive brakes were considered by the Douglas and BuAer engineers, as follows:

1. reversible propeller;
2. wing-mounted slatted brakes;
3. fuselage-mounted brakes;
4. parachute gear.

The reversible propeller option would have been highly favoured, as it had no weight or drag effect on the airframe. The idea was not new. The old Vought SBU-1 Vindicator dive bomber, which served aboard the US Navy carriers in 1940–2, with the US Marine Corps at Midway (and also with the Royal Navy, as the Chesapeake, and the French Navy, as the V-156, during the early years of the war) had been fitted with this device, to limit diving speeds. Reversible propellers were fitted to both the SBU-1 and -2, but the option could never be made to work satisfactorily and was never used. The Vindicator pilots had to glide bomb instead of carrying out true dive bombing, using the 'temporary' expedient of lowering their undercarriage wheels to slow the aircraft down![29] Experimenting continued in the Navy but no satisfactory production propeller had been developed that gave a sufficiently rapid rate of pitch change for the job required of it. There was clearly no time tolerance in the Destroyer-II's tight schedule to wait for a solution to appear, and this desirable option was therefore abandoned early on.

Wing-mounted slatted brakes would seem to have been the most obvious bet, Douglas having had wide experience both of the various designs, and of their associated problems. The famous 'cheese-grater' holes of the SBD Dauntless had become its particular identifying feature. The slatted type, originated by the Vultee V-72 Vengeance, and used most successfully on that aircraft in Burma, and also (despite persistent and inaccurate post-war reports to the contrary) by the North American A-36 Apache in the Mediterranean, was also available. Both were rejected.

Heinemann summarized the reasons for this as follows:

1. It had proven impossible, with wing-mounted dive brakes, to obtain sufficient drag, without the extension of these brakes to the full length of the wing, including the outer section. The effect of such brakes on the wing surfaces themselves caused a lower maximum lift and this was unacceptable to the new design, which required much higher wing loading and therefore cleanness.
2. All the varying types of wing-mounted dive brakes tested by Douglas during the 1940–4 period had given problems of severe buffeting, to varying degrees of intensity. The difficulties experienced in the prolonged development of the SBD Dauntless, although ultimately brought to a satisfactory conclusion, had been mirrored by those of other companies (for example, the SBU-1 Vindicator from Vought, and the SB2C Helldiver from Curtiss). This severe shaking of the aircraft when the brakes were extended had resulted in much poorer control of the aircraft in the dive, loss of stability, and some bombing inaccuracy.
3. Parachute retarding was only briefly considered as an option and was quickly discarded as impracticable.
4. Intensive design experimentation with the BTD-1 had shown that these heaving aircraft had confirmed that fuselage-mounted dive brakes would work very well.

Therefore, the fuselage-mounted dive brake more or less selected itself. The results in practice were found to be gratifying to the Douglas team. Heinemann claimed the following:

> With the fuselage-type brake it was found there is practically no adverse effect on the control of the BT2D in a dive. The wing lift is entirely unaffected and trim change has been found to be negligible. These brakes were soon found to have the added advantage of being excellent manoeuvring brakes for use during combat engagements, formation flying and let-downs from altitude.

Again, there was much discussion about the acceptable optimum dive angle. Generally, it had been found that, the steeper the dive, the greater the accuracy. With the new, 'denser' aircraft, and in the light of wartime experience that showed that a dive of 70 degrees was, in fact, the most common form of attack, the BuAer accepted this as sufficient for their needs. Douglas therefore no longer had to strive for absolute 'zero lift'. Although the press release claimed that the BT2D was 'capable of diving vertically', this was never, in fact, a requirement. The fuselage brakes effectively slowed the aircraft from speeds in excess of 500mph to under 300mph, enabling lower pull-outs and greater accuracy.

Stability and Control

The abandonment of the tricycle landing gear, so favoured by Douglas in such aircraft as the A-20 Havoc (known in Britain as the Boston), the DC-42 Skymaster and the A-26 Invader, as well as the ill-fated BTD,

Starboard broadside *(top)* **and starboard three-quarter frontal** *(bottom)* **view of the Douglas AD-1 Skyraider (BuNo 09102) of VA-176, now located at the front gate of NAS Oceana, Virginia Beach, VA.** Kevin R. Smith

caused much heartache at the time. It was the overriding desire to save weight that finally swung the design against a nose wheel, even though this was contrary to the overall concept of moving as much weight as possible to the forward end of the aircraft. A tricycle undercarriage would have helped this. According to Heinemann,

It is still difficult to determine the exact weight difference between the two types of gears; however, making the best possible allowances for bomb bay and wing changes it is believed a net gain of approximately one hundred pounds saving can be credited to the tail wheel gear.

The need to pack the maximum underwing attack ordnance into the area necessitated a rearward folding mechanism for the main landing gear.

These factors were tied in with the question of stability and control, always more relevant for carrier-based aircraft than for land-based machines. The small amount of space aboard a carrier imposed stringent limitations, which caused aircraft designers extra problems. One case affected by this was that of the Curtiss SB2C Helldiver, in which such considerations and Navy requirements led to almost terminal design problems. Meeting such demanding specifications had, hitherto, always required compromise on both sides. Although the Skyraider was ultimately to prove no exception to this rule, Heinemann stated that 'since hope springs eternal, it was felt that the flying quality requirements could be completely met in the case of the BT2D, provided that an all-out effort were made.'

He later went to say that

to obtain the necessary longitudinal stability, fundamental consideration was given to arrangement of all equipment and dead weight as far forward in the fuselage as possible … thus obtaining optimum tail length within the elevator size restrictions.

He obtained the desired elevator control forces by fitting an electrically controlled, adjustable stabilizer, which allowed a smaller elevator area to be built in. This resulted in lighter stick forces than a conventional, fixed stabilizer. Without this feature, the BT2D would have needed a power booster system, in order to obtain satisfactory stick forces. With the adoption of horn-type aerodynamic balances, combined with a short elevator chord, free-control longitudinal stability was improved.

Heinemann considered the twin problems of lateral and directional stability, and the associated control factors, as a single problem when designing dive bombers. His explanation was as follows:

This follows from the inseparable nature of these characteristics in both the low-speed carrier approach and wave-off condition and in the high-speed level flight and vertical dive cases. To obtain acceptable low-speed flying qualities, for example, it is essential to be able to pick up a dropped wing with either ailerons or rudder down to the stall. The required wing dihedral angle to accomplish this, however, is usually excessive for high-speed dives where application of rudder gives excessive roll and yaw. On the other hand, if the wing dihedral is too low, instability-in-roll will result in the flaps and gear-down cases.

The aim was to achieve the optimum wing- and tail-surface profiles that would result in positive stability and control about all axes, and throughout the whole spectrum of speeds (from terminal velocity dive to stall). A series of intensive wind-tunnel tests was conducted at both the Caltech facility and at the NACA Ames Laboratory situated at Moffett Field.

The achievement of aerodynamic balance on all controls, and the fitting of spring tabs to the rudders and ailerons, resulted in 'manoeuvrability and control harmony equivalent to modern fighter', according to Heinemann's press release. He also stated that, in order to 'eliminate the undesirable variations in control and trim, experienced with recent high-speed airplanes using fabric control surface

covering, metal-covered control surfaces have been developed for the Skyraider, which are actually lighter in weight than the fabric-covered surfaces used on the BTD.'

The BTD went a long way towards fulfilling Heinemann's lofty aspirations; exactly how far can be judged by a comparison of Douglas wartime dive bomber types (see the table below). In any case, he was able to point to a considerable increase in maximum bomb load, while this load, in terms of ton/mph, was enormously increased over the same aircraft. Take-off, climb and top speeds were also improved over both the SBD and the BTD.

According to Heinemann,

The Skyraider's most outstanding performance characteristic is its great load-carrying ability. Its low wing and power loading, high load factor, stability and control give it the added advantage of the manoeuvrability of a fighter so that it can protect itself against fighters. Its strength, manoeuvrability and vision also make it particularly well suited for ground machine-gun and rocket attacks.

This statement might be considered today to be hyperbole, written by the aircraft's proud originator. However, in the long term (fighter attributes apart), this early description of the Skyraider's chief merits proved time and time again to be accurate. The Spad would go on to do useful work in long years of front-line service, and its standard airframe would prove enormously adaptable, being repeatedly modified to fulfil a myriad of essential roles.

Comparisons of Douglas dive bomber types

	SBD-5	XSB2D-1	BTD	AD-6
Wingspan (m)	12.66	13.72	13.72	15.25
Length (m)	10.09	11.76	11.76	11.84
Height (m)	4.14	5.16	5.05	4.78
Empty Weight (kg)	2,905	5,651	5,851	5,429
Loaded Weight (kg)	4,245	7,381	8,228	8,213
Maximum Weight (kg)	4,853	8,682	8,618	11,340
Wing Loading (kg/sq m)	140.6	211.9	237.4	220.8
Power Loading (kg/hp)	3.5	3.2	3.6	3.0
Maximum Speed (km/h)	410	557	554	518
Cruising Speed (km/h)	298	290	303	319
Rate of Climb (m/min)	518	521	503	869
Ceiling (m)	7,780	7,435	7,195	8,685
Range (km)	2,520	2,380	2,380	2,115
Crew	2	2	1	1

CHAPTER FIVE

The Skyraider Described

Head-on portrait of Skyraider EA1E (ex-AD 5W) 135152 (N65164) at "Sun 'n' Fun", Lakeland, Florida, on 20 April, 1998. Frank A. Hudson

Both the new Douglas design and its immediate rival, the Martin Model 210, which became the XBTM-1 as well, were developed, although the latter finally shipped the Pratt & Whitney R-3350-4 Cyclone. Superficially these rivals ended up physically similar, both big machines for carrier aircraft.

Dimensions

The XBT2D-1 was 39ft 5in (15.25m) in overall length, had a wingspan of 50ft ¼in (15.25m) and a height of 15ft 7½in (4.76m). The wing area was 400.33 sq ft (37.19 sq m). Height to the tip of the tail-plane was 12ft ⅜in (4.64m), to the tip of the propeller, 15ft 8in (4.76m).

Weights

The first prototype (c/n 1913, BuNo 09085) weighed in gross at 16,372lb (7,427kg), 1,628lb (738kg) under the contracted design weight, the result of Heinemann's vigorous regime. These figures were so good that they upset predicted stability forecasts and, in anticipation of a negative reaction to this lighter weight, the wings on subsequent aircraft were moved forward 4in (10cm), further concentrating weight towards the nose.

The empty weight of the subsequent prototypes came out at 10,093lb (4,578kg), loaded weight at 13,500lb (6,124kg), and maximum weight at 17,500lb (7,938kg).

Wings

The new dive bomber featured a straight, low-mounted wing, of the NACA 2417 maximum lift series, of tapering section, with a 6-degree dihedral and a 6-degree sweep-back. The tapering section featured 4.2 degrees of low-speed 'wash-out', while a 4-degree incidence of wing root made for improved take-off ability. Wing loading was 33.7lb/sq ft (164.7kg/sq m) and power loading was 5.8lb/hp (2.7kg/hp).

Specification – XBT2D-1	
Powerplant:	R-3350-24W
Weights:	Empty 4,578kg (10,093lb); loaded 6,124kg (13,500lb); full 7,938kg (17,500lb); wing loading 33.7lb/sq ft; power loading 2.7kg/hp (5.8lb/hp)
Dimensions:	Length 12.01m (39ft 5in); height 4.76m (15ft 7½in); wingspan 15.25m (50ft ¼in); wing area 37.19sq m (400.33sq ft)
Performance:	2,500hp Max. speed 604km/h (375mph); at altitude 4,145m (13,600ft) Cruise speed 264km/h (164mph) Rate of climb 1,152km/h (3,680ft/min) Ceiling 7,925m (26,000ft) Range 2,500km (1,554miles)
Acceptance in service:	n/a

Breakdown of the major components of a Skyraider illustrates its simplicity of structure.

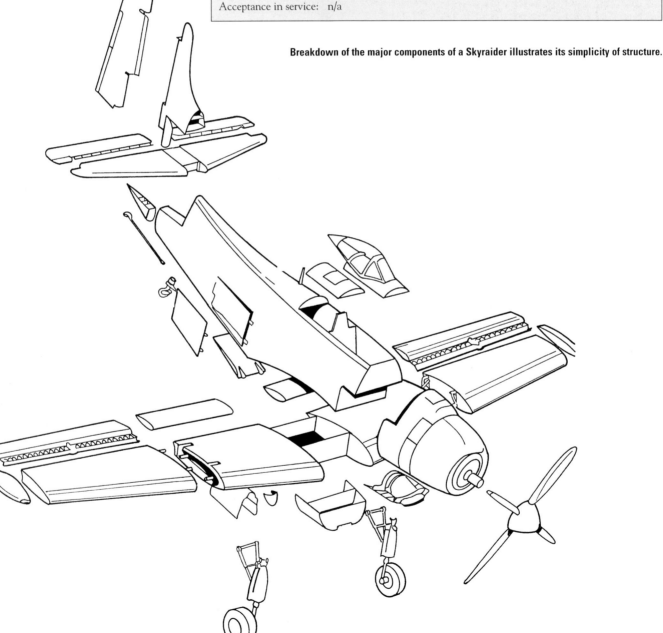

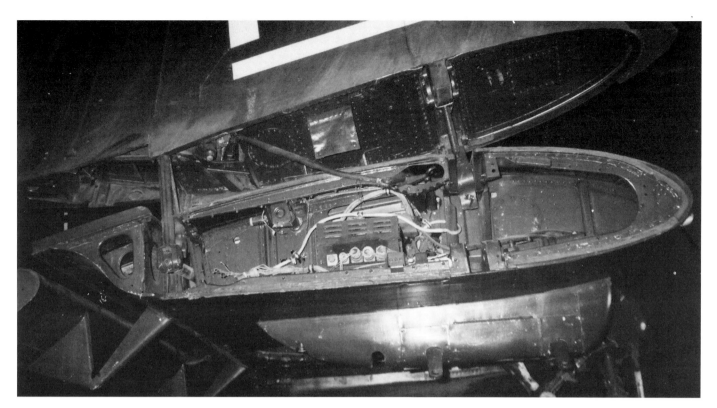

Wing-folding mechanism detail on the Royal Navy AEW-1 (AD-4W) WT 121 Skyraider at the Fleet Air Arm Museum, RNAS Yeovilton. Peter C. Smith

The outer wing panels folded inward hydraulically and, with wings folded, the maximum width was 23ft 11⅛in (7.29m). Folded wing height was 16ft 7⅜in (5.07m) with the wings fully folded inward towards the fuselage at an angle of 60 degrees; maximum height allowance for hangar-deck clearance during folding when the wings were temporarily passing through at 90 degrees was 19ft 4⅞in (5.92m). When the wings were unfolded and spread, ready for take-off, they were locked into place by the pilot, who

This rear-view shot of preserved French Skyraider F-AZDP *(below)* shows the wing jury struts that support the folded wing and *(right)* close up of canopy area. M. Hiscock

closed a handle that retracted locking rods, which were located on both wings, painted red and nicknamed 'beer cans'.

The ailerons were mounted only on the outer wing panels. Fowler area-increasing flaps were fitted on the broad centre-section in order to enhance low-speed operations. The standard navigation lights were fitted on the leading edges of the outer-wing extremities.

Empennage

The tail dragger design of the XBT2D-1 was another distinguishing feature, which, at first glance, appeared inadequate for a plane of such a size. A tall, narrow, vertical stabilizer, which joined the upper rear fuselage via a curved fillet, was complemented by two 9ft 11in (3.02m) lateral tail stabilizers placed well forward. Instead of conventional fixed stabilizers, the system

The massive and solid flaps and actuators on the Royal Navy AEW-1 (AD-4W) WT 121 Skyraider at the Fleet Air Arm Museum, RNAS Yeovilton. Peter C. Smith

was power-boosted by means of an electrically operated stabilizer control, mounted at the base of the tail section ahead of the rudder, which made possible these smaller-scale elevators.

Studies of the effect of high speed on the traditional fabric-covered control surfaces of contemporary aircraft showed that such types suffered inconsistencies in trim levels and control. To eliminate these factors as far as possible, the Douglas team utilized all-metal control surfaces. An unexpected bonus from this modification was that these were slightly lighter than the conventional type. Controls and spring tabs on the rudder and the ailerons featured aerodynamic balance.

Leading edge and wing-tip profile. Peter C. Smith

(Below) **Underwing detail and rear cockpit area of Skyraider 132683 (BuNo N39147) in natural finish on outside storage pad at the Planes of Fame Museum, Chino, 15 March 1998.**
Kevin R. Smith

Port side 'amidships' detail and wing flaps of the Douglas AD-4NA, supplied to the US Marine Corps during the Korean War and which was overhauled and then transferred to the French Air Force in 1960. They used it in strikes against Guerrilla forces in their African territories prior to Independence. In 1976 this machine was handed over to the Gabonese Air Force. When they had finished with her she was put up for sale and finally arrived at the Imperial War Museum airfield of Duxford, near Cambridge in 1991 where she is operated, strangely enough for a dive bomber, by The Fighter Collection. She has been repainted to resemble the USS Intrepid's VA-176 unit. Peter C. Smith

Close-up engine detail of the US Marines AD-4N (BuNo 126935) coded HB, Regd NX 2088G, at Aero Trader 1998. Kevin R. Smith

Powerplant

The R-3350-24W eighteen-cylinder, developing 2,500hp, was due to become available only in April 1945. Studies were made into the suitability of the Pratt & Whitney R-2800 engine as a back-up, but the first four prototype XBT2D-1s took to the air with the 2,300hp Wright R-3350-8 Cyclone 18 engine installed instead. This gave the aircraft a maximum speed of 375mph (604km/h) at 13,600ft (4,145m); a cruising speed of 164mph (264km/h), and a climb rate of 3,680ft/m (1,152m/min). The engine produced a service ceiling figure of 26,000ft (7,925m), and gave a range of 1,554 miles (2,500km). To reduce trimming usage, the engine itself was mounted with 4.5 degrees of downward thrust. The engine was mounted on a special, strong, but much-simplified mounting, also designed by Heinemann. This comprised a single solid forging with four profiled arms, which bolted directly on the main fuselage and combined relative lightness with inherent strength.

The prototypes were fitted with a hollow aluminium Aeroproducts A 642-G804/M20A2-162 hydraulically actuated, variable-pitch, constant-speed propeller with a diameter of 13½ft (4.11m). This prop was turned by a single-stage, two-speed supercharger. This unit was to give rise to governor over-speed problems early on in the testing programme, being prone to vibration. One of the prototypes (BuNo 09088) was accordingly fitted with an enlarged propeller spinner in an attempt to alleviate this vibration problem.

Behind the NACA nose ring, the engine was encased in an elongated cowling, the frontal part of which was hinged on a narrow central top panel. Two large access flaps opened upwards for easy maintenance access. Both the nose and the anti-drag ring at the rear of the cowl had cooling flaps. These were automatically controlled by actuators fitted to the landing gear, but the pilot could also open them manually if necessary. (Much later, the USAF tended to fix the nose flaps in a permanently open position during operations in the humid heat of Vietnam.)

The carburettor air scoop sat directly to rear of the cowling, in front of the cockpit. Cockpit heating and air-ventilation intake ducts were mounted on either side of it, and there was further access panelling opening all the way round. Below sat the massive oil cooler, which was protected below and aft by streamlined fairings,

Frontal view of the massive propeller of the Douglas AD-1 Skyraider, 09102, at the front gate of NAS Oceana, Virginia Beach, VA. Kevin R. Smith

through which the rearward-facing exhaust stacks projected. Both these fittings produced their own problems during early testing, along with backfires and cracks in the stacks themselves, and these led to unavoidable delays.

Fuel System

The main fuselage fuel supply was contained in a lozenge-shaped tank located abaft the pilot's seat. This tank had a 223-gallon capacity (later increased in the AD-1 to 340 gallons) and was self-sealing. The fuel-tank selector valve, fuel strainer and auxiliary fuel pump were located forward, below the firewall, with the engine-driven fuel pump forward of that, below the carburettor.

For additional range, the main fuel tank could be supplemented by a single Mark 12 external fuel tank, with a capacity of an additional 150 gallons, which could be carried on the central, centre-fuselage hard point, and by two Mark 8 wing-mounted external fuel tanks, of 300 gallon capacity, mounted on the underwing stations.

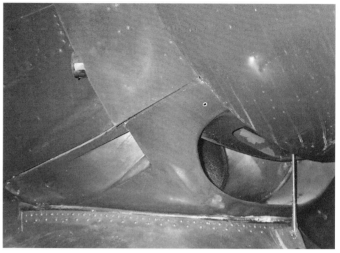

(Left) **Looking forward along the starboard fuselage showing engine exhaust detail on the Royal Navy AEW-1 (AD-4W) WT 121 Skyraider at the Fleet Air Arm Museum, RNAS Yeovilton.** Peter C. Smith

(Above) **Underside detail on the Royal Navy AEW-1 (AD-4W) WT 121 Skyraider at the Fleet Air Arm Museum, RNAS Yeovilton.** Peter C. Smith

Undercarriage

As another ploy to speed production, the first two prototypes were fitted with the main undercarriage struts and wheels, as the Chance-Vought F4U-1 fighter. On the basic A-1, the undercarriage width was 13ft 10¾in (4.23m), with the wheel centres 6ft 11⅜in (2.12m) from centre. Undercarriage length from wheel centre to tail-wheel centre was 22ft 2¼in (6.78m), which gave a wide wheelbase. The main undercarriage folded rearwards up into wells in the centre wing section where they were flat-packed and protected by their rearward folding

covers, the frontal parts of which were fitted with landing lights. The tail wheel was also fully retractable, folding away forward, and the arrestor hook was located to the rear of it. This latter had an automatic hold-down unit mounted internally in the rear fuselage above.

As with the engine and the prop, however, the undercarriage was to prove one of the weak links in an otherwise exemplary design. During trials at Alameda Naval Air Station, California, from May 1946 onward, and at the Patuxent River Test Center, Virginia, the XBT2D-1s undercarriage legs and supports soon began

collapsing on landing with unfortunate regularity. For a carrier aircraft this was disastrous, and hasty measures had to be adopted to rectify this problem.

The prototypes, along with the first two-score of the production AD-1s, were shipped back to El Segundo. Here, they were strengthened and the airframe itself was also modified to give a much sturdier wing-support section. The landing-gear pivot box was also re-cast, and it was hoped that these modifications had solved the problem; this proved not to be the case. Furthermore, these alterations resulted in an increase in weight of some 415lb.

Close-up detail of arrestor hook on the Royal Navy AEW-1 (AD-4W) WT 121 Skyraider at the Fleet Air Arm Museum, RNAS Yeovilton. Peter C. Smith

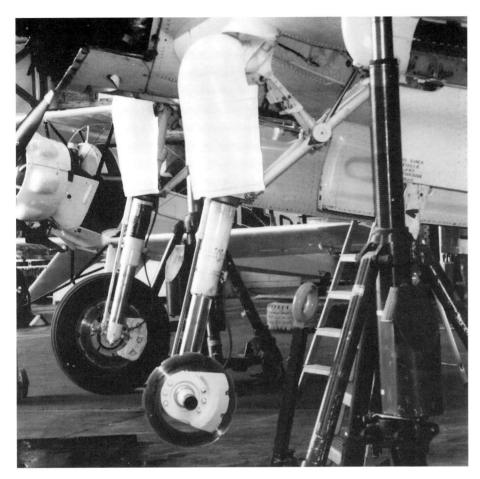

Close-up of the undercarriage equipment of the Douglas AD-4NA now at the Imperial War Museum airfield of Duxford, near Cambridge, via the US Marine Corps, the French Air Force, and the Gabonese Air Force. Peter C. Smith

(Below left) Close-up of the starboard wheel, wheel-well and landing gear of the Douglas AD-1 Skyraider BuNo 09102 of VA 176, at the front gate of NAS Oceana, Virginia Beach, VA. Kevin R. Smith

(Below) Close-up detail of tail wheel on the Royal Navy AEW-1 (AD-4W) WT 121 Skyraider at the Fleet Air Arm Museum, RNAS Yeovilton. Peter C. Smith

Cockpit Layout

The pilot sat in a bucket seat with an armoured headrest, under a clear-blown 'bubble' canopy, which slid back rearwards for access and egress. The armoured windshield had the Mark 20 Mod. 4 adjustable reflector gun-sight mounted centrally on a strong support arm, which was bolted atop the main instrument panel. The cockpit slide was electrically operated by means of either an internal handle mounted on the port side of the pilot's cockpit, which also locked it, or from outside by means of a simple Open/Close switch on the port side.

As a result of his own eyewitness observations with the fleet in the war zone, Heinemann had insisted on a simplified and cleaned-up cockpit, with emphasis placed on pilot compatibility. A 15 degree angle of pilot vision, both frontally and vertically, was therefore featured. The main instrument panel was laid out in a logical pattern and the two side consoles concentrated on engine controls (left), or radio and electrical controls (right). (*See* the diagram below.)

The upper fuselage in front of the cockpit was painted non-reflective black to reduce glare, and there was also an internal anti-glare shield. The fuselage hardpoint control was located on the forward right-hand side.

Dive Brakes

With the rejection of wing dive brakes and the adoption of the body-mounted version, Douglas dive bombers took on a whole new profile as they hurtled towards their target. Three hydraulically operated dive brakes were fitted, one on either side of the rear fuselage, and one underneath the fuselage abaft the cockpit.

All three dive brakes were metal panels set into recesses in the fuselage structure itself and hinged at the frontal end. The operating control was located on the left-hand side of the pilot's console and, when activated, the three dive brakes' operating cylinders worked simultaneously, but independently. There was no actual linkage between them.

When they were hydraulically actuated, it took under three seconds for all the brakes to open outwardly to a maximum angle of 80 degrees. Although they looked like barn doors left ajar, they worked without any hitches, and had no ill effects on wing lift or

KEY

1. rear vision mirror (2)
2. gunsight
3. t/o light
4. pilot's instrument panel
5. chartboard
6. armament panel
7. exterior light console
8. spare lamp container
9. seat actuating switch
10. rudder pedals
11. oxygen breathing tube and headset connections
12. anti-G connector
13. left-hand control panel
14. armrest
15. control stick
16. cockpit sliding enclosure control panel
17. landing gear control panel
18. right-hand control panel
19. windshield
20. canteen
21. seat belt and shoulder harness
22. headrest
23. microphone-headset

24. antiexposure suit vent provisions
25. kit bag
26. inertia reel
27. shoulder harness locking handle
28. pilot's relief tube
29. ash receptacle
30. circuit breaker panel
31. gunsight light elevation adjustment switch
32. hydraulic gauge and filler valve
33. landing gear audible warning relay and alarm

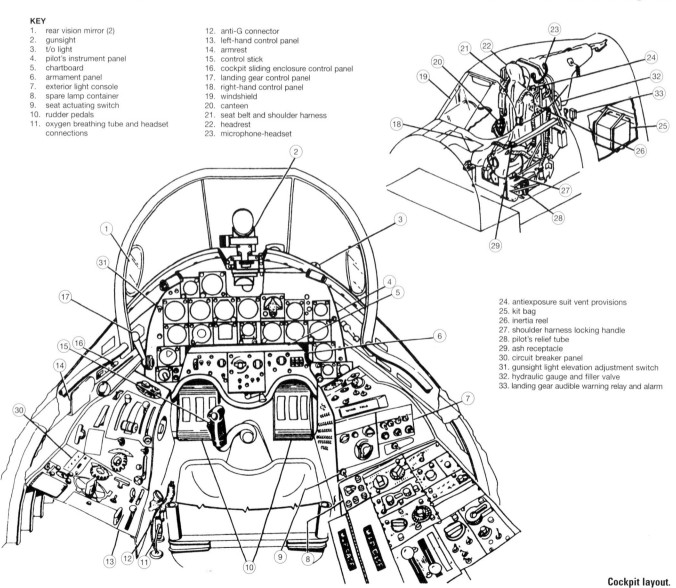

Cockpit layout.

The dive brake mounted on the under-fuselage, seen here fully opened. US Navy official photograph

(Below) An aerial view of three US Navy ADs peeling off into their dive attacks with fuselage-mounted dive brakes deployed. The Skyraider was one of the best-loved close-support aircraft ever, held in the same affection by hard-pressed American infantrymen in Korea and Vietnam as was the Junkers Ju. 87 Stuka by German ground troops in the Second World War. Both could count on accuracy of delivery and reliability when it was needed. US Navy official photograph, Washington, DC

(Bottom) Rear view of the United States Marine Corps Douglas AD-4B Skyraider, BuNo 132261 of VMA-121, being restored at USMC Air-Ground Museum, Quantico, CA, July 1998. This picture shows the massive recess for the fuselage-mounted dive brakes. Kevin R. Smith

control. In addition, only very slight trim alterations were necessary. With all three brakes extended, diving speed was cut from 500mph to 300mph (805–480km/h).

When exceptionally large bombs or other stores were carried on the central ventral position, which might impinge on the operation of the underside dive brakes, a manual locking valve prevented that dive brake from functioning. As a further precaution against accidental triggering of the dive brakes while on the carrier deck or runway ashore, the Skyraider was fitted with a solenoid safety lock.

When in an attack dive with all brakes fully extended, pilots were cautioned to leave them in the full-out position during levelling out, and not to retract them until the aircraft was flying almost straight and true. It had been found that, if the dive brakes were retracted before the aircraft had pulled up, the dive speed increased rapidly and there was a nose-down trim alteration that could prove terminal. Further advice was that the movable stabilizers were never to be used to help recover from such dives, as this would cause excessive loading on the aircraft's structure that could lead to its failure.

Armament

With the elimination of the internal bomb bay, underwing stowage was provided for the offensive ordnance. It was this decision, which resulted in unrivalled versatility, that was destined to give the Skyraider its longevity. As offensive payloads changed down the years – in type, weight, size, shape and function – these underwing stations were able to cope with every type with equilibrium. The oft-quoted fact that the Skyraider could tote more weaponry than the four-

engined Boeing B-17 Flying Fortress heavy bombers was the simple truth. As one USAF airman wrote, 'The A-1Es carry more weight on one wing than the F-100s on both.'[30]

Although the first prototypes were equipped with just three bomb racks for early trials, progression was soon made to increase the new aircraft's weapon-carrying capacity. Eventually, no less than fifteen external hard points were emplaced. One large Aero 3A ordnance pylon, with a 3,600lb (1,630kg) weight limit, was mounted on the centre-line under the fuselage and flanked outboard on the inner-wing section by two Mk 51 stations, which each had a 2,300lb (1,040kg) weight limit with 14in lugs, or 3,000lb (1,360kg) limited with 30in lugs. The other twelve Aero 14 stations were placed, six a side, outboard of these, and numbered 1 to 12 (from port outboard to port inboard, and starboard inboard to starboard outboard). These outboard stations had a 500lb (227kg) maximum limitation each, but with the proviso that neither total wing weight should exceed 2,500lb (1,130kg).

The other limiting factor for the outer-wing stations was the diameter of the ordnance carried, which dictated the realistic bomb load and, in effect, restricted it (other than the three 1,000lb M65 bombs on the inner pods) to a further four 500lb M64 or six 250lb M57 bombs per wing. The large diameter of the drop tanks (later utilized also as the 110 gallon Mk78 Mod 2 fire bomb) was also restrictive. The AD-4 was later capable of carrying one 2,000lb M66 bomb under each inner wing. The distances between pylons varied from 13.59in to 17.2in (34.5–43.7cm). Pylons 5 and 8 also had the limitation that any large-diameter ordnance hanging here restricted the ejection of the 20mm cartridges.

One of the more forward advances featured on the new dive bomber was the Douglas bomb ejector. The conventional release was becoming more and more outmoded for the type of ordnance being carried and the method of attack being utilized. Heinemann had given this problem much thought and the result was the new device. He later described it as follows:

Essentially, an electrically actuated, explosive charge in the rack pushed the store away from the diving plane into the airstream. Bob Rahn and Vance Breese flew many of the weapons-ejector test hops.[31]

This device was a great step forward. Without it, centre-line payloads, especially empty fuel tanks, would frequently hit the underside of the fuselage when released. The explosive charge almost totally eliminated the tendency for the Skyraider to nose-over when the large centre-line ordnance was jettisoned.

On the early prototypes (BuNos 09085-09109), underwing loads could be combinations of bombs, rockets, torpedoes, smoke canisters, drop tanks or napalm, up to a maximum of 8,000lb (3,629kg).

The in-built armament initially consisted of two M3 20-mm cannon mounted in both the wing stubs. This weapon fired a 5.5lb projectile and had a muzzle velocity of 2,330ft/sec (710m/sec) and a rate of fire of 400rpm. These 2M-3 cannon used percussion-primed ammunition. The magazines were mounted inside the wing,

Internal arrangement.

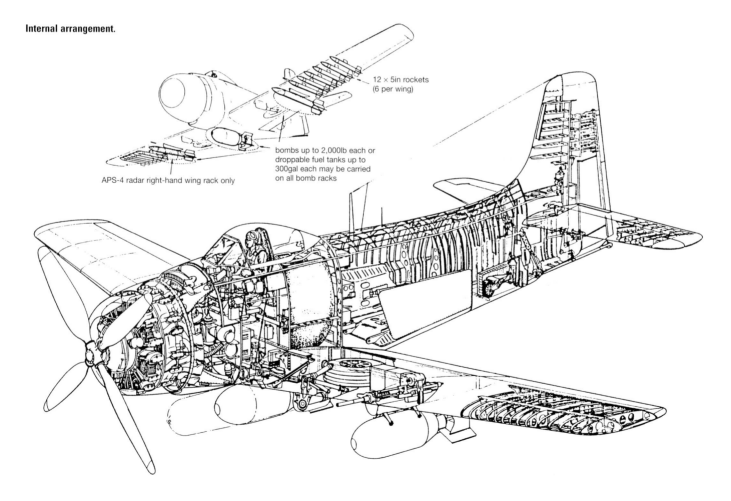

12 × 5in rockets
(6 per wing)

bombs up to 2,000lb each or droppable fuel tanks up to 300gal each may be carried on all bomb racks

APS-4 radar right-hand wing rack only

horizontally outboard of the cannon itself. They could hold 200 rounds each and were loaded from access panels atop the wing. The guns were fitted with an ARM/SAFE selection switch. This armament was increased to four wing-mounted cannon when the AD-4 came in, with the extra pair of guns being mounted in the outer-wing panels.

Comparisons

Comparison with contemporary and rival dive bombers is illuminating; see the table below.

Despite post-war claims that the Skyraider was by far and away 'the best dive bomber ever tested at Patuxent River', analysis of the figures shows that, in many areas, other dive bombers outclassed it. The Martin Mauler was marginally faster, the Vengeance had far greater reach, while the Buccaneer was the lightest, and had the smallest wingspan for carrier operations. However, what the Skyraider had in enormous abundance was hauling capacity. It was this factor, plus its overall versatility, which finally won the day.

The reasons why the Douglas Skyraider was so welcome in the fleet on its arrival were many and varied. The aircraft that it replaced was the Curtiss SB2C Helldiver, while its main rival should have been the Martin AM Mauler. One Navy pilot who flew all three dive bombers, as well as the legendary SBD Dauntless earlier, was Charles R. Shuford. His wide experience makes his account of the differences between the machines particularly valuable as a historical record.[32]

On active duty with the Navy, I flew the SB2C Beast from September 1944 until January 1947. In July 1950, the Navy released the AM-1 Mauler [Martin] to the reserves since this plane was not satisfactory for carrier duty. I flew this aircraft until July 1953. In July 1953, we received the F4U-Corsair (also known as the 'Bent Wing Widow Maker') and flew as an attack squadron using the wheels extended for dive brakes. In July 1955, the F4U was replaced with the Douglas AD-4 (also the -5 and the -6). I flew these until November 1962.

I flew the SBD Dauntless until advancing to the SB2C. Our introduction to fleet-type aircraft consisted of formation flying in groups of six, twelve, eighteen and twenty-four planes, and an opportunity to gain experience as a squadron leader. We practised procedures for making entrance to the landing pattern for final approach to land aboard a carrier. The majority of our time was spent on bombing technique. Approaches to the target, breaks, dive angle and rendezvous after the pull-out consumed several hundred hours of flight. Some of our land targets were manned so as to give us dive angle, range and deflection. We dropped cast-iron bombs that contained an elongated shot-gun shell so the puff of smoke would mark our drop.

At this stage we were flying three plane sections and six plane divisions. We usually broke from an echelon. Later we went to two plane sections with four plane divisions. I found this to be more desirable, especially when tight turns and evasive action was required. We tried to perfect our accuracy of bomb drops and obtain a dive angle of 65–75 degrees (although it felt as if we were perpendicular).

The SBDs we flew had the telescopic bomb sight, which restricted your sight and sometimes resulted in late and low pull-outs. The reflective sight was a great improvement and also served as a gun-sight.

I received orders to San Diego, California, to check out in the SB2C. Upon arrival in California I was sent to Oxnard, which was nothing but a motel with a landing strip. We had all types of fleet aircraft there. My commanding officer was Lieutenant Louis L. Bangs, fresh off the Enterprise, and Bombing Ten. The senior officer on board was Lieutenant-Commander J.D. Ramage, also of Bombing Ten. Ramage eventually made Admiral.

Having switched to the Beast from the Dauntless, I found the aircraft to be much to my liking as a dive bomber. Most of the problems had been worked out before my first flight. I especially liked the reflex gun sight. With the perforated flaps I had better control in a dive. With time in the aircraft I found that my accuracy in bombing improved. Pull-out required a higher altitude than with the SBD.

The Skyraider's normal cruising speed was a sedate 140 knots indicated airspeed, or three miles a minute over the ground, at an altitude of about 10,000ft (3,050m).

As a general rule (weather permitting) we usually approached a target at an altitude of 18,000ft or 20,000ft and made a high-speed run-in down to 15,000ft before making our break. During the run-in the divisions would take their interval on the lead so as to prevent over-running and so as to accomplish a rendezvous after pull-out.

The F4U Corsair was a joy to fly since it was light and fast. As a dive bomber it was not the best since it had no dive brakes. We extended the wheels to control our speed in the dive.

The Martin AM-1 Mauler was satisfactory in our operation as an attack squadron. With the

Comparison of US dive-bomber types

Model	DOUGLAS	MARTIN	CURTISS	VULTEE	BREWSTER	DOUGLAS
Ref	BTD	AM-1	SB2C	A-35B	SBN-1	AD-1
Name	DESTROYER	MAULER	HELLDIVER	VENGEANCE	BUCCANEER	SKYRAIDER
SEATS	1	1	2	2	2	1
WING CONFIGURATION	MID	LOW	LOW	LOW	MID	LOW
POWERPLANT	2,300hp (1,715kw)	2,957hp (2,218kw)	1,900hp (1,417kw)	1,700hp (1,268kw)	950hp (708kw)	2,400hp (1,790kw)
MAX SPEED	344mph (554 km/h)	367mph (591 km/h)	295mph (475 km/h)	279mph (449 km/h)	254mph (409 km/h)	366mph (589 km/h)
MAX RANGE	1,480 miles (2,382km)	1,800 miles (2,897km)	1,165 miles (1,875km)	2,300 miles (3,701km)	1,015 miles (1,633km)	1,900 miles (3,058km)
CEILING	23,600ft (7,195m)	30,500ft (9,295m)	29,100ft (8,870m)	22,300ft (6,800m)	28,300ft (8,625m)	33,000ft (10,060m)
MAX TAKE-OFF WEIGHT	19,000lb (8,618kg)	23.386lb (10,608kg)	16,616lb (7,537kg)	16,400lb (7,439kg)	6,759lb (3,066kg)	18,030lb (8,178kg)
OVERALL LENGTH	38ft 7in (11.76m)	41ft 2in (12.55m)	36ft 8in (11.18m)	39ft 9in (12.12m)	27ft 8in (8.43m)	38ft 2in (11.63m)
OVERALL HEIGHT	13ft 7in (4.14m)	16ft 10in (5.13m)	13ft 2in (4.01m)	15ft 4in (4.67m)	8ft 7in (2.64m)	15ft 5in (4.70m)
OVERALL SPAN	45ft (13.72m)	50ft (15.24m)	49ft 9in (15.16m)	48ft (14.63m)	39ft (11.89m)	50ft (15.24m)
ARMAMENT	2 × 20mm	4 × 20mm	2 x 20mm & 2 × 0.3in	6 × 0.5in (12.7mm)	1 × 0.3in (7.62mm)	2 × 20mm
ORDNANCE	3,200lb (1,451kg)	4,500lb (2,041kg)	2,000lb (907kg)	2,000lb (907kg)	500lb (227kg)	6,000lb (2,722kg)

VA-672 unfolding their wings to depart Navy Atlanta, Chamblee, GA, for their move to Dobbins AFB, Marietta. Charles R. Shuford

3,000hp Pratt & Whitney Wasp major 28-cylinder, four-row radial engine, it was fast. The bubble canopy provided excellent visibility and the dive brakes were very good. Around 160 of these were manufactured. They were not satisfactory for the fleet and therefore were given to the Reserves. Some of the planes we were assigned were equipped with Curtiss Electric propellers and some with Hamilton Standard propellers.

My reserve squadron had poor experience with the AM. We had a number of complete engine failures. Most of them resulted in fatalities. The engine had a habit of 'coughing' on the climb-out and the momentary silence was absolutely frightful.

How did the Skyraider compare with these types?

The Douglas AD was probably the better of all attack planes [propeller-driven] that I flew. Excellent for dive or glide bombing, it was able to carry a heavy load. It was comfortable to fly and had a good auto-pilot. Good for instrument flight.

On 22 February 1959, the US Navy moved from Navy Atlanta, Chamblee, to Navy Atlanta, Marietta, Ga [Dobbins AFB, home of Lockheed-Martin Aircraft]. With our ADs we made a big deal out of the last flight from Chamblee, which is now Peachtree Dekalb Airport, a county-owned facility. In June 1959, we were flying mostly AD-6s and these were taken away to be used in Vietnam. Thereafter we had AD-5s. These were a pleasure to fly. Years later I received a mailing from Time-Life books plugging their series on Vietnam. One illustration showed an AD-5 dropping napalm, and it turned out to be the one I first flew at Atlanta on 18 June 1960! [The Bureau numbers on the tail never change.]

Charles Shuford added one more pertinent remark, emphasizing that, no matter how good (or bad) an aircraft, ultimately, much rested on the pilot.

After so many years of flying attack aircraft, I have come to the conclusion that each pilot develops his own style of making his dive to get the maximum result. After the formation break, your own particular style takes over. After operating in a squadron for a period of time, you become familiar with each fellow pilot and know exactly what they will do in a given situation.

No. 2 Formation of AD-4s over Atlanta GA, September 1958. Charles R. Shuford

CHAPTER SIX

The Skyraider Joins the Fleet

The Experimental Unit, VX-1, based at Key West, Florida, was the test squadron for all new Navy aircraft. Here, an AD-1Q (BuNo 09366) is seen on 6 January 1949, equipped with the AN/APS-4 radar pod under its starboard wing. Although somewhat temperamental, this AEW radar was to be one of the longest-serving airborne radar sets in the US Navy, and was also utilized by the Royal Navy for many years. National Archives, College Park, MD

The Skyraider first became operational with a US Navy Squadron on 6 December 1946, when it joined VA-19A. Four months later, in April 1947, Carrier Qualification Tests began with VA-3B and VA-4B. The Skyraider soon began to equip other Navy attack squadrons, gradually replacing the Curtiss SB2C-5 Helldiver, which had been their mainstay. A study of the workings of two Skyraider units of the time gives a feel of how the new aircraft began to settle in.

VA-5B, with the Atlantic Fleet, and based at East Field, Norfolk, Virginia, received its first AD-1 on 22 September 1947. This was followed by two more the next day and four on 26 September.[33] On 5 January 1948, 50 per cent of all the squadron's enlisted personnel reported aboard the big new carrier *Coral Sea* (CVB-43) for preliminary training, in preparation for the ship's proposed shake-down cruise. At the same time, four AD-1 aircraft and four pilots were sent aboard. The other half of the squadron remained at Norfolk, but

changed places on 9 January, along with four relieving pilots. From 5 January to 17 January, the shore-based Skyraiders operated with the *Coral Sea*, so that 22 pilots were qualified in day carrier landings.

Repeated Accidents and Damage

The qualifications were not achieved without difficulty. Like all new aircraft, with new pilots, the Skyraider had its fair share of teething problems and accidents inevitably resulted. On 7 January 1948, Ensign Thor K. Stromsted, attached to VA-6B, was piloting AD-1 BuNo 09281 assigned to VA-5B. Ensign Stromsted was making his carrier qualification landings aboard the *Coral Sea* when his aircraft crashed into the barrier. The pilot emerged unscathed, but the damage suffered by the AD-1 led to its transfer to A&R. On the same day, Midshipman Rex R. Berglund,

also attached to VA-6B and flying an AD-1 (BuNo 09309) assigned to VA-5B, made a hard carrier landing, which resulted in 'wrinkled wings and fuselage. Damage to aircraft was such as to require a transfer of aircraft to A&R.'[34] It would seem that the Skyraider's reputation for toughness got off to a very shaky start; dive bombers were expected to be able to take this sort of thing in their stride.

Other weaknesses soon began to show up. On 12 January, Ensign Richard L. Robinson, flying AD-1 BuNo 09275 during carrier qualifications, made a 'normal carrier landing'. Despite this, the arresting hook broke, resulting in a barrier crash, and this aircraft joined the melancholy throng in A&R. It was quickly joined by a fourth Skyraider, BuNo 09260, which was flown by Lieutenant (j.g.) Edwin J. Walasek. He made a hard landing, which caused wrinkles in both wings of the aircraft.

On 17 January 1948, the entire squadron reported aboard the carrier and she sailed from Norfolk on the 19th for her shake-down cruise in the Caribbean. Problems with the ship soon changed that plan. On 30 January, the captain of the *Coral Sea* ordered the Skyraiders ashore to be temporarily based at McCalla Field Naval Air Station, Guantanamo Bay, Cuba. They flew back aboard the carrier on 6 February, and, after a short period at Cristobal, Panama, resumed operations in the Caribbean. This continued with joint operations with Tactical Air Control Squadron 2 from Carrier Battle-Group 5.

These early Skyraider operations took the form of simulated air-ground support missions, using the impact area on Culebra, Virgin Islands, as the AD-1's bombing range. They turned out to have been excellent preparation for the bulk of the AD's combat missions over the next quarter of a century – this aircraft, which was designed to crush enemy aircraft carriers and warships, in fact spent its entire combat career flying against land, rather than sea, targets.

The worrying engine problems continued. On 12 February 1948, AD-1 BuNo 09253, piloted by Ensign Struhsake, suffered complete engine failure. The pilot managed to ditch successfully and got clear, but the aircraft quickly sank and was a total loss. Again, the cause of the failure was undetermined. Exactly the same thing happened to Ensign Richard F. Johnston, while flying BuNo 09264 on 23 March. Investigations into the cause of the problem were hampered by the fact that on both occasions it was not possible to salvage the aircraft.

Deck-landing accidents also continued to take their toll. On 28 February, Lt Charles H. Napier flew AD-1 BuNo 09277 into the crash barrier of the *Coral Sea*; fortunately, neither he nor the machine was badly damaged! On 27 March, Ensign Richard T. Johnston landed AD-1 BuNo 09316 aboard the carrier; after successfully engaging number one wire, the arrestor hook broke, and the Skyraider crashed into the barrier.

Despite all these accidents, VB-5B was given a military and readiness inspection by ComAirLant (Commander, Aircraft, Atlantic Fleet), which resulted in a recommendation for a mark of 'outstanding' in readiness and 'excellent' in personnel and administration. Despite this, the Skyraider clearly needed to be reviewed, especially with regard to its powerplant and its arrestor hook equipment.

On 1 April 1948, VA-5B, commanded by Lieutenant-Commander James G. Hedrick, again took its Skyraiders to sea, based aboard *Coral Sea* (CVB-43) for a shake-down cruise. During the next four days, all the squadron pilots qualified in all phases of carrier day operations, without incident. On 5 April, the squadron returned to Naval Air Station, Norfolk, Virginia, re-embarking aboard *Coral Sea* on 10 May to conduct flight operations during a two-week Reserve Cruise in the New York area. However, their scheduled flight operations were curtailed by some fifty per cent due to inclement weather in the area; on 21 May, all the squadron's Skyraiders returned to Norfolk.

On 29 June 1948, the squadron, now commanded by Lieutenant-Commander Robert G. Randal, received its first AD-1Q. This month also saw another bad Skyraider accident in the squadron. On 15 June, Ensign Sammie O. Midgett, flying BuNo 09332, was on a routine training flight, when his aircraft engine suffered partial engine failure and then caught fire. It quickly became obvious to Midgett that he had no choice but to bail out, but he experienced difficulty in abandoning the aircraft. At the third attempt, the young ensign got clear of the cockpit but, as he went over the side, he failed to clear completely the empennage. His right leg struck the horizontal stabilizer, resulting in multiple fractures. By this time, the aircraft was at a low level and, by the time the pilot's parachute opened, he was only just above the water. The chute failed to break his fall, and Midgett suffered severe bruises and shock. Despite this, he had the presence of mind to inflate his life raft and use it while awaiting rescue. He spent an uncomfortable thirty-three minutes in the water in great pain, until an Air-Sea Rescue PBY-5A plucked him to safety and took him to the US Naval Hospital at Portsmouth, Virginia. The cause of the engine fire aboard his Skyraider was undetermined.

In autumn 1947, the sister squadron, VA-6B, was commanded by Lieutenant-Commander Rubin H. Konig. Equipped with the Curtiss SB2C-5 Helldiver, which was now getting a little long in the tooth, the squadron had been 'looking forward' to re-equipping with the new AD-1. It received its first Skyraider on 23 September 1947, followed by six more on 25 September, and one more on 28 September[35]. All the squadron's pilots attended the AD-1 Mobile Training Unit prior to the arrival of these aircraft, and

this was followed by familiarization on the Skyraider and qualification in FCLP (Fleet Carrier Landing Procedures).

On 1 October 1947, the squadron, now commanded by Lieutenant-Commander Glen B. Butler, from St Paul, Minnesota, had one AD-1 on its fully operational strength. However, over the ensuing three-month period, 'AD-1 aircraft were received steadily until the new AD-1 squadron complement of twenty-four (24) AD-1 aircraft and one (1) SNJ aircraft was reached on 23 December, 1947.'

In common with their companion Skyraider squadron that was also destined for the *Coral Sea*, VA-6B suffered more than its fair share of accidents with its new equipment. Events were to take the shine off their expectations.

On the morning of 17 October 1947, Ensign Charles C. Brown, Jr, USNR, 'inadvertently' landed his AD-1 (BuNo 09278) wheels-up at Naval Air Station Creeds Field, Virginia, while he was making familiarization landings. While the embarrassed Brown was not injured, his aircraft suffered Class 'C' material damage.

Pilot error could not be blamed in the next Skyraider incident.

On 4 November, Lieutenant Harvey Broadbent, Jr, USN, was flying an AD-1 (BuNo 09291) to the rendezvous point after taking off from Creeds Field, when the manifold pressure dropped to about 10. He succeeded in returning to the field and touched down about half-way down the runway. Severe application of the brakes was not quite enough to stop the aircraft and it nosed up gently in the grass about thirty feet beyond the end of the runway. The Skyraider suffered Class 'D' material damage only, but the cause of the initial failure, as well as that of the brakes, caused concern.

Throughout the first two weeks of December, Air Group 5 engaged in close air-ground support exercises in co-operation with units of the US Army at the Blackstone Army Air Field Bombardment area near Camp Pickett, Virginia. The Skyraiders practised glide bombing, rocket firing and making strafing runs with live ammunition, under the direction of an Army observation and control unit.

One interesting phase of their training at this time was described as follows:

During this training period the squadron began the adaptation of fighter-type tactics to the AD-1 aircraft. This tactical revision was necessitated by the superior performance characteristics of the new AD-1 aircraft and the loss of the protection afforded by a rear-seat gunner.'

On 19 January 1948, the squadron embarked aboard the *Coral Sea* for the shake-down cruise, being also based ashore at Guantanamo Bay, Cuba at the beginning of February, like VB-5B. Accidents continued to happen in this squadron too.

On the morning of 7 January, Lieutenant (j.g.) Robert G. Barnhart was making qualification landings aboard the carrier, when his Skyraider 'floated up the deck and engaged number ten wire'. The wire paid out enough to engage the barrier, but no serious damage was suffered by either

the aircraft to nose-over momentarily and then settle back to a three-point attitude, sustaining Class 'D' material damage as it did so. The accident was due to the normal hazards of carrier operations, as was the next incident, which happened later the same day.

Ensign Donald E. Kinney was making his second qualification landing aboard the *Coral Sea*, when he received a fast, high cut, and pulled back on his throttle. It is believed that he left a little throttle on and this, combined with the fact that he did not nose-over sufficiently, caused him to float on up the deck into the barriers at a speed of about 70 knots. The ship herself

B material damage was believed to be due to a progressive weakening caused by previous hard landings, and not by this landing in particular.'

Further food for thought was provided on 27 January, when, after a not particularly hard landing by Ensign Chandler V. Merrell, Class B damage was sustained by his AD-1, in the form of similar half-inch wrinkles in both the left and right wing roots. Again, the accident board was of the opinion that 'the plane may have been weakened by previous landings and that the number of similar failures indicates a weakness of design'.

The Skyraider was, subsequently, such a success story that its earlier failings tend to be ignored in histories of the aircraft. It would seem, however, that the Douglas team, in making supreme efforts to cut down on weight, may have gone too far in some areas, and that the tough arena of actual carrier operations quickly showed up weaknesses.

It was decided to test this point further. The captain of the *Coral Sea* ordered the two AD-1 squadrons ashore at Guantanamo, to conduct a series of experimental landings aboard the carrier. The aim was to find out exactly what was causing so many failures on the new aircraft, and the results of the tests 'revealed that a slightly faster, lower approach with a flared landing was necessary to prevent structural damage to the aircraft'.

One incident at this time revealed other difficulties. On 2 February 1948, Lieutenant James R. Langford was returning to Naval Air Station, Guantanamo, after a routine 'dive-bombing hop', when he found that he was unable, after repeated attempts, to extend the tail wheel of his AD-1. He was advised by the squadron maintenance officer to land with his dive brakes extended. He did this, and effected the landing successfully; the only material damage was some 9in of the bottom dive brake scoop being ground off before the aircraft came to a halt.

On 12 February, Ensign Joseph E. Puccini landed aboard the *Coral Sea* after a dive-bombing hop. As he taxied across the barriers, he was directed to the deck-edge elevator. Due to the prevailing high wind over the flight deck, Puccini had great difficulty in turning his AD-1, and an addition of throttle, in conjunction with holding the left brake, resulted in the aircraft rocking forward and the propeller striking the deck.

The Skyraider was designed to perform the rôles of both traditional dive bomber and torpedo bomber, a combination that had been suggested as early as 1942, and had been put forward by Admiral Halsey, and others. The two duties seemed incompatible, but the Skyraider proved it could be done. This is BuNo 122330, an AD-2, carrying a Naval torpedo under its fuselage, as well as a 2,000lb bomb and six 5in HVARs under either wing. Such enormous loads were toted by the Spad as a matter of routine. National Archives, College Park, MD

pilot or machine. On the same day, the C.O. himself, Lieutenant-Commander G.B. Butler, had completed his final qualification landing, and was being lowered to the hangar-deck level on the port deck-edge elevator. The taxi director then signalled to hold right brake and come forward with the port wheel. On complying with this, Butler's AD-1 caught its tail wheel on the outside edge of the elevator, and 30in of manifold pressure was not enough to break it loose. An additional 5in of manifold pressure was applied and, at the same time, the ship rolled to starboard. The tail wheel came loose suddenly, allowing

was rolling 10-15 degrees at this time, and a 40–42 knot wind prevailed over the flight deck, which did not help. The aircraft sustained Class 'B' material damage as a result of the barrier crash.

More worrying from the point of view of the Skyraider's durability and, therefore, its suitability for carrier work, was an accident that befell Ensign Walter J. Kuehn on 13 January. He received a similar 'cut' from the L.S.O. and dove for the deck. The tail hook engaged number one wire, but inspection after the landing showed a half-inch wrinkle in both the Skyraider's wing roots. According to the report, 'This Class

During the first part of March, the squadron and air group resumed intensive training in preparation for the operational readiness inspection, scheduled for the later part of the month. Glide bombing, rocket firing and strafing were emphasized, together with the perfection of carrier passes.

The basic problem had not gone away. On 4 March, Lieutenant (j.g.) Anthony S. Kalas made 'a normal approach and landing', but his Skyraider incurred a half-inch wrinkle in the port wing root. This

engaged number two wire and pulled out approximately fifteen feet of cable. At this point, the arresting hook parted at a point 3in from the swivel and the plane continued into the barriers, sustaining Class C material damage.

One final incident occurred on 17 March 1948. Midshipman Rex R. Berglund took off on a routine dive-bombing hop from the *Coral Sea*. Once airborne, he retracted his Skyraider's landing gear, noticing that the gear handle would not go completely into

Berglund's Skyraider's hydraulic pressure read 2,750 p.s.i., and he was instructed to break the hydraulic line in the cockpit, which led to the canopy closure accumulator, thus relieving all pressure on the system. He was then told to turn the selector to 'main landing gear only' and pump the wheels down with the emergency hand-pump system. This also failed to lower the gear and Berglund was then instructed to make a 'wheels-up' landing aboard, which he did 'in a very commendable manner'.

An AD-1 (BuNo 09286) in the flight markings of the National Air Test Center with radar configuration in flight on 6 December 1949. National Archives, College Park, MD

particular aircraft had popped rivets on previous landings, and it was the opinion of the subsequently convened accident board that 'the Class C material damage sustained in this case was not a result of pilot error but rather of design weakness'.

On the afternoon of 16 March, Ensign Richard C. Maxwell, Jr, made a 'normal approach and landing'. The tail hook

its 'up' position. He tried to lower the gear, but it would not extend. He completed the mission and then, prior to landing, tried again to lower the gear by flying at a slow speed, and then executing high 'G' pull-outs, and by operating various hydraulic mechanisms to loosen a stuck valve in case that was the cause of the problem. All his attempts to dislodge the landing gear failed.

The AD-1 suffered Class C material damage and subsequent examination revealed that the 'O' ring in the port main landing-gear actuating cylinder had deteriorated, thereby preventing sufficient flow of hydraulic fluid to the 'down' side of the piston to lower the landing gear.

It was clear that further substantial work would have to be done on the Skyraider if it was to justify the Navy's hopes for it as the premier carrier bomber for the post-war era. Various basic types were introduced, and subsequently improved and further developed in the immediate post-war period.

Tests and Trials

The service trials of the Skyraider confirmed that the aircraft was an excellent product, but they were far from uniformly good. The impression given by many post-war histories of the Skyraider is that the aircraft was designed overnight, and was perfect from then on. The Patuxent River reports of the period 1945–8[37] show clearly that this was not the case, and that a number of improvements had to be made.

Carrier landing tests with XBT2D-1 BuNo 09087 aboard the escort carrier USS *Charger* (CV-30) had consisted of approximately fifty landings, with various external configurations, and at various gross weights 'up to the maximum considered practical'. This aircraft was fitted with complete instrumentation to obtain data on arrested landing and catapulting loads and accelerations.

On 18 July 1945, the Chief of BuAer informed the President of the Board of Inspection and Survey that arrangements had been made for the allocation of XBT2D-1 aircraft, as follows:

XBT2D-1	Activity
09087	NAMC (Carrier Acceptability Test) from 15 August
09089	Service Test, NATC, Patuxent River
09090	NAMC (Powerplant Airplane)
09091	Armament Test, NATC, Patuxent River
09092	Electronics Test, NATC, Patuxent River
09093	Tactical Test, NATC, Patuxent River
09095	NavTorSta, Newport, Torpedo Trials

The trials aircraft were restricted to 400mph (644km/h) and 5G (at 15,600lb/ 7,075kg). Douglas advised that BuNo 09087 had the full required catapulting and arresting strength. Loading conditions up to those including one torpedo on the centre rack and one 1,000lb bomb on each wing rack could be tested, within the following restrictions:

1. Catapulting – maximum gross weight of 18,000lb and a maximum permissible average catapult acceleration of 2.8G (for aircraft considered as a deadload).
2. Arresting – maximum gross weight of 14,545lb and limited acceleration of 3.375G.

On 21 November 1946, the Director of the Chief of BuAer, Captain C.A. Nicholson, USN, requested the President, Board of Inspection and Survey, in Washington DC to conduct production and inspection trials on the model AD-1 aircraft 'as may be considered necessary. In view of the extensive testing of the model XBT2D-1 airplanes, it is suggested that the trials be brief in scope.'

He also noted that:

Since the first twenty AD-1 airplanes have few changes compared to the seven XBT2D-1 airplanes BuNos 09100–09106 now undergoing Service Acceptance Trials, and since the 21st and subsequent AD-1 airplanes will contain additional changes, it is designed that the subject trials be conducted with one of the later airplanes. It is anticipated that one will be available in January 1947.

He added the following rider:

In view of the urgent need in the Fleet for replacements for SB2C and TBM airplanes, it is requested that subject trials be expedited in order to permit early assignment of the airplane to the Fleet.

On 4 March 1947, Commander R.H. Prickett, USN, was able to advise the BuAer Representative at El Segundo that, under Contract Noa(s) 6530, Model AD-1 aircraft (BuNo 09155), allocated to the Research and Development Group of the Bureau, should be sent to the Naval Air Test Center at Patuxent River. He asked for the ETA.

On 5 February 1948, C.M. Lindsley of the Board of Inspection and Survey advised the Navy Department in Washington, DC, that the Service Acceptance Trials on the XBT2D-1 and the Production Inspection Trials on the AD-1 were overkill:

These two airplanes for all practical purposes are identical. It will expedite the conduction of trials if the Service Acceptance and Production Trials are conducted simultaneously.

This was agreed.

Project TED Nos. BIS 2177 and BIS 2192 covered the testing of the Model XBT2D-1 and AD-1 aircraft ordered under the original contracts, No(s) 743 and 6539. Fuel consumption tests were later cancelled, on 6 June 1948.

A Skyraider with a full ordnance load buzzes the tower of the NAS San Diego, June 1949. San Diego Aerospace Museum

A preliminary evaluation had been conducted on XBT2D-1 BuNo 09085, on 19 May 1945. The exhaust-flame visibility tests had recommended that flame dampeners be provided for the BT2D-1 in order to meet specification requirements. A detailed longitudinal stability investigation was made of XBT2D-1 BuNo 09100, and unsymmetrical loading tests and lateral stability tests for carrier take-offs and landings were conducted on AD-1 BuNo 09155. Performance characteristics of the AD-1Q were made using both BuNo 09352 and 09354, and these same aircraft were also utilized for carrier suitability trials.

The purpose of the Service Acceptance and Production Inspection Trials was to determine whether the AD-1 was acceptable for service and whether it met performance guarantees specified in Contract No(s) 6539, signed on 18 April 1945. The Combined Service Acceptance and Production Inspection Trials were conducted on AD-1 BuNo 09155, which had been assigned for the task on 4 March 1947, with Lieutenant-Commander G.T. Weems, USN, as the project pilot, Mr H.W. Hean as the aeronautical engineer, and Lieutenant-Commanders J.L. Genta, USN and D.C. Caldwell, USN, as senior project officers.

This aircraft mounted the Aeroproducts four-bladed, constant-speed hydraulic propeller, with blade design H20G-162-0, hub design A642-62, and a diameter of 13ft 6in (4.11m). The power ratings for the Wright Model R-3350-24W engine were listed as follows:

- Normal rated power: 2,100hp at 2,400rpm from S.L. to 5,500ft, 1,800hp at 2,400rpm at 15,000ft
- Military rated power: 2,500hp at 2,800rpm from S.L. to 3,500ft, 1,900hp at 2,600rpm at 14,800ft
- Take-off power: 2,500hp at 2,900rpm and 54ft Hg.

The scope of the trials included evaluation of the aircraft's performance as a bomber with the following:

A view of the quartet of ADs en echelon **flight on 23 April 1950, each carrying twelve HVARs. Nearest the camera is BuNo 123814 and, next to it, BuNo 123827.** National Archives, College Park, MD

1. Maximum speeds at sea level and at airplane critical altitudes for normal and military rated power.
2. Climb performance using normal and military rated power.
3. Take-off speed and minimum take-off distances in conditions of zero wind, and 25 knots wind.
4. Minimum speeds in both the landing condition and clean condition, power on and power off.

They also included evaluation of the aircraft as a scout, at maximum speed at sea level for military rated power. In addition, a qualitative investigation of the stability and handling qualities of the AD-1 loaded as a bomber, a carbon monoxide survey and miscellaneous tests were carried out, including the following aspects:

- trim tab characteristics;
- optical qualities of the windshield;
- airspeed indicator fluctuations in banked flight;
- take-off characteristics;
- ground-handling characteristics.

Some interesting results came out of this test programme. The aircraft failed to meet its performance guarantees in the following respects:

1. Maximum speed at engine military rated power at airplane high blower critical altitude, loaded as a bomber, was 259 knots, while the guaranteed speed was 280 knots.
2. Maximum speed at engine military rated power at sea level, loaded as a bomber, was 246 knots, while the guaranteed speed was 264 knots.
3. Maximum speed at engine military rated power at sea level, loaded as a scout, was 272.5 knots, while the guaranteed speed was 289 knots.

In the stability tests, the following results applied:

1. Longitudinal stability was satisfactory except for the static stick-free and stick-fixed stability in configuration PA, which were neutral for displacements below the trim speed.
2. Lateral stability was satisfactory except in one configuration, in which case dihedral effect was only weakly positive but acceptable. Aileron forces were light, especially at the higher speeds in some configurations. Aileron adverse yaw was undesirably high but acceptable.
3. Directional stability was good except in one configuration, in which case the control-free stability was weak.

The stability characteristics at high speeds were investigated by conducting dives to limit speed to determine whether the aircraft would meet the requirements of NAVER Spec SR-110A, of 7 April 1945. The following results were obtained:

1. The high-speed longitudinal characteristics were satisfactory except that an excessive push force (80lb) on the stick was required to hold the aircraft in a dive to limit speed, after it had been trimmed for zero control force in level flight in one configuration.

2. The high-speed directional stability characteristics were satisfactory except that the rudder-free directional stability was weak, and aileron adverse yaw was undesirably high.

3. The high-speed lateral stability characteristics were satisfactory except that aileron forces were objectionably light. On the first high-speed dive an aileron overbalance occurred at 240 knots V_1 at 24,000ft (7,315m) in a 30-degree wings-level dive. Investigation disclosed that a change in the pressure distribution caused by dents in the underside of both ailerons was the source of the overbalance. The dents were caused by the whipping action of rocket pigtails following rocket firing tests.

Stalls were investigated in both clean and landing configurations, power on and power off. Except for insufficient stall warning, the stalling characteristics were good. In all configurations tested, the stall was accompanied by a moderate roll and downward pitch of the nose. In the clean configuration, the stall warning consisted of a slight aileron 'nibble', a small amplitude rolling motion and a marked aft stick travel, all occurring about 2 knots above the stall speed. In the landing configuration, power off, the stall warning consisted of an almost full aft movement of the stick. No warning preceded the stall in the landing configuration, power on. Recovery was easily effected in all cases. The maximum altitude lost was 800ft (240m) in the landing configuration, power off. Control forces and control effectiveness were adequate, except for the power approach configuration, when aileron and rudder effectiveness were marginal.

The stall warning characteristics of the XBT2D-1 were therefore deemed 'inadequate', occurring 'too close to the actual stalling speed' of the aircraft. None the less, although 'unsatisfactory', they were acceptable, 'because of the excellent stall characteristics and control effectiveness for recovery'. It was noted that 'the opinion as to the adequacy of stall warning has been reassessed in light of the advanced stage of development of artificial stall-warning devices, and the warning which existed in the XBT2D-1 is now considered unacceptable.'

No problems were encountered with the carbon dioxide tests. Trimming controls were said to be readily accessible in the cockpit and their arrangement was satisfactory. Tab effectiveness was positive and satisfactory in all respects. Tab operation was easy, although the horizontal stabilizer control was too sensitive near the trim speed. Tab settings were positive.

The optical qualities of the windshield were satisfactory with no unusual distortion and no major obstructions to vision on the canopy or windshield. The rear-view

Skyraiders line up for take-off on the forward deck of the USS Antietam **(CV-36) on 15 October 1951. Two are already in position on the catapults, with three more moving up in readiness.** San Diego Aerospace Museum

mirror was adequate, and could be moved out of the way to enhance forward vision.

When a Mk. 5 external auxiliary fuel tank was mounted on the right bomb rack, undesirable airspeed indicator fluctuations were observed in level straight flight at speeds under 80 knots, and in the increased acceleration and angle of attack resulting from banked turns of 30 degrees or more at speeds below 85 knots. These fluctuations were as great as 20 knots, and were caused by a breakdown of airflow over the tank, which resulted in pressure changes at the total pressure source located under the right wing.

The flap setting was full down for all take-offs. Variations of directional trim with power and speed were not found to be excessive. The best rudder tab setting for take-off was determined to be 6 degrees nose right. The tendency of the tail to rise limited the power to approximately 31" MAP on turn-up with the brakes held.

Ground-handling manoeuvres on a dry concrete runway with a wood float finish consisted of a series of 360-degree turns, which were executed satisfactorily both to the right and the left, with wings both folded and extended. Cross-wind taxiing and parking were also performed without any hitches:

> Because of the tendency of the tail to rise it was not determined whether the brakes would be capable of holding the airplane against take-off power.

There were no ground-looping tendencies during landing.

The conclusion reached from these trials was that the AD-1 was

> acceptable for use as a service type aircraft, except for the following: 1. The variation of elevator control force with speed is excessive in dives to limit speed. 2. No perceptible stall warning exists in the landing configuration, power on.

The report added that the AD-1 did not meet the performance guarantees with respect to the following:

1. Maximum speed at engine military rated power at airplane high blower critical altitude, loaded as a bomber.
2. Maximum speed at engine military rated power at sea level, loaded as a bomber.
3. Maximum speed at engine military rated power at sea level, loaded as a scout.

The following recommendations were made:

1. Accept the model AD-1 airplane as a satisfactory service type.
2. Improve the elevator control force characteristics to lessen the build-up of control force with speed.
3. Provide adequate stall warning for the landing condition, power on.
4. Improve the airspeed system characteristics to prevent the airspeed indicator fluctuations.

A separate temperature survey on the engine installation of XBT2D-1 BuNo 09093 was conducted at Patuxent River between 20 October 1947 and 13 October 1948. Two engines – W-151802 and W-474741 – were fitted to this machine during this period. The first engine had 17.3 hours logged to it, but after only 19.2 test hours' flying it had be changed when the supercharger could not be shifted from the high blower. Special instrumentation fitted included a Brown Recorder-thermocouple installation for temperature measurement and a photo observer.

The cylinder temperature limits for these engines were as follows:

	Heads	Bases
Take-off power (5 minutes)	260°C	163°C
Military rated power (30 minutes)	260°C	163°C
Normal rated power to 70 per cent normal rated power (continuous operation)	246°C	163°C
70 per cent normal rated power and below (continuous operation)	232°C	163°C

Great difficulty was experienced in getting the engines to develop their rated power and also in obtaining and maintaining correct fuel flows in the carburettor. The carburettor had to be calibrated and adjusted by AEL Philadelphia four times during the tests. Cylinder-head temperatures were excessive for both the level-flight tests and the military rated power climb to service ceiling. Shifting from direct to alternate carburettor air at military rated power at both low and high blow critical altitudes resulted in losses of 370bhp and 320bhp respectively. Oil temperatures, fuel temperatures and accessory compartment temperatures indicated that the cooling was inadequate.

It was found that cooling of the accessory compartment was inadequate in flight

and during ground tests. Cylinder-head temperatures, oil temperatures and fuel temperatures were all excessive in flight. Cooling of spark elbows was inadequate during ground tests.

The conclusion reached was that the cooling of the powerplant did not meet the requirements of NAVAER E-59c, Specifications for the Measurement of Engine Installation Temperatures. Douglas were told to 'take the necessary corrective action'.

One further series of tests took place during this period, relating to the Radio Interference of the Airborne Electronic Equipment installed in XBT2D-1 BuNo 09092. Ground and flight tests were conducted between 26 June 1947 and 5 August 1947. The following installations were covered by these tests:

1. The receiver-transmitter, AN/ARC-1, ser. no. 38681.
2. The communications receiver R-23/ARC-5, ser. no. 48981.
3. The communications receiver R026. ARC-5, ser. no. 1731.
4. The UHF homing receiver AN/ARR-2, ser. no. 2697.
5. The X-band search radar, AN/APS-4, ser. no. 12184.
6. The AN/APX-2 IFF equipment, ser. no. 11391.
7. The Airborne Radio Altimeter AN/APN-1, ser. no. 19897.

The results were almost uniformly bad and it was concluded that the electrical and electronics installations in this aircraft did not meet the requirements, and that radio interference above the background noise level was present thus:

Equipment under test	Interference from
AN/ARC-1 (ground test)	AN/APS-4
AN/ARC-1 (flight test)	AN/APS-4
R-23/ARC-5 (ground test)	AN/APS-4
R-26/ARC-5 (ground test)	AN/APS-4 and fuel booster motor pump
R-26/ARC-5 (flight test)	AN/APS-4

It was therefore recommended that BuNo 09092 be 're-worked in conformity with the requirements of NAVAER installation specifications, to meet the requirements of Specification AN-I-24 and that particular attention be given to the provisions of NAVAER publication NAVAER 15-5Q-517, *Elimination of Radio Interference in Aircraft*.'

CHAPTER SEVEN

Experiments, Modifications and Improvements

As the AD programme developed, the versatility of the basic Douglas design was proven time and again. It lent itself to all kinds of specialist adaptations from the basic dive-bomber type. This, the key to the Skyraider's long lifespan, led early on to a wide variety of experimental types; some were stillborn after just one machine, while others led to subsequent developments and, ultimately, to use within the fleet.

XBT2D-1

In an early trial, a large spinner was fitted to Prototype No. 09088, one of the first four aircraft to be fitted with the R-3350-8 engine, in an attempt to improve that engine's performance. However, the -24 was soon generally available, becoming the standard powerplant for the early AD-1s and AD-1Qs, and this experiment was quickly deemed superfluous.

Another of the basic attack prototypes, fitted with the R-3350-24W engine, was also the subject of a 'one-off' experiment. After the introduction of the rocket projectile into service use with the fleet, Prototype No. 09094 was fitted with a pair of 5in rocket-launching tubes in place of its two 20mm wing cannon. These were intended specifically for ground attack against land targets rather than naval targets. Instead of firing them in salvo, as was the norm, a novel method of mounting was tried out, with single rockets firing in sequence.

The adapted aircraft could carry six spin-stabilized rockets internally, which were fired through the tubes that extended from the centre of the leading edge of the wings in the same manner as the cannon they replaced. The system worked well enough when it was tested at the Naval Ordnance Test Facility at Inyokern,[38] south-east of the China Lake Naval Weapons Centre, California, in the summer of 1948, but was not taken any further. Firing rockets sequentially had less impact than delivering them simultaneously *en masse*, when the delivering aircraft could hit with one heavy punch and then quickly be clear of the return fire. Underwing 5in HVAR, 5in RAM or 11.75 'Tiny Tim' rockets therefore remained the norm for such usage, on the Skyraider as on other aircraft.

A third basic attack prototype (BuNo 09018) was completed as a heavy-attack version, with extra armour protection and guns. It was given a more powerful engine in the shape of the 2,700hp Wright R-3350-26W. It was redesignated as the XAD-2.

XBT2D-1P

Douglas fitted out Prototype BuNo 09096 for a single-seat photo-reconnaissance rôle, with the AN/APT-16 ECM jammer in a pod under the port wing, and a Window aluminium foil dispenser in a dispenser pod under the starboard wing.

XBT2D-1N

Prototype BuNos 09098 and 09099 became test-beds for the three-seat, night-attack variant. This involved the most extensive physical modification, with a special cockpit being built into the fuselage for the bulky radar sets and for two radar operators, immediately abaft and below the pilot's cockpit, with a large access door on the starboard side. Conditions for the two radar men, seated side by side facing forward, were cramped, to say the least. An additional radar pod was mounted under the port wing, while, for illuminating targets located by the radar, a large searchlight was carried below the starboard wing, also mounted in an aerodynamic pod. Flash shields were fitted to the 20mm cannon muzzles. In compensation for this additional weight, and because they were deemed redundant in this configuration, the side-mounted fuselage dive brakes were omitted from these two aircraft and the recesses were faired over. Testing was conducted at Patuxent River in 1948.

XBT2D-1Q

The experiment that became the most relevant later in the Skyraider's long career was the fitting out of BuNo 09109, the last of the 25 prototypes built, as the first of the electronic countermeasures (ECM) aircraft. Extra accommodation, a starboard-side access door with an integral window, and a port observation window were built in for one extra crew member within the after-fuselage structure. Extra pods for both AN/APS-4 radar and a MX-356/A Window radar-jamming chaff dispenser were fitted below the port and starboard wings, respectively.

AD-1Q

The tests of the ECM prototype resulted in 35 AD-1Q aircraft (BuNos 09352-09386) being built. They represented the balance of the original BT2D-1 order, which totalled 277 machines, and they started joining the fleet in 1947. They carried an AN/APR-1 Search Receiver, an AN/APA-11 Pulse Analyser, and an AN/APA-38 Panoramic Adapter. An array of downward-pointing aerials was mounted below the after fuselage, with a small ECM blister prominent on the lower port side. To provide a flow of cool air for the ECM equipment, a small forward-facing air scoop was built in to the top of the rear fuselage

XBT2D-1W – Airborne Early Warning

The origins of the Airborne Early Warning system can be traced back to a British staff requirement of December 1943. The installation of an early warning system was requested, but, due to a lack of funds and of suitable radars and aircraft, nothing was done about it. It took the success in 1944–5 of the Japanese *Kamikaze*, the suicide-attack aircraft[39], against Allied warships, and the funding of the American Defence budget to get a related project under way.

In 1944, the Anglo-US Scientific Project Committee revived the British interest in this subject. Even with the huge resources at their command in the final drive on the Pacific in 1945, the American Task Forces were suffering grievous casualties at the hands of the conventional *Kamikazes*, and of the pulse-jet propelled Baka-manned missiles launched from aircraft. The fact was that, no matter how many standing combat air patrols were flown, it proved impossible to intercept all incoming raids in the warning time provided by the ships' radars.

The adopted method of early warning involved the placing of Radar Piquet Destroyers, at first singly, and then, as losses mounted, in pairs (for mutual support), far out from the main fleets, to give advance notice of incoming enemy flight. As well as being easy targets, and therefore taking heavy losses, the efficiency of these destroyers was limited by the range of their R/T sets, and the fact that, the further out the destroyer screens were placed, the greater circumference of patrols required and, therefore, the more destroyers needed. To provide radar cover on a screen of 60 miles radius, at least ten destroyers were required, and even this gave very little overlap. At this period of the war, the Americans had many hundreds of new and well-armed destroyers available. The British, on the other hand, not only had far fewer modern destroyers for the British Pacific Fleet, but their ships were also badly equipped, with anti-aircraft weapons that would not elevate above 55 degrees. They were forced to supplement their own destroyer pickets with light cruisers of the *Dido* class with heavier anti-aircraft armaments, and there were even fewer of these types available. The development of an Airborne Early Warning system seemed urgent for the Americans, and a dire necessity for the British.

In June 1944, the Massachusetts Institute of Technology was assigned the task of developing the AEW aircraft[10]. The working thesis was to develop radar equipment with enough power to detect a destroyer at 200 miles, and the ability to detect low-flying aircraft to the maximum range capable within the power output determined by the first requirement. In addition, the radar picture had to be relayed to the air control ship's Aircraft Direction Radar (ADR).

The intention of the Americans was that the crew of the AEW would play an entirely passive role. They would fly the aircraft on the allotted barrier, switch on and operate the equipment as ordered, but the personnel in the control ship's ADR would interpret the relayed radar picture, and decide on the action resulting from that interpretation, such as fighter direction.

The first prototype equipment was assembled at Mount Cadillac, Maine. A series of successful trials resulted, and the project was thereafter codenamed as the Cadillac One and Two Programs. In the Cadillac 1 scenario, the radar was to be fitted into an aircraft suitable for carrier-based operations, while Cadillac 2 was to fit the set into a larger, land-based aircraft, which would have its own Combat Information Centre (CIC). The high-powered radar set to be utilized in this role was developed by the Hazeltine Corporation, and was then produced by General Electric as the AN/APS-20.

At first, the early versions of the APS-20 radar operated on a low frequency (about 4 GHz). This was a deliberate choice, for various reasons: it proved less susceptible to weather attenuation, less 'bounce-back' reflection was encountered, and the picture was clearer. In choosing 'look-down' radar operations over the sea, they took into account the fact that the problem was less serious than over land, where the surface texture is less 'smooth', and reflects back more radiation. However, bad weather conditions at sea would cause adverse wind and wave rippling of the surface texture, and thus affect the efficiency of the AN/APS-20.

The frequency adopted enabled medium-sized aircraft to be detected at a range of 50 nautical miles. It had a 6ft scanner and a cavity magnetron, and each set weighed a ton and cost a million US dollars each. The magnetron caused many of the early problems of unreliability. It had been developed from an example fitted to a ground-based

radar and operated a very high rating. This factor, coupled with the fragile assembly of the cantilevered cathode, which did not stand up well to the hard usage of carrier-deck landings and operations, frequently caused the sets to fail through damage. A second hiccup resulted from the high-power operating mode, which meant that faults could not be checked out on the carrier decks, but had to wait until the aircraft was airborne, which delayed and complicated fault-finding.

In January 1945, eight months after the project began, the first AEW aircraft – a General Motors TBM Avenger – flew. In addition to the pilot, a single radar operator was carried. The radar information picked up was data-linked back, via an AT-53 downward-pointing antenna, to the base aircraft carrier as raw video, and mixed, allowing the ship to produce a radar map of its surrounding area.

By May 1945, 35 AEW Avengers were available to the Pacific Fleet, but the war ended without their participation. Although their radar sets worked reasonably well, the radar relay was disappointing and unreliable. When it failed, the whole system fell down; without an efficient relay, the aircraft were useless, because the aircrew were not trained to make use of the radar picture they were picking up. Post-war work continued on the radio relay problems at a more leisurely pace, and it was not until 1947 that they were overcome and AEW aircraft became part of the US carrier's aircraft complement.

The makeshift Avengers were followed into service in 1950 by the Grumman AF-2W Guardian, which carried the same APS-20 set. Only limited AEW protection was given by this aircraft, whose principal role was ASW. The Guardians were built to operate in pairs – the Hunter (AF-2W) would combine with the APS-20, while the Killer (AF-2S) was equipped with anti-submarine ordnance to finish off any detected submarine.

Douglas had also been working hard on the same problem from the last months of the war onward. The need for airborne radar warning, brought about by the arrival of the *Kamikaze* pilots, was urgent and BuNo 09107 was converted to this rôle. Again, extra accommodation for two radar operators was built into the fuselage, abaft and below the pilot's cockpit, under a large opaque fairing astern of him. The latest search radar set, the AN/APR-1, was mounted in a second large fairing built into the underside the fuselage. To compensate for the extra weight, no armament was fitted.

Redesignated as the XAD-1W, this aircraft continued to be tested, leading to the development of the circular ventrally mounted Radome. This was later also further tested on a single AD-2 aircraft (BuNo 122226), which was similarly adapted. These experiments led to the construction of three versions of the 'W' type – the AD-3W, AD-4W and AD-5W) – totalling 417 aircraft (see pages 66–7, 72, 105).

After the war, the Americans returned to isolationism, and even offered to sell back to the British their own idea for an AEW system! The co-operation of war time was over, so the Royal Navy determined to develop its own AEW capability, which it now saw as essential. Both the Admiralty and the Air Ministry had put forward AEW requirements at the end of the war, but there had initially been a dearth of scientists to go ahead with the programme, which was left to the Americans. In addition, post-war British defence budgets were even tighter than before. Plans to develop an AEW variant of the new Fairey Spearfish torpedo-bomber came to naught, and the project was cancelled.

AD-1

Some 217 AD-1s in the standard attack form were finally completed, with the first (c/n 1938, BuNo 09110) making its maiden flight on 5 November 1946, and the last being accepted by the Navy in August 1949. The leisurely pace of development was dictated by continuing post-war economies, which, by May 1950, had reduced production-line delivery to four per week (from a 1948-9 peak of six).

A single aircraft (BuNo 09195) was taken from the line and modified, with a square wheel-well replacing the old circular one and with full door coverings in place of the AD-1's strut covers. There was extra fuel bunkerage, which increased the total amount carried by 15 US gallons to 380 gallons (1,438 litres). This extended the useful range, and incorporated further fuselage and wing reinforcement, in the light of more adverse landing reports received from the earlier AD-1s and AD-1Qs operating at sea with the fleet. Cockpit controls were also re-vamped, in view of additional equipment, and according to squadron flying experience. The four

exhaust stacks protruding from the exhaust flaps changed to two groups of three, and the air scoop was changed. It had incorporated a series of adjustable flaps, but now it was lipped and more prominent, with two cockpit air ducts outboard a central intake aperture.

AD-2

Following the carrier-landing accidents experienced when the first AD-1s had joined the fleet, an improved version was needed. After tests, this need resulted in the AD-2.

The AD-2 appeared in 1948, and a total of 156 were built (BuNos 122210-122365). The powerplant was the R-3350-26W engine of 3,020hp. A re-worked engine cowling incorporated a new-style exhaust collector ring; the replacement of

the top group of three stacks by a twin allowed external identification. Other external alterations included a redesigned blade aerial, replacing the forward-leaning pole type of the AD-1 with a shorter aerial wire, which ran down to the top of the fuselage. A pitot tube was added to the front top of the vertical stabilizer. For long-range scout missions an extra 500 gallons of fuel were embarked, giving the AD-2 a range of 1,386 nautical miles.

The cockpit canopy was altered slightly at both forward and after ends, with a strengthened and extended head-rest with a flexible pivot aft, for more comfort. Other pilot aides were controls that were redesigned, with symbols of the functions they controlled being incorporated. Hinged doors were introduced for the undercarriage.

Overall length was down to 38ft 2in (11.63m), compared with 39ft 5in (12.01m) on the XBT2D-1. While other

Specification – AD-1	
Powerplant:	R-3350-24W
Weights:	Empty 4,656kg (10,264lb); loaded 7,241kg (16,000lb); full 8,178kg (18,030lb); wing loading n/a; power loading n/a
Dimensions:	Length 11.63m (38ft 2in); height 4.76m (15ft 7½in); wingspan 15.25m (50ft ¼in); wing area 37.192sq m (400.33sq ft)
Performance:	2,500hp Max. speed 589km/h (366mph); at altitude 4,115m (13,500ft) Cruise speed 328km/h (204mph) Rate of climb 1,110km/h (3,492ft/min) Ceiling 10,060m (33,000ft) Range 3,058km (1,900 miles)
Acceptance in service:	1946

Specification – AD-2	
Powerplant:	R-3350-26W
Weights:	Empty 4,784kg (10,546lb); loaded 7,379kg (16,268lb); full 8,284kg (18,263lb); wing loading 40.6lb/sq ft; power loading 2.7kg/hp (6lb/hp)
Dimensions:	Length 11.63m (38ft 2in); height 4.76m (15ft 7½in); wingspan 15.25m (50ft ¼in); wing area 37.192sq m (400.33sq ft)
Performance:	3,020hp Max. speed 517km/h (321mph); at altitude 5,580m (18,300ft) Cruise speed 319km/h (198mph) Rate of climb 853km/h (2,800ft/min) Ceiling 9,965m (32,700ft) Range 1,475km (915 miles)
Acceptance in service:	1948

a.

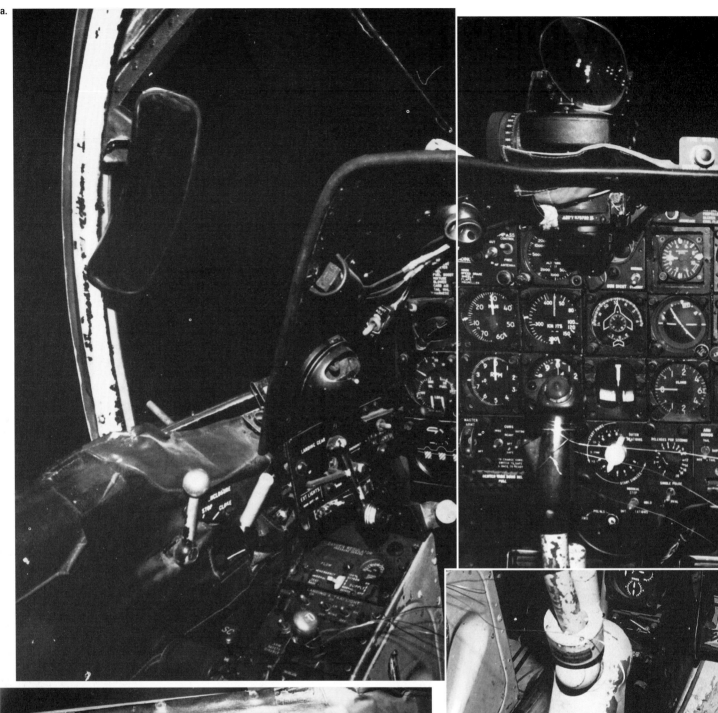

d.

e.

Detail, looking forward, of the cockpit of the A-1E 52-132649 at the USAF Museum, Wright-Patterson Airfield, Ohio

b.

c.

a. The port-side pilot's instrument panel and side panel layout.

b. The pilot's instrument panel.

c. The starboard-side pilot's instrument panel and side-panel layout, with reserve control stick and floor controls with console.

d. The lower port-side pilot's instrument panel and side-panel layout, with control stick and floor controls with console.

e. The port-side floor controls with console.

A busy scene aboard the USS Leyte **(CV-32) in May 1949. In the foreground, two AD-2s of VA-34 are held down on the pitching deck while their powerful (and unusual) ordnance load, a mix of three aerial torpedoes and twelve rockets, is checked out prior to an exercise.** National Archives, College Park, MD

Specification – AD-2Q	
Powerplant:	R-3350-26W
Weights:	Empty 5,062kg (11,159lb); loaded 7,775kg (17,140lb); full 8,683kg (19,143lb); wing loading 42.8lb/sq ft; power loading 2.9kg/hp (6.3lb/hp)
Dimensions:	Length 11.63m (38ft 2in); height 4.76m (15ft 7½in); wingspan 15.25m (50ft ¼in); wing area 37.192sq m (400.33sq ft)
Performance:	2,500hp Max. speed 510km/h (317mph); at altitude 5,580m (18,300ft) Cruise speed 330km/h (205mph) Rate of climb 789km/h (2,590ft/min) Ceiling 8,110m (26,600ft) Range 2,410km (1,497miles)
Acceptance in service:	1948

dimensions remained the same, the weights edged up to 10,546lb (4,784kg) empty, and 18,263lb (8,284kg) maximum, while wing loading went from 33.7lb/sq in (164.7kg/sq m) to 40.6lb/sq in (198.4kg/sq m). Speed was reduced from 375mph (604km/h) to 321mph (517km/h), but the service ceiling improved from 26,000ft (7,925m) to 32,700ft (9,865m). Stall speed was 65 knots.

From this batch, one aircraft (BuNo 122226) was selected to trial an improved engine-cooling system, which was under development, and was later fitted to the AD-3. On conclusion of these tests, the same aircraft was fitted with the experimental ventral Radome for the early warning variant (*see page 66*).

In common with all Skyraider types, a number of other experimental models were tested in the immediate post-war period. Two were believed to have been fitted out as pilotless, radio-controlled drones, packed with electronic measuring instruments. They were to be used to fly through the air over nuclear test sites in the aftermath of atomic bomb detonations, in order to gather radioactive data for analysis. They were given the unofficial designation AD-2D ('D' for data).

In a continuation of the electronic countermeasures programme, 21 aircraft (BuNos 122366–122372, and 122374–122387) were completed in the two-seat variant between September 1948 and April 1949 as the AD-2Q. Finally, one AD-2Q (BuNo 122373) was adapted on the production line to a target-towing trial machine. This Skyraider was ventrally fitted with a Mark 22 aerial target container as the AD-2QU at El Segundo. The theory was duly tested most successfully, which led to a general adaptation to carry this equipment.

In addition to normal military usage with the Navy and Marine Corps, in an effort to extend its potential for civilian duties, a United States Marine Corps AD-2 was fitted out with 250 gallon (946 litre) napalm tanks, modified to carry fire-retardant chemicals for spraying on forest-fire areas. Trials were conducted at Marine Corps Air Station El Toro in 1954, with Major Warren Schroeder piloting the aircraft in a series of test runs. Although these trials provided ample evidence that the Skyraider was perfectly adaptable for such a mission, nothing constructive came of them.

AD-3

The next move was to step up the performance of the AD-2. The initial proposal, in 1947, was to fit the Skyraider with a turbine engine. Five alternatives were given consideration – Douglas's own twin-turbine project, the twin Allison 500 engine, General Electric's TG-100, and two Westinghouse projects, the twin 24C and the twin 19XB. The proposal eventually led to the development of the XA2D-1 Skyshark. This [June 1945] project started out as a simple redesign of the Skyraider airframe to take the new powerplant, but rapidly evolved into a complete new project, resulting in a 22,966lb (10,417kg) attack plane powered by the 5,100eshp XT40-A-6 engine. This gave a significant increase in performance over the Skyraider, but the engine was continually problematic, and the project was finally abandoned.

The AD-3 designation continued to be used, this time to identify the AD-2 fitted with the Wright R-3350-26W engine. The basic design was cleaned up, with a strengthened fuselage and undercarriage, with the oleo gear having 14in (35.5cm) more movement. A better propeller was fitted and the new engine-cooling system was adopted, as well as a redesigned pilot's headrest, leading to a slight change in cockpit canopy profile. The AD-3 kept the same two 20mm wing cannon armament as the AD-2. The tail-wheel design was altered, and it no longer fully retracted into its lower fuselage well. The pitot tube was removed from the tail, while the rear part of the rudder was given a small ventral extension.

Total production of this type was 125 aircraft (BuNos 122729–122853). Of these, one AD-3 (BuNo 122853) was fitted with the 2,700hp R-3359-26WA engine, and

further modified, with an improved tail hook and a new-style windscreen. This aircraft was also fitted with the P-1 auto-pilot, and, with these alterations, became the prototype for the AD-4. Although the auto-pilot was a boon, care had to be taken later, when Skyraiders flying with the USAF and VNAF in South-East Asia were fitted with the G-2 compass. Re-setting this instrument while the P-1 was in use caused 'abrupt and violent rudder forces', which exceeded the Skyraider's design limits and could prove fatal.[41]

As always, there were variations on the basic theme.

AD-3N

The night attack variant was a three-seater built between September 1949 and May 1950. Only 15 (BuNos 122908–122922) were constructed, generally following the earlier versions.

AD-3Q

Ordered as the AD-3QU target tugs, these 23 aircraft (BuNos 122854–122876) were actually completed as two-seater ECM machines under the designation of AD-3Q. The operator's cabin was modified for

Specification – AD-3N	
Powerplant:	R-3350-26W
Weights:	Empty 5,209kg (11,483lb); loaded 8,185kg (18,044lb); full 9,607kg (21,180lb); wing loading 45.1lb/sq ft; power loading 3kg/hp (6.7lb/hp)
Dimensions:	Length 11.63m (38ft 2in); height 4.76m (15ft 7½in); wingspan 15.25m (50ft ¼in); wing area 37.192sq m (400.33sq ft)
Performance:	2,500hp Max. speed 476km/h (296mph); at altitude 5,580m (18,300ft) Cruise speed 317km/h (197mph) Rate of climb 689km/h (2,260ft/min) Ceiling 8,075m (26,500ft) Range 2,405km (1,496miles)
Acceptance in service:	1948

An AD-3N (BuNo 122922) seen at the Patuxent River Air Test Center on 21 November 1949. National Archives, College Park, MD

An AD-3N Skyraider (BuNo 122914) adapted for night-attack operations, one of only fifteen so converted. This one is pictured on 15 March 1951, at the Naval Air Test Center, Patuxent River, during an electronics test programme. National Archives, College Park, MD

greater comfort and the antenna display changed. When required they could be fitted with the Mark 22 aerial target system, which had been proven readily adaptable after trials with the AD-2QU. They were formed into flights of four aircraft for carrier work, and operated in pairs.

AD-3W

After successful trials with the XAD-1W, orders were placed for 31 three-seater AEW variants of the AD-5 (BuNos 122877–122907), known as the 'Guppy'. (Many war-built submarines of the *Gato* class were being streamlined at this time, and the same sort of streamlining was adopted for the Skyraider's aerodynamically shaped dome at the same time.) These

The appearance of the 'Guppy' was memorable, but uninspiring! However, it did an excellent and vital job. This is the Naval Air Test Center's AD-3W (BuNo 122878) seen over NAS Patuxent River on 9 November 1950, with the Electronics Test Flight. In the early 1980s, a lack of such AEW aircraft, due to government policy and cutbacks, cost the Royal Navy many ships and lives in the Falklands War. National Archives, College Park, MD

aircraft were completed minus the landing-gear fairings in an attempt to compensate for the weight of the Radome and equipment, and of the two operators seated side by side in their cabin. To help further with the aerodynamic problems that were caused by this vast carbuncle, a pair of small vertical stabilizer fins were fitted to the horizontal stabilizers. Two aircraft of the series (BuNos 122906 and 122907) were actually finally completed as AD-3Es.

The AEW system was still the most feasible way of detecting incoming enemy air attacks, but it was not the final solution. The sheer numbers of aircraft required to give total cover was as unacceptable as the destroyer radar piquet equation had been. In 1946, it was estimated that the type of antenna carried by carrier-based AEWs was capable of detecting incoming aircraft (at altitudes of between 500 and 3,000ft/150 and 915m) at only 60–70 nautical miles. With aircraft speeds increasing all the time, this was hardly sufficient. It was calculated from this estimate that a fleet would require six AEW aircraft stationed on a circumference 50 nautical miles out, spaced at intervals of 50 nautical miles; even then, there would be only a small overlap. In order to maintain round-the-clock cover of this type, 54 AEW aircraft would be required per fleet. While this would take a large chunk out of an American Task Force, it was totally unacceptable for a British Task Force, whose armour-deck carriers could only carry half as many aircraft of all types as their American counterparts.

Compromise was necessary, either by assuming (as at Okinawa) that all incoming attacks would be down a predicted axis from known enemy airfields, or by placing fewer AEWs closer in to the fleet and accepting the risks from low-flying intruders. The APS-20 had proved itself incapable of determining the height of the inward-bound interceptors; this meant that the ADR had still to do the job of vectoring intercepting fighters.

When the AD-3Ws first arrived in the Navy at the end of 1948, after trials with the Air Development Unit (VX-1), they were formed into two specialist squadrons: VAW-1 for the Pacific Fleet and VAW-3 for the Atlantic Fleet. In 1950, these two units were renamed as VC-11 and VC-12 respectively.

The aircraft were delivered from El Segundo to Norfolk Naval Air Station, Virginia, where their electronic equipment was installed and ground tested.

The cramped conditions of the two radar operatives aboard an **AD-3W Early-Warning Skyraider. This test aircraft was photographed on 3 May 1951.** National Archives, College Park, MD

They were then transferred to either the East or West Coast squadron bases, at Quonset Point or Alameda Naval Air Stations. Here, they were assigned and formed into four-plane detachments. After being trained up, they were assigned to carriers for operational duty.

With the Radomes, these Skyraiders were a different flying proposition from the normal Skyraiders, and had to be treated with care, not least because of the fragility of their vital equipment. Dives and fighter-type manoeuvres were out of the question, although vertical turns and wing-overs were allowed. Specifically banned, although it is hard to imagine that it was ever contemplated in a -4W, or in any other Skyraider variant, was an intentional spin!

With a sea-level maximum speed of 305 knots and a service ceiling of 36,000ft (10,970m), the aircraft had a range of 1,250 nautical miles and an endurance of 7.8 hours.

AD-3E and AD-3S Teams

The two AD-3Ws completed as AD-3Es (Search) were joined by two more aircraft (BuNos 122910 and 122911), converted from AD-3Ns into the AD-3S half of the two-plane Hunter-Killer team, to be employed against the growing Soviet

With a large searchlight carried in an underwing pod, the AD-3S formed part of a Hunter-Killer team able to track Soviet submarines and surface vessels by day and night. This aircraft is seen undergoing checks at the Boca Chica Naval Air Station, Florida, on 13 June 1951. National Archives, College Park, MD

(Below) The Hunter-Killer Team, pictured in action on 31 January 1950, with an AD-3E (BuNo 122906) in the foreground and an AD-3S in the background. This new method of anti-submarine warfare was being tested by VX-1 at Naval Air Station Boca Chica, Florida. National Archives, College Park, MD

(Bottom) The AD-3S (BuNo 122910) on 31 January 1950. This aircraft was one of a pair of AD-3Ns adapted to an exclusively anti-submarine warfare rôle. They were assigned to the Experimental Trials Unit 1 (VX-1) at Key West NAS, Florida. National Archives, College Park, MD

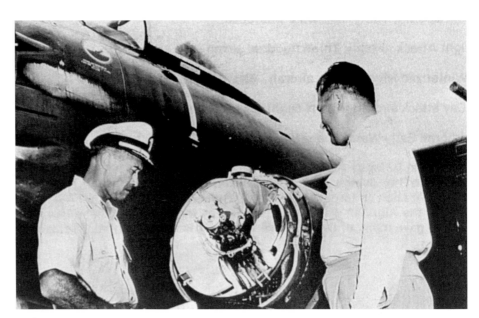

submarine threat. Although the basic concept was sound enough when tested by VX-1 at Boca Chica Naval Air Station in 1949–50, such a combination would prove heavy on carrier space and lacking in flexibility. Not surprisingly, plans were soon being put forward by both Douglas and the Navy to combine both rôles into one airframe.

Douglas had developed the AN/APS-31 Air-to-Surface (ASV) radar/scanner kit, which could be carried in a large pod under the left wing, with a powerful searchlight also mounted on an underwing pod. This version was trialled in one AD3S (BuNo 122910) in the winter of 1949–50, and flown by VX-1 at Boca Chica in 1951. However, its development was overtaken by the Navy's decision to equip or retrofit all AD-4Ws and AD-4Ns with a combined capability.

AD-4

The final modification to appear in the aftermath of the Second World War, which went into full-scale production, was the AD-4, following the testing of the modified AD-3. The main difference between this aircraft and the 372 AD-4s that followed (BuNos 123771–123006, 127844–127879, 128917–129016) was the addition of the APS 19A radar, which required a redesigned instrument panel. They were also equipped with P-1 auto-pilot and had a Mod ¼ Bomb Director. The pitot tube again reappeared at the top front of the vertical stabilizer, and a wider, flat, armoured, bullet-proof pilot's windshield was incorporated.

The three-hook bomb rack was another feature that first appeared with the AD-4. Designed by Douglas, this did away with the need for the sway-brace that was required on the old two-hook Navy type. The new design meant that the ordnance could be flush-mounted with the underwing pylons, giving a more aerodynamic and more secure loading. This improved rack was trialled in one AD-4, but was never adopted by the Navy.

A more successful innovation of the time was also Douglas-inspired – a redesign of the standard bomb shape, with the length-to-diameter ratio (the Fineness Ratio) becoming longer and sleeker at 8:3; these became the Aero 1A series. This format was extended to the whole range of standard bomb sizes – 250, 500, 1,000 and 2,000lb – and also to the 150-, 300- and 450 gallon drop tanks. From the AD-4 onwards, this new aerodynamically improved ordnance began to feature in the Skyraider's ever-increasing range of payloads.

This proved to be the largest production run of any Skyraider model; at the time, it was also expected to have been the last! The conventional Wright R-3350-25WA engine developing 3,020hp gave a top speed of 315 knots and offered a leaner user of gasoline, resulting in a range of 1,110 nautical miles. There was talk in 1947 of an 'improved AD' (the XA2D-1), to be powered by the General Motors Allison T40-A6 turbine-prop twin-section engine driving two 14in Aeroproducts propellers. This eventually metamorphosed into an entirely different aircraft altogether from the AD – the Skyshark – which ultimately did not make the grade.

As before, modifications and adaptations followed, with 63 aircraft being changed to the AD-4L designation, 28 others to the AD-4B, and BuNo 124006 becoming the prototype AD-5.

AD-4N

The three-seater (for pilot, ECM operator and radar plotter) night attack variant was also produced in considerable numbers; 307 were ordered in five batches (BuNos 124128–124156, 124725–124760, 125707–125764, 126876–127018, 127880–127920). All finally adopted the AN/APS-31 and Aero 3A searchlight pods for their S (Killer) mission. During the Korean war, many of these were further modified.

An AD-4NA, BuNo 126948, coded AK, starboard quarter front view, taken on 4 December 1958.
McDonnell Douglas

Details of the AD-4NA (AD-1D) Skyraider BuNo 126922.

(Above left) The non-slip wing-root walkway and the rear of bubble-type cockpit canopy.

(Above) In its day-attack configuration, the shelving that housed the original radar consoles remained. Note the inner fuselage walls, with internal bulged panels for lightness and strength.

In order to cool the electronics equipment crowded into the radar operators' compartment, the AD-4 had a forward-facing air scoop built into the top of the fuselage spine in a stalk-type fairing. Note the blade aerial abaft the air scoop. The rod in the starboard foreground is the folding wing prop.

(Above) Note the hydraulic brace to the rear and the electronically controlled sliding canopy.

The AD-4 introduced the 3,020hp, Wright R-3350-26WA engine with increased efficiency and reliability. Looking forward along the port nose, the two projecting plates are glare shields to aid the pilot's night vision from the flaring of the exhausts, which can be seen behind the engine cowling.

All pictures copyright Peter C. Smith

Final configuration of the AD-4N-1 (BuNo 124725) coded 725, on 18 December 1950. McDonnell Douglas, Long Beach

AD-4L and AD-4NL

A substantial step forward in strafing power was the doubling of the 20mm cannon armament from two to four, introduced in this mark from the 210th production AD-4 onwards. This was in response to combat operations beginning off the Korean coast. The second cannon was mounted on the leading edge of each wing, outboard of the folding hinge. In earlier aircraft this was a retro-fit.

The Korean conflict also forced the carrier air groups to operate in Arctic conditions, which necessitated the hasty fitting of anti-icing and de-icing equipment to 63 serving AD-4s. These 'winterized' modifications earned them the AD-4L designation. Heating boots were located on the leading edges of the wings, on the leading edges of the horizontal stabilizers and on the leading edge of the tail.

Douglas added the second wing gun to the outer section of each wing on one modified AD-4N (BuNo 124153), fitting it out with anti-icing and de-icing equipment following carrier exercises and aircraft tests in Alaskan waters. Trials proved successful, and a further 36 AD-4Ns

(BuNos 124725–124760) were similarly made over.

AD-4W

Some 168 three-seater AEW Skyraiders were built in five batches (BuNos 124076–124127, 124761–12477, 125765–125782, 126836–126875, 127921–127961). Those that served with American squadrons were all converted or built with the E (Search) capability. This comprised a AN/APS-20 Search Radar in the 'Guppy' Radome. Due to the fact that the post-war hiatus had resulted in no suitable British AEW aircraft being available, or even projected until 1952, the Royal Navy was forced to eat humble pie and reverse the 1945 decision to go it alone. Fifty aircraft of this variant were made available to Britain under the Mutual Defence Assistance Programme (MDAP), and joined the Royal Navy as the AEW-1.

AD-4Q

The two-seater ECM variant of the AD-4 totalled just 39 aircraft (BuNos 124037–124075), equipped with the modified

AN/APT-16 ECM system. The addition of the air scoop atop the fuselage for the ECM equipment necessitated moving the radio blade aerial further aft, and modifying it in shape to compensate, being backward-leaning.

AD-4B

The US Navy became locked in a bitter wrangle with the newly independent USAF. The USAF, eager to expand and fulfil its dream of total dominance by air power alone, saw new aircraft-carrier building being authorized by Congress as a threat to its exclusive role, and tried to prevent it. The Navy was anxious to point out the versatility of the aircraft carrier, which could go anywhere in the world on water, and bring power to bear from a base that was sovereign territory, and therefore immune to the restrictions suffered by foreign-based airfields.[42] It took the resignation of a whole flight of admirals to bring the government to its senses. In the event, the fact that the Navy could also carry nuclear weapons was significant, and, until a suitable new delivery system could be designed and built, the ever-reliable

Skyraider, whose lifting power was legendary, seemed the logical choice for a makeshift workhorse.

Twenty-eight AD-4s (BuNos 127854–127860, 127866, 127868–127872, 128937–128943 and 128971–128978) were further strengthened in the main fuselage area for this role. They were equipped with the Mark 51 centre-line ordnance ejector rack, capable of mounting the 1,700lb Mk 7 nuclear bomb, with a yield of 70 kilotons, as well as the Mk 43, Mk 57, Mk 101 ('Lulu') and Mk 104 ('Blue Boy') weapons. These awesome aircraft were given the new designation of AD-4B.

A new delivery method had to be devised – it became known as 'toss bombing', with the weapon being lobbed out and over the aircraft, using the combination of the Aero 18C Armament Control System in conjunction with the Mod 4 Bombing Director. This 'over-the-shoulder' method, once perfected, allowed slow aircraft to deliver their ordnance safely, and gave them a reasonable chance of getting clear of the subsequent detonation and radiation.

Following this programme, a further 165 AD-4Bs (BuNos 132227–132391) were built from scratch. One of these aircraft (BuNo 132363), piloted by Lieutenant-Commander J.S. Noonan, brought wider fame to the Skyraider by setting a new weight-lifting record for single-engine aircraft. On 21 May 1953, this aircraft was loaded with 14,941lb (6,77kg) of ordnance on its external hard points. Three M65 1,000lb bombs, six M177 750lb bombs and six M64 500lb bombs were mounted, plus extra fuel, resulting in a total take-off weight of 26,739lb (12,128kg).

Starboard stabilizer fins on the Royal Navy AEW-1 (AD-4N) WT 121 Skyraider at the Fleet Air Arm Museum, RNAS Yeovilton. Peter C. Smith

Specification – AD-4B	
Powerplant:	R-3350-26WA
Weights:	Empty 5,345kg (11,783lb); loaded 8,468kg (18,669lb); full 10,986kg (24,221lb); wing loading 46.6lb/sq ft; power loading 3.1kg/hp (6.9lb/hp)
Dimensions:	Length 11.96m (39ft 3in); height 4.78m (15ft 8¼in); wingspan 15.25m (50ft ¼in); wing area 37.192sq m (400.33sq ft)
Performance:	3,020hp Max. speed 515km/h (320mph); at altitude 4,570m (15,000ft) Cruise speed 315km/h (196mph) Rate of climb 908km/h (2,980ft/min) Ceiling 7,255m (23,800ft) Range 1,450km (900miles)
Acceptance in service:	1949

AD-5

By the end of the 1940s, it appeared that the Skyraider, with its adaptability and versatility, would continue to be the main workhorse of the fleet for several more years, but that its actual production life was nearing the end. In an era of Navy jet aircraft, the Skyraider was looking increasingly outmoded. Douglas made an effort to breathe new life into the design by proposing, at the end of 1948, the fitting of a turbo-compound R-3350 for extra power and lift, creating the AD-5. Military budgets were tight and the proposed new engine was both heavier and bigger than the existing power plant. Accommodating it would entail a complete redesign of the forward airframe. After examination and discussion, the Bureau of Aeronautics rejected the idea.

Undeterred, Douglas tried again. The first radical idea was dropped, and a new rôle was proposed, utilizing the R-3350-26WA engine. In December 1949, Douglas approached the Navy with the AD-5 purely as an anti-submarine warfare aircraft. Such a machine would combine the two separate roles of Hunter and Killer, as indicated by the S and E capabilities. This displayed good logic and, in principle, the Navy was in favour of the idea. Once again, however, a considerable redesign would be essential, including widening the forward fuselage to allow for side-by-side seating. In compensation, the now-redundant dive brakes could be dispensed with. The costs involved in such a re-working of the basic Skyraider design again gave the Navy pause for thought, despite the attractions of the concept. No final decision was forthcoming, and the matter rested there for the time being.

Developments to 1950

Designation	Rôle	Total	BuNos	Notes
AD-1	Attack	242	09110–09351	*1 to AD-2: 09195*
AD-1Q	ECM	35	09352–09386	
AD-2	Attack	156	122210–122365	
AD-2D	Drones	2	N/A	*Unofficial*
AD-2Q	ECM	21	122366–122372, 122374–122387	
AD-2QU	Target tow	1	122373	
AD-3	Attack	125	122729–122853	*1 to AD-4: 122853*
AD-3N	Night attack	15	122908–122922	*2 to AD-3S: 122910–122911*
AD-3Q	ECM	23	122854–122876	
AD-3W	AEW	31	122877–122907	*2 to AD-3E: 122906–122907*
AD-3E	Hunt	2	122906–122907	*Ex-AD-3W*
AD-3S	Kill	2	122910–122911	*Ex- AD3N*
AD-4	Attack	372	123771–123006, 128917–129016	*1 to AD-5: 124006; 36 to AD-4L: 124725–124760,127844–127879; 28 to AD-4B: 127854–127860, 127866, 127868–127872, 128937–128943*
AD-4N	Night attack	307	124128–124156, 124725–124760, 125707–125764, 126876–127018, 127880–127920	*100 to AD-4NA: 125742–125764, 126876–126883, 126903–126925, 126947–126969, 126988–127010; 38 to AD-4NL: 124725–124760*
AD-4W	AEW	168	124076–124127, 124761–124777, 125765–125782, 126836–126875, 127921–127961	*50 to RN*
AD-4L	Weatherized	63	123935, 123952–124005, 127845–127852	*Service mod*
AD-4Q	ECM	39	124037–124075	
AD-4NL	Weatherized	36	124725–124760	
AD-5B	Nuclear attack	193	127854–127860, 127866, 127868–127872, 128937–128943, 128971–128978, 132227–132391	*First 28 were modified AD-4*

CHAPTER EIGHT

Combat Over Korea

The US Navy Experience I

Communist North Korea's invasion of South Korea was a total surprise, and successful. It was clear that, until the leading nations' peacetime land and air forces could be mobilized, the only power that the UN could bring to bear on the aggressors lay with the ever-flexible maritime forces. Great Britain still maintained a reasonable-sized fleet at this time, and only British and US carriers could reach the threatened coast in time to be effective. A striking force was hastily assembled from their ships therefore, and those available in the area sailed to intervene.

Viewed from under the carrier's foredeck, an AD is launched from the USS Philippine Sea **(CV-47), off Korea, 1951. AD-4Bs from VA-115 and VA-65 operated from the** Philippine Sea. **Before sailing from San Diego, California, on 5 July 1950, she had embarked VA-115 as part of her Air Group 11 (CVG-11). Between 26 March and 2 April 1951, she disembarked CVG-11 in Japan, and embarked in their place three F4U-4B Corsair squadrons, as well as the VA-65 Skyraiders, all from CVG-2, which had previously operated from the USS** Valley Forge **(CV-45).** Roland W. Baker via Martin Bowman

Early Strikes

Striking Force 77[43] was placed under the overall command of Vice Admiral A.D. Struble, USN, and was based on two aircraft carriers – the American heavy carrier USS *Valley Forge* (CV-45) and the British light fleet carrier HMS *Triumph*. Their heavy-gun support was provided by two cruisers – the British 6in-gunned *Belfast* (flying the flag of Rear Admiral W.G. Andrews, RN), and the larger American 8in-gunned *Rochester*. Their screen of ten destroyers comprised the American *Shelton, Eversole, Fletcher, Radford, Maddox, Samuel N. Moore, Brush* and *Taussig* and the British *Consort* and *Cossack*.

A meeting held in Tokyo on 29 June between Admiral Joy and Generals McArthur and Stratemeyer decided upon the North Korean Air Force as the carriers' first major target.[44] It was estimated that this comprised 54 warplanes, all supplied by the Soviet Union, 33 YAK fighters and 21 Ilyushin bombers. Its main air bases were close to the Communist capital Pyongyang, and Vice Admiral Struble was instructed to take these out. Secondary targets allocated to the Allied naval aircraft were railway marshalling yards, which were channelling troops, munitions and supplies south to reinforce the invading armies, and the associated bridges.

Task Force 77 sailed on 1 July for the west Korean coast and the area off Pyongyang, reinforced by a signal from the Commander Naval Force, Far East, which extended its brief:

CINCFE authorizes you to continue strikes past the first day in view of the rapidly deteriorating Korean situation. Highest priority to be given to rail facilities in vicinity of Kumchon, Sariown, and Sinanju.

At 0545 on 3 July, the first attacks were launched. The Fleet Air Arm had the honour of making the first strike, with twelve Fairey Firefly and nine rocket-armed Supermarine Seafires being launched. They hit hangars and installations on Haeju airfield, and then turned to the railways and bridges as their secondary targets. Many hits were scored and they all returned to the *Triumph* at 0815. When the *Valley Forge*'s turn to strike came, her striking force – 16 Chance-Vought F4U Corsairs of VF-54, each with eight 5in rockets, and the 12 AD Skyraiders of VA-55 under the command of Lieutenant-Commander N.D. Hodson – was launched at 0600. Each Skyraider was armed with two 500lb bombs and six 100lb

Enemy aircraft on the field were strafed and set afire, and there were no casualties among any of the American aircraft from return AA fire, which was light.

In the afternoon, VA-55 went back for a second dive-bombing strike, this time taking the Pyongyang rail marshalling yards. They claimed to have destroyed 15 locomotives, with ten others damaged, as well as many wagons; their bombs also exploded on the roundhouse, repair sheds and station, and tore up sections of rail track. They also targeted rail and road bridges over the River Taedong, but only scored a succession of near misses.

four managed to return to the *Valley Forge* safely, but one of them had suffered damage to its flaps-actuating gear, and its flaps could not be lowered on the landing approach. After 'a high and fast approach', it 'took a cut, landed wheels first and bounced over the protecting barriers into the planes parked forward. One AD and two F4Us were totally destroyed while three ADs, one F4U and two F9Fs were damaged.'[45]

This high rate of achievement against North Korea continued throughout the first month, at the end of which Task Force 77's aircraft claimed to have destroyed 38 enemy warplanes and to have damaged another 27,

AD-4B from VA-115 and VA-65 – landing back aboard. Roland W. Baker via Martin Bowman

bombs. They were escorted by eight F9F2 Grumman Panther jet fighters, which were being used for the first time in combat by the US Navy.

The Skyraiders met with poor weather conditions en route to the target zone, which helped shield them from the enemy defences. The ADs' target was Pyongyang airfield itself, and they made a fast approach, with a final pushover into their attack dives from 7,000ft (2,130m). One bomb scored a direct hit on the enemy fuel-storage farm, starting a satisfactory fire, while all three hangars on the field were hit and the runways badly cratered.

The next day was American Independence Day, and AD-55's Skyraiders celebrated with their own brand of fireworks against the same targets. This time, their bombs dropped a span of the bridge. Ten more locomotives were claimed as destroyed, and attacks were also made on North Korean gunboats on the Taedong, and left burning. In total, eleven North Korean warplanes had been destroyed and one damaged.

In return, the Skyraiders suffered their first combat casualties. Anti-aircraft fire was heavier than on the previous day, and four ADs were hit over the target area. All

all except two on the ground. In knocking out the North Korean Air Force right at the beginning of hostilities, the Skyraiders had made a significant contribution.

The Skyraider as a Torpedo Bomber

One unexpected outcome of the Navy's involvement in the Korean War was the Skyraider's only chance to function in one of its original roles, as a torpedo bomber! The background to the story involved all three services.

On 1 November 1950, the Chinese Communists sent in their armies across the Yalu River to save the North Koreans from total defeat. The United Nations forces were quickly beaten back by weight of numbers, and, by 4 January 1951, the Communists re-took the South Korean capital of Seoul. Although a counter-offensive freed the city again by 18 March, a further Communist counter-attack temporarily halted the United Nations advance. The war settled down to a bloody stalemate, reminiscent of the First World War trench warfare in Flanders. In the meantime, General Douglas McArthur

Bay on the Yellow Sea. The rivers' water level was partly controlled by eighteen sluice gates built on top of a massive concrete dam, which held back the waters of the Hwachon Reservoir. This structure had been built by the Japanese in the early 1940s, when Korea was under their control, as a means of providing fresh water for the city, but, lying as it now did behind Communist lines, it represented more of a threat than a salvation to the population. If the Communists controlled the sluice gates, they could raise them, or even destroy the dam, and flood Seoul. This would also deny the armies of the United

had flooded the River Roer, General Ridgway wanted early on to pre-empt any such control, and had called for the Hwachon Dam sluices to be taken out totally. He asked the USAF to repeat the RAF's dambusting exploits, and, accordingly, attacks were made by Boeing B-29 heavy bombers using 6 ton bombs. Their attack was a total failure. The US Eighth Army had, meanwhile, thrown pontoon bridges across the Pukhan to continue its advance and, on 9 April, the Communists duly raised the sluice gates and released the flood water exactly as predicted. Two bridges were immediately affected, one being totally

AD-4Bs from VA-115 and VA-65 – the batman directs a Skyraider back on board after a mission.
Roland W. Baker via Martin Bowman

Hook down, undercarriage down, heads down! Safely back aboard, even if the landing is not a perfect three-pointer. Roland W. Baker via Martin Bowman

was summarily sacked by President Truman for proposing to bomb China in retaliation. The commander of the US Eighth Army, General Matthew B. Ridgway, took over as Commander, Far East.

The lines of the two opposing armies straddled the original frontier and, although Seoul was in Allied hands, it was threatened, not only by the Communist armies, but by another, more insidious danger. The South Korean capital stands just west of the confluence of the Han and Pukhan Rivers, before they flow into Asan

Nations any opportunity to re-start an offensive, and advance north of the flooded rivers against Communist positions. On the other hand, the Communists could close the sluice gates totally, making the river easily fordable for their own advancing hordes. Either way, whoever controlled the great sluices, 20ft (6.10m) in height and 40ft (12.20m) in width, controlled the destiny of the battlefield in mid-Korea.

No doubt influenced by his combat experience in Germany at the end of the Second World War, when the Germans

washed away, the other withdrawn under threat of collapse, and the advance ground to a halt. Exasperated, Ridgway again called on the US Air Force to do something, but his request was turned down; even its biggest bombs were powerless against such a massive structure.

Ridgway tried another tack, and two attempts were made to storm the dam using special assault forces. Both attempts failed. A general offensive followed and troops of the Eighth Army seized the area around the Hwachon Reservoir for a

AD-4Bs from VA-115 and VA-65 – a four-plane formation stacked up over the Philippine Sea. Roland W. Baker
via Martin Bowman

A Navy Skyraider armed with three 1,000lb bombs takes off from the carrier USS Valley Forge **(CV-45) for a
strike on Communist targets in Korea, on 26 April 1951.** National Archives, College Park, MD

short period. A team of US Marine engineers was rushed forward to sabotage the sluice gates and lock them open permanently. However, before they could do any more than make an inspection, on 22 April 1951, the Communist army again threw the Americans back and re-took the dam. Ridgway was back where he had started!

Within three hours of receiving the request for help, *Princeton* despatched a striking force of six AD4 Skyraiders, each armed with two 2,000lb bombs. They had a fighter escort of five F4U Corsair fighter-bombers of VF-193, for flak-suppression runs ahead of the bombing attack. The Skyraiders duly carried out the assault with considerable élan, and one bomb hit and

targets. The Soviet Union still had some old battleships in full commission at this period, and also had a large and growing number of 15,000 ton cruisers of the *Sverdlof* class built. Against these, until guided tactical atomic weapons could be developed, the torpedo was still the most effective counter-measure. Thus it came about that the Skyraider was finally seen, for the only time in history,

An AD-1 of VA-195 unfolds its wings aboard the carrier USS Princeton **(CV-37) off the Korean coast preparatory to a strike mission.** McDonnell Douglas, Long Beach

The Army now turned to the Navy for help. A request was sent to the commander of Task Force 77, Rear Admiral Ralph A. Ofstie, for his aircraft to try and destroy at least two of the vital sluice gates, to lessen the potential danger of further flooding. Operating with this task force was the attack carrier USS *Princeton* (CV-37), commanded by Captain William O. Gallery. Aboard, she had VA-195, under the command of Lieutenant-Commander Harold G. Carlson.

holed the dam, but all the sluice gates remained unscathed.

There remained one final hope. Among her ordnance inventory the *Princeton*, like all attack carriers, carried a small complement of the Mark 13 aerial torpedo. Despite the advent of the air-launched rocket, and its successful application in the last two years of the Second World War against smaller and lightly armed shipping targets, it was still a fact that this weapon was relatively ineffective against larger warship

fulfilling the combined rôle of dive and torpedo bomber for which it had originally been developed ten years earlier.

Captain Gallery proposed that the torpedoes should be utilized in a second attack by the *Princeton*'s Skyraiders against the stubborn sluice gates. His idea was taken up with alacrity, even though very little training had been done in this rôle. Neither was there any opportunity for further practice, as the mission was scheduled for the following morning. The hazards faced by torpedo bombers were well known, and the dam was well defended, with anti-aircraft guns placed in the hills surrounding the natural amphitheatre of the reservoir valley. Only a comparatively short lead-in was available once the attacking force had cleared this barrier, and there was little time to line up with the obscure, 40ft (12.20m) wide targets.

A strike force of eight Skyraiders was launched from the *Princeton* on the morning of 1 May 1951. It comprised five VA-195 aircraft and three VC-35 Skyraiders, under the overall command of CAG-19, Commander R.C. Merrick. For flak suppression, a strong force of twelve F4U Corsairs from both VF-192 and VF-193, armed with VT fused bombs, was also launched.

On arrival over the target zone, at 1130, they met only light anti-aircraft fire. Once the Corsairs had dropped their ordnance on those guns that revealed themselves, the Skyraiders were able to make relatively untroubled approaches to the target at very low level. A photographic Grumman F9F Panther jet from VC-61 took pictures. All eight torpedoes were launched from the bombers; one proved to be a dud, while another veered off course and failed to strike the target. The remaining six ran 'hot and true', and detonated on or near their targets.

Not all the warhead explosions that resulted were on target, or produced the desired results, but one direct hit punched a hole 10ft (3m) in diameter through one of the sluice gates, while others took out one sluice gate completely. The Skyraiders had done all that had been asked of them, without loss. As they left the scene, water was pouring through the gaping apertures, and the threat of further flooding had been eliminated.

After this attack, unique in naval aviation history, VA-19 was proud to carry the title of 'Dambusters'.

Princeton's Skyraider Missions

The Hwachon Reservoir attack, although the most spectacular, was only one of many daily strikes being mounted by VA-19's 'Able-Dogs' at this period. Almost continually in action, the Skyraider was proving itself an invaluable weapon in the United Nations armoury. It was up against superior numbers; the enemy's Soviet-supplied T-34 tanks were proving too tough for the

Seen under the wing of a Navy AD-4 Skyraider from VA-195, under Commander Harold G. Carlson, USN, the torpedoes launched at low level explode as they hit the sluice gates of the Hwachon Dam, on 1 May 1951. This famous strike marked the last combat use of the aerial torpedo against an enemy target. National Archives, College Park, MD

few American tanks, and even the American 2.36in bazooka anti-tank rockets bounced off their armoured hides. Six years earlier, the Germans had found that only precision bombing had any effect on these monsters, and the Americans were now discovering the same. On the Eastern Front, it was the Junkers Ju. 87 Stuka that had the accuracy to deliver this type of attack; the piston-engined Skyraider, as much a subject of scorn as the Stuka, was now proving itself the superior aircraft in this rôle, outstripping even the USAF jets.

The ADs were not only up against a fanatical enemy, it was now also the summer monsoon season. There was persistent fog over their operating area, with low ceilings, which made dive bombing impossible: Many scheduled flights were cancelled or delayed because of poor visibility and/or low ceilings either over the force or in the

target area. On one replenishment day the fog lasted all day and was so thick that visibility was seldom greater than 200 yards. In addition to the fog, pilots were further plagued by heavy haze and smoke in the vicinity of the front lines, which often reduced visibility to less than one mile.[46]

None the less, the Skyraider strikes continued. On 29 April, *Princeton* launched a typical 22-AD mission, which made strikes along the front and against Communist supply routes in the immediate rear of the front. It destroyed 60–70 enemy-held buildings, 45–75 fuel drums, three ox-carts and three enemy-occupied villages, inflicting about 125 casualties on the enemy. On the next day, in addition to the 2,000lb bomb attacks on the dam, interdiction flights along the front in support of the still-withdrawing UN troops were made from Seoul to Kowon. They claimed the

Ordnance expenditure Korea – *Princeton* April 1951

Bombs (lb)	No.	Fuses	No.
2,000 GP	214	AN-M103A1	115
1,000 GP	309	AN-M139A1	1,400
500 GP	327	AN-M140A1	172
250 GP	944	AN-M168	7,556
100 GP	3,883	AN-M100A2	8,913
350 DB	4	AN-M101A2	317
260 Frag.	4,540	AN-M102A2	450
Napalm tanks	1,552	AN-M166	620
Thickener	57,540	M115	88
Mk 13 torpedoes	8	M116	4
Rockets 6.5 ATAR	835	M117	30
Rockets 5.0 HVAR Mk 6	1,338	M125A1 (6 Hr)	23
Rockets 5.0 motor	2,170	AN-M230	2
Rockets 3.5 head Mk 8	4	T4E1	2
Rockets 3.25 motor	4	M157	2,946
Fuse rockets Mk 149	1,338	M157	2,946
20mm cannon ammo	165,592		
.50 cal m.g.	573,750	Flares Mk 6	102

destruction of two enemy barracks, two gun emplacements and caused an estimated 300-plus casualties among the enemy's ground forces, as well as destroying four locomotives, 3,035 wagons, one building, 50–75 fuel drums, a truck and two ox carts. Two photo-reconnaissance missions were also flown, one over the Chongjin area and one from Wonsan to Kowon.

On 1 May, while the dam sluice was being breached, there were similar strikes in the Sanchon area and along the front above Seoul, which destroyed two more enemy gun emplacements, a supply dump and eleven trucks. At the same time, photo reconnaissance was conducted over the Chuuronjang area and the transportation facilities in the Hamhung area.

The *Princeton* replenished at sea that evening and next morning was back striking hard at the advancing enemy columns. Eighteen Skyraiders were launched and attacks made in the Wonsan, Hungnam areas, and again along the front line above Seoul. Two more enemy artillery pieces were knocked out, as well as twelve trucks and sundry smaller vehicles, and a bridge was dropped. Photo flights covered the areas west of Kowon and north of Pyongyang. After replenishing again, *Princeton* moved further north to follow up on what the photographs had revealed and launched another 24 AD strikes against Communist transport systems at Songkin, Kilchu and Sinpungni, claiming the destruction of one gun position, two complete bridges, while

knocking a span out of a third, as well as sections of vital railway track.

On 5 May, an even greater effort was made and no less than 29 Skyraiders took part in interdiction strikes against the enemy supply routes in the Kowon and Yonghung region, north of Seoul and in the eastern front area. Four railway bridges and one road bridge had spans knocked out, while five rail cars and more than twenty wagons were burnt.

No less than 30 Skyraiders were despatched from the *Princeton* on 6 May, an incredible achievement and one that reflected the gravity of the military situation ashore as fresh Chinese armies continued to smash into the UN forces. The ADs hit Communist transport from Songjin to Wonsan and, again, bridge spans were demolished, locomotives and wagons destroyed, fuel dumps blown up and road vehicles strafed.

The ordnance material expended during this period of non-stop air support can perhaps be estimated from the figures for one month's operations from the *Princeton*. (See the table above.)

Guided Missiles

GMU-90

In those desperate days, conventional dive-bombing and strafing attacks were not the only contributions made by the

carrier-based Skyraiders to the discomfort of the enemy.

The idea of hitting heavily defended targets by means of remote-controlled aircraft packed with high-explosives had long intrigued airmen, and a great deal of research in this field had already been done in the 1920s and 1930s.[47] Contrary to many American accounts, it was not they, but mainly the Italians and the Germans who had pioneered this work; indeed, the Italians were known to have used such devices in combat as early as 1942.[48]

Once research in the field was fully funded in the USA, during the Second World War, some significant advances were made, albeit with little success. Postwar, research continued and the latest manifestation of one particular type of guided aircraft (as distinct from missiles such as the Bat or the Pelican) was trialled by the USA's Guided Missile Unit, GMU-90. The AD-2D drone aircraft had played a rôle in monitoring radiation from the fallout of the atomic bomb tests against warships at Bikini Atoll; subsequently, specially modified Grumman F6F-5K Hellcat fighters were fitted out as drones. The Hellcats were fitted with a remote-controlled television guidance device, and armed with a single 2,000lb bomb affixed to the underside of the central fuselage.

A team of two AD-4Ns monitored the take-off and subsequent aerial television control of the F6F-5K. The equipment was mounted in the after cabin, and the two-man operating team guided the aircraft to the target area, standing off from the danger zone and controlling the final dive into its objective. Although tests proved 'patchy', and not very accurate, it was decided to combat-test the device. CV-35 was selected for the job.

Operations of Boxer's GMUs

Following the pioneering work of GMU-90, the carrier *Boxer* (CV-21) was despatched to join Task Force 77, which sailed from Yokosuka, Japan on 23 August 1952.[49] In addition to her normal Skyraider complement, which comprised the 16 AD-4s and 23 pilots of VA-65, commanded by Commander A. Sherwood, she had aboard the three AD-4Ws of VC-11's Detachment 'A', commanded by Lieutenant J. Waddell, and Detachment 'A' of VC-35, commanded by Lieutenant R. W. Taylor, with four AD-4NLs and one AD-2Q.

The *Boxer* rendezvoused with Task Force 77, now commanded by Rear Admiral A. Soucek in the carrier *Essex* (CV-9) on 26 August 1952. Air operations commenced on the next day, with a total of 86 combat sorties (56 of them by the Skyraiders) being launched by the *Boxer* Air Group; their targets were in the vicinity of Chosen, and inland storage and supply areas south-west of Wonsan. In all, 66 tons of ordnance were dropped on supplies and troop areas.

by the simultaneous launch of the controlling AD-4N from the starboard catapult.[50] The first Skyraider kept pace with the drone, which was radio-controlled through its launch and into its initial climb to the required altitude by the second controlling AD-5N (piloted by Lieutenant Taylor), which waited on the deck. When the drone was safely aloft and cruising, Taylor's controlling Skyraider was launched, climbing quickly to a position above and behind the F6F-5K. It re-

aircraft fire, a signal was sent. This controlled the Hellcat's ailerons and flaps, sending it diving into the target. The 2,000lb bomb caused a large detonation and raised clouds of earth, dust and smoke over the area of impact, but it was not until the photo-reconnaissance aircraft had over-flown the target that results could be ascertained. The pictures were returned to the carrier, and careful analysis of them indicated that the bridge was no longer standing after this first attempt.

27 August 1951. Four Skyraiders from the carrier USS Boxer (CV-21) fly over the Japan Sea on their way to demolish an enemy bridge west of Wonsan, Korea. These dive bombers are carrying a bomb load equal to that of a Second World War Army B-17. Flying the Skyraiders are Naval Reserve pilots formerly based at **NAS Dallas, Texas.** McDonnell Douglas, Long Beach

On the next day, 28 August 1952, the weather was poor. Strikes did not commence until 1230, when a further 43 combat sorties, including 27 by the ADs, were launched against targets in the Songjin-Kilchu area. They delivered 23 tons of ordnance into the No 2 hydro-electric plant at Chosan and south of the Ambyon reservoir.

The significance of this day was the fact that it marked the first GMU attack. One of the six F6F-5k drones was launched from *Boxer's* port catapult, accompanied

assumed control and placed the drone on a heading towards the selected target – the Hungnam bridge, a strategic crossing that had so far defied repeated USAF attempts at its destruction.

The camera in the Hellcat's cockpit sent a fuzzy but clear enough picture to the controlling AD-4N's monitor to enable Taylor's crew to control the drone with a reasonable degree of accuracy. It was steered to the bridge and then, from a safe distance outside the zone of heavy anti-

Following this success, VC-35 continued operations against other worthwhile targets, mainly rail bridges and tunnels, which could only be demolished by heavy ordnance delivered with great accuracy.

The second F6F-5K drone attack was made on the following day, 29 August, as part of some 112 combat sorties flown from the *Boxer*. The bulk of these sorties (78 in total) were made by the Spad. The targets were a large rubber factory, military billeting

Skyraiders operating from the Bon Homme Richard **(CV-31) off Korea.** Ron McMasters

and troop barracks at Pyongyang; 81 tons of ordnance were deposited.

Operations were curtailed during the next two days due to necessary replenishments and bad weather, but began again on 1 September. On this day, from 0430, a total of 130 combat sorties were flown (88 of them by the ADs), against industrial and mining installations at Chongjin. There, thermo-electric plants, transformers, iron-works, barracks, warehouses and supply buildings were wiped out, while, at Musan on the Tumen border, an ironworks was totally destroyed. This day also saw the launch of two drones, numbers 3 and 4,

Rarin' to go! A Skyraider with prop spinning and a very mixed load of ordnance stands ready for take-off on the deck of its carrier off the Korean coast. A Chance-Vought F4U Corsair, wings folded, is spotted on the side of the deck. San Diego Aerospace Museum

which were guided in by the AD-4Ns to make excellent attacks.

The final two F6F-5K drones were launched the following day, 2 September, making a total of six such sorties.

These six missions by F6F-5K drones were absolutely unique in the history of both the US Navy and the Skyraider, and were never repeated in combat. Lieutenant Taylor's VC-35 has a valid claim to a special place in the annals of naval aviation.

On 2 September, the Skyraiders of VA-65 flew several missions, with 72 combat sorties being contributed to the total of 84 conventional strikes flown. The weather closed in on the next day and, on 4 September, the carriers *Boxer* and *Essex*, escorted by the destroyer *Park*, departed from Task Force 77 to return to Yokosuka. Forty-seven of *Boxer's* aircraft flew ashore to Atsugi airbase on 4 September.

During this intensive period, the *Boxer* Group Skyraiders had flown 401 sorties, offensive and defensive, with VA-65 totalling 3,213 flight hours. This worked out at 4.9 flights per pilot and an average

of 12.85 flight hours per pilot. VC-11 had contributed 40.5 flight hours (6.7 hours per pilot and 2.8 flights per man), while VC-35's 'Hush-Hush' missions gave figures of 62.9 hours total flying time, or 10.5 hours per pilot with an average sortie rate of four per pilot.

Such figures were typical for Skyraider squadrons during the Korean conflict.

Additional Armour Protection

As the enemy flak intensified, so the need for greater Skyraider aircrew protection became the dominant factor in the decision as to whether or not they continued combat operations. This increasing danger was exacerbated by the zeal and courage of the Navy and Marine Corps Spad pilots themselves. They persistently pressed down low to ensure accurate delivery of their payloads, especially when conducting road and rail cut missions, where precision was essential. This technique was

actually against official policy. Loss and damage rates became so bad that the BuAer estimated in late 1950 that attrition would use up their whole stock of ADs with nine months!

In the light of this crisis point, and with the AD-4 production line due to finally close in 1951, Lieutenant-Commander Hank Suerstedt, the BuAer AD Project Officer, Marine Corps Major Ken Reusser, of the Bureau Armament division (who had been the driving force in getting an extra two 20mm cannon into the Spad), and Douglas Aircraft Corporation's senior naval representative in Washington, Bob Canaday, got their heads together. Their aim was to effect some kind of rescue, and persuade the Navy to place a fresh contract.

The Senior Plans Officer was not enthusiastic. The Pentagon had already undertaken a detailed evaluation of the Soviet ground-attack aircraft *par excellence*, the Ilyushin IL-2 *Shturmovik*, which was the most heavily armoured ground-attack plane ever produced and had earned itself a legendary reputation in this rôle. The aircrew of the IL-2 were encased in an armoured-steel box of enormous strength. The American technical experts concluded, however, that the adoption of such protection for the Skyraider was out of the question; the extra weight would have too adverse an effect upon the AD's performance. Suerstedt's initial request was therefore rejected outright and he was told to mind his own business. In fact, his letter was sent back endorsed 'Zapateros a tus zapatos', which translates as 'Cobbler, stick to your last'!

Undeterred, the Douglas company made a detailed study of its own. The experts carefully analysed the bulk of the Skyraider's ground-fire hits, and came up with a pattern of the most common type of structural damage. They made a small model of the Skyraider and passed Lucite rods through the simulated flak entrance and exit holes to illustrate the concentration. Having concentrated on the main problem areas, the Douglas team then came up with a proposed solution. The vulnerable areas as indicated by the model could be covered by sheets of a new material, a compound of steel and duraluminum, which was strong but comparatively lightweight; this would provide the necessary protection. Each sheet was an eighth of an inch to half an inch thick, and weighed about 600lb.

The Navy agreed to tests of the new armoured sheets. These were conducted at the Naval Proving Grounds of Dahlgren, Virginia, Patuxent River, Maryland and Quonset Point, Rhode Island. The performance of the new armour was impressive, for, although a .50-calibre bullet could penetrate the ½in plate, its velocity was so retarded that it caused little or no damage. A 20mm HE incendiary shell hit was found to cause extensive dishing of the plate and to crack it, but the armour totally excluded the damaging fragments.

Douglas refined the sheets so that specially formed sections could be produced. These could be tailored to fit precisely the areas of the Spad that were considered most vulnerable. These were the under section of the main central wing and fuselage section, where the pilot and the main fuel cell needed protection; the under and side sections around the engine and along the central fuselage; the pilot's headrest, and so on.

The problem of obtaining enough aluminium (which was then scarce) to manufacture this new composite armour was eventually solved with the direct (if largely unofficial) collaboration of Lieutenant-Commander Williard Nyburg, a special assistant for military production in the Office of the Secretary of Defense, Washington, DC. The Marine Corps was won over and Douglas flew out the armoured sections to Korea to field-fit them on their ADs. Loath to be seen to be playing second fiddle to the Marines, the Navy followed suit, and the adoption of the armour spread. The Douglas AD-4 line was re-started, the first of four such re-starts through the years; Heinemann had been shrewd enough to keep the machine tools and plant in reserve after each close-down.

There was a final footnote to this remarkable initiative, so reminiscent of Heinemann's original ploy with the BuAer back in 1944, which kept the Skyraider flying. Ironically, Lieutenant-Commander Suerstedt, who had played such a significant part in this achievement, was appointed Commanding Officer of Navy Skyraider Squadron VF-54, relieving Lieutenant-Commander Paul Gray. He was soon leading his squadron into low-level combat action in Korea, thus metaphorically putting his money where his mouth had been!

SKYRAIDER MEN – Ron McMasters, USN

The Korean War saw the first full-scale involvement of the 'Spad' on a combat basis and she fully proved her worth. Among the American aircraft carriers operating off the coast between May and December 1951, flying missions against Communist targets ashore was the *Bon Homme Richard* (CV-31) had embarked VA-923 equipped with the Skyraider. Ron had flown the Curtis SB2C Helldiver both aboard carriers, in the Mediterranean and North Atlantic during 1947, and from shore bases as a Naval Reserve pilot in 1948, but it was with the Skyraider, after once more being called to the colours, that he flew his first combat mission.

Ron hailed from northern Carolina, where he was born on 5 March 1924. He enlisted in the Navy in September 1943, but did not finally graduate from flight school until April 1946. After serving with the Helldiver, he took discharge in November 1947, but the Berlin crisis of July 1948 saw him recalled to service for the first time and it was not until June 1950 that he was again discharged from duty. He remained flying with the Navy reserve forces and the invasion of the Republic of Korea again saw his return to duty when he was recalled for the second time in September 1950.

After training on the AD, his tour duty with VA-923 followed, where he flew fifty combat missions. On return he became an AD instructor at the Fleet Air Gunner School, NAS El Centro, California, and he was not again discharged until June 1953. Once an aviator, always an aviator, and Ron continued to fly with the Naval Reserve until he retired in 1965. His naval career won him two Air Medals as well as various Theatre medals.

These calls on him naturally caused frequent interruptions to his education but he persevered and finally completed college, majoring at Fresno State University and emerging from College with honours in Criminology, achieving both Bachelor and Masters degrees, in 1959. He joined the California Highway Patrol and served as a patrolman between 1953 and 1959, following which he organized the Law-Enforcement Education programme at Bakersfield College in 1959.

Following this Ron moved into administration and he was eventually to retire as a Dean of Students in 1984. Resident now in Tehachapi, off Highway 58 south-east of Bakersfield, Ron had meanwhile met and married his wife Jessie, and they had two children, who, in turn, have presented them with four grandchildren and one great-grandchild! Ron keeps himself fully occupied in several ways. He plays golf, helps friends build and remodel their houses, cooks for the Church Youth Groups in their Summer and Winter Camps.

Night Operations

The Hunter-Killer anti-submarine team of AD-4N and AD-4Q, with its main base at San Diego NAS, provided four-plane sections for each of the carriers assigned to operations off Korea. However, although they dutifully patrolled in this guise throughout the war, they were not troubled by any Communist underwater attacks. The threat only remained in case Soviet-supplied (and, possibly, Soviet-manned) submarines should put in an appearance.

The main duty of the various radar-equipped Skyraiders was to become night harassment, for which their equipment made them particularly suitable. Navy and Marine Corps Spads pounded enemy supply columns, rail networks and other communications ceaselessly throughout the hours of daylight. At night, hordes of forced-labour coolie battalions would be organized to repair the bomb damage, while columns of blacked-out vehicles thundered south with their ammunition, troops and supplies. The AD-Ns were called upon to attack and disrupt this nocturnal enemy traffic. From 1952, four special night-attack units, VC-11, VC-12, VC-33 and VC-35, started to fly 'Moonlight Sonata' and 'Insomnia' missions.

To supplement their radar, the Skyraiders were each equipped with four 1,000,000-candlepower flares to illuminate targets located on their scope. They then utilized up to 3,000lb ordnance payloads, with 500lb and 250lb bombs, or napalm, along with their 20mm cannon (soon increased in number from two to four) to destroy any enemy transport. Later, VC-35 pioneered the use of the 2.75in 'Mighty Mouse' rockets in this night rôle. As dive bombing was out of the question, this, and the low-level approach, became the norm for this type of work; the equipping of each AD-4N with three seven-rocket packs under each wing enormously increased the hitting power.

Night combat was no sinecure in those days. Take-offs and landings, sometimes in a damaged state, were both more hazardous after dark. The Essex class carriers were equipped with a single red mast-head light. For landing on, the LSO used illuminated bats to guide the aircraft in, while the carrier deck was briefly illuminated with shaded 'dust-pan' lights along the deck edges, and small shielded 'pin' lights set in the carrier's deck to outline the landing area. It required a great deal of skill and nerve to land the Spad back aboard a heaving carrier deck after a mission over enemy territory which might have lasted several hours. For the night harassment units, such difficulties became a regular fact of life.

The Kitchen Sink

On the afternoon of 23 June 1952, one of the strongest carrier-based attacks of the Korean conflict was mounted against the vital Sui-ho electricity-generating plant, and the Fusen One and Two and the Kyosen power stations on the Yalu River, deep in hostile territory. Three aircraft carriers – the Boxer, Philippine Sea and Princeton – took part in this classic assault, putting a powerful striking force that included 35 Skyraiders in the air. Despite the fact that the main Communist concentration of MiG-15 jet fighters lay less than 40 miles away from the target, the Skyraiders pressed home their attack with skill and determination and deposited 90 tons of bombs exactly on all the targets.

One Navy pilot, Commander M.K. Dennis of VA-195 from Princeton, was quoted in the press as saying, 'We dropped everything on them but the kitchen sink.'[51] This was construed by other AD men as a challenge to their capabilities and plans were made to re-affirm the Spads' 'honour' forthwith. Two of VA-195's mechanics got together with the carrier's maintenance department, who showed a great deal of resourcefulness in coming up with a genuine kitchen sink, complete with S-bend piping and all fitments! The sink, duly labelled in block letters, was lashed firmly to a 1,000lb bomb mounted on the centre-line of Lieutenant (j.g.) Carl B. Austin's AD and, on 29 August 1952, he took off with it in place on a combat strike over Pyongyang. The kitchen sink was successfully dropped over the North Korean capital through heavy flak. Whether the commissars displayed any sense of humour about the episode will never be known!

Order of battle US Navy carrier units – Korea

SQUADRON	CAG	CARRIER	TYPE	FROM	TO
VC-35	2	Boxer (CV-21)	AD-4, AD-4N, AD-4Q	May-53	Jul-53
VF-54	5	Essex (CV-9)	AD-4, AD-4N, AD-4Q	Aug-51	Mar-52
VF-54	5	Valley Forge (CV-45)	AD-4	Dec-52	Jun-53
VF-94	1	Valley Forge (CV-45)	AD-4, AD-4N, AD-4Q	Dec-51	Jun-52
VF-194	1	Boxer (CVA-21)	AD-4	May-53	Jul-53
VA-35	3	Leyte (CVA-32)	AD-2	Oct-50	Jan-51
VA-45	4	Lake Champlain (CVA-39)	AD-4	Jun-53	Jul-53
VA-55	19	Princeton (CVA-37)	AD-4	Jan-51	Aug-51
VA-55	5	Valley Forge (CV-45)	AD-4	Jun-55	Nov-55
VA-55	2	Essex (CV-9)	AD-4	Jul-52	Jan-53
VA-65	2	Boxer (CVA21)	AD-2	Sep-50	Oct-50
VA-65	2	Boxer (CVA-21)	AD-4	Mar-51	Sep-51
VA-65	2	Valley Forge (CVA-45)	AD-2	Dec-50	Mar-51
VA-65	2	Philippine Sea (CVA-47)	AD-2	Mar-51	Jun-51
VA-75	7	Bon Homme Richard (CVA-31)	AD-4	Jun-52	Dec-52
VA-95	19	Princeton (CVA-37)	AD-4	Apr-52	Oct-52
VA-95	9	Philippine Sea (CVA-47)	AD-4	Jan-53	Jul-53
VA-115	11	Philippine Sea (CVA-45)	AD-2	Aug-50	Mar-51
VA-115	11	Valley Forge (CVA-45)	AD-4	Mar-51	Mar-51
VA-115	11	Philippine Sea (CVA-47)	AD-4	Jan-52	Jul-52
VA-155	15	Princeton (CVA-37)	AD-4	Mar-53	Jul-53
VA-195	19	Princeton (CVA-37)	AD-4	Dec-50	May-51
VA-702	101	Boxer (CVA-21)	AD-1	Mar-51	Oct-51
VA-702	14	Kearsarge (CVA-33)	AD-4	Sep-52	Feb-53
VA-728	15	Antietam (CVA-36)	AD-2	Oct-51	Mar-52
VA-923	102	Bon Homme Richard (CVA-31)	AD-3	May-51	Nov-51
VA-923	12	Oriskany (CVA-34)	AD-3	Oct-52	May-53

CHAPTER NINE

Combat Over Korea

The US Marine Corps Experience

Surprisingly, in view of the Skyraider's reputation as the close air support aircraft *par excellence*, and the fact that it was the United States Marine Corps that had specialized in and made this rôle its own, and had perfected it in the Second World War, the Spad and the Marines spent very little time in each other's company. In fact, it was not until 1951 that the USMC received any Skyraiders on its inventory at all, some five years after it had joined the Navy squadrons (*see* the table below). The Korean War brought about the USMC conversion, when, due to the dire circumstances, the reserves had to be mobilized.

Marine Corps Outfits Receive the Skyraider

The first Marine Corps outfit to receive the Skyraider was the Reserve Squadron of VMF-251, equipped with the old Chance-Vought F4U Corsair fighter-bomber and

Grumman F8F Bearcats. Assigned to Marine Air Group 13 (MAG-13), they were ordered to mobilize on 1 March 1951, and were then transferred to Marine Corps Air Station El Toro to undergo conversion training on the AD-1. Subsequently, they were, more appropriately, redesignated as Marine Attack Squadron 251 (VMA-251) because of this.

In a similar manner to VMA-251, Marine Attack Squadron 121, (VMA-121) based at NAS Glenview, Illinois, under the command of regular officer Lieutenant Meanwhile, in June, the second reserve squadron was mobilized, VMA-121 (formerly VMF-121) at Glenview Naval Air Station, Illinois, Under the command of regular officer Colonel P. B. May, USMC., once assembled this unit was also converted to the Skyraider and although their conversion came later, they got into the action sooner. Their nickname was the 'Wolf Raiders' but they soon became known as the 'Heavy Haulers' in

deference to the record bomb loads they deposited on the enemy, and never was a better choice made. With the Skyraider they were to enhance their reputation and, indeed, so successfully did they apply themselves that their name was to become one of the many associated with the AD itself!

In June 1951, the squadron was alerted and the reservists were called back to the colours. Once the personnel had assembled, the whole of VMA-121 was transferred to El Toro as a complete unit and commenced training on the AD-2. This took the best part of the autumn and then, once the unit was ready for combat, the squadron was allocated to Marine Air Group 33 (MAG-33).

The officers and men of VMA-121, now equipped with the AD-3, arrived in Japan on 18 October 1951. Three days later, they flew their Skyraiders to one of MAG-3's forward operational airstrips in Korea, codenamed K-3, near Pohang. This was

US Marine Corps Skyraider deployment			
Unit	From	To	Notes
VMA-121	1951	1952	First Marine Skyraider squadron
VMA-151	1951	1957	
VMA-211	1952	1957	
VMA-212	1954	1957	
VMA-225	1954	1957	
VMA-251	1953	1957	Ex-VMF-251
VMA-324	1954	1958	
VMA-331	1954	1958	Last Marine Skyraider squadron
VMA-332	1954	1956	
VMA-333	1954	1956	
VMC-1	1952	1956	Became VMCJ-1
VMC-2	1953	1956	Became VMJC-2
VMC-3	1952	1956	Became VMJC-3
VMAT-10	1952	1953	
VMAT-20	1952	1957	
VMCJ-1	1956	1958	Ex-VMC-1
VMJC-2	1956	1958	Ex-VMC-2
VMJC-3	1956	1958	Ex-VMC-3

A US Marine Corps AD-4N (BuNo 12572) from VMC-3, based at El Toro Air Station, California, seen here on 20 February 1950. The USMC came late to the Spad, and left early, but, during the Korean War period, operated most variants in most configurations in both 'Hot' and 'Cold' war scenarios. National Archives, College Park, MD

the only airstrip made of concrete in the area, and thus the only one believed to be capable of bearing the weight of the heavily laden Skyraiders as they took off to join the grim battle. (Later, even greater loads were carried by the Marine Corps ADs working from strips of pierced-steel planking closer to the front line, in response to the needs of comrades on the ground.)

Sorties and Losses

The first Marine Corps Skyraider sortie was on 27 October 1951, and from then on the unit was in almost continuous action. Its rôle was, as usual, the direct close support of US Marines ground forces, who were fighting a terrible war, heavily outnumbered and in appalling conditions that at times resembled the static trench warfare of the First World War rather than the more mobile fighting of the second conflict. Like the pilots operating from the carriers offshore, the Marine Corps Spad jockeys found themselves more and more flying interdiction missions against strategic targets, flying round the clock in rail- and bridge-cut missions against the heavy concentrations of Communist anti-aircraft guns that guarded such vital targets. They were also required to target enemy ammunition dumps and road transport. It was demoralizing work – the Communists mobilized an army of peasants every night to repair any damage inflicted the day before – and the Skyraiders' task appeared endless.

On 20 April 1952, the squadron switched bases to K06 field at Pyongtaek. In May, the squadron was reassigned to MAG-12, but their main duties continued as before, with the unit under the overall control of 5th Air Force.

When the bitter Korean winter closed in, the Marine Skyraiders based ashore suffered much more than their Navy counterparts in their heated hangars. With temperatures plummeting to minus 35 degrees, engines would have frozen solid overnight had special precautions not been taken. Like the Luftwaffe Stuka ground crew on the Eastern Front during the Second World War, the Marine Corps engineers came up with specially built engine coverings, 'nose hangars' as they were dubbed. They also pumped hot air all night through flexible ducts directed towards the engines, ignition systems, hydraulics and oil and fuel pipes. The well-worn phrase 'Keep 'em Flyin' was never more hard earned than by VMA-121 in Korea.

An AD-2 (BuNo 122310) of VA-702, flying from the carrier USS Boxer (CVA-21). It carries the unit markings and the name 'Jinx' under its cockpit cowling. A wing panel is being replaced on a land airstrip after flak damage over the target. Note two Chance Vought F4U fighter-bombers in the background, still in use by the Marines in Korea. National Archives, College Park, MD

During the combat sorties, whether in winter or summer, flak continued to be the main hazard, especially the Soviet-supplied 85mm mobile cannon, which threw a wall of 25lb shells up to a height of 25,000ft, and the 37mm automatic cannon, which had a rate of fire of 160rpm. This combination, and the Communist tactic of concentration of up to 2,000 such weapons around the main target areas, led to many Spad losses. The situation had become so serious by autumn 1952 that the Commanding Officer of Navy Task Force 77, Rear Admiral Apollo Soucek, gave instructions that dive-bombing attack pull-outs must be made at 3,000ft.

Folding its wings aboard the carrier Leyte (CV-32) while operating in Korean waters, this AD-3 (BuNo 122799) was photographed on 12 November 1950. The aircraft, tail-coded K, carrying 503 on her nose and with a green spinner, belonged to VA-35. National Archives, College Park, MD

This new official policy would seriously affect the accuracy of such attacks.

The Marines continued to barrel in lower than the official height, and in one typical incident during that summer, Second Lieutenant Edward (Ted) Uhlemeyer, Jr, took a heavy anti-aircraft shell hit. It tore away a whole central segment of one wing, and the impact of the detonation was so strong that it completely inverted the AD, knocked out most of his aileron controls and jammed his landing gear shut. Despite his desperate situation, Uhlemeyer managed to regain control by supreme physical effort, using both arms and legs to move the control stick and flip his aircraft right way up once more. He was so composed that he even managed to deliver his two 1,000lb bombs, which by some miracle were still in place on the underwing pylons, into the enemy target. With this weight gone, the plucky Spad held together long enough to carry its brave and resourceful pilot back safely to base.

The Spad continued to be loaded to the limits and on one memorable sortie a Marine Corps AD lifted off with a bomb load comprising three 2,000lb and twelve 250lb weapons – a total of 9,000lb of ordnance payload. The greatest single-day ordnance delivery made by any unit in the Korean War – 156 tons on target – was achieved by VMA-121 in June 1953. By the end of its combat period, VMA-121 had become the squadron that could boast the heaviest weight of ordnance delivered against enemy targets in the whole Korean conflict.

Justifying the Skyraider's Position

What did the troops on the ground in Korea think of the Skyraider? Their opinion was the one that really counted if the Spad was to justify its retention in the front line at a time when jet aircraft were increasingly dominant. Its position had to be earned.

Army General Mark W. Clark described very precisely the ideal close-support aircraft, from the infantryman's viewpoint in Korea.[52] It should

(a) carry a 9,000lb load of ammunition – bombs, rockets, bullets, etc;
(b) have sufficient accuracy and stability to hit the target;
(c) have adequate communications with ground officers directing their strikes;
(d) carry enough fuel to give it at least two hours over the battle area;
(e) take off in 3,000ft (900m);
(f) operate in any kind of weather, day or night.

The AD was really the only aircraft fighting in Korea at that time which fulfilled all those requirements. But of course it was not only the wrong type of aircraft that the USAF was deploying, but the wrong type of attitude. While the main priority of the USAF was to stay alive in the air, hence their preference for jet fighter-bombers, the Lockheed F-80 and the Republican F-84, the foot soldier in desperate need for

(Above) **Impressive line-up of the US Marine Corps Air Group Skyraiders, (carrying Tail code AK), at Osan Air Base, Korea, in 1952. Beyond the Spads, (with WS codes) are Marine Corsair fighter-bombers.** James V. Crow

(Below) **US Marine Corps Air Group Skyraider displaying a full wing load of rockets.** James V. Crow

support had a rather different view of close-air support.

> To the guy on the ground it doesn't make much sense for a fighter-bomber to come within a few miles of its target only to jettison its bomb load and go upstairs to fend off an attacking fighter force. Once committed to a task, say the ground men, the fighters should stick with it to the end … If protection from enemy fighters is needed, send along a few jets without bomb loads for that purpose, but first of all see that the support planes stick with the assignment rather than a rule book.

The Marine Corps Skyraider flyers, in contrast, lived, breathed and, above all, believed in close air support. The Skyraider had the unique ability to deliver ordnance on over one hundred passes during a single sortie; it was exactly what the boys on the ground were looking for. One report reflected the point of view of the 'dough-boys':

> We want no more of these jet jockeys. They don't have enough fuel to stay in our areas long enough to find out where we are having trouble. And they don't have enough firepower to do any real good. Give us those Marines … [53]

Other Skyraider Units

The other Marine Air Skyraider outfit that saw combat action in Korea was Marine Composite Reconnaissance Squadron 1 (VMC-1). It had been equipped for a specialist rôle with the AD-2Q and AD-3N variants and reached the battle zone on 15 September 1952. VMC-1 was based at Marine Air Strip K-16 under the direct command of Marine Air Control 2. Its intruder missions operated over the areas of the front where the Communists had a strong radar net. The ECM aircraft duly blocked and confused the enemy while the AD-4Ns went in to complete the job against defined targets.

Meanwhile, VMA-251 had completed its training, had converted to the AD-3, and was assigned to MAG-15 on 3 January 1952. However, it only followed VMA-121 out to Korea via Japan on 4 June 1952, flying in two echelons to Marine Air Base K-6, at Pyongtaek. They arrived on 5 July as part of MAG-12. The war, however, was stumbling to an unsatisfactory stalemate and the unit saw very little action.

In the period January to April 1952, VMA-121 was working out of K-3 airstrip,

Frank C. Kleager, VMA-121's Operations Officer, told me that:

> The airstrip was not overly a long one (how long I don't know), but one day we decided to see how much of a load we could fly off the strip with. We loaded two ADs with 10,400lb each and away we went. The west end of the runway had about a 50ft drop into a rice paddy. That gave us just enough 'slop' so that we could raise the wheels and remain airborne for a successful mission.[53A]

Colonel May was enthusiastic about the Skyraider, stating in an interview at that time that:

> It's an excellent plane for the operations we're carrying out in Korea. It's the first time that the Navy and the Marines have used a plane particularly designed for close-air support work. With this plane, we can fulfil Marine aviation's rôle to support troops on the ground. We had been using planes designed for other types of work than close air support, and they haven't always proved suitable. The AD was built strictly for close air support work. You can't do a damned thing behind enemy lines unless you have a plane that can carry a big load and get down to the ground and deliver it, and have enough speed and manoeuvrability to get out and come back again. This plane has that![53B]

The unit soon named its aircraft, and the Marine flyers embellished their machines with 'I'll Take You Home Again', 'Lady Luck', 'Chi Town Jack' and 'Nancy O', along with 'Kit Ann Curse'. They soon earned a formidable reputation.

During an attack by VMA-121 on Sariwon airfield, the flying Leathernecks reported that twenty-five bombs had actually landed on the target area. HQ was not convinced; it had heard tales like that before. A photo reconnaissance aircraft was despatched to disprove this statement. When it returned and the photo analysts got the full results, they found that the eight Marine Corps Skyraiders had, in fact, cut the runways fifty-six times! They had also damaged other airfield installations, so much so that Sariwon was later abandoned by the Communists.

Order of Battle US Marine Corps squadrons – Korea

Unit	Types	From	To
VMA-121	AD-4N, AD-4W	Oct 51	June 52
VMA-251	AD-3, AD-4B	Jun 53	July 53
VMCJ-1	AD-2Q, AD-3N	Sept 52	July 53

One of the last US Marine Corps Skyraiders, BuNo 133885, from VMA-331, seen in flight on 4 November 1955. National Archives, College Park MD

CHAPTER TEN

The AEW

The Royal Navy Experience

On 1 October 1951, the Royal Navy had set up No. 778 Squadron, Fleet Air Arm, specifically to evaluate the American electronic equipment under British operating conditions. The Royal Navy was considering the American AEW concept of using the Skyraider purely as a passive reception and transmitting vehicle, hoping to stretch its limited resources by utilizing its aircraft of this type more efficiently. The British intended (despite the known technical difficulties) to use the AEW as an airborne radar platform in every sense of the word, with the additional capabilities and duties of control of the Combat Air Patrols, vectoring out strikes and detecting surface targets at extreme ranges.

After purchasing the AD-4W, the Royal Navy bypassed the normal process of acceptance trials with the A&AEE and the Service Trials Unit (No. 703 Squadron), considering that its long service with the US Navy was enough to have proven the aircraft's capabilities. Apart from C(A) trials (some of which were conducted with the private company, Scottish Aviation Ltd), only selective catapult trials at Farnborough Royal Aircraft Establishment were carried out, to test compatibility.

Once the first four AEW-1s had been put through their paces, No. 778 Squadron was, on 7 July 1952, redesignated as a fully operational squadron, No. 849. It would have an HQ Flight, and there were also plans for four carrier-based flights – 'A', 'B', 'C', 'D' and 'E' – once sufficient aircraft were to hand. Whereas other Fleet Air Arm squadrons were formed to join specific carriers, and disbanded upon completion of

each ship's commission, the AEW squadron remained in permanent commission. Its officers were appointed on two-year tours of duty, and its flights were allocated as needed when carriers were paid off and others were commissioned for service.

Deliveries

The 50 AD-4W Skyraiders allocated to the Fleet Air Arm under the terms of the MDWP (Mutual Defence Weapons Programme) formed two distinct groups.

Twenty brand-new aircraft were diverted from the El Segundo production line and delivered directly to the Royal Navy by the Douglas Aircraft Company. Four of these (c/n 7584 to 7587, BuNos 124774–12477) were taken at the end of 1951, and became WT 944–WT 947. First flown between June and August 1951, they transferred to Norfolk NAS, where they were given a protective weather coating to protect them during their sea voyage. On 26 October, all four were embarked aboard the transporter *American Clipper* for passage to the United Kingdom.

King George V Docks, Glasgow – one of the initial quartet of Skyraiders to arrive in the UK under the Mutual Defence Program is unloaded from the freighter American Clipper **on 9 November 1951.**
Arthur Pearcy Archive, by courtesy of Audrey Pearcy

The AD-4Ws, now classified by the Royal Navy as AEW-1s, were offloaded by crane at Glasgow's King George V docks on 9 November, and the following day there was a handing-over ceremony on the quayside. Rear Admiral W.F. Boone of the US Navy, Deputy Commander-in-Chief, Eastern Atlantic, handed over the four Skyraiders to Rear Admiral W.T. Couchman, Royal Navy, Flag Officer, Training. The four aircraft were then transported to Royal Naval Air Station (RNAS) Abbotsinch, where they arrived on 10 November 1951. There, the protective coatings were stripped away and the aircraft were made serviceable. They then flew from Renfrew airfield to HMS *Seahawk*, the RNAS Culdrose in Cornwall, where they joined the establishment of No. 778 Squadron, Fleet Air Arm, the Royal Navy's first AEW squadron.

The Skyraider became unique in that it was to be the last piston-engined aircraft (other than helicopters) to serve in the Royal Navy. At 25,000lb, the Skyraider was also among the heaviest type of aircraft ever operated by the Navy, and had one of the greatest ranges of British carrier aircraft.

Fourteen more brand-new Skyraiders (c/n 7961 to 7974, BuNos 127946–127959), which first flew between October 1952 and February 1953, were subsequently transferred (127946 and 127949 via Quonset Point NAS) to Norfolk NAS, where they were given the usual protective coatings and prepared for shipment to the UK. They were subsequently embarked in two batches, on 26 January and 13 March 1953, aboard the Royal Navy aircraft carrier *Perseus*. It transported them to Glasgow for unloading, and then they were transported to Abbotsinch at various dates in February and March, becoming WT 948 to WT 961.

The fifteenth aircraft (c/n 7975, BuNo 127960) first flew on 21 February 1953, before transferring to Norfolk NAS for shipment preservation on 3 March and was not finally embarked aboard the freighter *American Venture* until September 1953. The last new AD-4W (c/n 7976, BuNo 127961) was first flown on 18 March 1953, duly transferred to Norfolk NAS for shipment preservation, and embarked aboard the transport *Green Mountain State* on 15 September 1953. These two aircraft became WT 962 and WT 963, respectively, and both went straight into store at Abbotsinch. On 7 September 1956, WT 963 was given into the hands of the Receipt and Despatch Unit (RDU); on 1 December 1957, it was de-preserved and

August 1957 it arrived at Culdrose and No. 849 Squadron's HQ Flight. An even longer hibernation awaited WT 963. On 1 December 1957, it was de-preserved and delivered to RNAS Culdrose, where it was on the strength of the Aircraft Holding Unit (AHU). On 13 March 1958, it was transferred to the Naval Aircraft Radio

A pair of AEW-1 Skyraiders, WT 945 (302) and WT 946 (303) display their full early markings in Royal Navy service. Arthur Pearcy Archive, by courtesy of Audrey Pearcy

Installation Unit (NARIU), Lee-on-Solent, for equipping, returning to RNAS Culdrose eight days later and joining No. 849 Squadron on 6 October 1958.

The remaining 30 AD-4Ws had already seen much service with the US Navy, one (BuNo 125772) with VX-1, the remainder with VC-11 and VC-12, who arranged their delivery in two batches – 19 in 1952/53, and 11 in 1954/55. They were all given a full overhaul at NAS Quonset Point or NAS Alameda and were then ferried by VC-31 and VC-32 pilots to NAS Norfolk, and then loaded on to ships for Glasgow docks.

Royal Navy WV 102 to WV 106 were transported aboard the carrier *Perseus* in

February 1953, together with the first batch of the new AD-4Ws. Next came WV 177 to WV 180, which were transported aboard the carrier *Perseus* on her second supply trip, in March 1953, along with the second batch of the new AD-4Ws.

The first former US Navy AD-4W, WT 966, arrived with a batch of stores on board the *Perseus* in May 1953. It was not joined by any more until the next batch arrived in the UK – five refurbished aircraft, WT 112, WT 121 and WT 967 to 969 shipped on the freighter *Green Mountain State* in September 1953, these reaching NAS Abbotsinch on the 25th. Five ex-US Navy aircraft (BuNos 124097, 124112, 124121, 124761 and 126849) had their BuAer serials changed easily to British serials by the replacement of the first three digits with WT; this short-cut led to complications, however, since it resulted in allocations of numbers already belonging to other RAF aircraft! WT121 was an English Electric B. 2 Canberra on order (fortunately subsequently cancelled), while WT 761 was a Hawker Hunter F. 4 already in existence! Three further ex-US Navy aircraft – WT 761 and WT 964 and 965 – arrived aboard the freighter *American Venture* the same month.

Two years elapsed before a further two deliveries were made, again of refurbished aircraft. In November 1955, the freighter *J. Robinson* delivered WT 097, WT 849, WT 985, WT 987 and WV181. The following spring, in April 1956, the final six US Navy-supplied Skyraiders – WT 984, WT 986 and WV 182 to WV 185 – arrived in the UK, embarked aboard the freighter *Francis McGraw*. (*See* the table on page 74.)

Training

The CO designate of No. 788 Squadron, Lieutenant (later Lieutenant-Commander) John Treacher, RN, along with his allotted aircrew and senior technical ground staff were sent to the USA in the summer of 1951, to undergo a three-month familiarization and conversion course at NAS Quonset Point and Norfolk. The pilots flew with the American VC units, and operated the aircraft under full service conditions. The radar staff got to know the capabilities and the limitations of the one-ton AN/APS 20A set, and its tactical applications, which differed quite significantly from the Royal Navy requirements.

Admiral Sir John Treacher recalled what this entailed.[54]

> The reason for the Royal Navy choosing to have this particular aircraft to be supplied under the MDWP (Mutual Defence Weapons Programme) was, in fact, because shipborne radars were unable to detect the presence of low-flying aircraft – those coming in 'under the radar' – and the cost of providing a ring of escorts was prohibitive. By the end of the war, Westinghouse and Grumman had produced an initial development aircraft which had proved the concept. Housing an improved version of the radar in the much more capable AD-3 resulted in a system that was deployed by the USN until replaced by the Grumman E2-C and in the RN until replaced by the AEW Gannet, largely on the grounds of removing Avgas from carriers.
>
> The Skyraider was the last piston-engined carrier aircraft to be designed by the legendary Ed Heinemann at Douglas. It incorporated all

A beautiful shot of Royal Navy AEW-1 Skyraider WT 966 (coded 411) of No. 849 Squadron, banking over St Michael's Mount and the Cornish shoreline. Arthur Pearcy Archive, by courtesy of Audrey Pearcy

Mass formation flight from the Royal Navy's AEW-1 Skyraiders. Arthur Pearcy Archive, by courtesy of Audrey Pearcy

the lessons learned during the Pacific War and Heinemann had introduced every weight-saving device possible in order to enhance overall aerodynamic performance. The result was a rugged dive bomber with a huge load-carrying capacity, plenty of endurance and considerable agility as well as steadiness in a steep dive.

I first flew the AD-3 in the summer of 1951, while attached to US Navy Squadron VC-12, based at Quonset Point, Rhode Island. This was a preliminary familiarization with the 'basic' Skyraider in its dive-bomber configuration, prior to flying the AEW version. My previous experience of USN aircraft had been in the Grumman Avenger, which had been widely used by the RN during the war and which had proved both a successful torpedo bomber and all-round AEW aircraft.

As was only to be expected, the Skyraider had all the good attributes of USN carrier aircraft – a solid airframe with a rugged undercarriage, good all-round visibility plus such new additions as an electrically operated cockpit hood and full electric controls for seat movement. All this was behind the latest version of the Wright radial engine.

The AD-3 was a delight to handle and, without any underwing stores, had the agility to give any fighter aircraft a run for its money – something the Avenger could never claim! Moving on to the AEW version was still to enjoy all the basic characteristics of the original, but the huge Radome and the massive range of electronic equipment packed into the fuselage, together with the two operating bays for the observer/controllers, gave the feel of a fully-laden aircraft in the air.

Overload tanks were available to give extra endurance to the four and a half hours' fuel carried internally. Hence, comfort – for all the crew – was important and at first we did not think the 'hard hat' helmets with boom or throat microphones were a help, although over time we came to appreciate them.

The first aircraft for the RN came by sea to the Clyde in November, where they were unloaded and towed to the RNAS at Abbotsinch [now Glasgow Airport] for preparation and test flying before joining No. 778 Squadron at Culdrose. This squadron had been formed to introduce AEW to the RN and train the first operational crews. Two full crews had been with me in the USA, the second pilot assisted me with the test flying and the conversion of new pilots as they joined, while the senior observers and aircrewman dealt with the training of the 'back-seat' operators. They were to be, in effect, fully fledged 'Direction' officers, in that they were empowered to take fight aircraft under direct control for the interception of the enemy aircraft detected by the early warning radar.

This technical equipment was highly complex in itself and also in its relay capability to the ship. A brilliant technical officer had joined us in the USA and, within a short time, he had mastered the entire electronic system and he was able to oversee the installation of all the servicing equipment and to build a training model.

772 Squadron began flying its ADWs at Culdrose before the end of 1951 and, by early 1952, was training new crews for the fleet. In February, I took an aircraft to Farnborough for tests to establish deck-landing parameters for the arrestor wires and catapults and then aboard the carrier HMS *Eagle* for live deck-landing trials. They were all normal.

Training continued throughout the first six months of 1952, during which time four crews, who were to comprise the first AEW flight scheduled to embark in *Eagle* later in the year, were qualified. To recognize the transition from a purely training rôle to operational status, the squadron was given an 800 designation and 778 Squadron became 849 Squadron on 1 July 1952.

While No. 849's squadrons HQ flight was planned as a shore-based unit, the other flights were destined to be self-contained carrier-borne units. Each of these flights had a theoretical establishment strength of four AEW-1s , for which five complete crew were provided – a total of 16 officers and 62 other ranks – with command being vested in a senior Lieutenant (A) or Lieutenant-Commander (A), who was either a pilot or an observer. When not embarked, the flights were returned to *Seahawk* for continued training and maintenance. Although the initial aircrew had been trained in the USA, an Operational Training School was set up at the Headquarters Base, commanded by the squadron executive officer, with six officers and nine observers undergoing training as replacement aircrew. The pilot course was of 20 weeks' duration, with 180 hours spent flying and 350 hours on ground instruction. Similarly, the observer course was 21 weeks long, with a total of 123 hours flying and a 420 hours of ground instruction.

The original *Seahawk* tail codes given to the AEW-1s were CW, but this was changed to CU in January 1953. (In 1956, under a major reorganization of Fleet Air Arm codes, the '300' series aircraft codes changed to the new '400' series. Because of various carrier allocations, some Royal Navy Skyraiders carried a total of six different code designations during their nine-year service with the Royal Navy. The BuNo, fortunately, remained the same.)

Operations and Exercises

When they returned home and first formed 778 Squadron at HMS *Seahawk*, Culdrose, on 1 October 1951, there were no AEW-1s on hand, and it was two months before the first of these aircraft arrived at Abbotsinch. In February 1952, the first four AEW-1s, CW/301-304, undertook carrier trials aboard the new carrier, HMS *Eagle*. In addition, a significant number of simulated operations were undertaken in conjunction with the Joint-Anti-Submarine School, Eglinton and the RN Aircraft Direction Station, Kete. They also took part in joint service manoeuvres during Operation *Castanets* at RAF St Eval, with the AEWs practising both the early-warning detection of both air and surface contacts, and the vectoring out of strikes against ship targets.

The first major exercise in which the AEW was involved had been *Mainbrace*, a large-scale exercise held in northern waters, with the Skyraiders of 'A' flight operating from the carrier *Eagle*, which was to remain their home for six years. Another major event was the Coronation Review for the newly crowned Queen Elizabeth. Admiral Treacher recalled these first carrier operations by the AEWs.[55]

In September, the squadron embarked a flight, which included those of us who had been in the USA, in *Eagle* for autumn deployment, which included a major NATO maritime exercise in northern waters. Operating by day and night and in weather that grounded all the other aircraft in the carrier group, the flight demonstrated the huge extension to the reconnaissance area covered by 200-mile radius radar, as well as the detection of low-flying aircraft. Conditions were such that, when some smaller naval units failed to make a rendezvous, the Skyraider flight was called upon to locate them. Not an AEW function, but a demonstration of just one of the capabilities of this remarkable aircraft and its radar. Our aircraft were invariably ranged on deck and there was nothing the wind or weather could do to reduce the serviceability, which remained at near 100 per cent.

Building up the operational flights toward the target of one for each operational aircraft carrier meant four flights with four crews (four pilots, four observers and four aircrewmen, plus an air electrical officer, and air engineer and supporting maintenance crews). All the pilots were experienced and well carrier-qualified, and the same applied to the rear-seat men. They almost invariably adapted quickly to their new rôle and the aircrewmen revelled in finding a new challenge at a time when their skills and experience were proving difficult to place.

Training and the introduction of the new aircraft as they arrived in Scotland was a task well met during the remainder of 1952 and the first half of 1953. By the time of the Coronation Review of the Fleet in June, the squadron was present with sixteen aircraft in the Fleet Air Arm flypast, the highest number of any squadron.

While the Fleet Air Arm was making the transition to jets, 849 Squadron was, perhaps, 'left behind' with its piston-engined equipment. But while the ADW was an ungainly bird and deprived of most of her natural agility, the remarkable capability of the radar and the multitude of other rôles she was able to perform made her a much-valued member of all carrier air groups. The absence of AEW in the Falklands conflict cost the Navy dear.

Lieutenant-Commander Treacher handed command of the squadron over to the late Lieutenant-Commander M.J. Baring at the end of July 1953. As the AEW-1s continued to arrive in the United Kingdom, so more flights could be formed by 849 Squadron. By October 1953, enough Skyraiders (39) had been disembarked for

Royal Navy AEW-1 Skyraider WT 954 (310/J) landing aboard the carrier HMS Eagle **in 1954. It carries the marking of 'A' Flight, 849 Squadron, Fleet Air Arm.** Arthur Pearcy Archive, by courtesy of Audrey Pearcy

Douglas AD-4W Skyraider as Royal Navy AEW-1 WT 954 (310/J) takes off from the flight deck of the aircraft carrier HMS Eagle **in 1954, carrying the identification codes of 'A' Flight on its engine cowling.** Arthur Pearcy Archive, by courtesy of Audrey Pearcy

Royal Navy AEW-1 Skyraider WV 105 (320/Z) takes the wire as it lands aboard the aircraft carrier HMS Albion in the Mediterranean, 1954. Arthur Pearcy Archive, by courtesy of Audrey Pearcy

the squadron to be brought up to establishment. (*See* the table opposite.)

In the meantime, the construction of the rest of the new carriers (*Ark Royal, Albion, Bulwark, Centaur, Hermes* and the rebuilt *Victorious*) was seriously delayed by lack of funds, and by the adoption into their design of new carrier features. These had all originated in Great Britain, and included an angled flight deck, mirror landing aids, steam catapults, and so on. This meant that the AEWs were ready well before there were carriers to receive them (other than the *Eagle*, and, as a temporary measure, the light fleet carrier *Ocean*). The Admiralty therefore decided to cut back the number of flights and, on 5 July 1954, No. 849 Squadron disbanded 'B' Flight completely, allocating two of its Skyraiders to each of 'A' and 'C' Flights as Front-Line Immediate Reserve (FIR) aircraft, and then redesignating 'C' Flight as 'B' Flight, and 'D' Flight as 'C' Flight. Only 'A' Flight was therefore embarked (aboard the *Eagle*) at this early period, the remainder operating from shore bases. Even so, this did not prevent a serious shortage of aircraft, due to lack of spare engines; this finally resulted in 'A' and 'B' Flights being reduced back to four aircraft each, and 'E' Flight becoming 'D' Flight.

A fine study of AEW-1 Skyraider WV 105 (320/Z) aboard the aircraft carrier HMS Albion in the Mediterranean in 1954. Arthur Pearcy Archive, by courtesy of Audrey Pearcy

AD-4Bs from VA-115 and VA-65 – crew members with AD-5W, coded 45. Roland W. Baker via Martin Bowman

(Above) **BuNo 134520 serving with VA-165 on the deck park of the carrier USS** Intrepid, **October 1966.** Jim Sullivan via Walt Ohtrich and Nick Williams

Douglas AD-6 Skyraider, BuNo 139769, of VA-176, wings folded, aboard its carrier. Arthur Pearcy Archive, by courtesy of Audrey Pearcy

A series of action photographs of AD-4Bs from VA-115 and VA-65 operating from the USS Philippine Sea (CV-47) off Korea, 1951. Before sailing from San Diego, California on 5 July 1950, she had embarked VA-115 as part of her Air Group II (CVG-II). Between 26 March and 2 April 1951, she disembarked CVG-II in Japan and embarked in their place three F4U-4B Corsair squadrons, as well as the VA-65 Skyraiders from CVG-2, ex USS Valley Forge. Roland W. Baker via Martin Bowman

(Top) **Good starboard broadside view of a US Navy Skyraider from VA-176 of the USS** Intrepid **(CV-11), nose-coded 404.** Arthur Pearcy Archive, by courtesy of Audrey Pearcy

(Above) **US Navy Douglas AD-6 Skyraider (BuNo 139665) of VA-122.** Arthur Pearcy Archive, by courtesy of Audrey Pearcy

US Navy Douglas Skyraider in deep blue finish, nose-coded 515. Arthur Pearcy Archive, by courtesy of Audrey Pearcy

Douglas A-2H Skyraider, tail-coded AD 415. Arthur Pearcy Archive, by courtesy of Audrey Pearcy

Royal Navy AEW-1 Skyraider 415/CV at Culdrose. Bob Turner

Skyraider A-1E, BuNo 133862, of the USAF, seen here at Scott AFB, July 1966. Nick Williams

(Top) **US Navy AD-6 Skyraider (BuNo 132598) at China Lake Test Centre.** Arthur Pearcy Archive, by courtesy of Audrey Pearcy

(Above) **A camouflaged USAF A-1 (BuNo 132415) at Hanscom AFB in July 1968.** Nick Williams

Heavily laden A-1E Skyraider, BuNo 134990, of the USAF. Nick Williams

(Above) Checkerboard cowling on this US Navy Skyraider, BuNo 135188, on a desert airstrip, 27 March 1970. Arthur Pearcy Archive, by courtesy of Audrey Pearcy

(Above left) Douglas AH-1 (former AD-6) Skyraider, BuNo 139732, of VA-165. Arthur Pearcy Archive, by courtesy of Audrey Pearcy

(Above) A Navy Skyraider shows off her clean lines and deep blue paint scheme. US Navy Official

Two former Gabonese/French/American AD-4 Skyraiders, still bearing the colours of their last unit, await new owners at this French air park. SIRPA/ECPA Fort d'Ivry

The Amicale J.P. Salis A-1D F-AZDP resting between shows at its home base of La Ferté Alais during the annual airshow there in May 1998. M. Hiscock

Now owned by the Fighter Collection at Duxford as G-RAID, this A-1D was previously based in France as F-AZED. It is seen here landing at La Ferté Alais in May 1991. M. Hiscock

Here is one interesting machine, the Gate Guard at the USAF Museum at the famous conversion and training base, Hurlbert Field, Florida, home of the 'Jungle Jims'. One of the few former AD-5Ns (A-1G) supplied to the VNAF, she was later assigned to the USAFs famous Special Operations Wing where she carried ID code 57-598. She was brought back to the States in 1973 and has been placed on display there ever since. Kevin R. Smith

Royal Navy AEW-1 Skyraider deployment

RN serials	Modified to	c/n	BuNo	First flight	Transport	Arrival NAS	Delivery by	Notes
WT097	WT943	7403	124097	01 Jul 50	*J. Robinson*	21 Nov 55	US Navy	WT097 was incorrectly applied to WT943
WT112	WT982	7418	124112	01 Oct 50	*Green Mountain State*	25 Sep 53	US Navy	WT112 was incorrectly applied to WT982
WT121	WT983	7427	124121	24 Jan 51	*Green Mountain State*	25 Sep 53	US Navy	WT121 was incorrectly applied to WT983
WT761	-	7571	124761	16 Jan 51	*American Venture*	16 Sep 53	US Navy	Original serial should have been WV108. WT761 was a duplicate serial carried by an RAF Hawker Hunter F.4.
WT849	-	7832	126849	01 Jul 52	*J. Robinson*	21 Nov 55	US Navy	Original Serial should have been WV109
WT944	-	7957	127942	13 Jun 51	*American Clipper*	10 Nov 51	Douglas Aircraft Company	Re-allocated BuNo 124774
WT945	-	7958	127943	19 Jul 51	*American Clipper*	10 Nov 51	Douglas Aircraft Company	Re-allocated BuNo 124775
WT946	-	7959	127944	18 Aug 51	*American Clipper*	10 Nov 51	Douglas Aircraft Company	Re-allocated BuNo 124776
WT947	-	7960	127945	30 Aug 51	*American Clipper*	10 Nov 51	Douglas Aircraft Company	Re-allocated BuNo 124777
WT948	-	7961	127946	20 Oct 52	*Perseus*	19 Feb 53	Douglas Aircraft Company	
WT949	-	7962	127947	01 Oct 52	*Perseus*	19 Feb 53	Douglas Aircraft Company	
WT950	-	7963	127948	01 Nov 52	*Perseus*	20 Feb 53	Douglas Aircraft Company	
WT951	-	7964	127949	05 Nov 52	*Perseus*	19 Feb 53	Douglas Aircraft Company	
WT952	-	7965	127950	01 Nov 52	*Perseus*	20 Feb 53	Douglas Aircraft Company	
WT953	-	7966	127951	25 Nov 52	*Perseus*	19 Feb 53	Douglas Aircraft Company	
WT954	-	7967	127952	02 Dec 52	*Perseus*	19 Feb 53	Douglas Aircraft Company	
WT955	-	7968	127953	12 Dec 52	*Perseus*	31 Mar 53	Douglas Aircraft Company	
WT956	-	7969	127954	01 Dec 52	*Perseus*	20 Feb 53	Douglas Aircraft Company	
WT957	-	7970	127955	01 Jan 53	*Perseus*	31 Mar 53	Douglas Aircraft Company	
WT958	-	7971	127956	24 Feb 53	*Perseus*	31 Mar 53	Douglas Aircraft Company	Crashed Culdrose 13 April 1957
WT959	-	7972	127957	01 Jan 53	*Perseus*	31 Mar 53	Douglas Aircraft Company	
WT960	-	7973	127958	09 Feb 53	*Perseus*	30 Mar 53	Douglas Aircraft Company	
WT961	-	7974	127959	21 Feb 53	*Perseus*	31 Mar 53	Douglas Aircraft Company	
WT962	-	7975	127960	01 Feb 53	*American Venture*	15 Sep 53	Douglas Aircraft Company	
WT963	-	7976	127961	18 Mar 53	*Green Mountain State*	25 Sep 53	Douglas Aircraft Company	Crashed Culdrose 12 Feb 1960
WT964	-	7420	124114	01 Dec 50	*American Venture*	15 Sep 53	US Navy	
WT965	-	7430	124124	30 Jan 51	*American Venture*	15 Sep 53	US Navy	
WT966	-	7575	124765	01 Mar 51	*Perseus*	15 May 53	US Navy	
WT967	-	7581	124771	01 May 51	*Green Mountain State*	25 Sep 53	US Navy	
WT968	-	7578	124768	03 May 51	*Green Mountain State*	25 Sep 53	US Navy	
WT969	-	7413	124107	12 Oct 50	*Green Mountain State*	25 Sep 53	US Navy	
WT984	-	7849	126866	01 Aug 52	*Francis McGraw*	24 Apr 56	US Navy	
WT985	-	7410	124104	01 Oct 50	*J. Robinson*	21 Nov 55	US Navy	
WT986	-	7409	124103	01 Sep 50	*Francis McGraw*	24 Apr 56	US Navy	
WT987	-	7937	127922	01 Aug 52	*J.Robinson*	22 Nov 53	US Navy	
WV102	-	7428	124122	01 Jan 52	*Perseus*	19 Feb 53	US Navy	
WV103	-	7391	124085	26 Apr 50	*Perseus*	20 Feb 53	US Navy	
WV104	-	7486	124080	22 Mar 50	*Perseus*	19 Feb 53	US Navy	
WV105	-	7419	124113	17 Nov 50	*Perseus*	19 Feb 53	US Navy	
WV106	-	7392	124086	01 May 50	*Perseus*	20 Feb 53	US Navy	
WV107	-	7416	124110	19 Oct 50	*Perseus*	31 Mar 53	US Navy	
WV177	-	7407	124101	24 Aug 50	*Perseus*	31 Mar 53	US Navy	
WV178	-	7417	124111	30 Oct 50	*Perseus*	31 Mar 53	US Navy	
WV179	-	7421	124115	01 Dec 50	*Perseus*	31 Mar 53	US Navy	
WV180	-	7422	124116	21 Dec 50	*Perseus*	31 Mar 53	US Navy	
WV181	-	7850	126867	01 Aug 52	*J. Robinson*	22 Nov 55	US Navy	
WV182	-	7582	124774	01 Oct 52	*Francis McGraw*	24 Apr 56	US Navy	
WV183	-	7850	124772	01 Apr 52	*Francis McGraw*	24 Apr 56	US Navy	
WV184	-	7829	126846	01 Jun 52	*Francis McGraw*	24 Apr 56	US Navy	
WV185	-	7587	124777	01 Oct 52	*Francis McGraw*	24 Apr 56	US Navy	

RN code letters			
A *Ark Royal*	E *Eagle*	O *Ocean*	Z *Albion*
B *Bulwark*	H *Hermes*	R *Ark Royal* (later)	A *Albion* (later)
C *Centaur*	J *Eagle*	V *Victorious*	CW *Seahawk* CU *Seahawk* (later)

Royal Navy AEW-1 Skyraider WV 105 (320/Z) being towed aft by a tractor aboard the carrier HMS Albion **in the Mediterranean in 1954.** Arthur Pearcy Archive, by courtesy of Audrey Pearcy

The Four Flights

Apart from taking part in the normal peacetime exercises and training, the Skyraiders gained limited 'hot'-war and combat experience. In November 1956, 'A' Flight, still operating from the *Eagle*, provided Early Warning for the fleet during Operation Musketeer, the Suez Operation. The operation was proceeding satisfactorily until political decisions aborted it before it achieved final success (in much the same way as Desert Storm would be terminated forty years later). The affair also served to confirm both the versatility of the Skyraider, and its popularity. Captain D.H. Frazer, RN, recalled that, 'in addition to the radar equipment in the AD-4W, if one observer was left out it was possible to stack 1,000 cans of beer in the cabin. This was done during the Suez operation in 1956 when the troops ashore were thirsty!'[56]

Duties in November 1954 included a detachment of two aircraft to Gibraltar, where they undertook trials of a new radar reflector buoy. Further sea service aboard both the modernized *Eagle* and the smaller *Bulwark* followed, for a short interval, before a return to Culdrose in reduced strength, and a final transfer to the Fairey Gannet in February 1960.

'B' Flight spent the first five months of its career shore-based at Hal Far RNAS, Malta, working with the Mediterranean Fleet, and was then relieved by 'C' Flight. In January 1954, it joined 'A' flight aboard the *Eagle* before being disbanded and re-formed with 'C' Flight. The new 'B' Flight was again based ashore at Malta and subsequently served aboard *Ark Royal* and then *Victorious* before returning to Culdrose and re-equipping with the Fairey Gannet in 1960.

A Skyraider AEW-1, WV 177 of 'C' Flight, No. 849 Squadron, landing aboard the aircraft carrier HMS Albion, **1955.** Arthur Pearcy Archive, by courtesy of Audrey Pearcy

Skyraider Men – Admiral Sir John Treacher, KCB

The commander of No. 849 (AEW) Squadron from 7 July 1952 until 20 July 1953, John Treacher had a long and distinguished career in the Royal Navy. He was born in Chile on 23 September 1924, where his father, Argentine-born Frank Charles Treacher, was then working. The young John returned home and was educated at St Paul's School. He entered the Royal Navy in the summer of 1942, before his eighteenth birthday. After traditional training at HMS *Frobisher*, Treacher saw considerable war service as a young officer, both aboard the battleship HMS *Nelson* and the light cruiser HMS *Glasgow*, during the war, in the Mediterranean and home waters; the latter ship, for example, carried out bombardments in support of the US Army at Omaha Beach during the Normandy landings in 1944. He also served aboard small ships, the old destroyer *Keppel* on Russia Convoys, and then aboard the new sloop *Mermaid*.

Treacher had volunteered for aircrew during the war, but was not sent for training until 1946. In 1947, he qualified as a naval pilot and, while serving with 800 Squadron, flying the Seafire 47 from the carrier HMS *Triumph*, took part in the Korean War operations. On return to the UK, he converted to jets and became senior pilot in the trials squadron, No. 703, before flying the basic Skyraider with the US Navy. In 1951, he was appointed Commanding Officer of No. 778 Squadron, which was formed to train crews for the fleet. His appointment to form and command the Royal Navy's only front-line Skyraider Squadron followed in July 1952.

Treacher attended the Naval Staff course in 1954 and then served on the Naval Staff in Washington, DC, before being appointed as the Executive Officer of HMS *Protector*, the South Atlantic and Falklands Island Guard Ship, from 20 August 1955, being promoted to Commander on 31 December 1956. He served on the staff of the Flag Officer Flying Training at HMS *Heron*, the Royal Navy Air Station at Yeovilton, from July 1957 to May

1959, before becoming Commander (Air) aboard the carrier HMS *Victorious* from May 1959 to October 1961. She had just spent many years being almost completely rebuilt and had recommissioned in January 1958, with a full-angled deck and state-of-the-art radar and equipment. She was able to operate the latest naval aircraft, being the first to carry the new Supermarine Scimitar.

Treacher introduced carrier aviation to the Indian Navy as head of the team that worked up their first carrier, the INS *Vikrant* (formerly HMS *Hercules*) with British Hawker

Sea Hawks and French Alize ASW aircraft. He was promoted to full Captain on 30 June 1962.

His next appointment was as Naval Assistant to the Third Sea Lord and Controller of the Navy, from October 1962 to December 1964, before going back to sea as Commanding Officer of the frigate HMS *Lowestoft*, taking command of the vessel in December 1964. In May 1966, he was appointed Director, Naval Air Warfare, holding this important post for two years at a critical time for the Navy. More sea time followed, when he became the Commanding Officer of the carrier HMS *Eagle* from November 1968.

On leaving *Eagle*, he was promoted to Rear Admiral and appointed Flag Officer Carrier and Amphibious Ships, on 7 July 1970. He served in this post until June 1972, when he was appointed Flag Officer, Naval Air Command. This was followed, on October 1973, by appointment as Vice Chief of Naval Staff. On 1 December 1973, he was promoted to Vice Admiral, and in the same year was elected a Fellow of the Royal Aeronautical Society. He was appointed a full Admiral on 15 December 1975, and awarded the KCB in the Birthday Honours List of the same year.

Admiral Treacher completed a most successful naval career with his last appointment, as Commander-in-Chief Fleet (all ships world-wide, including submarines and FAA aircraft). With this came his NATO appointment as ACCHAN (with SACEUR and SACLANT, one of the three major NATO Commands), until he left the Navy on 30 March, 1977, aged fifty-two.

After leaving the Navy, Sir John joined National Car Parks, serving as Director until 1985. He joined the board of Westland in 1978, and was Deputy Chairman between 1986 and 1989. He also served as one of the non-press members of the Press Council between 1978 and 1981 and as a director of SBAC between 1983 and 1989.

Currently, Sir John lives in Bayswater, London, and enjoys travel, shooting and photography.

The flight was renowned for its prominent insignia of a brown and yellow bee on a square white panel on both sides of the engine cowling, from 1958 to 1960. In response to an inaccuracy in an American book, which stated that the insignia was a wasp, Lieutenant R.A.J. Mersom, RN, wrote his 'Ode to the 'Bee':

The Sky is known both far and wide,
With squadron cyphers on its side;
In 849 our Flight did roam;
Four flights at sea, HQ at home.

Four flights of four, a letter for a name.
A through D, each one gained fame;
On each cowl, there was a letter,
'B' Flight went just one better.

Placed right there for all to see,
That is no wasp, it is a BEE!

A 'B' Flight Skyraider AEW-1 showing its 'Bee' badge in close-up. Arthur Pearcy Archive, by courtesy of Audrey Pearcy

The story of 'C' Flight largely mirrored that of 'A', with sea service aboard the *Eagle*, shore-based operations from Malta, including a brief sojourn aboard the light carrier *Glory* in 1953, before becoming the new 'B' Flight. 'D' became the new 'C' Flight, and joined the new carrier *Albion* in August 1954, for catapult trials, then briefly embarked aboard her sister ship, *Bulwark*, for mirror landings. It was back to the *Albion* in July 1955, then a period of land-based operations before returning to the same carrier to take part in the Suez landings in 1956, and several other commissions, including a Far Eastern cruise in 1958. In 1959, it returned to Culdrose and gradually re-equipped with the Fairey Gannet during 1960.

The brief life of 'E' Flight was spent at Hal Far, Malta, where it spent five months before returning home to become 'D'

Flight. 'D' Flight also joined the *Eagle* in 1953 and then undertook detailed trials of the AN/APS-20 radar at RNAS Eglinton, before becoming the new 'C' Flight. When 'E' Flight, in turn, became the new 'C' Flight, it undertook deck trials aboard the *Bulwark* before being land-based at Hal Far, Malta, relieving 'C' Flight. In 1956, embarked aboard the *Albion*, the flight cruised to the Far East and conducted exercises in the Indian Ocean. After intervals at Culdrose, two commissions aboard the *Bulwark* followed in 1957 and 1958.

'D' Flight, commanded by Lieutenant-Commander P.G.W. Morris, RN, at this period had five crews, each comprising a pilot and two observers. Their back-up was a maintenance crew of 37 ratings; their duties were equally divided between A&E and L&R, with four officers' stewards, three aircraft handlers, one cook and one safety equipment rating. There were no technical officers, and this work rested with the senior ratings of the flight.

WT 959 of 'C' Flight revving up and unfolding its wings prior to take-off from the deck of the aircraft carrier HMS *Albion*, **1956.** Arthur Pearcy Archive, by courtesy of Audrey Pearcy

Duties and Rôles

The AEW-1s were expected to supplement their primary function of guarding against low-flying attacking or shadowing aircraft by either reporting such contacts to the carrier, or by vectoring their own airborne fighters to deal with the threat. In service, however, they were given the extra rôles of AEW, strike direction, surface search, mail delivery, ambulance, and so on. In fact, 'D' Flight renamed itself the 'Wells Fargo and Anyplace Airline', and its commanding officer was inspired to

Commanding Officers of No. 849 Squadron

	HQ	A	B	C	D	E
CO	Lt-Cdr J.D. Treacher	Lt W. Holdrige	Lt A.W. Sabey	Lt H.G.L. Llewellyn	Lt-Cdr D.T. Andrews	Lt-Cdr N. Ovenden
From	07 Jul 52	20 Jan 53	Feb 53	01 Jun 53	07 Sep 53	01 Dec 53
CO	Lt-Cdr M.J. Baring	Lt M.W.P. Betts	Lt-Cdr G.P. Sabin	Lt-Cdr D.W. Winterton	Lt-Cdr N. Ovenden	
From	20 Jul 53	06 Jan 54	07 Jan 54	19 Oct 53	15 Oct 54	
CO	Lt-Cdr C.B. Armstrong	Lt-Cdr G.P. Sabin	Lt-Cdr R.M. Shave	Lt-Cdr H.G.L. Nash	Lt-Cdr A. Baillie	
From	18 Dec 54	05 Jul 54	05 Jul 55	25 Jan 54	05 Jan 55	
CO	Lt-Cdr D.G. Frazer	Lt-Cdr C.B. Armstrong	Lt-Cdr R.C. Ashworth	Lt-Cdr R.M. Shave	Lt-Cdr W.L. Shepherd	
From	01 May 56	31 Aug 54	07 May 55	16 Jun 54	6 June 9156	
CO	Lt-Cdr F. Bromilow	Lt-Cdr G. Legg	Lt-Cdr R.G.G. Hubbard	Lt-Cdr D.T. Andrews	Lt-Cdr P.G.W. Morris	
From	13 May 57	04 Jan 55	02 May 56	05 Jul 54	07 Oct 57	
CO	Lt-Cdr A.G.B.Phillip	Lt-Cdr A.D. Hooper	Lt-Cdr J.W. Wickham	Lt-Cdr D.A. Fuller	Lt-Cdr T.G. Butler	
From	09 Apr 59	04 Jan 56	01 Apr 57	04 Dec 55	06 Dec 58	
CO		Lt-Cdr R.H.S. Menzies	Lt-Cdr B.H. Stock	Lt-Cdr N.G.T. Taylor		
From		05 Sep 56	23 Jul 58	05 Apr 57		
CO		Lt-Cdr B.J. Williams	Lt-Cdr C.R. Mellor	Lt-Cdr P.A. Woollings		
From		10 Sep 56	27 Aug 59	18 Aug 59		
CO		Lt-Cdr C.R. Mellor	Lt-Cdr D. Levy			
From		17 Apr 58	29 Feb 60			
CO		Lt K.W.C.Readings				
From		17 Aug 59				

433 of 'B' Flight No. 849 Squadron lifts off from the angled flight deck of the aircraft carrier HMS Victorious **in 1960.** Arthur Pearcy Archive, by courtesy of Audrey Pearcy

write the poem (*see* page 2) that sums up the Skyraider's nine-year rôle in the Royal Navy.

Lieutenant-Commander Percy Morris had the following recollections:[57]

The Skyraider was a splendidly reliable aircraft. It performed its rôle excellently. Perhaps, as a pilot, I most appreciated its deck-landing characteristics. It was so much more easy to land on than the planes of the Firefly era. You could see the deck centre line on the final approach almost as well as in a jet. The undercarriage also was very robust, like the Avenger. After a heavy landing the Skyraider would extend its oleos, give itself a shake and taxi forward, when slightly older British aircraft would possibly need 'Jumbo' [the British name for the flight-deck mobile crane] to pick up the pieces! The auto-pilot was also a boon. You could use two hands on a map without having to hold the stick between your knees in bumpy air.

The Skyraider did not like being catapulted. The result, too often, would be a radar failure. To avoid this, the Skyraider would be ranged right aft and do a free take-off after the jets had been catapulted.

The accessibility of much of the radar equipment was handy. A radar failure after launch could often be rectified by one of the observers scrambling up the tunnel and giving suspect items an educated clout! Radar failure was sometimes frustrating. The jolt on arresting would fix the fault and leave the technicians little to work on.

No. 849 HQ at Culdrose always produced very well-trained and skilled observers. They did the

navigation, report of contacts and interceptions. We, during our world cruise, had little success with the 'Bellhop' equipment[38] which would have allowed low-level interception to be carried out on board in the Ops Room. We in 'D' Flight felt that we could do as well, or better, with the APS 20C than our American friends with the APS 20F, the equipment later fitted on the AEW Gannets. One problem with the APS 20C was that it was not stabilized in a turn. This meant a

tactical advantage in doing steeply banked turns to minimize the loss of radar picture.

One 'D' Flight experiment to extend the AEW's range of duties even further came to an abrupt end. The idea was that, with all the radar equipment stripped out, and the scanner and Radome removed, the 'Sky' would make an excellent troop transport. (As it turned out, *Bulwark* was on her last commission as a carrier, and was ultimately fitted out for just such an amphibious troop transport rôle.) One aircraft was modified; the senior pilot took her up, but very rapidly brought her back down again. The Skyraider flew 'nose-down tail-up' the whole time she was in the air, no matter what the pilot did. A signal was despatched to the Douglas plant at El Segundo seeking answers to this dangerous conundrum, and the reply was that, with the AD-3, -4 and -5Ws, the extra weight imposed by the radar equipment and two operators had meant the re-positioning of the wings on the fuselage, in order to compensate. This had thrown the aircraft's balance dangerously out of kilter, and the 'good idea' was promptly shelved!

Bulwark's sister ship, the carrier HMS *Centaur*, then became 'D' Flight's home for a brief period. Sea Slug missile trials took place in the Mediterranean, with the Skyraiders, again working from Hal Far,

A Douglas AD-4W Skyraider in the guise of Royal Navy AEW-1 WT 987 (432/V) takes off from the angled deck of HMS Victorious **in 1960.** Arthur Pearcy Archive, by courtesy of Audrey Pearcy

aiding the trials ship HMS *Girdle Ness*, before a last cruise aboard the *Albion*, which proved to be the very last AEW commission to the Far East. On 16 December 1960, after its return, the Flight was disbanded at Culdrose and the AEW-1 finally left the Royal Navy's front-line squadrons after nine solid years of service.

A Long Life

During the nine years, the Skyraider had begun to show its age, but it had kept performing. Casualties over that long period were rare. Two aircraft crashed with three days of each other – WT 963 in a field near Exeter on 12 February 1960, and WV 183 aboard the *Albion* on 9 February 1960. There were also some accidents (*see* the table below).

There was a continuing shortage of spares, accentuated by the final commissioning of the new carriers, and only tem-porarily alleviated by further small deliveries from the USA in 1955 and 1956. The AEW-1 seemed destined to suffer the fate of all Skyraiders, being assigned to a number of supplementary duties (not all official!). Although the detection of low-flying incoming 'hostiles' remained its prime rôle, it was also called upon to function as a directing aircraft for anti-submarine hunts and weather reconnaissance. Its bulk enabled it to become a jack-of-all-trades when required, with ship-to-shore transfer of supplies and stores as well as personnel becoming a large part of its carrier duties.[59]

In order to keep enough of the Skyraiders operational, there was a great deal of 'shuf-fling' of aircraft between flights, especially in the latter years. Several aircraft were 'cannibalized' in the end, in order to keep others flying. Airframes were refurbished at RNAS Donibristle, while the responsibility for engine overhauls was handed over to the specialist centre at Treforest, north-west of Cardiff, of British Overseas Airways Corporation (BOAC, the forerunner of British Airways). The upgrading and modernization of the AEW-1's radar and radio equipment remained the duty of the Naval Aircraft Radio Installation Unit (NARIU) at Gosport and Lee-on-Solent.

The Skyraiders continued to serve with the fleet until 1959/60, by which time their replacement, the Fairey AEW-3 Gannet, had begun to arrive. A gradual transition period followed. Two AEW-1 Skyraiders were reserved to become permanent memorials – WV 106/CU-427 (BuNo 124086) was retained at Culdrose, before being finally transferred to Yeovilton; the other (WT121/CU-415, BuNo 124121) went to the Fleet Air Arm Museum at RNAS Yeovilton. After many years on display outside, it has now been brought under cover to take its place in a proposed new hangar and display funded by the National Lottery.

This was not quite the end of the active life of some of the AEW-1s, however. For a few, a reprieve was at hand.

AEW-1 accidents

Date	Flight	Ship/Base	Location
21 June 1956	A Flt	*Eagle*	Mediterranean
24 November 1956	A Flt	*Eagle*	Mediterranean
22 September 1959	B Flt	*Victorious*	North Sea
20 November 1959	B Flt	*Victorious*	Mediterranean
24 February 1960	HQ Flt	*Seahawk*	Culdrose

Officers and men of No 849 Squadron, Fleet Air Arm with their AEW-1s lined up at HMS Seahawk, **with the Squadron Badge and Battle Honours.** Arthur Pearcy Archive, by courtesy of Audrey Pearcy

CHAPTER ELEVEN

Further Diversification

On 25 June 1950, the North Korean army, without provocation, crossed the 38th Parallel and invaded South Korea. This clear act of aggression was to prove to be the catalyst in the first remarkable Skyraider revival. In the absence of a delegation from the Soviet Union, the United Nations passed a resolution to intervene. The US Navy was the only strong force available to the UN; accordingly, American aircraft carriers in the vicinity were soon making combat strikes against

look more attractive in Washington, DC. Funding was increased to deal with the situation and, with this slackening of the defence budget purse strings, a fresh look was taken at the Douglas plan. As a result, the AD-5 was approved, funded and quickly put in hand.

Despite increased production and a renewal of the earlier temp on the lines at El Segundo as Douglas responded to this new situation, none of the resultant aircraft – the AD-5 and AD-6 series – saw combat,

Changes

Modification for the AD-5 involved more than a simple tinkering with the basic design; a complete re-working resulted in a radically different machine. The single-seat dive bomber metamorphosed into a two-seat day-attack aircraft of great potential, rather than the ASW machine originally envisaged. A mock-up was inspected and approved as early as October 1950, and work began.

AD-5 Skyraider (BuNo 132674) ready for the off. Nick Williams

North Korean targets, with great effect. As time went on, and it became obvious that the UN forces were in for a long, hard, slog, and that the Skyraider was fulfilling its duties with more than adequate efficiency, fresh orders were placed for the AD-4. The old plans for a new variant, so brusquely rejected a few months earlier as a waste of limited resources, now began to

although they were completed in time to take part in Korea, where fighting did not end until 27 July 1953. Many Navy and Marine Corps units in the theatre began to re-equip with the aircraft from 1952 onwards, but they did not take part in any fighting. The new types were, however, to enjoy a long and very useful service life, and many were to earn laurels in a later conflict.

The two crew members were seated side by side rather than in tandem; this basic fact involved changes to the aircraft's fuselage, cockpit, instrumentation and aerodynamic balance. The prototype for this modification was a standard production-line AD-4 (BuNo 124006), with a fuselage 9in wider than normal; the width had been added from the leading edge of the wing to the trailing edge, by extending the fuselage out to the wing root, and then blended it back into the original contour.

The fuselage was also strengthened, and lengthened by 1ft 11in (58.4cm), to compensate for the new configuration, which had dramatically shifted the Skyraider's centre of gravity. The two dive brakes were omitted completely from the two side fuselage locations, although the ventral dive brake was retained. The engine was moved forward by 8in, the vertical tail surface area was increased by a substantial 50 per cent, and the leading edge of the fin was fitted with an air scoop. The forward-facing pitot tube was relocated at a lower level on the leading edge of the fin.

In addition to the standard Aero 14 hard points, 12 of which were retained, two new, enlarged and redesigned Mark 51 forward-raking underwing pylons, more capable of carrying the 11.5in Tiny Tim rockets, were fitted, with an additional one on the centre line, while the four wing-mounted 20mm cannon became the norm.

The new, broader and longer, rearward-sliding canopy featured two flat, forward-sloping bullet-resistant centre sections, with angled side panels. The pilot and co-pilot were seated behind this, shoulder to shoulder, with an anti-glare rack shield fitted internally. The pilot had his flight instrument panels on the left-hand side while the co-pilot acted as navigator and also had the radar bombing instrumentation on the right-hand side of the cockpit. Two hand-grip, angled control columns were provided; the navigator's could be unshipped and stored to the rear of his seat on later models. Radio controls, the co-pilot's throttle and other ancillary instruments were located on a centre console between the two men.

The stub blade antenna was initially located atop the centre section of the canopy while the long, glazed rear section, with upward- and outward-opening hatches, housed the two radar operators, who were also seated side by side. Both centre and rear glazed segments were tinted very dark blue, to protect the sensitive equipment from sun glare; to the rear, the canopy was blanked off with a solid, curved fairing. The antenna was soon relocated atop the after fuselage.

Wing span was increased to 50ft 9in (15.47m), length increased to 40ft 1in (12.22m) and overall height increased to 15ft 10in (4.83m). Weights mushroomed and now came out at 12,313lb (5,581kg)

Specification – AD-5	
Powerplant:	R-3350-26W
Weights:	Empty 5,581kg (12,313lb); loaded 8,528kg (18,799lb); full 11,340kg (25,000lb); wing loading 47lb/sq ft; power loading 3.2kg/hp (7lb/hp)
Dimensions:	Length 12.22m (40ft 1in); height 4.83m (15ft 10in); wingspan 15.47m (50ft 9in); wing area 37.192sq m (400.33sq ft)
Performance:	3,020hp Max. speed 501km/h (311mph); at altitude 5,485m (18,000ft). Cruise speed 322km/h (200mph) Rate of climb 701km/h (2,300ft/min) Ceiling 7,925m (26,000ft) Range 1,935km (1,202miles)
Acceptance in service:	1953
Numbers Cancelled:	443

empty, 18,799lb (8,528kg) loaded with maximum all-up weight of 25,00lb (11,340kg) compared with the XBT2D-1s 17,500lb (7,938kg) a few years before. Wing loading now was 47lb/sq in (229.3kg/sq m) and the maximum speed, with the R-3350-26W 3,020hp engine, was pulled down still further to only 311mph at an altitude of 18,000ft (501km/h at 5,485m). Range was down to 1,202 miles (1,935 km).

This aircraft first flew in its new configuration on 17 August 1951, and the first AD-5 built as such from scratch (BuNo 132478) soon followed. After successful trials, the US Navy placed orders that resulted in the construction of 212 basic AD-5s in three batches, (BuNos 132392–132476, 132637–132676 and 133854–133929). The last aircraft were accepted into service in April 1956.

Conversion Kits

The proven value of this aircraft was further increased by the supply of various 'bolt-on' conversion kits, which enabled the large fuselage area below the much bigger canopy to be quickly adapted for a variety of rôles, as follows:

1. Photo reconnaissance, with up to five cameras fitted.
2. Ambulance, for casualty evacuation, with either a single Stokes litter for serious casualties, or up to four basic stretchers fitted, one above the other, two on either side of the inner fuselage. In this rôle, a hoisting rig with ratchet loading hoist was carried, along with

limited medical equipment; if necessary, oxygen was piped in from the right-hand cockpit console.
3. Cargo transport, by the addition of a mechanical hoist capable of carrying a maximum of 2,000lb (908kg) of military stores.
4. Troop transport, with bench seating capable of accommodating twelve fully equipped soldiers (the '12-in-1').
5. Target tug, with the normal towing equipment and drones.
6. Passenger transport, with four rearward-facing bucket seats, each of which was equipped with its own individual oxygen regulator and safety harness. This was mainly employed for top brass transportation to and from airfields and rear-area bases.

Such versatility also led to a Navy requirement, in 1953, for the AD-5 to be adapted as an in-flight refuelling tanker, to replenish Navy jets such as the Cougar and the Panther, and thus extend their mission range. Douglas looked into this and reported that such a conversion was not practicable as specified. They did come up with a working alternative in the carrying of a self-contained external fuelling tank, the 'buddy' store, in conjunction with a trailing fuel hose and nozzle. This concept became part and parcel of the AD-5's vast repertoire.

More Permanent Variants

The internal kits sufficed for the numerous ancillary tasks that came the Skyraider's way in the 1950s but, as before, the basic

AD-5Ns in close-up echelon formation at 500ft (150m) over the Atlantic Coast on 22 June 1955. National Archives, College Park, MD

133757–133776, 135139–135222 and 139556–139605).

AD-5Q

Douglas took one AD-5N (BuNo 135054) and modified it as a four-seater ECM (electronic countermeasures) aircraft. Trials followed, and another 50 AD-5Ns were subsequently provided with similar kits for in-service conversion to this new rôle. These aircraft carried the AN/APS-16 ECM transmitter pod and associated equipment and, from 1948 onwards, operated in four-plane detachments assigned to carriers from two specialist squadrons, one for the Pacific Fleet and one for the Atlantic Fleet.

AD-5S

A single aircraft (BuNo 132479), assigned to the Naval Experimental Test unit VX-1 at Key West, Florida, was equipped as an experimental ASW test-bed. Equipped with the Magnetic Anomaly Detector (MAD) instrumentation, it undertook a series of trials in this guise, but no production requirement resulted.

The All-Weather Squadrons

The arrival of the all-weather squadrons gave the fleet an extra dimension. Originating with the composite squadrons (VC), which had a mixed bag of aircraft in their complement, these developed into full all-weather attack and fighter units (VFAW). For a long period, their main workhorse was the AD-5.

The squadron that originated as VC-4 at NAS Atlantic City, New Jersey, in July 1948, and was redesignated as VFAW-4 on 2 July 1956, which arrived at Quonset in May 1958, can be taken as typical. By 1 July 1957, commanded by Commander John E. Odell, Jr, USN, this squadron listed its main functions as follows:

To intercept and destroy enemy aircraft during all conditions of weather and visibility. Provide all-weather air defense of the carrier task force. Provide all-weather air defense for other surface forces. Provide Mk-90 attack capability within all detachments deployed aboard CVSs having the Mk-90 weapon capability.

On the squadron's strength at that date were between 57 and 59 pilots, with 26 AD-5s, along with two TV-2s and one SNB-5.

model was also adapted for further missions in a series of more permanent variants.

AD-5N

This was a night attack aircraft, with the usual extra compartment built into the central fuselage to house the two operators and their specialist equipment, which comprised a searchlight, a flare dispenser and a sono-buoy. They carried both the search radar and powerful illumination in the form of an Aero 3B elongated pod carried under the wing on the pylon. Douglas produced one aircraft (BuNo 132477) to test this configuration and then built a total of 238 more aircraft of this variant in two batches (BuNos 132480–132636 and 134974–135054).

AD-5W

The AEW version of the AD-5 was a four-seater with the usual AN/APS-208 pod, commonly known as the 'Guppy' Radome, which was mounted under the fuselage section immediately abaft the engine. The rear canopy was redesigned as a 'solid' all-metal covering, with small semi-circular windows, abaft the forward two-seater cockpit. Almost all the usual underwing ordnance points were omitted from this type, with just one pair being retained for additional fuel drop tanks.

The normal arrangement was for a detachment of four such aircraft to be assigned to each carrier. A total of 218 of this variant were finally produced, in four batches (BuNos 132729–132792,

These Skyraiders, as well as being responsible for developing the loft-bombing techniques for the Navy's Atomic Bomb delivery at that time,[60] ran a continuous training programme to train pilots in all-weather flight procedures and also provided detachments for carrier commitments, as required by COMNAVAIRLANT. Between 1 July and 20 September 1957, VFAW-33 had the following detachments at sea to take part in the NATO Exercise 'Strike Back'.

Detachment	Carrier	Aboard from
38	USS *Tarawa* (CVS-40)	16 Aug–24 Oct 1957
45	USS *Essex* (CVA-9)	16 Aug–24 Oct 1957
51	USS *Leyte* (CVS-32)	29 Aug–28 Nov 1957
52	USS *Valley Forge* (CVS-45)	20 Sept 6 Dec 1957

Each of these detachments consisted of seven officers, 30 enlisted men and four AD-5s. From 10 October, detachment 51 participated in the anti-submarine phase of two more NATO exercises, 'Haystrike' and 'Red Epoch', in conjunction with the Sixth Fleet. On 5 November, the squadron received 13 F2H aircraft, and began training teams on this machine in addition to its normal AD commitments.

Similar deployments followed in the first quarter of 1958, although the AD-5 units had been reduced to nine aircraft, with the following detachments:

Detachment	Carrier	Aboard from
52	USS *Valley Forge* (CVS-45)	1 Jan–31 Mar 1958
51	USS *Leyte* (CVS-32)	27 Jan–24 Feb 1958
38	USS *Tarawa* (CVS-40)	6 Jan–3 Feb 1958

They participated in the NATO Exercise *Springboard One* between 6 January and 3 February, as well as inter-ship exercises. By the end of June, the transition period from all-weather attack to all-weather fighter squadron had just about been completed, and the Skyraider had been phased out of this squadron. Only a solitary AD-5 remained on its strength, and the attack rôle was taken over by VA(AW)-33.

By mid-July 1957, VA(AW)-33 was commanded by Captain R.M. Bruning, USN, who had relieved Commander W.L.

Pack, USN, on 12 July. It was based at NAS Atlantic City, NJ, as part of the Atlantic Fleet, and its aircraft strength consisted of 42 AD-5Ns, along with two TF-1Qs, an A2F2 and an SNB-5. There were several active detachments aboard carriers at sea, as follows:

Detachment	Carrier	Aboard from
36	USS *Randolph* (CVA-15)	4 Jun 1957–4 Jan 1958
37	USS *Roosevelt* (CVA-42)	13 Jun–6 Mar 1958
43	USS *Saratoga* (CVA-60)	Returned 22 Oct 1957
42	USS *Forrestal* (CVA-59)	Returned 21 Oct 1957
33	USS *Intrepid* (CVA-11)	Returned 21 Oct 1957

These detachments took part in NATO Exercises 'Strikeback' and 'Pipedown'. Detachment 33 was under Lieutenant-Commander S. Takis as Officer-in-Command, with five pilots, 41 men and four AD-5N aircraft; detachment 42 had Lieutenant H.T. Gower as Officer-in-Command, with eight pilots, one air intelligence officer, 51 men and seven AD-5N aircraft; detachment 43 was under Commander C.G. Tidemann, with eight pilots, one air intelligence officer, 50 men and seven AD-5N aircraft. All these detachments returned to the squadron on 21/22 October.

This establishment was maintained in early 1958, changing slightly at a Skyraider strength of 38 AD-5Ns and one AD-5Q, increased to nine AD-5Q aircraft by the end of March, while detachment 45 was deployed to the USS *Essex* (CVA-9) on 3 January and detachment 43 to the USS *Saratoga* (CVA-60) on 4 January. By April, the squadron had 37 AD-5Ns and 11 AD-5Qs on its strength, and detachments 33, 36 and 42 had deployed to the carriers *Intrepid*, *Randolph* and *Forrestal* once more, on 20 May, 28 June and 23 April, respectively. This was their pattern; for full details of their subsequent deployments, see Appendix III.

By concentrating the all-weather attack firepower in one unit, expertise could be built up in this specialist area, and training of new aircrew could be assimilated, with sea experience gained by the periodic detachments from the squadron to the attack carriers of the fleet.

Nuclear delivery was an added burden and responsibility for the Skyraider (*see* page 123).

AD-6

There was a continuing need for a single-seater day-attack Skyraider and the AD-6 continued to be produced concurrently with the new AD-5 two-seater airplane. The AD-6 was powered by the Wright R-3350-26WD 2,700hp engine, and its overall span, height, weights, wing area and speed were almost the same as those of the AD-4B; its length was slightly less, at 38ft 10in (11.84m) overall, and wing loading was 45.2lb/sq in (220.8kg/sq m) compared with 46.6lb/sq in (227.7kg/sq m). The rudder was about 3 sq ft larger in total area than the AD-5 and had a markedly stiffer feel, due to the increased spring tension in the controls.

Range was much improved, increasing from 900 miles (1,450km) to 1,316 miles (2,115km). As well as the usual Mk 8 300-gallon (1,363-litre) drop tanks mounted under the wings when required, an extra pair of 155-gallon (704-litre) fuel tanks were provided in the after cockpit compartment and an extra 12.5 US gallons (930lb or 422kg) of oil could be carried in a small tank mounted above this in a small tank. Oil supply was always the limiting factor with any Skyraider sortie. The 38.5-gallon oil sump proved insufficient, and auxiliary oil tanks had to be fitted for long-range ferry flights. The dive brakes, deleted from the AD-5, were retained on the AD-6, whose rôle continued as before. The pilot's control stick was shorter and required a very different operating technique.

This mark was based upon the AD-4B and retained that aircraft's nuclear capability. It was fitted with the Mod 4 Bombing Director, and capable of carrying the Mark 7 'Blue Boy' nuclear device (which was fitted with a folding ventral fin for deck clearance when mounted on the Skyraider).

The AD-6 also incorporated many other of the improvements introduced with the AD-5. It was armed with two (later four) 20mm wing cannon, and had the larger forward sweeping ordnance pods, for example, making it capable of toting both the AGM-12A and AGM-12B Bullpup missiles, as well as LAU-3A and LAU-6 Zuni rocket pod clusters. Other ordnance carried included the following: up to four 750lb M177 bombs; the 500lb Mk 82 Low Drag General-Purpose (LDGP) bombs, fitted with snake-eye fins and with 18in or 36in 'Daisy Cutter' fuse extensions; the 250lb and 100lb white phosphorous bombs ('Willie Petes'); BLU-1 napalm canisters;

Specification – AD-6	
Powerplant:	R-3350-26WA
Weights:	Empty 5,429kg (11,968lb); loaded 8,213kg (18,106lb); full 11,340kg (25,000lb); wing loading 45.2lb/sq ft; power loading 3kg/hp (6.7lb/hp)
Dimensions:	Length 11.84m (38ft 10in); height 4.78m (15ft 8½in); wingspan 15.25m (50ft ¼in); wing area 37.192sq m (400.33sq ft)
Performance:	3,020hp Max. speed 518km/h (322mph); at altitude 5,485m (18,000ft) Cruise speed 319km/h (198mph) Rate of climb 869km/h (2,850ft/min) Ceiling 8,685m (28,500ft) Range 2,115km (1,316 miles)
Acceptance in service:	1953

Douglas AD-6 Skyraider (BuNo 134536) of VA-176. Arthur Pearcy Archive, by courtesy of Audrey Pearcy

5in LAU-10A Zuni and LAU-59 rocket pods; SUU-11 A/B containing the GAU-2B electrically driven, six-barrelled 7.62mm Gatling gun, with 1,500 rounds of either ball, tracer or armour-piercing ammunition, and with a rate of fire of either 3,000 or 6,000rpm; and SUU-14 A/A cluster bomb dispensers with six tubes banded in an inverted triangular pylon-mounted unit. These fire assortments of CBUs included Gravel.[61]

As well as BLU-1 (unstabilized) and VLU-27 (stabilized) fire bomb pods containing napalm and other flammable liquids, another especially powerful addition to the Spad's armoury in Vietnam was the BLU-76/B fuel air explosive bomb (FAE). This canister of 30in diameter, containing a highly combustible liquid, was fitted aft

with fins and T-fins 42in in diameter, for stability in descent, as well as with a parachute to slow its rate of descent, to give the low-level delivery aircraft time to get clear. At the forward end, the container tank was fitted with a long, tapering cone, with an ejectable nose in front, giving an overall length of 167in (4.24m). With the various fittings (tie blocks, arming lanyards, and such) all-up weight of this device was 2,600lb (1,180kg).

Its workings were crude enough – impact crumbled the thin casing, releasing the liquid into the air, and a 0.03-second fuse retarded the flash combustion long enough for the resultant gas cloud to spread, for maximum impact. The effects were devastating, particularly against concentrations of enemy troops – the device

was described as having the explosive power of 10,000lb of TNT.

The AD-6 thus incorporated both low-level and all-weather capacity to become an all-round attack aircraft of great versatility. As its ground-attack rôle became more significant, additional armour plating was worked in around the pilot. This extra protection consisted of side panes abreast the forward canopy extending down to the wing roots, and underneath protection covering the centre section, with moulded armour panels leading up to the engine firewall. These modifications were designed to give increased protection from ground fire.

Once again, additional strengthening was introduced, with double-thickness skin around the wheel wells. The wing structure was made more resilient around the usual trouble spots of the landing gear, with reinforcement of the wing skin above. This had become necessary because of the ever-increasing loads being imposed on the aircraft. The AD-6 had a sink rate of 23 feet per second, almost double that of the AD-1, and could therefore slam down harder and more often on carrier decks than its relatively delicate ancestor. To help in this, the aircraft was fitted with a hydraulically raised tail-hook mechanism. The single cockpit was again redesigned to incorporate these additions, and given improved lighting.

In 1966, the AD-6 became the first aircraft to feature the Stanley 'Yankee Extractor' extraction rocket device for emergencies. This device was designed so that it could even be used while the aircraft was still on the deck. A rocket device was fitted behind the pilot's rear-of-seat armour shield. When activated by the pilot pulling hard on a lanyard, the canopy was blow clear away in the single-seat model. In the case of the tandem two-seat variant, the A-1E, a canopy cutter was activated, which carved two separate holes that were sufficiently big for both crew members to pass through.

The extraction rocket was then automatically ejected upwards, uncoiling the trailing pendant lines. Once clear, the rocket ignited and the pilot's seat folded down and away; his seat belt and shoulder restraint straps opened up, releasing him as he was lifted clear of the cockpit, and then the rocket separated from the pilot and his parachute automatically opened. The two parachute lines were prevented from fouling the rocket by the fitting of a swivel.

The Yankee rocket itself was spin-stabilized by two angled nozzles.

A large anti-collision beacon was later added to the tip of the tail and retrospectively fitted to earlier models on an extension. Static discharge booms also appeared in pairs outboard on the elevators of the horizontal stabilizers, and in triples on the trailing flaps of the main wings.

In total, 713 AD-6s were built, in four batches (BuNos 134466–134637, 135223–135406, 137492–137632 and 139606–139821). They saw widespread front-line and combat duty with both the US Navy and the US Marine Corps, and later, when the jokes abruptly stopped, with the VNAF and the USAF. Uniquely for the 'Able-Dog', no sub-variants of this mark were built.

An AD-6 of VA-145 in flight over the Philippines while operating from the carrier USS Hornet (CVA-112) during the WesPac cruise, February 1957. National Archives, College Park, MD

An AD-6 tanker belonging to the US Navy's VA-104, fuelling a Chance-Vought F-8U-1 Crusader during exercises over the USA, 26 November 1957. National Archives, College Park, MD

AD-7

The final mark of the remarkable Skyraider to be built by Douglas at El Segundo was the AD-7. Outwardly, it was almost identical to the AD-6, sharing the same span, length, height and wing area, heavy armour protection for low-level close support work, and a potential nuclear capacity. The main difference was its adoption of the Wright R-3359-26-WB engine, which required strengthened engine mounts. This engine gave the AD-7 a maximum speed of 343mph (552km/h) at a height of 20,000ft (6,095m), with a reduced service ceiling, down to 25,400ft (7,740m). Range was also slightly reduced, to 1,300 miles (2,090km), although rate of climb improved, from 2,850ft per minute (869m per minute) to 3,230ft per minute (985m per minute).

Further undercarriage strengthening was also undertaken. This area was always the Spad's most vulnerable point, especially as its duties had expanded over the years. The outer wing panels and fittings also had to cope with ever-increasing loading demands, such as the extra pair of M3 20mm cannon that were fitted to the AD-6. The introduction of the Multiple Ejector Racks (MER), which were fitted to the AD-6 and AD-7 and were capable of carrying six bombs, confirmed the need for such reinforcement.

The Navy placed orders for 240 of this version.

(Around this time, the aircraft was beginning to be referred to in the Fleet by the affectionate nickname of 'Spad'; this seems to have derived from its vintage, which led jet pilots to compare it to the French First World War stalwart of the same name.)

Another duty that came the way of this Spad variant was that of flying tanker. In this configuration, a drogue hose and paying-out winch was fitted, and three streamlined tanks with 300-gallon capacity were carried, one under the fuselage and one on either wing, on the large Mark 51 ventral pylons to port and starboard. This equipment proved successful and was retro-fitted to many AD-6s.

Armistice and 'Ceasefire'

The end of fighting in Korea led to an armistice in July 1953; at about the same time, the expected arrival of the Spad's jet replacement, the XA4D-1 prototype of the Skyhawk, happened. (This aircraft proved to be of equal longevity, making its first flight, coupled with the usual premature cut-backs in the defence budget.) Despite this, existing orders were such that the peak of Skyraider production at El Segundo was actually reached in June 1954, when 59 machines were completed. Nonetheless, the original AD-7 order was severely cut, and only 72 of this type (BuNos 142010–142081) were built.

The ceasefire in Korea failed to bring about a complete halt to Communist expansion in the Far East. As the Communists continued to lay plans for further aggression, the West could not afford to lower its guard, and a strong US Seventh Fleet was its main guarantee of the continued independence of such places of Nationalist Chinese Taiwan. Beijing seemed to hold international law in contempt, and have little respect for human life. Indeed, on 23 July 1954, an unarmed Cathay Pacific DC-4 transport plane, flying

Specification – AD-7	
Powerplant:	R-3350-26WB
Weights:	Empty 5,486kg (12,094lb); loaded 103,490kg (22,795lb); full 11,340kg (25,000lb); wing loading 56.9lb/sq ft; power loading 3.8kg/hp (8.4lb/hp)
Dimensions:	Length 11.84m (38ft 10in); height 4.78m (15ft 8½in); wingspan 15.25m (50ft ¼in); wing area 37.192sq m (400.33sq ft)
Performance:	HP n/a Max. speed 552km/h (343mph); at altitude 6,095m (20,000ft) Cruise speed 314km/h (195mph) Rate of climb 985km/h (3,239ft/min) Ceiling 7,740m (25,400ft) Range 2,090km (1,300miles)
Acceptance in service:	1956
Numbers Cancelled:	168

in International Air Space over waters adjacent to Hainan, was subject to an unprovoked attack by two Red Chinese fighter aircraft. They not only shot the transport plane into the sea, but also repeatedly strafed it on its way down, killing ten of its civilian crew and passengers.

A search was ordered for any survivors from the DC-4 and the aircraft carrier USS *Philippine Sea* (CV-47) was ordered to sea from Manila to carry out an air sweep of the area. She had embarked three Skyraider units: VC11, an AEW outfit equipped with AD-4Ws, VC-35,

equipped with AD-4Ns, and VF-54, equipped with AD-4s, and under the command of Commander Christian Fink, USN. Along with British seaplanes from Hong Kong and American amphibians from the Philippines, some 16 Skyraiders from the *Philippine Sea* quartered the seas off Hainan between 24 and 26 July, on a rescue box-search. They failed to locate any survivors but, on the 26th, did flush out enemy fighters hoping to repeat their earlier massacre.

The Skyraiders flew in a stepped-up echelon of four-plane boxes, with each box in

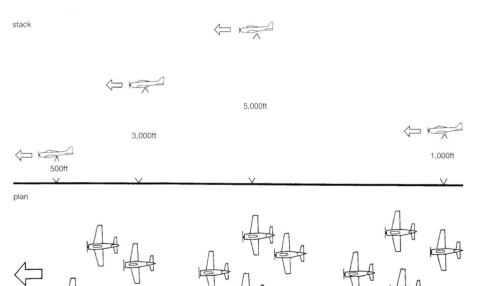

The Hainan Island incident – 26 July 1954 – battle formation.

tactical offset formation (below). They consisted of a four VF-54 lead, commanded by Lieutenant-Commander Paul Wahlstrom, with Lieutenants (j.g.) Richard Ribble and John Damian, and Ensign John Zardus, flying at 500ft (150m) altitude. Behind and above this section, stacked at 3,000ft (900m), followed four more ADs, led by Lieutenant-Commander William Alexander, with Lieutenants (j.g.) Richard Korsgren and John Rochford, and Ensign Richard Crooks. Another 2,000ft (600m) higher and, again, behind this group were three more Skyraiders, led by Commander George Duncan, the Carrier Air Group (CAG) Commander, with Lieutenant Roy Tatham and Ensign Richard Neubauer, one aircraft of this section having aborted the mission. Five miles astern flew two AD-4Ns, piloted by Lieutenants Max Puckett and William P. Robinson, escorting a lone AD-4W AEW, piloted by Lieutenant Peter Choreff, which was acting as radio link to the carrier. At 10,000ft (3,050m) above this wedge of Spads flew two Chance-Vought F4U Corsair nightfighters of VC-3.[62]

The Skyraider force spent the first part of its mission flying some 12 miles (19km) off the eastern coast of Hainan Island. This was well within International Air Space, even though the Communists had extended their territorial waters claim to four times that of the rest of the world, claiming 12 miles instead of three. The American rescue flights were therefore deliberately non-provocative in their conduct. This cut no ice in Beijing and, while the American formation was making a 180-degree turn at the northern boundary of its search zone, two Lavochikin LA-7 fighters of the Chinese Air Force appeared above and behind the lead flight of VF-54 and dived down on them, making firing runs. Three of the Skyraiders were subjected to a hail of fire.

The Communist pilots had concentrated on the highest flight, and thought they had been presented with four sitting ducks; they hoped to take these out, and then dive down to deal with the other sections in turn, using their height advantage. Lieutenant Tatham (a former fighter instructor) was the first to sight the Communist fighters closing in; after thinking they might be the two Corsairs, he realized their hostile intent and shouted warnings to his companions, who immediately broke and avoided being hit. Tatham himself reacted quickly and got astern of one of the attackers, firing at him with his 20mm guns. He was soon joined by Ensign Crooks, and they saw the enemy fighter fail to recover from his dive, and plunge into the sea.

The second LA-7 narrowly missed Lieutenant-Commander Alexander, who did a hard left turn and got clear. His wingman, Lieutenant (j.g.) Rochford, got astern of the enemy at 3,000ft, but failed to hurt his target, having forgotten to arm his guns, which were still set to 'safe'! By the time Rochford got two of his wing cannon firing, the two enemy aircraft were pulling out 800ft above the ocean after a 360-degree spiralling descent. He ran out of ammunition, but the lower section of Skyraiders suddenly appeared, blazing away at the Chinese fighter, followed by the two Corsairs of the top cover. This ended the matter, and the second Lavochikin shortly afterwards joined its companion at the bottom of the South China Sea off Tonkon Point.

Thus, the Skyraider notched up two more fighter kills to add to its remarkable record. There was protest from China (and from left-wing supporters in the West), but the entire action – from unprovoked assault to successful defence, and shooting down of the aggressors – had actually taken place more than 12 miles from the Red Chinese coastline. It was therefore deemed legitimate.

The Last Skyraiders

The US forces learned from this incident that it was vital to keep up their guard, and the Spad continued to play a full part in this. The number of Navy squadrons equipped with the new versions of the Skyraider continued to grow, peaking, by September 1955, at 29. To the uninitiated eye, the sight of the Skyraider being catapulted off the deck of a *Forestall* class carrier varied little from the launches from the *Franklin D. Roosevelt* a decade earlier Although the traditional overall deep navy blue colouring of the Spad had been replaced, on 23 February 1955, by the new gull grey and gloss white paintwork, little else seemed to have changed.

The US Marines Corps, its rôle severely curtailed, peaked at 15 Spad squadrons. From 1956 onwards, it gradually discarded the AD, until, by 1958, the last one had left its ranks with its retirement from VMA-331.

In California, Douglas held a ceremony as the final Skyraider (BuNo 142081), the 3,180th, was completed and formally rolled out at El Segundo on 18 February 1957. Its acceptance into the Navy's VA-215 Squadron, as the last piston-engined attack aircraft, marked the end of an era. The aircraft served long and hard and, in 1965, ended its days with the 'Spad School', VA-122 at Quonset Point.

Developments 1950–7

Designation	Rôle	Total	BuNos	Notes
AD-5	Attack	212	132478	
			132392–132476	
			132637–132767	
			133854–133929	
AD-5N	Night attack	239	132480–132636	
			134974–135054	
AD-5W	AEW	218	132729–132792	
			133757–133776	
			135139–135222	
			139556–139605	
AD-5Q	ECM	53	135054	
N/A	Conversions from AD-5Ns			
AD-5S	ASW	1	132479	
AD-6	Attack	713	134466–134637	
			135223–135406	
			137492–137632	
			139606–139821	
AD-7	Attack	72	142010–142081	Last Skyraider BuNo 142081

Delivering the Goods

No matter how excellent its design, and how dedicated its pilots, the Skyraider's entire *raison d'être* was the placing of ordnance where it would be most effective. The dive bomber, and the Skyraider in particular, was able to do this because it was designed specifically for the job; their aircrew were trained, too, and dedicated to the task. This was the result of a deliberate policy over two decades, in which the US Navy had emphasized the accuracy of dive bombing as a necessary skill to achieve the precision required to sink fast-moving targets. Navy dive-bomber pilots lived and breathed dive bombing.

The failure of 95 per cent of land-based heavy and medium bombers to achieve results anywhere near as good as those of the dive bombers was a clear indication that they had got it right. It is certainly worth looking at the techniques that were taught to and practised by trainee Skyraider crews in the 1960s.[63] First, the fundamentals had to be learnt.

The Firing Run

The first fundamental consideration was to fly the correct dive angle (flight path). The most common error – flying a convex flight path to the bomb-release point – could be avoided by initially aiming short of the target, and then allowing the 'pipper' (at the centre of the aiming sight) to move up to the correct aiming point by the time of release. Two factors affecting accuracy of ordnance delivery were wind drift, which applied during the dive, and wind correction, which applied after release, and these had to be compensated for. The following wind factors had to be taken into consideration:

1. the wind (or moving air mass) moving the Skyraider with the same velocity and in the same direction as the wind;
2. the motion imparted to the aircraft by the wind, which was further imparted to the ordnance as it was released from the Skyraider;

3. the wind further imparting its direction and velocity to the ordnance itself after firing.

These forces, if not compensated for, resulted in errors of both range and deflection. To mitigate this, the following corrective measures were taken by the Skyraider pilot:

1. he determined from aerology the wind velocity and direction at the ordnance firing altitude; and then
2. he determined the relative wind along the chosen dive-attack axis.

The following method was taught: the pilot would use the standard Mark 6A plotting board and take 0 degrees as the target-dive axis. The true index was rotated from 0 degrees to the relative angle indicated. Using a speed ring appropriate

to the wind velocity, a dot was placed along the true index, and the true index was returned to 0 degrees. A line was drawn horizontally from the dot to a point intersecting the true index line. Another line was drawn vertically from the dot until it intersected the index line perpendicular to the true index line. The length of the line from centre of the board to the intersection of the horizontal line with the true index was the 6 and 12 o'clock or range wind component. The length of the line from the centre of the board to the vertical line intersecting the index line perpendicular to the true index was the 3 to 9 o'clock deflection component.

The following example was given: target axis 60 degrees and wind 310 degrees/18 knots. The wind is thus 110 degrees to the left of the target axis. Place the true index on 0 degrees and then rotate 110 degrees to the left, or to 250

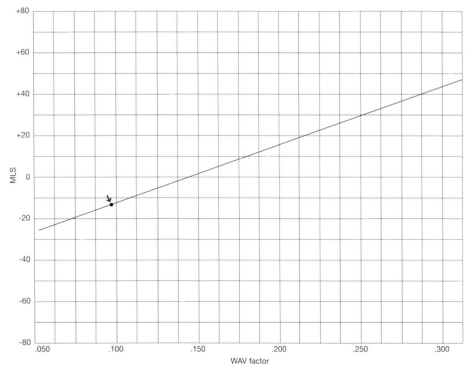

Ordnance delivery – WAV factor.

degrees. Place a dot along the true index line at the 180 knots speed ring, which corresponds to 18 knots of wind. Rotate the axis to 0 degrees. Draw vertical and horizontal lines from the dot to the true index and index line perpendicular to it and read wind components as follows: range component 6 knots, deflection component 17 knots.

Once the wind components were known, the proper corrections had to be applied in order to fire the ordnance effectively. These were applied as follows;

Altitude correction table

Altitude (ft)	Altitude correction (mils)
50	2.2
100	3.1
150	3.8
200	4.4
250	4.9
300	5.4
350	5.8
400	6.2
450	6.6
500	6.9

Displaying its unique 'barn door' side-opening fuselage-mounted dive brakes and a formidable array of rocket ordnance, a US Navy Skyraider commences a shallow dive. US Navy official photograph

1. Range component mil correction – determined from consulting the wind correction tables available to all the squadron's pilots. This mil correction was added or subtracted to or from the mil lead used basically for the 70-degree, 50-degree or 30-degree dive to be used. This gave the 6 to 12 o'clock position.

2. Deflection component mil correction – obtained by using the same method.
3. The corrections were applied by setting the correct mil lead into the gun-sight.

This was done by taking the basic mil lead for the type run to be employed and adding or subtracting the range wind mils. The dive was then entered with the pipper into the wind so that the Skyraider was drifted during the dive to a point where the pipper was vertically even with the target, but off horizontally the number of mils required to give correct deflection correction. Thus, if a 45 mils deflection correction was required, and the wind was from 8 o'clock relative to the dive axis, it was necessary to enter the dive with the pipper perhaps 70 mils from the target so that, by the time release altitude was reached, the pipper was 45 mils at 9 o'clock from the target. Experience aided in entering the dive offset the proper distance from release position, so as to be drifted to the right spot at release altitude.

4. A further aid in determining corrections was to use the sight as a range-finder. For example, 1 mil is 1ft at 1,000ft or 1 yard at 1,000 yards. For 30-degree and 70-degree dives, the slant

The impressive bomb load of the 'Able-Dog' -4B amounted to 8,000lb (3,630kg) worth of mixed 'cookies', giving an incredible all-up weight of 20,000lb (9,070kg) gross.
McDonald Douglas, Long Beach

range is 1,000 yards and 1 mil will subtend 3ft on the target along the 3 to 9 o'clock axis. For a 50-degree dive, the slant range is 1,200 yards and 1 mil would subtend 3.6ft along the 3 to 9 o'clock axis. Thus, if the wind is such that it results in a 10 knots range component and 19 knots deflection component, the wind correction for the range component needs to be made by setting plus mils into the gun-sight, as appropriate. For the deflection component, the aiming offset was 47 mils or 170ft into the wind along the 3 to 9 o'clock line. This distance of 170 could be judged by using the standard dimensions of a training target, which had an inner circle of 75ft radius and an outer circle of 150ft radius.

Release and Recovery

The Skyraider had to be in balanced flight at the point of ordnance firing: 'Trim the aircraft and do not stand on the rudders.' There had to be only one-G force on the Skyraider at release point. Excess positive G forces caused short drops, and negative G forces caused drops to fall beyond the target: 'In order to preclude the applications of G forces at release, pause momentarily before initiating recovery until the bomb is clear of the aircraft.' Each release altitude was calculated to prevent the Skyraider from going below a designated altitude above the target, if 4.5G was smoothly applied on recovery.

Cosine table

Dive angle	Cosine
0	1.000
5	.996
10	.985
15	.966
20	.940
25	.906
30	.866
35	.819
40	.766
45	.707
50	.643
55	.573
60	.500
65	.423
70	.342
75	.259
80	.174

The firepower of the Skyraider was legendary; here, a mixed load of rocket projectiles is displayed as the aircraft banks away from the camera. US Navy official photograph

Common Errors – Effects and Corrections

1. Incorrect release altitude – this tended to be high, with corresponding short drops. Pilots had to develop rapid instrument and gun-sight scan: 'Remember the altimeter lags in a dive.'
2. Incorrect dive angle – generally, the dive angles tended to be shallow, with corresponding short drops. Calibration flight on raked targets had to be utilized to establish consistent dive angle, using reference points initially.
3. Incorrect firing speed – generally, firing speed tended to be low, with corresponding short drops. This could be caused by incorrect entry altitude and/or airspeed and shallow dive angles.
4. Incorrect mil lead – generally, wind corrections were incorrectly made. Previous runs had to be analysed and definite corrections made. The pilot had to be aware that shallow dives resulted in a low release airspeed. When an error produces another, the mil correction was additive also: 'Fly the airplane all the time and think! Don't just take the elevator down.'
5. Nil release or multiple release – occasionally, the Skyraider itself would not be functioning correctly. More often, however, it was the pilot who was not functioning correctly: 'Know your ordnance panel. Double check the switches. Using the wrong pickle is not uncommon, but is inexcusable. Remember, in combat you may not get another chance.'
6. Corrections for errors in dive angle and/or speed – it was acknowledged at the training school that not every dive could be perfect. It was therefore necessary to estimate errors in dive angles and speed, and to correct them accordingly. As a very rough guide, the

November 1970: these three Skyraiders in echelon formation show clearly the varied payloads that the Able-Dog could carry. McDonnell Douglas, Long Beach

Skyraider pilots were told that 20 knots of speed, 5 degrees of dive angle and 200 yards of error in slant range release altitude caused 10 mils of impact error. A fast, steep dive could be compensated for by releasing high. This was considered desirable, otherwise a low pull-out could result. Only one error could exist – if a dive was 5 degrees shallow, even with a correct speed and altitude, the bomb would still fall short of the target. By moving the pipper in the 12 o'clock direction, it would be possible to compensate for the dive-angle error.

Trainee Skyraider pilots had their attention drawn to the phenomenon known as 'target fixation'. This was well known to all dive-bomber pilots, and the cause of many a fatal accident over the years. The only way this could be avoided was through the awareness of the pilot. 'When a pilot is involved in a dive attack, there is no margin for lapse of mental facilities.' The following basics were laid down during periods on the training ranges:

1. Do not enter a dive unless the location of the aircraft ahead is known.
2. Aircraft loaded with ordnance should not be operated in proximity to antennas (radio or radar) due to the possibility of ignition of certain weapon components by electromagnetic radiation forces. [Considering that one of the principal Skyraider targets in Vietnam was NVA radar installations, surely many combat pilots ignored that particular cautionary note on their way down!]
3. There will be a minimum 30 second interval between aircraft.

The Dive

For the actual dive, the rudder trim required at 190 knots was very nearly correct at release airspeed: 'Make certain you do not exert pressure on one rudder pedal at release. Rudder trim should occasionally be checked during pull-out.'

Although rudder trim was permitted to be adjusted during the dive, the elevator trim was not. The Skyraider men were

114

advised that the reason for this was 'design and structural limitations, plus the possibility of the trim running away'.

The importance of getting the Skyraider on to the correct glide or dive path as early as possible was stressed, in order that necessary corrections could be made in time. The initial point of aim was at 6 o'clock and into the wind (60 mils short for 30-degree glide approach, and 40 mils for a 50-degree glide). For a trainee pilot's first dive-bombing attacks, either a reference point on the ground or on the Skyraider itself could be used to help estimate the correct roll-in point. On the Skyraider, such points were listed as the following:

1. for 30-degree glide bombing – between the inboard and outboard guns;
2. for 50-degree glide bombing – the Mk 51 bomb rack;
3. for 70-degree dive bombing – a point half-way between the inboard gun and wing root.

It was stated that, after a little practice, 'it should be possible to estimate the angle without these crutches.' It is interesting to see how this compared with dive-bombing practice in the Second World War and the Korean War. New Zealander Bob Browning, who flew the Vultee Vengeance dive bomber in Burma, recalled that they would line up with a yellow line painted along the engine cowling, while an RAF Vengeance pilot, Flight Sergeant L.R.M. Tibble, recalled the procedure used by his unit in combat in 1944, thus:

We approached the target from a direction which allowed it to pass under the port wing and, as it appeared tight to the side of the fuselage, selected bomb doors open and allowed the target to

continue towards the rear to a count of ten. We then selected dive brakes out, made a tight downward turning and inverted turn to either port or starboard back towards the target, having, of course, arranged in advance the return course to base to be adopted following final pull-out. It was essential to settle in the dive immediately to allow as long as possible, to ensure that the entire craft was pointed directly towards the target without any slip or skid. The path of the aircraft had to align with the fore/aft axis of the craft.

In Tibble's opinion,

It really was a matter of instinct ... the best dive-bomber pilots dived themselves at the target and reacted instinctively ... with dive bombing, one felt that the aircraft was only a vehicle to help one to hit the target oneself... in the 70-degree-plus dive angle, the pilot himself was virtually standing in a crouched position on the rudder pedals.[64]

This is further confirmed by the account of US Navy Dauntless pilot, Rear Admiral Paul A. Holmberg, who fought at the Battle of Midway in 1942:

During my training there were some instances where pilots crashed because of their inability to determine (until too late) when to commence their pull-out. I observed that it was easy to become engrossed in, and transfixed by what one sees of the earth or sea as they are approached in this manner. Those pilots whose practice bombing scores were best were most often the ones who were well co-ordinated physically (baseball players, golfers, etc, who could throw or strike balls with a bat). Dive bombing, then, was almost an art.[65]

In the 1960s, the Skyraider pilots were following a well-trodden path. Warning was given:

Recovery from dive and glides should be executed with stick forces alone. As you recover, pull the nose up to a 45-degree climb but commence lowering the nose as the speed drops below 200 knots. NO NEGATIVE OR ZERO Gs.[66] Gain as much altitude on recovery as possible. Climb at 140 knots utilizing 2,200rpm and 30in settings. MAP will decrease during the dive, however, the throttle should not be adjusted until the climb has been established at 140 knots.

On this part of the trainee Skyraider pilot's learning curve, it was emphasized that

consistency is the word in angle calibration. Through practice, the ability to dive at a

A US Navy NAOTS (Naval Aviation Ordnance Test Station) Skyraider (BuNo 123869) coded 869, carrying two 1,000lb bombs on its underwing stations. National Archives, College Park, MD

Dive delivery table

Type delivery	IAS	5 degrees dive angle/error	200 yards s/r error
30-degree glide bomb	+20 knots: 72ft over	Steep: 90ft over	Too close: 132ft over
	−20 knots: 90ft short	Shallow: 120ft short	Too far: 126ft short
50-degree glide bomb	+20 knots: 34ft over	Steep: 74ft over	Too close: 68ft over
	−20 knots: 31ft short	Shallow: 84ft short	Too far: 63ft short
70-degree dive bomb	+20 knots: 18ft over	Steep: 43ft over	Too close: 22ft over
	−20 knots: 21ft short	Shallow: 47ft short	Too far: 10ft over
30-degree glide rockets	+20 knots: 24ft over	Steep: 36ft over	Too close: 10ft over
	−20 knots: 24ft short	Shallow: 45ft short	Too far: 12ft short
50-degree glide rockets	+20 knots: 24ft over	Steep: 35ft over	Too close: 5ft over
	−20 knots: 28ft short	Shallow: 43ft short	Too far: 5ft short

predicted angle consistently is acquired. Entry altitudes and speeds, release altitudes and speeds, and correct dive angles combine to complete a smooth, professional dive.

Different scenarios were practised for the three main angles of attack, and these were continually worked on during training.

30-Degree Glide-Bombing Procedure

A 90-degree turn entry was normally used to position the Skyraider for a glide-bombing run. Assuming the aircraft was heading into the wind during its bombing run, a downwind leg was first flown past the target at a sufficient distance to allow a cross leg to a point downwind of the target, which would place the Skyraider in a position elevated 30 degrees from its objective. This downwind leg was flown at an altitude of 6,500ft, or by climb to that altitude. The target was allowed to pass close enough so that it was obscured by the wing about mid-way down it. Should a late or a premature turn-off be made on the downward leg, the cross leg could be adjusted so that the Skyraider arrived in the proper position, 30 degrees elevation from the target:

The target should appear between the inboard and outboard guns and the roll-in should occur as the target passes under the leading edge of the wing.

Just prior to the 90-degree turn, the pilot rolled into the target, set his throttle to 30in and set his propeller control to 2,200rpm. At that point, the trim tabs were pre-set.

At the roll-in point, the airspeed was 190 knots and the altitude 6,000ft. The armament switch was placed 'On' after it had been ascertained that the other applicable switches had been placed in the proper positions for bombing, and the sight was set on the proper mil lead, with the sight light on. If the glide angle appeared shallow, the pipper in the sight was placed above the target, and the Skyraider was flown up to the target to make a steeper angle. Alternatively, should the angle appear too steep, the pipper was placed further below the target than normal so that the Skyraider was flown down to a shallower angle before the firing altitude was reached.

The ball was kept in the centre and the wings level while flying the pipper up to the bull's-eye, and it was held on for several seconds prior to release in order to establish a straight flight path. Should the pipper drift off target to one side or the other, the Skyraider was flown back to the windline[67] by dropping the nose slightly, banking towards the target until the pipper was back on the windline and then raising the pipper back to the bull's-eye.

Any attempt to kick the Skyraider on target by use of the rudders would prove ineffective, and the pilot was warned that this could damage the aircraft structurally. Wind correction was made by placing the pipper into the wind and holding it. If the wind was constant, the mil lead could be held constant once the airspeed in the dive had stabilized.

Once the mil lead was set into the sight, the release – 'pickling' the bomb, by firing the explosive charges on the ordnance pylons selected – was made at around 1,800ft, with wings level, the pipper on the target (or into the wind), the ball in the centre and a speed of 320 knots. Once the ordnance had been 'pickled', a steady pull-out followed, using 4.5Gs straight ahead, until the Skyraider's nose was well above the horizon. Trainees were warned that attacks should never be made below 1,000ft, although of course this rule was not always observed in the heat of combat. The idea was to make the most rapid ascent possible to get back to altitude quickly.

Pilots converting airspeed to altitude for the quickest ascent were admonished:

A shallow climb will result in the requirement for more power to reach your original altitude. Do not add power until airspeed reduces to below 200 knots because the propeller will act as a brake. At 4,500ft, commence turn back to the downwind leg while continuing to climb.

For the variations for 50-degree glide bombing and 70-degree dive bombing, see the diagrams opposite.

Night Bombing

The same general procedures could be followed for bombing at night, but one added precaution was the use of the gyro horizon on pull-out, where there was no visual horizon.

On dark nights, it was important for the pilot to turn his attention immediately to his instruments, once the ordnance had been fired, and to execute his pull-out by means of these. When bombing was conducted on a single light, such as a smoke float in the water, where there were no other reference points, it was of vital importance that continuous reference was made to the gyro horizon while actually in the run. It was particularly easy to become disoriented over the sea, and quite possible for a pilot to lose track of his own wing position. Trainee Navy

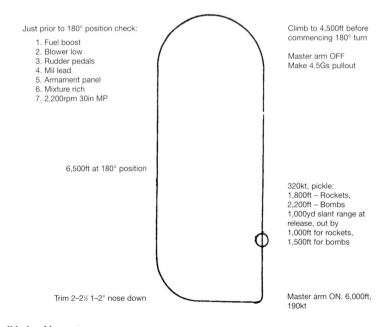

Just prior to 180° position check:

1. Fuel boost
2. Blower low
3. Rudder pedals
4. Mil lead
5. Armament panel
6. Mixture rich
7. 2,200rpm 30in MP

6,500ft at 180° position

Trim 2–2½ 1–2° nose down

Climb to 4,500ft before commencing 180° turn

Master arm OFF
Make 4.5Gs pullout

320kt, pickle:
1,800ft – Rockets,
2,200ft – Bombs
1,000yd slant range at release, out by
1,000ft for rockets,
1,500ft for bombs

Master arm ON. 6,000ft, 190kt

30° glide-bombing pattern.

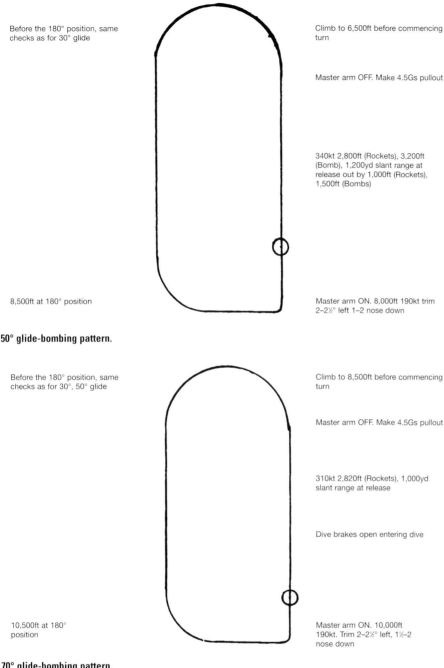

Before the 180° position, same checks as for 30° glide

Climb to 6,500ft before commencing turn

Master arm OFF. Make 4.5Gs pullout

340kt 2,800ft (Rockets), 3,200ft (Bomb), 1,200yd slant range at release out by 1,000ft (Rockets), 1,500ft (Bombs)

8,500ft at 180° position

Master arm ON. 8,000ft 190kt trim 2–2½° left 1–2 nose down

50° glide-bombing pattern.

Before the 180° position, same checks as for 30°, 50° glide

Climb to 8,500ft before commencing turn

Master arm OFF. Make 4.5Gs pullout

310kt 2,820ft (Rockets), 1,000yd slant range at release

Dive brakes open entering dive

10,500ft at 180° position

Master arm ON. 10,000ft 190kt. Trim 2–2½° left, 1½–2 nose down

70° glide-bombing pattern.

Skyraider pilots were therefore reminded of the following:

The bomb-sight installed in the AD provides three (3) different reticules, ranging from the minimum sighting datum of a pipper and a partial mil ring to a complete pipper, ray, mil ring presentation. Selection is easily accomplished by a knob, located on the gun sight. Each pilot will develop, through practice, the preference for certain reticules. A general rule to remember is that, as the lighting conditions decrease, so should the reticule illumination.

The actual level of illumination was obtained by selecting the reticule with the least presentation of rings and rays by the pilot exercising proper control of the sight rheostat. The pilot was advised always to check the rheostat settings prior to turning on the sight, because turning on a sight set for high-level illumination, at night, would seriously impair the pilot's night vision at the critical moment of his attack and, in all probability, ruin the attack completely.

Rocket Firing

The techniques employed in rocket firing – the entry into the run, the run itself, the pull-out and the climb back to altitude – were all much the same as in bombing. The dive angle, however, tended to be much shallower (30 degrees) than in bombing. It was noted that variation in dive angles gave less range error when rockets were employed than when bombs were fired. The entry altitude for rocket attack was 6,000ft and release height was 1,800ft, which again corresponded exactly with that laid down for glide bombing.

Flares

At sea (and, later, on night missions over Vietnam), flares formed a very important part of the night-patrol Skyraider's equipment:

There will be many times that, without flares, the other ordnance may as well be left on the ship.

This did not imply that flares were used on every night mission, because there were many nights when there was still enough natural illumination, especially in the tropics. However, on a dark night, sub-hunting in the cold and black wastes of the North Atlantic, flares were essential.

The most versatile flares in use at the time were the Mark 6, which were used with a 500ft drop delay. This delay before illumination was long enough to allow the Skyraider deploying the flare to clear it and be in position to make its attack immediately after ignition, yet it was short enough to permit quick and accurate illumination where it was needed. The Mark 5 flare was also used; it would ignite after 90 to 120 seconds, which apparently caused 'an uncomfortable delay while awaiting illumination'.

Each Skyraider had time to get in at least two well-illuminated runs before a second flare needed to be used. The technique was, as the first flare flickered out at about 1,500ft, for the second Skyraider of the attack team to retain its altitude and release over the target, adjusting for wind,

Among the later weapons that the Spad added to its inventory was the PAVE PAT II, the development of the
BLU-76/B fuel air explosive munition. Here, an A-1H is seen at Kirtland AFB, New Mexico, in 1968. National
Archives, College Park, MD

Starboard front quarter view of a Skyraider, coded 401, laden with a mixed range of ordnance on its
underwing stations, marking the 20th anniversary of its entrance into the Navy, El Segundo, 1967. McDonnell
Douglas, Public Relations, Santa Monica

and transmitting 'Flare away, 3,500ft.' With practice, it was found that a target could be illuminated almost continuously with a maximum economy of flares (*see* the diagram).

The glide attack run in such cases was made below the flare as the candle floated down from 3,000ft to 1,500ft. The final attacks, using a long-burning or late-igniting candle, could be below or alongside the flare, but this usually caused no problem, as the slightest wind would tend to drift the flare to one side of the target. If the target was a well-defended, pre-briefed one (like a Soviet *Kresta* Class cruiser), it was recommended that a time delay and a below-the-minimum-altitude flare-release point be adopted, which would illuminate the target without revealing the attacking Skyraider.

Another danger for the attacking AD was overcast, which reflected the light and silhouetted the aircraft, quickly making it an easy target. Although the Navy training had operations at sea firmly in mind, Skyraiders faced exactly this situation over the enemy-ridden jungles of Vietnam. The recommendation was that, when operating in such overcast conditions, 'extreme care must be used in employing flares. Indeed, they shall be used only in an emergency.'

The principle was to drop flares into the wind so that wind effect would cause them

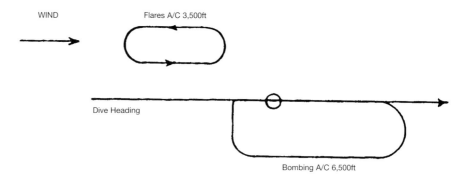

Practice bombing pattern using flare illumination – 2 to 4 aircraft.

to drop with, or normal to, the bombing line, in order to give silhouette illumination to the target:

> Flares dropped directly over the target give little depth perception to the bombing pilot, and a small amount of wind will cause them to drop out of effective illumination range prior to the exhaustion of the flares.

It was obviously dangerous to drop a flare so that a pilot had to execute his pull-up into its light, and thus reveal himself to the enemy.

The Skyraider team technique was for the section to approach the target with 1,000yd separation gap and a 500ft step-up between the two ADs. The first Skyraider would release its flare directly over the darkened target at 3,500ft in level flight. No attempt was made to make allowance for wind drift on this first drop, unless it was accurately known. On release, the first pilot transmitted 'Flare away, 3,500ft, turn left' (or 'right', depending on terrain), and immediately commenced a turn to be in position for a 30-degree glide attack. The section leader then established the axis of

'Cherrie', a USAF A-1E Skyraider, BuNo 132624, armed with ten SUU-14/A cluster bomb containers en route to the target zone in South Vietnam on 20 January 1966. US Air Force Official

(Above) **Ideal Spad bait, this convoy of Vietnamese army trucks was located proceeding along Route 1A, the key north to south artery of supply for the invasion forces, in the vicinity of Dong Hoi on 9 February, 1967. Thirteen empty vehicles were headed north, seven loaded vehicles were moving south and were given a good working over by the US Air Force Skyraiders.** Department of Defense, Washington D.C., courtesy of Robert C. Mikesh

North Vietnamese regular army tanks and vehicles exploding and burning under low-level attack by USAF Skyraiders in April 1968. Often depicted in the western media as a popular uprising against a corrupt regime, in fact the Vietnamese war was an act of aggression by a Communist nation against its democratic neighbour and fought with ruthlessness and in contravention of all signed treaties and United Nations conventions. For a time the Spads helped hold the line. Department of Defense, Washington D.C., courtesy of Robert C. Mikesh

attack by transmitting, 'Dive heading 270 degrees, recover to left'.

The flare temporarily destroyed the pilot's night vision, so caution had to be used on recovery from the glide under a brilliant flare into the blackness. The pilot had to make full use of his instruments on the turning climb-out, and this sometimes caused vertigo because, although the attack was completely visual, the night pilot had to scan his airspeed indicator, altimeter, and altitude indicator frequently and quickly. To judge altitude above sea level for the pull-out depended on a seaman's eye, the pressure altimeter and an estimate of terrain height: 'No formula can be given to substi-

tute for the pilot's judgement, which must be gained by practice and experience.' (This could, of course, also be applied to dive-bombing technique.)

As a general rule for flare-dropping, no Skyraider pilot ought to have pressed his first run in below 1,000ft without excellent night visibility, especially when he was toting the heavy loads the AD was capable of lifting. This would invariably result in mushing, or make for critical airspeed in the climb-out. A 30-degree glide angle sufficed for accurate bombing and strafing under such circumstances, and yet gave a safety margin in speed of approach to the wave-tops or the ground. A 40-degree

angle of approach was considered to be the absolute maximum for night attacks.

50-Degree Plus Angle of Attack with Bombs and Rockets

A 60-degree to 90-degree approach was considered essential for 50-degree runs; apart from that, the technique was about the same as for 30-degree runs. Again, a downwind leg was flown to a position abeam the target, at an altitude of 8,500ft, or climbing to that height. The target was then allowed to pass a point in line with the Mk 51 bomb rack, and entry airspeed was

190 knots at 8,000ft. The pipper was placed 40 mils short at the 6 o'clock position and flown up to the bull (no wind). Release height was 3,300ft for bombs and 2,800ft for rockets, with pull-out altitudes of 1,500ft for bombs and 1,000ft for rockets.

Napalm

This ordnance was not a weapon of sea warfare, but the technique of delivering it was taught to Navy Skyraider pilots. This was because of the US Navy's long tradition of supporting troops ashore with close air-support operations, which started in the Pacific Campaigns of the Second World War, and had been emphasized by its almost exclusive tasking in this respect during the Korean War. In fact, the training was to serve the Navy well in its subsequent employment over South-East Asia. The following is an extract from the training manual:

> One factor that makes napalm so effective is the accuracy with which it can be delivered. Since there is no danger to the aircraft from bomb blast, it can be dropped from any altitude. This means that a pilot can fly in low and fast and deposit the napalm on the target. The low-altitude delivery is especially effective against buildings for the aircraft can be flown directly at the structure at high speed, level flight, release the bomb and pull out. It is practically impossible to miss the target using this means of dropping. Against enemy troops, the low-level high-speed delivery is effective also because of the tendency to spread the burning napalm over a wide area. Ground controllers are less reluctant to direct a napalm attack close to friendly lines than they are to call in a close strike with fragmentation bombs. They know that the napalm can be dropped with extreme accuracy and that its effects will be limited to a known area, whereas the effects from a fragmentation bomb are sometimes unpredictable, in addition to the fact that releasing at 1,000ft above the terrain does not provide reliable accuracy.

Napalm could be released in a dive just as conventional bombs were, but it was found that its accuracy by such delivery was poor. The trajectory of the napalm bombs then in use was unpredictable, and they often tumbled in flight. It was therefore deemed much more efficient to release napalm utilizing the low-level technique, with an approach speed of 240 knots, at a height of about 100ft, and using 22 mils to place the ordnance exactly as required. If the target was a building, this level high-speed drop permitted a great deal of leeway. As the napalm canister would proceed horizontally, or almost, for a considerable distance after the drop, release anywhere within a reasonable distance would normally result in a direct hit. Later, advances in napalm bombs produced a non-tumbling bomb fitted with a proximity fuse.

Strafing

The Skyraider was armed with four 20-mm cannon, firing belted percussion rounds. Although these were of an old type, the method was still deemed effective against enemy infantry. Strafing runs were usually conducted at low angles of approach, between 20 and 45 degrees. The guns were bore-sighted at 1,200yd and were, ideally, fired in short bursts. The technique recommended was for the initial rounds to strike short of the target and then for them subsequently to be 'walked up to the target'. Should the first rounds hit over, a steeping of the dive was necessary, which, in turn, meant more speed, requiring a smaller lead angle; a smaller lead angle meant an even steeper dive, leading to a vicious circle. This could become dangerous close to the ground if the Skyraider pilot concentrated too closely on the target and got too steep and too low.

The opening rounds were squeezed off at about 1,500yd slant range, and, as the range shortened, the lead angle reduced to zero. As the range approached and then passed through the distance at which the guns were bore-sighted – 1,200yd – the hits crossed the target. In other words, where the starboard gun shells were hitting to the left of target when inside bore-sight range, they then hit to the right of target when outside bore-sight range. When firing tracer, it appeared that the rounds were over when, in fact, hits were being made: 'If you can see the actual

An excellent view of Armée de l'Air **armourers loading clips of 20mm cannon rounds into a French Skyraider of the 20th** Escadre de Chasse 'Aurers-Nementchas', **based at Les Salaines, south of Bone, Algeria, 1963.** SIRPA/ECPA Fort d'Ivry

impact of the rounds, you have the only accurate information on sighting adjustments necessary.'

It was recommended that tracers should not be loaded or used in the fleet:

> Use of tracers at night gives the gunners on the ground an ideal aiming reference. The use of HE and HEI heads will facilitate spotting at night and enable the pilot to correct his aim.

(Above) **Skyraider of the Gabonese Air Force at Libreville airport. The former French colony used these aircraft (secretly flown by French pilots) on anti-insurgency strikes and patrols.** SIRPA/ECPA Fort d'Ivry

Close-up of a Gabonese Air Force Skyraider at Libreville airport, showing in detail the starboard wing cannon and rocket load, with standard weapons for counter-insurgency strikes against Libyan-backed guerrilla forces. SIRPA/ECPA Fort d'Ivry

Nuclear Weapons

The varied equipping of the versatile Skyraider turned this already impressive aircraft into a serious contender. Both the US Navy and the US Marine Corps Skyraiders were assigned the nuclear delivery rôle, both utilizing the low-level navigation approach at wave-top or terrain-hugging heights to within range of the target. This was followed by the 'loft' form of ordnance delivery, which gave the aircraft at least a nominal degree of immunity from the blast of its own weapon, and a slim chance of survival.

Scenarios that might have seen the Skyraider thus employed are still under wraps, but an escalation of the Vietnam conflict with Soviet intervention, a Communist Chinese invasion of Taiwan, and resumption of all-out war in Korea are just some of the flash-points that might have seen the Seventh Fleet employing such weapons as a last resort. An all-out Soviet attack in Europe, coupled with a main-fleet sortie from Murmansk into the vital North Atlantic sea routes, might have called for tactical use against main surface units, if all else failed. Different techniques would have been employed to deliver nuclear weapons from the Skyraider, all based on the 'over-the-shoulder' method of ordnance release. Conjecture is useless, but such nuclear-weapon delivery techniques were learned and practised.

With the adoption of a nuclear weapons capability, the US Navy conducted a series of experiments to determine the best method of delivering such weapons to the enemy. The Skyraider was the natural choice, if only for its endurance. If people looked askance at the choice of a slow, propeller-driven, single-engined aircraft to carry nuclear weapons against a sophisticated enemy air defence, it was because they overlooked the less obvious features of low-level operating and endurance.

Testing of the practicality of this choice was carried out during a series of special trials, as Project OP/V219/X22, conducted in 1951 by the experimental trials unit, VX-3, of the Operational Development Force, based at NAS Atlantic City. The aim of this hush-hush unit was to evaluate the lob-delivery system, utilizing the AD-4 and AD-4Q, fitted with three external fuel tanks to give maximum bunkerage.

The actual test facility was Putnam Target Centre, Jacksonville, Florida.

For the first of the long-distance, low-level flight trials, VX-3 had 25 pilots and five aircrew on establishment and they took it in turns to fly non-stop at under 200ft, up and down the eastern coast of the United States. The average flight time was an incredible 11½ hours. For a single-seater, this sort of duration placed enormous stress on the pilot, but it was found to be practicable. Personal discomfort had to be dealt with and the trial Skyraiders were fitted with an essential modification – special relief tubes for the discharge of personal waste; these were fitted to all the nuclear-armed ADs over the years.

A second series of tests was carried out from Putnam by VX-3 in 1952, this time with 34 pilots and four aircrew; these trials pushed flight times up even further, to a maximum of 13½ hours.[68] Over such durations, minor irritations, which could be endured on normal, short combat sorties, became major problems. Simple modifications – such as altering the pilot's 'Mae West's inflatable design to prevent collar chafing, adding extra cushioning for the pilot's seating, and a new type of light-weight helmet to lessen headaches, plus extra Aspirin for the same problem – were duly made.

It was not just aircrew comfort that had to be improved for such missions. The Skyraider also needed to be adapted if it was to carry out this rôle proficiently. Conventional D/F did not function properly at such low altitudes, so, for obtaining ground-station bearings to aid navigation, the aircraft were fitted with OMNI equipment. However, the pilots still had to depend on their own prepared route maps for distances.

Following the acceptance of the X22 trials recommendations, the Navy went nuclear courtesy of the AD. Basic training patterns for the low-angle loft, lay down delivery and medium-angle loft were drawn up for training of aircrew in this specialized form of flying. Basically, in order to thwart the enemy radar, a long, low approach was practised to get in under the radar blanket. Routes had to be carefully planned to

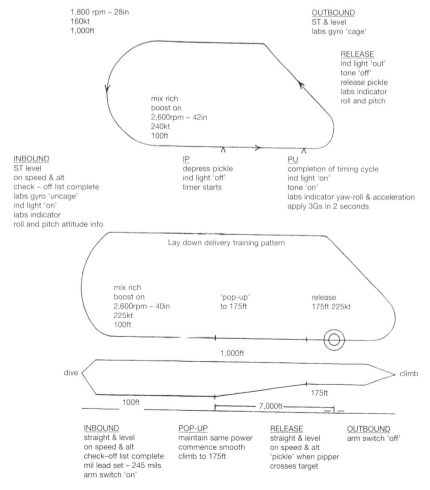

Nuclear bombing – low angle loft delivery pattern.

Nuclear bombing – medium angle loft delivery pattern.

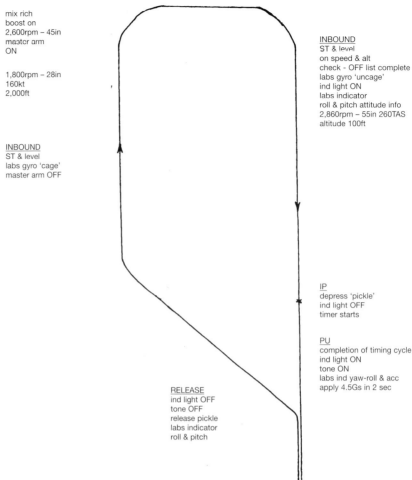

mix rich
boost on
2,600rpm – 45in
master arm
ON

1,800rpm – 28in
160kt
2,000ft

INBOUND
ST & level
labs gyro 'cage'
master arm OFF

INBOUND
ST & level
on speed & alt
check - OFF list complete
labs gyro 'uncage'
ind light ON
labs indicator
roll & pitch attitude info
2,860rpm – 55in 260TAS
altitude 100ft

IP
depress 'pickle'
ind light OFF
timer starts

PU
completion of timing cycle
ind light ON
tone ON
labs ind yaw-roll & acc
apply 4.5Gs in 2 sec

RELEASE
ind light OFF
tone OFF
release pickle
labs indicator
roll & pitch

penetrate enemy air space and take advantage of the ground contour. In those pre-Stealth days, invisibility meant survival. Such an approach path for the slow AD could mean six or seven hours' flight time, on average. For these practice flights, heights of around 100ft were the norm, straight and level with the engine mix set rich, and boost on to give 2,600rpm, for 225 knots airspeed to within 7,000ft of the target. This caused great strain, but it was essential if the Skyraider was to survive long enough to have any effect. The long and wearisome flights that were made in practising this approach were nicknamed 'Sandblowers' by the butt-weary AD crews.

In an actual attack scenario, a long approach would be made and then, as the release position was neared, the Labs Gyro Uncage' indicator light would go 'On', the engine would be set to 2,860rpm at 55in, 260 true airspeed (TAS), then the pickle would be depressed, the indicator light

Ron McMasters resting on a conventional freefall bomb mounted on his tethered Skyraider aboard his carrier. Ron McMasters

would go out and the timer countdown would commence. The AD would pop up ('highball') to 175ft altitude in a smooth climb for the final delivery run. The timing cycle now completed, the indicator light would go back 'On', accompanied by the warning tone.

The actual lob was done by making a three-quarter loop with an upright recovery on the opposite course to the run-in (a one-half Cuban eight, nicknamed by the Skyraider pilots the 'Truman Eight' after the former president), with the ordnance tossed at the highest peak. This was the yaw, roll and accelerate (YRA) sequence, which applied 4.5Gs in two seconds. On release, the indicator light and alarm tone both went 'Off' and the Skyraider, turning back 180 degrees on its former course, then executed a sharp 45-degree turn climbing up to 1,000ft to clear the impact area and avoid the worst concussion from the atomic blast wave.

This form of nuclear-weapon delivery practice method is best illustrated in graphic form (see the diagram on page 123 and above).

Carrying nuclear weapons presented some problems, due to their size, length and weight. The Skyraider's loading limit was set at 17,500lb, and the size of the nuclear bomb necessitated a special Skyraider modification, with the disabling of the under-fuselage dive brake. According to former US Navy pilot Chuck Mullaney:

Once again this was nuclear thinking. The early nukes (they were A-bombs then) stretched back into the dive brake, and the stabilizing fins could be damaged by the extended lower brake.

The Spad had an enduring career. I feel that this was largely due to its range, and its ability to deliver a nuclear weapon with an all low-level profile. The range would be 1,000 miles round trip, or 2,000 one-way. The Spad mission profiles were strictly low-level. There was no low-high-low involved. I feel that surviving the blast was remote in any case. In the 50s and 60s, any nuclear delivery was deemed worthwhile.

CHAPTER THIRTEEN

Target Tug

The Swedish Experience

Its exposed parts flimsily covered, former AEW-1 Skyraider, WV 185, stands forlornly outside the hangars of Scottish Aviation at Prestwick airfield in 1962, awaiting conversion into a target tug. This aircraft never flew operationally with any active service flight once it left the US Navy, and ended its days as SE-EBI with the Svensk Flygtjanst, before being given to the Swedish Air Museum. Arthur Pearcy Archive, by courtesy of Audrey Pearcy

In 1961, the three Swedish Defence Forces found themselves in urgent need of aircraft versatile enough to act as target tugs, and suitable for their other requirements. The Swedish Defence Ministry cast around for appropriate aircraft capable of doing this job without breaking its budget, which was urgently required for front-line aircraft. As so often before, the faithful Spad fitted the bill and, when it was known that the Royal Navy was disposing of its AEW-1s, negotiations were opened with the Ministry of Defence in London. These resulted in a deal whereby 13 of these redundant Skyraiders were purchased (12 operational, one spare).

The aircraft needed to be converted, so that they could carry out their new duties, and be brought up to a new specification issued by the Royal Board of Civil Aviation (Swedish Civil Airworthiness Authority).

Scottish Aviation Ltd, based at Prestwick, and with an earlier knowledge of the Skyraider from Royal Navy service, was awarded the contract to refurbish 12 of the purchased aircraft, and convert them to target tugs. They were awarded Class B British registrations for their temporary British residency and this enabled two of the selected AEW-1s, WT 987 and W 951, to be flown direct from RNAS Culdrose up to Prestwick as G-31 3 and G-31 2. The rest followed more sedately, covering the shorter distance from RNAS Abbotsinch by road.

The conversion involved the removal of the Radome, the vertical fins, arrestor hook, wing slats and other military hardware, including radio equipment. Once this was done, the aircraft were given a thorough overhaul and then fitted out for their new rôle. This involved the fitting of

updated civilian radio and electronics (VHF/VOR/ILS glide-slope, marker beacon, radio altimeter, intercom systems). The former observer's cabin was refitted with a towing winch and associated equipment, and seating for the operator.

Three types of towed targets were at that time being used by the Swedish Air Force and the Skyraiders were fitted to deal with them all. The strut target was mainly used for anti-aircraft training for the Swedish Army and Navy's ground- and ship-based guns as air-defence training. The wing target and the arrow target were more for aerial combat practice by the Swedish Air Force in air-to-air training.

As always with the Skyraider, other duties were found for the aircraft, besides target towing. Electronic countermeasures was added to the repertoire with the fitting of a

(Top) **The conversion process from AEW to target tug took place at the Prestwick hangars of Scottish Aviation Limited, prior to their sale to the Swedish Air Force in 1962. The conversion prolonged the active service life of the aircraft and led to many being saved for posterity. Here, a former 'A' Flight veteran WT 959 (424/A) undergoes the transformation.** Arthur Pearcy Archive, by courtesy of Audrey Pearcy

(Above) **Three of the twelve former Royal Navy AEW-1 Skyraiders, purchased by the Swedish government for use as target tugs, undergoing conversion in the hangars of Scottish Aviation at Prestwick during 1962.** Arthur Pearcy Archive, by courtesy of Audrey Pearcy

radar-jamming 'Sune' pod under the port wing. This was later upgraded when it was replaced by the more advanced 'Petrus' pod.

The dark blue ('Midnite') paint that had been the AEW-1's trademark all its working life was stripped off, and the aircraft were re-painted in bright yellow, with their British Class B Civil registrations in black. In this condition, they were test flown and then delivered by air direct to Sweden. Here, they were re-registered and allotted their Swedish registrations, which replaced the British markings, by *Svensk Flygtjanst AB* (Swedair Limited) at Bromma. The delivery dates were as shown in the table, right.

Swedish Skyraiders flight data

Class B Reg.	First flight	Swedish Reg.	Delivery date
G-31-4	7 September 1962	SE-EBA	14 September 1962
G-31-5	11 October 1962	SE-EBB	23 October 1962
G-31-6	6 November 1962	SE-EBC	27 November 1962
G-31-7	30 November 1967	SE-EBD	15 January 1963
G-31-8	–	SE-EBE	25 January 1963
G-31-9	13 February 1963	SE-EBF	1 March 1963
G-31-10	7 March 1963	SE-EBG	26 March 1963
G-31-13	–	SE-EBH	29 August 1963
G-31-11	4 April 1963	SE-EBI	26 April 1963
G-31-12	1 May 1963	SE-EBK	21 May 1963
G-31-3	28 July 1962*	SE-EBL	19 June 1963
G-31-2	20 Jul 1962*	SE-EBM	9 July 1963

* Ferry flight from RNAS Culdrose to Prestwick

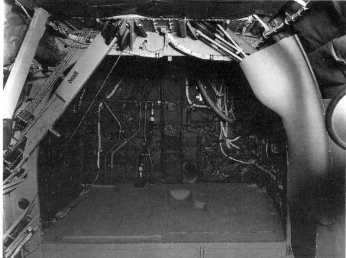

(Above) **Cockpit layout of a Royal Navy AEW-1 Skyraider after conversion to a Swedish target tug.** Arthur Pearcy Archive, by courtesy of Audrey Pearcy

(Above right) **Looking aft from the pilot's cockpit into the former radar compartment of a Swedish Skyraider converted to a target tug by Scottish Aviation at Prestwick in 1962, showing winches and wires.** Arthur Pearcy Archive, by courtesy of Audrey Pearcy

The spare aircraft (WT 849) was shipped by sea in 1963 in its original, unconverted state, and put into store. When the first casualty occurred, with the loss by fire of SE-EBH at Lulea in September 1968, this aircraft was assigned as its replacement. Taken from storage in 1969, it was given the full conversion treatment by Swedish Airworks Limited at Bulltofta, and registered as SE-EBN. However, it did not last long, being destroyed at Midlanda

The winch operator's observation dome on the port side of a converted target-towing Skyraider of the Swedish government. Arthur Pearcy Archive, by courtesy of Audrey Pearcy

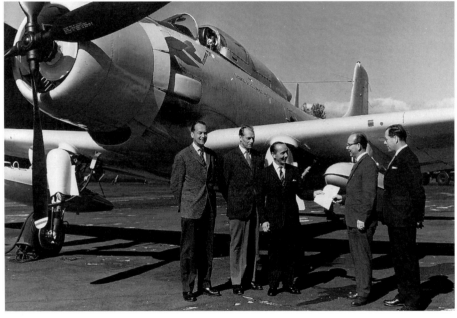

(*Above*) **September 1962. In the colours of the** Svensk Flygtanst AB, **the former WV 185 carries the ID code of SE-EBA of its new owners, and is seen here at Prestwick airfield, Scotland.** Arthur Pearcy Archive, by courtesy of Audrey Pearcy

Mr Arne Holmgren (second right) formally accepting delivery of the first Skyraider for the Swedish Air Service from Mr D. McConnell, Contracts Manager of Scottish Aviation Limited. Also in the picture (left to right) are Captains Olle Holger and Richard Osabahr, Chief Pilots of Swedish Air Services Limited, and Mr H.G. Hart, Scottish Aviation's Assistant Sales Manager. Arthur Pearcy Archive, by courtesy of Audrey Pearcy

in 1971. By this time, plans were being mooted to replace the Skyraiders with the new custom-built Mitsubishi MU-2F (MU-2B-20), as well as two Lear Jet 24s. However, these new aircraft were just not capable of duplicating the Spad's overall carrying capacity and were unable to perform the ECM duty it had also carried out. Four of the Skyraiders (SE-EBF, SE-EBK, SE-EBL and SE-EBM) had to be retained after 1974 to perform this rôle, until suitable replacements could be found.

This prolonged the Swedish Skyraiders' life for a further three years, at a time when most of their equally venerable companions were broken up at Malmo as surplus to requirements, from 1974 onwards. This second stay of execution was important, as it ultimately led to the aircrafts' preservation and salvation. Three others, SE-EBB, SE-EBC and SE-EBI, were allocated to Swedish Air Museums and put into store, pending restoration and display.

Swedish Skyraider details

Swedish Civil Reg.	US BuNo	British Class B Reg.	Royal Navy No.	Notes
SE-EBA	127950	G-31-4	WT952	Scrapped Malmo 1974 onward
SE-EBB	127947	G-31-5	WT949	Luftfartmuseet Stockholm-Arlanda
SE-EBC	127960	G-31-6	WT962	Svedino's Bil Och Flygmuseum, Sloine
SE-EBD	127948	G-31-7	WT950	Scrapped Malmo 1974 onward
SE-EBE	127954	G-31-8	WT956	Scrapped Malmo 1974 onward
SE-EBF	127955	G-31-9	WT957	Crashed Lulea-Kallax 25-2-76
SE-EBG	127942	G-31-10	WV182	Scrapped Malmo 1974 onward
SE-EBH	127957	G-31-13	WT959	Destroyed by fire, Lulea, Sept. 1968
SE-EBI	127945	G-31-11	WV185	Airmuseum Sweden 3-9-73
SE-EBK	126867	G-31-12	WV181	Pacific Fighters, Chino – N4277N
SE-EBL	127922	G-31-3	WT987	National Warplane Museum – N5469Y
SE-EBM	127949	G-31-2	WT951	Cham S. Grill, Medford, Or. – N4277L
SE-EBN	126849	N/A	WT849	Delivered unconverted. Converted Sweden, Reg. 1969. Replaced SE-EBH. Destroyed Midlanda in 1971

CHAPTER FOURTEEN

Combat Over Vietnam

The US Navy Experience II

The End of the Skyraider?

By the end of the 1950s, it seemed as if the day of the Skyraider was almost over as far as the United States was concerned. The US Marine Corps had flown its final missions with the Spad in 1958, the Navy was still finding good employment for the aircraft in specialist rôles, but numbers had decreased sharply from the heyday of 1955. Further surplus-to-requirements disposals were taking place, the most significant being the sale of 93 ADs to France, under the auspices of the Mutual Defence Air Programme. (This deal stretched the programme to the limit, as the French wanted the aircraft for what the Americans regarded as 'colonial' wars. The sale went through, but the Americans' generosity was not to be reciprocated when they, in their turn, urgently requested some of the aircraft back from the French!)

Under the terms of a wide-ranging review of the military, which took place in 1962, all surviving variants of the Skyraider

A Skyraider (BuNo 129667) of the VA-85 landing aboard a British aircraft carrier. The 'Heavy Hauler' or 'Able-Dog' operated from all manner of carrier decks and jungle airstrips for almost 30 years, mounting strike after strike against Communist aggressors in both Korea and Vietnam. Long after piston-engined aircraft elsewhere had been declared unfit for combat operations, the Skyraider's enormous ordnance-lifting power, its ability to strike at small targets accurately and, above all, its ability to 'linger' over the combat zone awaiting targets of opportunity at the request of the troops on the ground, was everything required in a close-support airplane. US Navy official photograph

were formally redesignated as the A-1 by the US Department of Defense (*see* the table). At the time, this changing of designation did not seem to be important – only 12 Navy squadrons remained operational with the aircraft, and the Skyraider was not expected to figure on the lists of the US military forces for much longer anyway. However, as so often before, the unexpected happened!

Change of Skyraider designations September 1962

new designation	old designation
A-1D	AD-4N
A-1E	AD-5 (attack role)
A-1G	AD-5N
A1-H	AD-6
A-1J	AD-7
EA-1E	AD-5W
EA-1F	AD-5Q
UA-1E	AD-5
	(utility rôle – target tugs)

Retaliatory Air Strikes

Since October 1964, the training detachment from the Navy's VA-152 squadron had been working in the USA and, later, in South Vietnam, training Vietnamese pilots in the use of the A-1s they had purchased. However, no 'official' combat missions had been undertaken by American Navy personnel. This all changed abruptly in August 1964, with the Tonkin Gulf incident. On 2 August, North Vietnamese motor torpedo boats ('MTBs' in Britain, 'PT' boats in US parlance) made a series of unprovoked attack runs against the American destroyer *Maddox* (DD-731), operating in International Waters. Two days later, on 4 August, similar attacks were made against the destroyer *Turner Joy* (DD-951). The American President ordered retaliatory air strikes against the naval bases that housed these units, and the Americans were thus provoked into entering the shooting war against the Communists once more.

The first US Navy Skyraider operations over Vietnam came on 5 August 1964, with Operation 'Pierce Arrow'. The carrier *Ticonderoga* (CVA-14) launched her VA-52 Skyraiders and the *Constellation* (CVA-64) launched VA-145s in support, both units being equipped with the A-1H and A-1J. They struck at five separate North Vietnamese naval bases and an oil storage depot at Ninh, which was the torpedo boats' main source of fuel. It was estimated than 25 of the enemy ships were sunk or severely damaged in these attacks, but this day's operations also saw the first Skyraider casualty of the Vietnam War, when a VA-145 Spad (BuNo 139760), piloted by Lieutenant (j.g.) Richard C. Sather, was lost to AAA fire over the target area. A second Skyraider of this squadron also took hits, but was able to make it back to home base.

Initially, the Navy's Spads were restricted to 'tit-for-tat' actions, in which a Communist attack would result in a slap on the wrist in the form of an air strike. This pattern of response seemed only to lead the aggressor to increase his actions. US politicians showed themselves unwilling to grasp the nettle, and, while a more determined approach might have been effective in deterring the Communists once and for all, this was avoided, and hit-and-run raids were the order of the day for the Spad pilots.

The situation changed in February 1965, when several American advisors were killed by the Viet-Cong and a number of South Vietnamese villagers were massacred. This led to the authorization of further carrier strikes. On 11 February, VA-125 joined VA-95 and VA-215 in Skyraider strikes launched respectively from the carriers *Coral Sea* (CVA-43), *Ranger* (CVA-61), and *Hancock* (CVA-19), which had all joined the Seventh Fleet. These strikes were made against North Vietnamese army barracks and support facilities, which the Spads hit square and solidly, without any AD losses.

Douglas AH-1 (former AD-6) Skyraider, BuNo 139732, of VA-165. Arthur Pearcy Archive, by courtesy of Audrey Pearcy

Lieutenant-Commander Ed Greathouse of VA-25 ready for launch from the USS Midway **(CVA-41) in 1965, armed with everything he could carry, including the bathroom plumbing. This was listed as VA-25's secret weapon!** San Diego Aerospace Museum

By May 1965, American aircraft carriers were patrolling on Dixie (South) Station off South Vietnam, to strike at the Viet-Cong guerrilla armies, and on Yankee (North) Station, for strikes against the North Vietnamese war machine, which was feeding the aggression against its democratic southern neighbour. Skyraiders operating in these waters were usually adorned with the badge of 'The Tonkin Gulf Yacht Club' on their rear fuselages.

As well as strikes against specified targets north of the so-called De-Militarized Zone (DMZ), which was ignored by the Communists, the Skyraiders also flew rescap missions, providing combat air patrol cover for helicopters searching for shot-down pilots. These missions, later known as CSAR (combat search and rescue), soon involved the Skyraiders in brushes with both the enemy jet fighters and Surface-to-Air

Missiles (SAMs). The North Vietnamese were deploying these in increasing numbers thanks to Soviet supply.

Skyraiders Against MiG-17s

The zenith of the Skyraiders' performance over Vietnam was undoubtedly the shooting down of enemy MiG-17 jets – a feat they performed not once, but twice!

The first instance took place on 20 June 1965. While on a rescap mission over North Vietnam itself (operations over land were known as 'feet dry', while those over sea were 'feet wet'), four A-1Hs of VA-25, operating from the carrier *Midway* (CVA-41) as 'Canasta' flight, were searching the Dien Bien Phu region for a shot-down F-105 pilot. The flight was led by Lieutenant-Commander Edward Greathouse, with

Lieutenant (j.g.) James Lynne as his wingman, and with the second section of Lieutenant Clint Johnson and Lieutenant (j.g.) Charles Hartman. Each Spad carried four pods of 2.75in rockets, and they were flying at an altitude of 10,000ft (3,050m), about 1,000ft below the cloud level. Visibility was good, although stratus layers of cloud up to 1,500ft-thick (460m) blocked out the sun above them. The two sections were flying a parallel course about 50 miles (80km) north-west of Thanh Hoa, 90 miles (145km) south of Hanoi, and well within MiG range of the Communist airfields there. Some miles ahead of them, a force from VA-196 was taking a similar course.

The two pairs of A-1Hs were in formation, about half a mile apart, when they received a warning message from the radar covering destroyer off the coast that enemy aircraft ('Bandits') had been picked

An AD-6 coded NE 570, BuNo 142048, of VA-25 from the carrier USS Midway **(CVB-41)
unleashes her cargo of 'cookies' over Viet-Cong positions.** McDonnell Douglas, Long Beach

up after taking off from one of the airfields. These hostile contacts rapidly closed the gap between them and the Skyraiders, which were on a north-westerly heading, and the controller aboard the destroyer issued a second warning soon afterwards: 'Two Bandits, 6 o'clock, four miles'.

Despite the warning, the Skyraiders were surprised by two MiG-17s, which appeared in right echelon, 500ft above and one mile astern of the right-hand A-1H (Hartman). Hartman described them as 'a pair of silver machines',[69] but was unable to communi-

cate this vital information to his wingman (Johnson), whose own aircraft had suffered radio failure. Greathouse and Lynne had also spotted the enemy at 7 o'clock, and, as they sped by, thought that the aircraft of VA-196 were the MiGs' appointed victims. However, when they reached a position some two miles ahead of the Skyraider formation, the enemy jets, warned by their own ground control that they had overshot the Spads, did tight turns and made head-on attack runs toward them, closing at a combined speed of 600 knots.

The action now developed very quickly. The Spads executed the standard split-S turns as an instinctive survival manoeuvre, and headed for the ground. Hugging the deck at varying altitudes, from 50 to 500ft, the Skyraiders followed the line of a river valley to the south-east at their best speed of 225 knots. One MiG now closed with Hartman, who dumped his two 300-gallon drop tanks. Fortunately for him, this made his Skyraider rear up, with the result that the surprised MiG pilot, who, thinking he had a sitting duck in his sights, had opened fire, completely missed. He then pulled up and headed off to the north, out of the battle, apparently low on fuel.

The second MiG was made of sterner stuff and attacked, and the fight deteriorated into a whirling mêlée as the various aircraft careered round in tight circles, while each side tried to get a shot at the other. Confused, the Communist pilot pulled up and made a determined direct run at Greathouse and Lynne's flight, apparently forgetting the other two Spads, which were now on collision course. This mistake gave Hartman and Johnson their opportunity, and they pumped out ninety and fifty rounds of 20mm respectively into the oncoming MiG at point-blank range. Its cockpit disintegrated, and at high speed, and flying straight and level, the enemy aircraft passed between the two AD-1Hs, before veering over on one wing and crashing into one of the ridges on the starboard side of the valley. The whole battle had lasted three minutes.

Following this action, Hartman and Johnson deservedly received the Silver Star for their shared kill, while Greathouse and Lynne both got DFCs. Another legend was added to the Skyraider's impressive history.

Personal Accounts

Chuck Mullaney was serving with VA-152 aboard the carrier USS Oriskany (CVA-34) in 1965. This squadron was responsible for the rescue of about a dozen pilots shot down in North Vietnam. At the end of the 1965 cruise, VA-152 was the most highly decorated propeller squadron since Second World War, its awards largely for rescue work. As Mullaney himself remembered:

This was not without cost. A Spad squadron at that time consisted of 12 airplanes. VA-152 lost 13 aircraft. Seven of the original pilots were killed, and one was a prisoner of war for seven and a half years.[70]

First Combat Sortie

Chuck Mullaney recalled his first combat sortie in that area:[71]

My first mission over North Vietnam was a Rescap. Rescaps could be loosely placed in three categories. One category was where we rendezvoused with the HU-16 somewhere between the De-Militarized Zone (DMZ) and Dong Hoi, and just waited for someone's luck to run out.

Another category was when there was a pilot/r/o shot down and we proceeded to a specific rescue scene where we were to further aid in an ongoing rescue effort. The third category was rescap for an Alpha strike, which involved an airborne helicopter and enough airplanes that you were pretty sure someone was going to get shot down.

This mission was in the first category. That made it a nice gentle introduction to the combat world. The air intelligence briefing informed us of what activities were under way and where we could expend our rockets rather than bring them back aboard the carrier. Rockets were slid into a catch of sorts when placing them on their rails. They could, and did, slide out of their catch on an arrested landing and while they generally went harmlessly down the angle deck after they came loose, they could easily stray to the right and wreak havoc on the bow. In the Spad's case, since we were the last aircraft in the recovery, there was always a good number of jets parked forward.

The rockets that we carried in this particular case were 19 2.75s in a single pod. The centre rocket fired first and broke a shatterable dome, and then the other 18 followed in the next second. I believe they were called LAU-19 pods, but my memory doesn't serve me well enough to swear to this. Since these were not to be brought back aboard the carrier, we were to expend them on a flak installation in the south end of Tiger Island. The rescap was uneventful, so my wingman and I proceeded to the island to unload our four pods that we each carried. I rolled in at 6,500ft and I had no idea where the site was. As soon as I was established in the dive I felt a jolt under my plane. I could immediately see muzzle flashes very close to the spot I had chosen as the flak site. Since they were kind enough to designate the target I continued the dive. But the following will demonstrate how slow the Spad was in a dive. I had time to change my mil lead from rockets to guns, adjust the aim, strafe for about 1,000 to 1,500ft, readjust the mil lead to rockets, change the aim point, readjust the dive, and fire the rockets. Then I tried to make the smallest profile I could imagine and get out of there. My wingman stated that the rockets seemed to hit right on the muzzle flashes and he did not receive any fire in his dive. Perhaps I hit the flak site, perhaps not. But putting 76 hand grenades in one site sure made it likely.

My experience with this flak site was certainly an eye-opener. In spite of knowing that aircraft get hit, it gets closer to home when it is you. Their fire was accurate enough to jolt my Spad in what I would say was their first clip of 37mm's – they were very accurate. It drove home the point that this was indeed a combat

cruise, and not a training operation. I felt that I had covered myself well with the inclusion of strafing, but, later in the cruise, I would never have pulled out as high as I did. I learned vulnerability early, and I know it was beneficial as time went on.

Chuck Mullaney recalled another mission, which took place in late June, or early July, 1965. It began in the Air Intelligence Briefing Room aboard the Oriskany.

The briefing was more elaborate and with greater attendance than normal, as this was going to be a major strike on a bridge in North Vietnam. It was to be a joint Navy and Air Force strike, with some 80 aircraft involved. The most significant thing that I remember about the briefing was that the Air Force had preliminary photos, hence suspicions, that a new missile emplacement had gone in just south of Vinh.

The four Spads were to be rescap for this affair. Our ordnance load was four rocket pods containing four 5-in HVARs in each pod. We had the usual 750 rounds of 20mm. This was about as light an ordnance load as we ever carried, but we were strictly rescap on this occasion. Our fuel load was 2,280 internally, and 2,680 in a 400-gallon drop tank on the centre station. This gave us an endurance of eleven to eleven and a half hours, depending on our activity.

I remember on the cat shot that I heard 'missile away' over the UHF. I do not know if this was a bona fide announcement, on guard channel, or a smart Alec in the tower editorializing over the Spad's slow end speed off the catapult of 110 knots. I suspect the latter; however, it was to be prophetic!

The XO was leader of the flight, and I was leader of the second section. At some point we split up, and the leader went to cover the seaplane, and my wingman and I went to cover the rescue helicopter. We joined up on the helicopter, which was a single-engine jet type (whose designation I have forgotten), and, at 135 knots, it was fairly easy to fly wing on it. The actual strike commenced about an hour after we joined on the helicopter. At this point, the chatter on the strike channel was as intense as you could imagine in a combat situation. The chatter gave me the impression that two aircraft had been hit, but it turned out that we were dealing with the ejection of one F-105 pilot. Just about this time, an F-105 came right between my plane and the rescue Helo. It was the fastest-moving thing I had ever seen in my life. It also got the attention of the helicopter gunner, who up to this time was whiling away the time by aiming his 50-calibre machine gun at me. After the passage of the Thud he just sat down in the door!

The 105 pilot came down some 50 miles south-east of Hanoi. His wingman/leader had stayed with him in the descent, consequently we were able to proceed directly to him. Since he was in the water, we though we had an excellent chance of retrieving him, but it appeared that he had drowned after hitting the water. The helicopter crewman had gone in the water to do what he could. At this time it was 45–60 minutes after the strike and the chatter was strictly among ourselves.

While the six aircraft (four Spads, a Helo and a HU-16) were working to rescue this Thud driver, a MiG alert came over the strike common. I acknowledged the MiG alert, which came from a destroyer near by. The exchange went pretty much like this: 'Locket Flight, you have a MiG alert,' (followed basically by the co-ordinates of Phuc Yen). I acknowledged: 'Locket 586 – Roger – who is my fighter cover?' 'Wait one …Your fighter cover is Locket 586 and flight.'

In the ensuing exchanges I ascertained that there were no jets airborne, and explained to the radarman on the destroyer what kind of planes we were and that he would have to vector my section to visual acquisition of the MiG. He sounded pretty young, but also very professional. He seemed to have a little trouble grasping that we had no radar ourselves. I commented that technologically we had one more engine instrument than a World War II fighter and that oriented him as to what he was dealing with.

The MiG went west from Phuc Yen for his climb, leaving us climbing straight into the sun.

We shifted blowers about 12,000 and continued climbing, with directions from the destroyer. About 17,000 I caught one glimpse of the MiG, but I kept losing him in the sun and advised the destroyer of this. The radarman kept vectoring us until the MiG turned north and then he became steadily visible about 5,000ft higher than we were. I doubted very much that we frightened him, but I turned north after him, knowing that catching him was out of the question. I would say that in less than a minute the destroyer announced 'Missile away'. I now had a full grasp of the MiG's mission. He sucked us up into the missile envelope and withdrew.

A quick split-S took us back down to the surface and we proceeded back to the rescue effort. The helicopter crewman was still trying to extract the downed pilot, and we just orbited while this was going on. In about 30 minutes we were advised that some cargo junks had been recently spotted down at Vinh. Since we were the only ones airborne, we seemed to be the people to be given this information. The XO switched wingmen with me and sent us down after the junks. The wingman switch gave me a pretty inexperienced pilot to deal with for the next part of the day.

Vinh had a remarkable amount of flak around it so I decided to come out of the sun ALA the aforementioned MiG. Vinh Harbor is shaped like a big C with the opening to the east. The junks were reported on the southern part of the C, on an elongated spit protruding northward. I had been briefed for just one pass and then to head

out to sea due to the flak plot. We rolled in about 6,500ft and the junks were just as reported. Probably 20 to 24, tied to the pier/sea wall. About 3,000ft a large smoking telephone pole went by my right wing about 100ft away. My wingman announced, 'Chuck, I think I saw a missile.'

Things happen fast in these circumstances and three thoughts transpired at once: hit the junks, get me out of there, get my wingman out of there. Due to his inexperience I immediately transmitted, 'Hit the junks but don't pull out – go down to the water.' I know I said it twice, and possibly three times. By then I was rippling off my rockets, followed by strafing down to about 1,000ft.

The flak started up by then, but it was half-hearted, and mostly in front of me. So my estimation is they were thinking in terms of jets to hit their set-up. I didn't feel too smart, walking into two SAM set-ups in one day. I had no options in the MiG encounter, and in a poor country like Vietnam, a junk was a remarkably tempting target. Four Spads came back to the carrier unscathed, so I'll leave it as an educational experience.[72]

Mullaney's encounter with the MiG was to be repeated on other Skyraider missions as the days went by, and culminated, on 20 June 1965, in the first MiG kill by the Spads of VA-25.

Rescap Mission from Yankee Station

A second MiG kill followed on 9 October 1966. Four A-1Hs from VA-176, one of two Skyraider units working from the carrier *Intrepid* (CVA-11), were operating with a helicopter on a rescap mission from Yankee Station, stationed south-east of Hanoi and standing by to pick up any casualties from a big three-carrier strike into North Vietnam. The leader of the flight was Lieutenant-Commander Leo Cook, VA-176's ops officer, with Lieutenant (j.g.) James 'Pud' Wiley as his wingman, and the second section was led by Lieutenant Peter Russell, with Lieutenant (j.g.) Thomas Patton.[73]

Sure enough, a McDonnell F-4 Phantom from the strike was hit and went down 20 miles south-west of Hanoi. The helicopter was ordered 'feet dry' to search for the downed pilot and VA-176's Spads followed him in over the coast, in two pairs, one covering the helicopter at 9,000ft, the other some distance behind as back-up. The whole slow-moving group flew towards the massed AAA and SAM sites waiting for them. They made it through the flak, with the rear pair making suppression strafing runs, and no missiles were

A Douglas A-1H, converted from a former French AD-4NA by Jack Spanich, indicated by the dorsal air scoop and large door in the central fuselage. It is painted to resemble A-1H BuNo 1235326, from VA-176 from the carrier USS *Intrepid* (CV-11), which, piloted by Lieutenant (j.g.) Tom Patton, shot down a MiG-17 over Vietnam on 9 October 1966. Arthur Pearcy Archive, by courtesy of Audrey Pearcy

SKYRAIDER MEN – Captain Chuck Mullaney, USN, Rtd

Chuck Mullaney served in the United States Navy for eleven years and spent his entire time in Squadrons. His enviable record was a total of 4,050 military flights, including 250 carrier-deck landings, and, for sheer mileage, his total of some 3,000 flying hours in the Spad takes some beating!

Chuck Mullaney was born on 11 November 1935, in Boston, Massachusetts, and educated at assorted junior colleges around Texas. He spent two years in college at the University of Connecticut before graduating, and joined the Navy on 28 September 1955 as an officer cadet. He met and married Ann Lasiter at Corpus Christi, Texas, on 22 March 1957. The couple had three children – first Rick, Cindy two years later, and, after three more years, Daniel.

Mullaney's Naval flight training was done on a variety of aircraft, as was usual in those days. He spent 800 hours flying T-28s, with a further 250 hours on the SNJ (the Navy version of the T-6 Texan or Harvard), the SNB, and T-33s. During his Navy career he also flew the A3D and the F9F-8. Most of his time in combat was spent flying the Skyraider, including his duty over Vietnam with VA-152 from the carrier *Oriskany*. In that period he was awarded the DFC, eight Air Medals, Navy Commendation Medals and several Group Citations. He outflew everyone in the squadron as far as combat hours went. A schedule officer once told him that, with his rank and experience, he was the most usable pilot in the squadron. He could lead the entire squadron or fly wing in a two-plane section.

On leaving the service, Mullaney joined American Airlines, on 2 May 1966, as a pilot. In the next 30 years, he clocked up a further 20,000 or so hours flying six different airliner types. He retired from commercial flying on 10 November 1995, but still flies his own light aircraft for fun.

Mullaney confesses to being 'a hopeless blue-collar workaholic', and, when his hobby of carpentry stopped being enough for him, he took up farming: 'Started fooling with cattle the same time I went with the airline and I still farm 400 acres.' He lives on his ranch near Celina, Texas, and periodically renews his old Navy friendships at a gathering in Dallas of a group called 'Friends of the Fighter Aces'.

(Right) **Chuck Mullaney in April 1966, with his 'Ace of Spades' Spad showing 95 bombing missions over Vietnam.** Chuck Mullaney

Award ceremony for the 'Ace of Spades' squadron, April 1966, on their return home from their tour of duty off Vietnam. Chuck Mullaney

fired at them. However, the enemy had other things up his sleeve and a warning was soon received that four MiG-17s had scrambled from a Hanoi airfield, and were on their way south.

The four enemy jets were soon sighted by Cook and Wiley, and they went down on the deck. The enemy jets followed, and the AD-1Hs were immediately fighting for their lives. Three MiGs homed in on Wiley and the other on Cook and only crazy manoeuvring at low level saved them for the moment. Wiley even managed to get in a snapshot at one of his tormentors and score hits, which caused it to break off, but there were still two more jets with twice his speed in tow. The lead pair's luck could not last much longer and they radioed for help, but no protecting American jets were available to offer the Spads protection. Lieutenant Russell therefore signalled to his leader, 'We're on our way with two Spads and a Helo!'

The 'rescue party' duly arrived on the scene and made a head-on attack against two of the MiGs, with Russell scoring hits this time at very close range. The other MiG was down on the deck and, fortunately, the enemy pilot had not observed the second Skyraider (BuNo 137543) piloted by Lieutenant (j.g.) Tom Patton, which was some miles astern and still at 9,000ft (2,740m) altitude.

Seeing his team-mate in dire trouble, Patton unhesitatingly put his Spad into a power dive, using his height advantage to build up to a respectable speed of 350 knots, and duly 'bounced' the MiG. As he came down, the enemy pilot got sight of him, broke off his own attack and nosed up to gain some altitude in order to punish this impertinence! However, the Spad's speed had built up sufficiently by this time to close the gap to within 500ft (150m) of the enemy jet and Patton began pumping out 20mm rounds from his four wing cannon into this sitting target. Still firing, he continued to close to within 100ft (30m) of the MiG. Two of Patton's cannon jammed, the other two ran out of ammunition, but bits were flaking off the predator. Patton then fired his Zuni ground-attack rockets at the MiG as a final gesture.

Patton was rewarded for his audacity, for, although the rockets near-missed, the startled MiG-17 broke away, flipped over and went vertically into the ground; its shocked pilot ejected clear and followed his aircraft down by parachute. All four Skyraiders and the Helo eventually got out

safely, although the downed Phantom crew was never located.

For their heroic work, which resulted in one MiG destroyed and one heavily damaged in the wing, for no friendly losses, Patton received the Silver Star and his three companions the DFC.

Night-Harassment Missions

As in Korea, the Spads also flew night-harassment missions in Vietnam, with special metal shields fixed above the exhaust stacks to block out glare, and aid night vision. Chuck Mullaney recalled one night mission, explaining exactly what such an action involved:

Hard targets, rescaps, and road reconnaissance were the Spad's three missions. Hard targets were rare, and the rest of the missions were roughly one-third rescap and two-thirds road reccies. Road reccies were basically to ensure that nothing of a supply nature moved. As one wag put it, on night road reccies, 'If you saw a light, you put it out.' Two factors determined my conduct of road reccies. First was the bomb load. The daylight bomb load was usually two 1,000lb bombs on the inboard stations and six 500lb bombs on the outboard stations with six 267lb fragmentation bombs between each 500-pounder. Always on board were 1,000 rounds of 20mm. Second was the system that the Skipper demonstrated when I flew a road recce as his wingman. He hunted around the southern panhandle of North Vietnam until he found a bridge. Then we bombed that bridge with our two 1,000-lb bombs. This got rid of our biggest weight and drag factor and we were somewhere near manoeuvrable with the remaining 5,000lb of ordnance. At night the 267-lb fragmentation bombs were replaced with phosphorous flares.

On night missions we went over the beach as sections (two-plane flights). Once over the beach we split up to do our reconnaissance individually, so we could operate lights out, while hoping for a target. On this particular night I was checking out a highly regarded Lieutenant that had come to our squadron about a week prior. I briefed for the cross the beach procedure and then split up and find something of consequence to drop the two 1,000 pounders on, and then spend the rest of the night looking for lights, road interdiction, or another bridge. We did as briefed, with my wingman taking an area to my north. On this particular night, overhead was something that could only be called a 'bomber's moon'. The sandy reaches north of Cape Mui Ron were virtually clearer than daylight. Some 20 to 30 minutes of lazing around rewarded me

with a two-lane concrete bridge on the fringe of a forested area just north of which the sand went on for about ten to twelve miles. As I remember, there were no pockmarks around it, so it must have been undetected to this point. A two-lane concrete bridge was the most substantial target that I had ever seen on a road reccie and I was pretty happy. Since I was invisible to the flak people, and not being the best bomber in the world, I decided to take my time and ascertain that I got the bridge. I climbed up to 6,500ft and made a textbook left-hand roll-in and dropped one 500-pounder and checked my hit. Fifty to one hundred feet at 6 o'clock.

I climbed back up to 6,500ft and repeated the procedure with a correction, dropping another 500. The next bomb hit about fifty to one hundred feet at 12 o'clock. I figured that I could remember the picture, so I climbed back to 6,500ft and did the classical left-hand roll-in. I released a little lower this time, since I figured that with the dropping of two 1,000lb bombs plus two 500s for insurance, the pull-out would not be as deepened as the previous two runs. When I looked back this time I could see that I had dropped the bridge.

Now that the work was done it was time for confirmation. For a variety of reasons we carried a hand-held 35mm camera. One purpose was confirmation of target damage. To obtain a photograph I finally had to illuminate the target. This was done by dropping a phosphorous flare, and then coming down under it to photograph the bridge. In the process of doing this, I also illuminated myself. The picture taking went awry immediately due to a couple of near misses. The patience of the flak people had been tried to their limit, and when I finally became visible every 37mm within range opened up on me. The flak was largely in front of me. I feel the reason for this was that the gunners had no idea how quickly the Spad decelerated. At the beginning of the photo run I had 210 knots, by the time I was outside the sphere of illumination I was down to 140 knots. I was happy with my work, and I figured that the photo F-8s could come by and take a picture if the staff or anyone were so inclined.

Summing up the AD

During three and a half years of intense and honourable front-line combat over Vietnam, the Skyraider had constantly confounded the enemy and refuted its critics. The final Navy mission was flown on 20 February 1968, appropriately by VA-25, which was then embarked aboard the equally veteran carrier, *Coral Sea*. In all those years of combat, a total of 40 US

Navy Skyraider pilots paid the ultimate price of freedom, and did not return.

On 10 April 1968, the US Navy conducted a formal ceremony at Naval Air Station LeMoore when the A-1 was finally retired. The Navy Spads might be officially dead, but they still refused to lie down, and the last actual combat launch of the A-1 was by VAQ-33 with an EA-1F flight on 28 December 1968.

To sum up the Navy's regard for the AD, Chuck Mullaney gave the following pertinent and valued observations and opinions of the Skyraider during its final period of activity:[74]

The Spad was vulnerable, due to its mission, but it was not without protection. There was ½in of

plate from the accessory section of the engine to back behind the pilot. This plate weighed 1,100lb. The Spad went out of the Navy inventory in 1968 for reasons I can only guess at. I feel it should not have, due to its road recipe ability. There were Spads over the southern panhandle of North Vietnam virtually around the clock. To launch at midnight and recover at 0730 was a normal mission. This translates to 5½ hours of preventing unhampered supply movement in an assigned sector.

The Navy A-1H and A-1J Skyraiders were able to carry a countermeasure in the form of the standard ECM pod, the AN/ALQ-81, which was sufficient to block out the radar controls of the North Vietnamese Soviet-supplied Surface-to-Air (SAM) and Anti-

Aircraft (AAA) radar sets. This pod came complete with an in-built ram air turbine placed at the front for its electrical system. The system plugged in, and a small ECM control and monitor box was attached to the port side of the pilot's console.

Range was always a problem, as Chuck Mullaney related:

Our squadron configured the external fuel to a 400-gallon tank on the centre line. The downside was the endurance was cut back from 13½ hours to 11½ hours. The upside was the freeing up of the two inboard racks for larger bombs rather than having just one on the centreline. It also bypassed the ¼in fuel lines that were installed coming from the inboard pylons. They were a modification to permit air-to-air refuelling. On

Against a hostile force operating deep in another nation's territory, like the Japanese in Burma or the Red Chinese in Korea, the Western allies quickly found that a strategic rôle was demanded from their close-support aircraft if they were to fend off the invasion of South Vietnam, and stop the movement of supplies. High on their list of priorities, as always, was the dropping of enemy-controlled bridges for road and rail traffic. This photograph dates from 13 June 1967; US Navy pilots have destroyed this highway bridge and cratered its approach to a ferry crossing in air strikes directed at the important Phu Qui crossing, 35 miles (56km) south-west of Thanh Hoa. US Navy official photograph

occasions it was difficult to establish suction through these big lines. The centre line still had the small diameter lines that never gave a suction problem.

Our bombing runs were generally made at 40 degrees without using dive brakes. In my reading about SBDs I have become aware that the 60-degree dives that we practised in the late 50s were more effective. The steep dive had given way to glide bombing and I am not sure why. Mechanically speaking, however, the bottom dive brake was deactivated. None the less, with the side brakes open, a 60-degree dive was a minimum acceleration manoeuvre that left you 'hanging in the straps'. These brakes were roughly two foot by six. I guess dive bombing just became a lost art.

One remnant of World War II that we employed was the Thatch weave. The four possible moves from a Thatch weave could be executed in radio silence, or radio failure for that matter. The leader could direct reversals of 90-degree turns with simple wing-dip signals. But it was done on the radio, since our UHFs were a considerable improvement over the SBD and SB2C radios. The weave was employed continuously when escorting the HU-16 or the helicopters.

In the realm of insight, I have a couple of observations. The first is that you seem to have a total acceptance of the enemy trying to kill you, but you go through the ceiling when *Americans* make what seems like a determined effort to wipe you out. This happened a couple of times, though I imagine that in combat it is a universal experience. Your own mistakes find you more forgiving of your own stupidity (as opposed to that of others), but not by much. Mistakes generate a change in the conduct of tactics or whatever, or a serious vow not to make that error again.

But least understandable, to me anyway, was the absolutely euphoric feeling that you had when you went 'feet wet' heading back to the carrier. To be completely objective, you only had 24 hours guaranteed on your life span, and then you were back over the beach again. But the 24-hour reprieve seemed to be the best thing that ever happened to you. I do not know if others had this feeling as I never discussed it with any of my squadron mates.

Of course, no such respite came the way of the USAF or VNAF Skyraider aircrews operating from air bases ashore. They were surrounded and often directly attacked by an almost invisible enemy. Theirs was a very different and, in some ways, more personal war, even though they too saw it from the cockpit of a Spad.

US Navy Skyraider squadrons

Squadron	From	To	Type	Notes
VA-1L	1948	1948	XBT2D-1, AD-2	ex-VT-58
VA-15	1950	1965		
VA-16	1955	1958	A-1H	
VA-24	1947	1949		ex-VA-1B
VA-25	1947	1968	A-1H, A-1J	ex-VA-2B
VA-34	1948	1950		
VA-34	1948	1950		
VA-35	1949	1959		ex-VA-3B
VA-42	1947	1948		ex-VA-3B
VA-45	1947	1957	AD-4B	ex-VA-4B
VA-52	1959	1966	A-1H, A-1J	
VA-54	1949	1957	AD-2, AD-4, AD-4L, AD-4Q	ex-VF-54
VA-55	1949	1957	AD-4	
VA-64	1947	1948		ex VA-5B
VA-65	1947	1959	AD-2, AD-4	ex-VA-6B
VA-74	1949	1949		
VA-75	1949	1963	AD-4	
VA-92	1955	1957		
VA-94	1949	1949		
VA-95	1952	1965	AD-1, AD-4NA, AD-4, AD-4L, A-1J, A-1J	
VA-96	1956	1958		
VA-104	1953	1959		
VA-105	1952	1958		
VA-114	1948	1949		
VA-115	1949	1967	AD-4, AD-4Q, AA-1H, A-1J	ex-VA12A
VA-122	1959	1967	A-1H, A-1J	RAG
VA-125	1950	1962	AD-2, AD-3, AD-4, AD-4B, AD-4NA, AD-4Q, AD-5, AD-6, AD-7	ex-VA-26
VA-126	1958	1958		
VA-135	1961	1962		
VA-144	1959	1959		
VA-145	1950	1968	AD-2, AD-4, AD-4L, AD-4Q, A-1H, A-1J	ex-VA-702
VA-152	1959	1968	A-1H, A-1J	
VA-154	1948	1948		
VA-155	1951	1958	AD-4, AD-4L, AD-4Q	ex-VA-728
VA-165	1960	1966	AD-1H, AD-1J	
VA-174	1949	1949		
VA-175	1948	1957		
VA-176	1955	1966		
VA-194	1946	1949		ex-VA-19A
VA-195	1947	1959	AD-1, AD-4	ex-VA-20A
VA-196	1951	1966	AD-4NA, AD-4Q, A-1H, A-1J	ex-VF-194
VA-215	1955	1966	A-1H, A-1J	
VA-216	1955	1959		
VA(AW)33	1955	1960	AD-5W, AD-5Q, EA-1E, EA-1F, A-1E	ex-VC-33
VAAW-35	1950	1960	AD-1, AD-2, AD-2Q, AD-3, AD-4, AD-4B, AD-4L, AD-4N, AD-5, AD-6	ex-VC-35
VAQ-33	1950	1969	AD-4NL, EA-1E	ex-VAAW-33
VAW-11	1949	1960	AD-3, AD-4W, AD2Q, EA-1F	ex-VC-11
VAW-12	1949	1961	AD-4W, AD-5W	ex-VC-12
VAW-13	1949	1968	EA-1F, AD-4, AD-4L, A-1H	
VF(AW)4	1955	1958	AD-5	ex-VC-4

CHAPTER FIFTEEN

Combat Over Vietnam

The USAF Experience

Training of almost every USAF pilot to fly the Skyraider in combat between 1964 and 1972 was carried out by 4400 Combat Crew Training Squadron (CCTS). This outfit, commanded by Colonel Benjamin H. King, was based at Elgin Air Force Base's No. Nine Auxiliary depot, Hurlburt Field, located close to Fort Walton Beach, just to the east of the US Navy Air Base of Pensacola, Florida. This unit trained foreign personnel in COIN operations earning itself the epithet 'Jungle Jim'. With the involvement of USAF pilots, the 4407 CCTS handled the intake, and prepared them for the transition from jets of 700-plus mph (1,125km/h), to ground-strafing piston-engined Skyraiders. It was a rôle reversal for which many volunteered with a wry sense of humour, while others found themselves rather perplexed to be assigned to it.

The USAF's First Involvement

The USAF became involved in Vietnam on 4 November 1961, with Operation 'Farm Gate' at Bien Hoa Air Base. After President Kennedy had authorized the use of CCTS personnel for on-the-spot training of VNAF personnel in Vietnam itself, on 11 October 1961, Detachment 2A, comprising 151 officers and men, was despatched from Hurlburt on 4 November, its aircraft carrying VNAF markings. Step-by-step American direct participation in the combat fighting progressed from flying as 'advisors' with Vietnamese aircrew, through flying missions accompanying VNAF cadets still awaiting their Stateside training, and flying missions in company with VNAF aircraft, to independent combat sorties.

The USAF Skyraiders differed from those modified for service with foreign services in that they retained the auto-pilot gyro horizon indicator, but dropped the Navy's all-weather external radar and associated radar scope from the right-hand side of the control panel. Conversely, much extra radio equipment was embarked. Among other improved navigational instruments, they had UHF, VHF and FM radio equipment, and grew a whole host of external antenna. Mounted atop the fuselage abaft the cockpit to port was an FM

'Firebird' over Vietnam, a good air-to-air view of a heavily laden Spad on the prowl over the battleground.
US Navy official photograph

622 whip antenna for air-to-ground communications, while the UHF antenna projected to starboard. Mounted further back and centrally was the stub blade AN/ARC-27 UHF antenna., although sometimes the ARC-1 was fitted instead, with the TACAN (AN/ARN-21) positioned behind it, followed by the radio-compass loop aerial behind a circular fairing, and a radio-compass sensing aerial strung to the leading edge of the vertical stabilizer. The AN/ARA-25 UHF homing antenna was

while the FM homer was positioned under the rear fuselage. USAF equipment also included an XM-47 mine dispenser, which was not released to MAP recipients of the Spad. The USAF Skyraiders also differed from those supplied to the VNAF in that most retained their tail hooks.

For Air Force men, flying a Navy plane could lead to unexpected problems. For example, there are several cases on record of USAF pilots starting to take off while the aircraft's wings were still in the folded

In the case of the two-seat AD-5 (A-1E), some modification to the controls was considered necessary by the USAF. This was to give credibility to the 'Vietnamese-flown – American-advised' rôle under which the use of the Skyraider had been sanctioned by Congress. There was an additional (removable) throttle control lever fitted at the central console position, directly connected to the pilot's throttle on the left-hand console. This extra control lacked throttle stops and friction locks, but enabled the co-pilot to make left-handed adjustments. Likewise, a 'spare' control stick grip, complete with is own gun trigger, bomb release and trim tab control, featured, while a few A-1Es also had rudder trim control, which worked on manual selection of a trim selector switch.

In theory then, the American instructor/advisor sat alongside the Vietnamese pilot. In practice, the majority of combat operations were conducted by the American pilot. The Vietnamese assistants were progressively downgraded, first to the rôle of passive spectator, then, when trained VNAF pilots became proficient enough to work with their own Skyraider squadrons, being substituted by untrained personnel just to fill the seat. These unfortunates were given the humiliating nickname of 'Sandbags' by the American airmen!

Combat over Vietnam. An A-1E of the USAF, BuNo 132665, dropping a bomb on an enemy position. McDonnell Douglas, Long Beach

housed at the extremity of the starboard wing, with the AN/ARN-12 marker beacon being similarly located to starboard, while the AN/APN-22 radio altimeter had a similar position mid-way along the starboard horizontal stabilizer. From the lower starboard side of the rear fuselage extended the horizontal FM homing antenna, with the AN/ARC-44 VHF-FM radio above it,

configuration![75] A special safety feature had to be introduced to prevent this occurring. The wing-pin lock door and the wing-fold handle were deliberately left in the 'wings unlocked and folded' position; they obstructed the pilot's legs, and thus gave him a timely hint to unfold the wings and lock them securely *before* attempting to lift the Spad off the ground!

Increasing Intervention

The establishment of 1 Fighter Squadron (Commando) FS(C) at Bien Hoa airfield, was a significant escalation in American intervention in South-East Asia. It was originally planned to have three American Skyraider squadrons in place, to provide the necessary 'stiffening' of the VNAF units and, in the words of General Joseph H. Moore of 2 Air Division, to 'lead by example'. The first detachment of 1 FS(C) was based at Bien Hoa on 8 July 1963, as part of 34 Tactical Group, but its first A-1Es did not arrive there until 1 May 1964. The squadron was commanded first by Lieutenant-Commander John M. Porter, and subsequently by Lieutenant-Commander William R. Eichelberger.

Originally activated on 17 June 1963, the redesignated 1 Air Commando Squadron, Composite, became part of 6251 Tactical Fighter Wing on 8 July 1965, being switched to 3 Tactical Fighter Wing from 21 November 1965. By 8 March 1966, the unit had become part of 14 Air Commando

Wing. Its original duties were the training of VNAF pilots, but these soon expanded to incorporate more active participation in the war. They flew psychological warfare missions, then photo-reconnaissance missions, and, finally, full bombing combat missions.

On 15 August 1967, now commanded by Lieutenant-Commander James R. Hildreth, the unit was redesignated as 1 Air Commando Squadron, Fighter, before being reorganized as part of 56 Air Commando Wing, on 20 December 1967. This wing was itself redesignated at 56 Special Operations Wing. On 15 August 1967, the unit was redesignated yet again, becoming

Reeves, were assigned in August 1967. Their initial duties were to fly A-1H AND A-1J Skyraiders from their storage field at Davis-Monthan over to the US Navy IRAN facility at Quonset Point, Rhode Island, for refurbishment, and then to fly them back to England. Gradually, a further 14 pilots arrived and, under the command of Lieutenant-Commander Repp, a proper training programme began. This continued until February 1968, when they were transferred by C-141 via the Survival School at Clark AFB to Pleiku, Vietnam. Under the command of Commander Wallace A. Ford, their establishment strength was 25 pilots with 135 airmen. Three

mounted over a three-day period between 18 and 20 January 1965, as a pre-emptive strike, prior to the defoliation runs by Ranch Hand C-123 Provider transport planes equipped with Agent Orange chemical sprays. Some 395 tons of bombs, including a large number fitted with delay-action fuses, were delivered into an area of 18,500 acres, which concealed an entire enemy regiment and its equipment. Operations continued throughout the spraying period, placing a further 372 tons of ordnance and 85,000 rounds of 20mm cannon fire into the enemy concentrations, while the vulnerable transports went about their deadly work.

A USAF AD-6, BuNo 152243, in the usual camouflage paint scheme used in South-East Asia. McDonnell Douglas, Long Beach

1 Special Operations Squadron, and Lieutenant-Commander John A. Saffell, Jr, assumed command on 20 December 1967. On 5 January 1966, 1 Air Commando began operating from Pleiku Air Base.

Meanwhile, a second USAF Skyraider squadron – 6 Air Commando squadron – was being formed at England Air Force Base as part of 1 Air Commando Wing. The first two pilots of this squadron, William 'Bill' Constantine and James 'Jim'

weeks later, in mid-March, the squadron's 20 aircraft were unloaded at Cam Ranh Bay from the escort carrier transport ship, and the squadron was in business.

One unusual, and controversial, operation in which USAF Skyraider participated was the provision of very heavy bombing and strafing attacks on a main Viet-Cong base complex hidden in the Boi Loi woods 25 miles north-west of Saigon, close to the Cambodian border. The attacks were

As an extension of this operation, the USAF Spads were back over the area again on 31 March, this time dropping napalm to ignite the 1,200 gallons of diesel fuel dumped by C-123s in order to start forest fires. This proved a damp squib, as tropical thunderstorms stopped the conflagration almost as soon as it had started.

The Hoboes, as the 1 SOSs were nicknamed, after their call-sign, pioneered the use of their 500lb napalm tanks in a more

Close-Support Operations

On the whole, more conventional close-support operations proved to be 1 SOS's forte. Operating close to the enemy from forward operating locations (FOLs), they were able to give good and almost instant support to Allied ground forces. But the cost was high. In one such mission, carried out on 10 March 1966, in relief of an Allied Special Force Camp in the A Shau valley, close to the Laotian border, six A-1Es were despatched. The Allied garrison, 20 Americans and 375 South Vietnamese, had the day before reported themselves to be surrounded by an estimated 2,000-strong Viet-Cong force. The enemy had the approaches to the camp ringed with 20 major anti-aircraft guns, plus thousands of light automatic weapons, all of which dominated the only aerial approach route, which was 1 mile wide and 6 miles long. The Spad pilots had already made one attempt to bring help, and had christened this approach 'The Tube'. The Communist gunners were ready and waiting for the Skyraiders, and one American pilot said it was like 'flying inside Yankee Stadium with the people in the benches firing at you with machine guns'.

In command of the striking forces was Major Bernard F. Fisher, who flew with wingman Captain Francisco (Paco) Vasquez. Bad weather, with very low cloud and drizzle, had forced them back the day before. This time, however, Fisher located a hole in the murk, and led his five companions down through it to make low-level attacks. They emerged beneath the cloud layer at a height of about 800ft, with the tops of the hills invisible on either side of them.

The final approach called for a low-level straight flight, running the gauntlet of everything that could be thrown. This terminated in a hard left turn, during which the pilot had a small window for 'bombs off', before continuing his 180-degree about face to repeat his ordeal back down the tube to safety.

The Skyraiders were talked down by one of the American radiomen at the base, who gave them up-to-date details of the swarming enemy's location along the southern face of the hills. Despite this, there was little the six pilots could do to improve their position once they had committed.

Several of the Skyraiders were badly hit. Captain Hubert King had his windscreen shattered and was forced to break off and crash-land back at Pleiku. Undaunted, the remaining Spads completed the first strike

As in Korea, although jet aircraft were used predominantly for air strikes, to good effect, there was still a need for an aircraft that could carry large amounts of heavy ordnance, and yet still have the ability to loiter 'on-call' in the target zone. The rationale of the Stuka and the Dauntless of the Second World War was seen still to be a valid concept, even two decades or more later. The Douglas Skyraider was the last of the dive bombers in this classic tradition, and later adaptations of the 'Able-Dog' served well in this rôle. Here, a USAF Spad, BuNo 132593, heads out on another mission over South Vietnam in 1965. USAF official photograph

effective way, by converting them to supply pods. Each tank was fitted with a parachute to slow its descent, and packed with stores and equipment. Even so, due to their relative frailty, the converted tanks had to be released at very low level (from 50–250ft), which made the Skyraider a sitting duck. Tactics were evolved by 1 SOS whereby preliminary strafing was conducted at dusk and the supply droppers – each A-1 could carry up to eight of these converted tanks – followed up. The first such missions were conducted in November 1966, to help the friendly forces that were occupying an area west of the squadron's airfield. Again, although the theory was good, results were

disappointing. The Skyraider canisters tended to be scattered over a wide area, making their retrieval under the enemy's nose very dangerous. Some converted tanks, on which the parachute had failed, made hard landings and the ammunition they were carrying detonated and was wasted.

Night interdiction sorties also became part and parcel of the 1 SOS's duties, as they had for its Navy counterparts. Their undersides were painted with black gloss paint, and, almost invisible, the aircraft patrolled up and down the Ho Chi Minh trail in an effort to restrict the flow of supplies being fed down to the Viet-Cong and NVA from north of the DMZ.

and turned back into the cone of fire to make a second run. On the way back in, the Skyraider of Major Dafford W. Myers took a serious hit from a 37mm cannon, which knocked his engine out and filled his cockpit with smoke and fumes. Myers radioed, 'I've been hit and hit hard.' Fisher was in close contact and confirmed back, 'Rog, you're on fire and burning clear back past your tail.' Myers' aircraft was far too low for him to consider baling out as an option and decided to try and put his burning machine down at A Shau itself. Fisher talked him down as he had nil visibility forward, and the airstrip at the base was under continuous shelling as he made his glide approach. Despite all the odds, Myers made it almost down on to the tiny strip, but, at the last moment, realized he would not be able to stop in time. Again guided by Fisher, he retracted his undercarriage, then tried and failed to release his belly fuel tank; he settled down on the strip anyway, the gas exploding on contact and covering his aircraft in a sheet of flame. Incredibly, Myers survived both the blind belly landing and the fire, managed to extract himself and took cover at the edge of the airstrip, still under fire.

Having witnessed Myers' escape, Major Fisher reported the situation to the Command Post, who advised that a rescue helicopter would be sent for Myers. Fisher decided that it would arrive too late, and would, anyway, stand little chance of survival. He therefore made the decision to go in and get his squadron mate himself. With enormous bravery, he landed his own

Douglas A-1E Skyraider, No. 52-133905, 1 ACS. Arthur Pearcy Archive, by courtesy of Audrey Pearcy

Skyraider under enemy fire and plucked Myers from under the enemy's nose, while his four remaining comrades – Vasquez, Captain Jon Lucas, Captain Dennis Hague – conducted strafing runs to cover him, even after they ran out of ammunition. During this phase, Captain Lucas' A-1 suffered heavy flak damage.

Fittingly, Fisher was one of only two Skyraider pilots in Vietnam to receive the Air Force Medal of Honor. His gallant mount, BuNo 32649, survived this, and other hair-raising missions, and now resides on display at the Air Force Museum at Wright-Patterson field in Ohio.

6 SOS

On 1 August 1968, 'Fighter' was dropped from 6 ACS's title (to the disgust of most of the pilots), and it was redesignated as 6 Special Operations Squadron as part of 633 Special Operations Wing. They were soon in heavy combat and, among the 12 pilots lost in action, was Commander Ford, who was killed on 24 May 1968. Some casualties resulted from accidents rather than from enemy AAA fire. At least two Spads suffered damage through their wing cannon misfiring, and starting fires. Pilot John Hayes was forced to bale out of No. 065, while Stretch Ballmes managed to land his Skyraider safely at 200 knots with one wing almost burnt through after a similar misfire. The fact that the Skyraider's wing-mounted 20mm cannon still used percussion-primed ammunition, at a time when this had long been replaced by electrical priming, was believed to have been behind these incidents. Stocks of percussion-primed 20mm dated back to the Korean War, and it was not always in the best condition. The brasses sometimes failed to eject, causing instant percussion on the next round to the jammed one, and a wing fire followed. The same accident was thought to have led to the loss of John Hayes and Jack Ford of the same unit, although both were officially listed as Killed in Action (KIA).

Meanwhile, between 25 October and 15 December 1967, half the aircraft of 1 SOS were redeployed to Nakhan Phantom in Thailand for clandestine operations in that country. The rest of the squadron

An Air Commando A-1E Skyraider takes off. USAF Museum via Hugh V. Morgan

(Above) **Loading ordnance on a USAF A-1E.**
USAF Museum via Hugh V. Morgan

USAF A-1E dropping bombs on Viet-Cong positions.
USAF Museum via Hugh V. Morgan

joined them on 20 December 1967 and they continued operations from there until December 1972. Their rôle flying search and rescue (SAR) missions made them well known, but they also conducted close-support and direct-strike combat missions. Typical Skyraider ordnance carried on SAR missions over South-East Asia comprised four CBU-25 canisters containing multiple HE bomblets, two CBU-22 canisters with smoke bomblets, two AN-M47 white phosphorous (WP) smoke bombs, two LAU-3 pods, each containing 19 HE rockets, two LAU-59/68 pods with seven white phosphorous marker rockets each, plus 720 rounds of 20mm for each of the four M-3 wing cannon, and a SUU-11 minigun with 1,500 rounds of 7.62 ammunition. The Spad could thus cover all eventualities, and frequently did!

On 15 November 1969, 6 SOS, whose call-sign 'Spad' had become synonymous with the Skyraider in Vietnam, ceased to be. Its surviving pilots had been mainly transferred to Nakhon Phanom ('Naked Fanny' to the Spad aircrew), split between 1, 22 and 602 SOS Squadrons. Although

USAF Skyraider units – South-East Asia

Unit	Dates	Type	Bases	Call-signs	Notes
1 ACS	17-6-63	A-1E	Bien Hoa		
			Qui Nhon	TC	Became 1 SOS
1 SOS	1-8-67 to	A-1E/G/H/J	Nha Trang		Ex- 1 ACS
	15-12-72		Pleiku		
			Nakhon Phanom	TC	
6 SOS	1967/9	A-1E/G/H/J	Pleiku	ES	
22 SOS	1968/70	A-1E/H/H/J	Nakhon Phanom	TS	
56 SOS	10-69 to 1972	A-1H	Da Nang	TC	
602 ACS	1964	A-1/E/G/H/J	Pleiku	TT	Became 603 SOS
602 SOS	1970	A-1/E/G/H/J	Udorn	TT	Ex- 603 ACS
			Nakhon		
			Phanom		

the sanctioning of a third Skyraider-equipped Air Commando Squadron had been officially halted by a nervous Congress, who preferred the diverting of extra A-1s to the VNAF instead, another new unit was formed, somewhat surreptitiously. This new Skyraider outfit was 56 Special Operations Squadron, Operating Location Alpha Alpha (OCLAA), under Commander James Wold, formerly of 6 SOS. The A-1Hs of 56 Special Operations Squadron were operating from Da Nang airfield from 1970 and continued to mount strike missions through to 1972.

For two gruelling years, 22 SOS worked from Nakhon Phanom. Its call-sign 'Zorro' was a welcome sign to battle-weary American troops, cut off and surrounded in the jungle, that strong, lingering and accurate help was on the way.

603 SOS

The other famous USAF Skyraider squadron was 602 ACS, known as the 'Fireflies' after their call-sign. It worked out of Pleiku from 1964 onwards, and was later redesignated 603 SOS, moving to Udorn airfield and then to Nakhon Phanom, Thailand. Like the other USAF Spad units, its pilots flew search and rescue missions (known as 'Sandy', again after a call-sign, and the Air Force's equivalent to the Navy's rescap missions) in support of rescue helicopters, at great personal risk. The job of the Skyraider was to locate and plot the exact position of any shot-down aircrew, and then to protect such survivors from enemy attack by providing air cover. These duties changed to those of 'On-Scene Commander' when the rescue helicopter arrived, co-ordinating the successful recovery of the pilot from the jungle, directing additional air strikes against the enemy should they threaten the operation, and giving protection to the helicopter by escort and strikes throughout the mission. Only an aircraft with the Spad's ability to loiter over an area for many hours could combine such diverse duties so successfully.

One of these Sandy operations, flown by 603, produced the second Air Force medal men. Their commanding officer, Lieutenant-Colonel William A. Jones III, was flying as 'Sandy-1' on 1 September 1968, in a two-plane formation – his 98th combat mission of the war. The objective of his search was a downed McDonnell F-4 Phantom jet north-west of Dong Hoi. A faulty positional fix from the F-4's companions had led Jones astray, wasting precious time and fuel before a North American F-100 Super Sabre re-directed him to the correct location. While flying a low criss-cross pattern to visually ID the pilot, Jones' aircraft took splinters from a single 37-mm shell air burst, but he stuck to his task and was rewarded by a signal from the man on the deck. The Communists, following their usual tactics, had used the Phantom pilot as bait and ringed him with light flak guns. Jones made low-level attack runs against those he could see, hitting them with rocket salvoes and 20mm cannon fire. In reply to one of these, a 14.5mm weapon, scored a hit, which detonated Jones's Yankee rocket; it burst into flames, but, fortunately, failed to ignite the system.

Despite severe burns to his head, shoulders, arms and hands, and constant pleas from his wing-mates to abandon his burning aircraft, Jones, with great presence of mind, extinguished the blaze in his cockpit by blowing away his canopy, then adjusted for manual bale-out. That done, he turned back to his task and carefully plotted the Phantom pilot's exact location

A mixed load of ordnance on its way for delivery. Low-angle side view of two A-1s from 1 Special Operations Squadron in flight over the jungles of South-East Asia, October 1972. National Archives, College Park, MD

The classic USAF Rescue Mission, or 'Sandy'. An H-3 helicopter en route to pick up a downed pilot deep in enemy-held territory is given escort and support by a pair of A-1s from the 1st Special Operations Squadron over Vietnam. US Air Force official photograph

before taking his damaged aircraft back on the 150-mile (240km) leg to base. He was guided in by Captain Paul Meeks, and landed safely. He was adamant in conveying the location and plot of the Phantom to his rescuers before allowing them to take him from his charred and blackened cockpit and into hospital. Fortunately, the story had two happy endings – the pilot was subsequently rescued, and Jones survived his surgery, and deservedly was awarded the Air Force Medal of Honor.[76]

A heavily armed USAF 'Spad' heads out on another mission.
US Air Force official photograph

Other Work

Another rôle to which the versatile Skyraider was assigned in USAF service was that of Forward Air Controller (FAC). Patiently circling over suspected enemy troop concentrations, or working the sky ahead of Allied ground patrols, the A-1 pilot became both aerial observer and firepower support controller. He would sight the hidden enemy and forestall his ambushes by radio warning to his colleagues on the ground, and he would direct heavy air strikes at VC and NVA concentrations and break up enemy strongpoints ahead of the advance.

Apart from Sandys and other special missions, the USAF Skyraiders' role was mainly that of close-support aircraft, and, like their Navy counterparts, they excelled in it. One more mission serves to illustrate their work during those many years of intense combat.

The Viet-Cong tactics alternated between the classical guerrilla methods of surprise, concentration of overwhelming force against selected weak points, and terror. Whether they sought a major confrontation, as they did in the set-piece battle of Khe Sanh, or whether they simply

SKYRAIDER MEN – Major Bernard F. Fisher, USAF

The worthy holder of one of only twelve Air Force Medals of Honor, Major Bernard F. Fisher was born in San Bernardino, California, on 11 January 1927. Soon after his arrival, his family moved to Clearfield, Utah, where he was raised, attending the Clearfield and Kaysville schools. On his eighteenth birthday, the young Fisher became subject to the V06 program of the US Navy in March 1945, and was called up for war service. He served briefly at the end of the Second World War, and took his discharge in March 1946, to resume his academic career. He attended Boise Junior College between 1947 and 1949, and then majored in Fine Arts at the University of Utah from 1949 to 1951. He served with the Air National Guard from 1947–50, before volunteering for the Air Force and commencing officer training in 1951.

On 10 January 1953, Fisher received a US Air Force ROTC commission and enrolled as a student officer at Marana, Arizona, for primary flying training. This was followed by Basic Flying School instruction at Williams Air Force Base, Arizona, the Instrument School at Moody AFB, Georgia, and the Day Fighter School at Tyndall AFB, Florida, where he flew the F-80. On graduation, he became a jet-fighter pilot and steadily progressed through Air Defense Command.

On the successful conclusion of his training, Fisher joined his first operational squadron, as a pilot in 42 Fighter Interceptor Squadron (FIS) based at O'Hare Field, Chicago, where he flew F-86Ds. Between squadron duties, he also attended the Squadron Officer School at Maxwell AFB, Alabama. He continued to serve with this squadron, which, in August 1955, had been redesignated as 63 FIS, until December 1955, when he was assigned to 339 FIS, then based at Chitose AFB, Japan, where he completed a full tour of duty.

In the mean time Bernard had met and married Realla Jane Johnson. The couple had five sons – Bradford, William, Robbin, Timothy and Scott.

Bernard Fisher's next move was to the Interceptor Controller School from where he was assigned to 801 Aircraft Control and Warning (AC&W) Squadron, then based at Malstrom AFB, Montana. In 1959, he attended the USAF Instructor School at Connolly AFB, Texas, before transferring to 29 Air Division as a weapons controller. In February 1961, it was back to jet jockey, with his assignment to 20 FIS as Flight Commander, where he flew the F-101B. Now a Captain, Fisher's next appointment was to 310 FIS, which was equipped with that notorious pilot-killer

the F104-Starfighter. While with this unit, based at Homestead Air Force Base, Florida, Fisher twice survived complete engine failures on this aircraft. On both occasions, it would have been safer, and quite proper, for him to have baled out, but he had twice elected to stay with his aircraft and nurse it back to earth in safe condition for examination. For these courageous decisions he received recognition from the Air Force in the form of the Air Medal. He survived it all to make Major.

Not content with these two flirtations with death, Fisher volunteered for combat service in Vietnam in 1965 and was one of the 1,000-plus mph men who had to learn to deal with the rather more sedate, if much more reliable, prop-driven Skyraider. On completion of his conversion training, and time with Jungle Jim, he was assigned to 1 Air Commando; between July 1965 and June 1966, he flew a total of two hundred combat sorties with that famous squadron. His rôle was to train Vietnamese pilots, but Major Fisher went on to do much more than that.

On 19 January 1967, President Lyndon Johnson presented Fisher with the Medal of Honor at the White House; he was only the forty-eighth recipient, and the first living recipient of that award since the Second World War (the four awarded in the Korean War being posthumous).

After his time in Vietnam was up, Fisher was assigned as Flight Commander of 496 FIS, then based at Hahn AFB, Germany, and flew F-102As into RAF Alconbury, England, in 1968. A colleague who helped re-fuel his aircraft there described him as 'very low key'. This earnest, dedicated and modest man now lives in quiet retirement.

As well as the Medal of Honor, Bernard Fisher earned the Silver Star, the Distinguished Flying Cross and the Air Medal with six Oak Leaf Clusters for meritorious service in the face of the enemy.

Bernard Fisher, USAF, with his crew chief. USAF Museum via Hugh V. Morgan

took advantage of prevailing weather and night-time conditions to eliminate small posts, as at Dong Xoai, they always held the initiative, and the Allies had to respond to it. As often as not, it was the Skyraider that was most able to offer an immediate and meaningful counter, to hold the line until help could be summoned.

The defence of Dong Xoai on 10–11 June 1965 is a typical example of the USAF's hazardous work at this period.

Dong Xoai was a Special Force Camp, located in Phuoc Long Province, some 50 miles (80km) north-east of the South Vietnamese capital of Saigon.[77] It held a small garrison composed of a Regional Forces company of about 100 men, some 300 Civilian Irregular Defence Group (CIDG) personnel, a scout car platoon with four armoured cars and a platoon of 105mm howitzers. The tiny American presence totalled a nine-man Seabee construction team and 28 instructors. It was an easy target for the Viet-Cong to score a propaganda victory at little cost, and create one more headline in the Western media to undermine the already weakening political will against their aggression. At twenty minutes after midnight on 10 June, using the darkness to achieve total surprise, and a 500ft (150m) ceiling of low cloud cover to shield them from any interference from the air, a regiment of VC, heavily armed with automatic weapons, machine guns, 75mm recoilless rifles and flame-throwers, erupted out of the night and quickly overran the compound's outlying defences. Further groups of VC infiltrated the surrounding area, occupying all access roads and strategic buildings. Dong Xoai seemed doomed.

Airborne help was quickly on the way. Despite the conditions, a C-47 arrived in under an hour to drop illumination flares and enable the defenders to see their attackers. It was joined in 20 minutes by a pair of VNAF A-1Hs. They found the VC had already overrun the camp's airstrip and was preparing for a final assault on the American compound itself. Despite the illumination from the two C-47s, the enemy succeeded in quickly making inroads into the compound – its final fall seemed only a matter of time. The VNAF Skyraiders were unable to carry out any attacks due to the low cloud shrouding the whole area, and could only prowl around above the murk, hoping for a break.

At 0430, two more 2nd Air Division A-1Es were scrambled from Bien Hoa airfield, piloted by Captain Richard Y. Costain and

Two A-1Es, BuNo 133893 closest to camera. USAF Museum via Hugh V. Morgan

Captain Doyle C. Ruff. They could see fires from the burning camp through the clouds from time to time, and heard the radioed appeals for urgent assistance from the hard-pressed little garrison. Despite the fact that the minimum altitude laid down to safely drop 260lb fragmentation bombs was 1,000ft (300m), both pilots decided to go in under the cloud and make their attacks while there was still time.

Relying totally on their instruments, both pilots plunged down into the gloom using the burning fort as their aiming point. They were met by a hail of anti-aircraft fire from at least six automatic cannon, plus light weapons, up through the overcast from the VC, whose aim was partly guided by the Spads' incoming engine noise. Both released twelve fragmentation bombs in level flight, making a series of runs in a rectangular pattern through the clouds. Every time they dropped down to establish their position, a hail of flak met them, but their deliveries were perfectly accurate and on target.

A forward air controller directed Costain, who made two deliberate dive-bombing passes through the scud from 5,000ft (1,500m), again achieving the kind of accuracy that only the Skyraider could deliver at such a time. Fighting on the ground was almost hand to hand and there was no room for error. The VC now launched a final desperate charge up over the walls of the fort, eager to reach a decision before the lightening sky exposed them to retribution. With their normal disregard for their own casualties, they swarmed forward and again the defenders called urgently for 20mm cannon fire, to smother the attackers.

To comply would mean exposing the two A-1Hs dangerously, as they would need to make their low-level runs below the clouds, and would thus be clearly silhouetted by the flares, providing the VC gunners with easy targets at almost point-blank range. Again, the two USAF pilots unhesitatingly accepted the risks and commenced their strafing runs in patterns below cloud level. Together, they pumped some 15,000 rounds of 20mm cannon shell into the milling ranks of the Communist troops.

Each pass was met by intensive ground fire, but the two A-1Es had evidently been given charmed lives. During one such pass, Ruff, who pulled seven Gs on his instruments, became temporarily disorientated and almost flew into the ground, but somehow pulled up in time. Each pilot then made a deliberate dive at a high angle against fixed machine-gun positions, pulling out low and up into the cloud cover. Costain took two .50-calibre machine-gun bullets into his engine, and a .30 calibre machine-gun bullet in his left wing tip on his final strike, which was made at a height of 400ft.

These two brave Spad pilots had saved the day. With the dawn, almost continuous close-air support missions began over the beleaguered garrison. No less than 35 A-1Es and two dozen A-1Hs from both the USAF and VNAF teams took part, joined by strikes by 37 F-100s and 11 B-57s. The garrison had concentrated their defences in a single building and the commander of the 5th ARVN Division gave the Spad pilots *carte blanche* to strike at anything or anyone moving outside the compound or on the surrounding roads, certain that they could only be VC. Between 0600 and 0800, strafing was conducted at a low level by a further eight A-1Es against the schoolhouse in which the Communists had set up their heavy machine guns; ten other buildings were demolished, which had, similarly, become nests for the enemy.

By now, a relief column of ground troops was on its way to lift the siege and, at 0940, with again both USAF and VNAF Skyraiders giving instant pre-strike air cover and close support, helicopters carried the 1st Battalion of the 7th Regiment,

with four American advisors, into a clearing north of the town. The enemy instantly turned its full attention on this unit, and pulverized it with overwhelming fire and mass attacks. Despite intensive close-support attacks, which covered the plantation area with dead VC, the Allied outfit was largely destroyed.

This was a harsh introduction for some USAF pilots to the realities of combat in Vietnam. Major Oscar Mauterer was one who earned his spurs the hard way:

Mauterer had never practised theatre daylight tactics, let alone flight tactics and procedures. Nor had he ever flown before with the multiple bomb rack which was loaded on his A-1E. On his first dive-bomb pass, Mauterer was unaware that his master light switch failed to turn off his navigation lights, and as he went in he made a perfect target pulling out at 1,000ft. On his second run, he put four 100-pound GP bombs directly on a gun emplacement located only fifty yards from the north-west wall of the fort, still with his plane lit up like a Christmas tree. After finally turning the lights off, he made two more bombing runs, then strafed the north-west wall of the fort since it was already overrun by the VC. On one strafing run, Mauterer turned directly into a .50-calibre gun and fired down its muzzle until he had to pull out a few feet above the trees. Although he took six rounds from automatic-weapon ground fire, Mauterer never wavered in his strikes.[78]

In what was later described as 'some of the roughest anti-aircraft fire of the war', many of the A-1Es were taking hit after hit from .50-calibre multiple machine guns. One UH-1B was shot down, but the Skyraider attacks were unremitting.

In the afternoon, another three-plane Spad strike was gallantly led by Captain Richard D. Head through the overcast, which stretched up solidly from 800 to 4,000ft. Release height of 1,200ft was the recommended minimum for the three A-1Es 260lb fragmentation bombs, but, like his companions before him, Head ignored the rule book. He banked and drove down into the driving rain to commence his attack.

At 800ft, Head levelled off and the three A-1Es stormed towards the enemy straight and level, passing through intermittent cloud. He was silhouetted against the cloud, and hit after hit thumped into his solid little aircraft, which shrugged them off. A larger cannon shell punched a hole through his right wing, and his right aileron was shredded, but Head, undeterred, continued to make low-level passes, strafing with his own

cannon no less than 13 VC heavy machine-gun emplacements. Both his companions also took numerous hits before Head returned to Bien Hoa.

Meanwhile, on the ground, the battle continued to go against the South Vietnamese army. The Americans were airlifted out of the compound by helicopter and the battered fort was temporarily abandoned to the enemy, which was now estimated at three battalions; another helicopter was shot down. The Skyraiders dropped napalm, general-purpose and fragmentation bombs, and 60 tons of incendiaries on the enemy, and fired off thousands of rounds of 20mm cannon shell and rockets. The VC body count steadily rose but in reply no less than 13 A-1Es were hit by anti-aircraft fire, and damaged to varying degrees.

That night, the enemy resumed the attack under cover of darkness after regrouping, and hit the advancing 52nd Ranger Battalion. Called upon yet again, two A-Es provided air support until 2100 that night, and the Rangers broke back into Dong Xoai. All through the night of 10/11 June, the faithful Spads were overhead, bombing the VC whenever they were exposed by the flares from four C-47s.

Next morning, the Allies resumed the counter-offensive, with the Skyraiders again much in evidence. Nineteen A-1Es took part in a morning strike against enemy positions. In the end, the Communists melted back into the jungle, having slaughtered some 150 of their own civilian countrymen in the initial mortar attacks on the town. They left behind them some 700 dead, but took their less badly wounded away with them.

The American Commander-in-Chief in South Vietnam, General William C. Westmoreland, had no doubt about the Spad's part in this victory. As he told Lieutenant-General Joseph Moore, commander of the 2nd Air Division,

The performance of your strike pilots in providing close air support for the Dong Xoai 9–11 June operations was singularly outstanding. Working under adverse weather conditions, your pilots displayed true professionalism and delivered their weapons with precision. They, in fact, turned the tide of the battle.[79]

By April 1968, 1 Special Operations Squadron, was based at Nakhon Phanom Royal Thai Air Force Base, Thailand, and took part in missions in support of Project 'Muscle Shoals'.

Clandestine Mission – Son Tay 20/21 November 1970

One of the most secretive missions in which the USAAF Spads participated was the daring plan to rescue almost 100 American POWs incarcerated in the Viet-Cong prison hell of Son Tay, with its merciless Communist guards and polluted water. The Special Assistant for Counterinsurgency and Special Activity, Brigadier General Donald D. Blackburn, had been given special permission from the Joint Chiefs of Staff to undertake this hazardous action. After detailed discussions with the various Military Commands involved, and also with representatives of both the Central Intelligence Agency and Defense Intelligence Agency at Eglin AFB in Florida and in Washington, DC, it was decided that such a mission, although very risky, was viable.[80]

The raid was mounted by the 432nd Tactical Reconnaissance Wing based at Udorn, Thailand, where civilian tents had sprung up whose occupiers kept themselves strictly to themselves. A force was drawn up comprising two C-130E Combat Talon unconventional warfare aircraft, an HH-3E, and five HH-53 helicopters (plus two UH-1s for back-up units) with 92 specially trained assault troops embarked. Led by Colonel Arthur 'Bull' Simons, an Army Ranger, they left the base at 1150 that night and headed deep into enemy territory. Son Tay was just 28 miles (45km) north of Hanoi, the Communist capital and the most heavily defended area of North Vietnam. Their airborne escort and assault force consisted of five F-105s and ten F-4 Phantom jets, but given pride of place were the five A-1Es from the 1 SOS from Nakhon Phanom, specially loaded with the awesome BLU-76/B fuel air explosive weapons to cover the daring assault.[81]

The A-1Es had trained with the C-130s for some time for their special and vital rôle in this mission, with the big transports providing the navigational assistance to and from the target, and pallets of napalm canisters, which were to be used to form a flaming pool of fire to act as a marker beacon for the other aircraft. The Spads were equipped with specially configured napalm canisters to do the same job, in case the slow C-130s were unable to carry out their part of the plan. The Skyraiders were also tasked with creating a diversion by bombing a vital bridge close to the POW camp, to prevent enemy reinforcements from

Going downtown! A quartet of USAF Skyraiders heading purposefully over the Mekong river on another mission against the Viet-Cong. San Diego Aerospace Museum

reaching the area. Should the worst happen, the five A-1Es were to carry out low-level strafing attacks with their 20mm cannon on any approaching enemy columns.

Only a select few of those taking part knew the real objective of their mission. During training, theories had ranged from an attack on Fidel Castro in Cuba to a rescue mission in one of the African dictatorships. The choice of codename for the operation – Operation Ivory Coast – deliberately lent itself to this deception.

All seemed to go according to plan. The first C-130 dropped its napalm as arranged, and the second led in the five A-1Es, and dropped its napalm as they broke away and successfully dropped the bridge as planned, before taking up their patrolling circuit above the sea of flames, ready to intervene further if required. Then the helicopters went in. Regretfully, what the special forces found at Son Tay was not emaciated American POWs to be rescued, these had been spirited away by the Communists on 14 July to another camp, but a Soviet Training Unit populated by Russian advisors and their pupils, North Vietnamese sappers. Their training base and the old POW camp were on adjacent sites. The American raiders decided to make them pay, and killed many, including the Camp Commandant, before making their way back to the helicopters and safety.

An F-105 was damaged by one of the 16 SAMs fired off at the Americans by the Communists, and was forced to ditch over Laos. The empty rescue helicopters went to the aid of the aircrew and, at dawn, five more A-1Es from Nakhon Phanom, led by Sandy Low, arrived to lend their support. It was he who located the downed airmen. While his three wingmen strafed the immediate area to keep the enemy away, Low supervised the two helicopters, who picked up one crewman apiece and took them back to safety at Udorn. This ended a raid that was bold in its planning, and brave in its execution, and failed only because of a lack of up-to-date intelligence.

Final Days

By the autumn of 1971, 1 SOS had 28 Skyraiders on its strength and had reached its peak, but another year of combat attrition, with few replacements, halved this strength. On 7 November 1972, it became the last USAF unit to fly the A-1 in combat. A total of 104 USAF Skyraider pilots had died in combat over South-East Asia, the final casualty being Major Ezekiel 'Zeke' Encinas. With the American pull-out, all 19 remaining Skyraiders of this unit that were still active were handed over to the VNAF, before moving to Kadena Air Base.

CHAPTER SIXTEEN

Combat Over Vietnam

The VNAF Experience

Supplying the VNAF

Despite the obvious aggression of Communist-led North Vietnam, with active Soviet backing, against South Vietnam, the Geneva Accord had specifically ruled out either nation's patrons from supplying them with jet aircraft, hoping thus to limit the conflict. The US State Department was more dedicated to honouring this agreement than Moscow or Beijing, or Hanoi, and this was the key that led to the Skyraider's introduction into that theatre; the restrictions applying to propeller-driven combat planes were less stringent.[82] Thus, when the elderly (and unsuitable) aircraft with which the VNAF was equipped started to suffer unacceptable accident rates, the decision was taken to allow them to stock with surplus AD-4 aircraft.[83]

At first, only strictly limited re-supply was considered, with 1 Fighter Squadron being allowed just six Skyraiders. These were the first Spads to be delivered to the Vietnamese Air Force (VNAF), arriving in Saigon on 23 September 1960, to replace

the ex-French and ex-American Grumman F-8F Bearcats. They were followed by a second batch of 25 Skyraiders, which arrived in May 1961, allowing 2 Fighter Squadron similarly to refresh its complement, along with providing some spares.

These initial shipments soon escalated into a flood of Skyraiders as the war situation rapidly deteriorated. The supply of AD-4s was quickly exhausted and, in early 1960, AD-6s were also authorized for release, even though they were still in service with the US Navy.

Supplying the Skyraiders to South Vietnam was one problem; finding enough pilots who were sufficiently well trained to fly them into combat was another. Indeed, it was the lack of skilled aircrew that caused the worst headaches early on, given the USA's initial intention to remain neutral and outside the conflict. The first six English-speaking pilots from 1 Fighter Squadron VNAF to be selected – Captains Huy, Pham-phu-Quoc and Nguyen-quang-Tri, and First Lieutenants Nguyen-ngoc-Bein, Nguyen-van-Chan and Nguyen-van-

Long – were sponsored under the Military Assistance Programme (MAP). They were sent to Naval Air Station Corpus Christi, Texas, where they joined 301 Aviation Training Unit (ATU). Since they had already had considerable experience (a minimum of 800 hours) with the much smaller Bearcat, conversion training was limited to 40 hours flying. Their instructor on Skyraiders was Lieutenant Kenneth E. Moranville. On completion of this training, the six men transferred to VA-122, based at LeMoore NAS, San Diego, for a further 40 hours tactical flight training with the Replacement Air Group (RAG) based there, before returning to Bien Hoa.

Meanwhile, Lieutenant Moranville had volunteered to head a US Navy team consisting of four chiefs and two petty officers with specialist AD knowledge. It was seconded to MAAG in Saigon, in order to oversee the transfer of the Skyraiders to 1 Fighter Squadron. The aircraft arrived via escort carrier, from Quonset Point NAS, where they had been fully re-activated, and painted in modern light grey, complete with the Vietnamese national and squadron markings. The original BuNos were retained, but with had the first digit '1' omitted, a policy followed later by the USAF. The Skyraiders were then given a preservative coating, to keep the salt out during the sea voyage, when they would be stacked on the flight deck of an American escort carrier being used as an aircraft transport.

Unloaded at Saigon docks, the ADs were towed through the streets of the city to the Tan Son Nhut air base, where the preservative covering was stripped off, and they were given a full check by Moranville's team. The Lieutenant took one of the Skyraiders of this first consignment aloft with a full ordnance load, and gave a stunning demonstration of her firepower to the Vietnamese dignitaries, including VNAF Chief of Staff Nguen-xuan-Vinh, assembled below. Making low-level passes

Three Vietnamese Air Force A-1H's, fully armed, head out along the Mekong Delta on an attack sortie. National Archives, College Park, MD

The first Vietnamese pilots to train on the Skyraider are seen here with their American instructors. From left to right: Commander Clark, Lieutenant K. Morranville, Captain Huy, First Lieutenant Bien, First Lieutenant Chan, Captain Quoc, Captain Tri and First Lieutenant Long. Robert C. Mikesh

at a target on the airfield itself, Moranville dropped his bombs and then brought his demonstration to a fitting finale: 'I simultaneously fired eight pods full of rockets, 152 in all. They completely obliterated the target.'[84] When all six aircraft were airworthy, they were flown out to Bien Hoa, where their pilots eagerly awaited them.

At first, the relatively small numbers of pilots competent to fly the aircraft, ground technicians able to maintain them, and suitable spare parts all limited the value of the Spad in VNAF service. The South Vietnamese Army always retained final control over air operations and, being less well versed in close air-support techniques, tended to misuse the VNAF Skyraiders. At best, the complex chain of command led to serious delays, so that the tactical situation had invariably altered from the time the air support was required, to the time when approval for it was received. In one typical incident, in 1961, a call for an AD strike against enemy forces, opportunely exposed at a vital river crossing in Phuoc Thanh, was held up for three hours while the local governor was sought, to

give his personal approval of the mission. The delay rendered the action fruitless.

These problems were exacerbated by other internal political considerations, as the coup-wracked South Vietnamese government, led by the justifiably nervous President Diem, was reluctant to allow such potent war machines too far from their immediate control. At first, the units were restricted to Bien Hoa airfield in the immediate vicinity of Saigon, although four other airfields were capable of handling them. He also restricted their offensive armaments to only their 20mm wing guns and, on 4 March 1962, they were forced to fly against the Viet-Cong, near Tan Son Nhut, in this condition. The strikes, although accurate, ultimately accounted for just 25 of the enemy, when bombing might have proven more effective.

Initially, limited numbers and lack of proper maintenance, rather than the capabilities of the Skyraiders themselves, or their Vietnamese pilots, restricted the aircrafts' value in the field of battle. Many were forced to stand idle on their airfields, due to poor logistics. That was soon to

change. However, on 26 February 1962, the Skyraiders' copybook was somewhat blotted, when an attack was made by two AD-6s against the Presidential Palace. It was a grudge strike against the head of the Secret Police, the President's brother Ngo Dinh Nhu, rather than a full-scale coup against President Diem himself. One of the Skyraiders was shot down by flak, while the other fled to Cambodia and crash-landed. Four A-1Hs were similarly used, more successfully this time, in a real coup at the beginning of November 1963; this time, it resulted in Diem's overthrow and execution.

Reorganization of the VNAF

At the start of 1963, as part of a more general reorganization of the VNAF, the two Skyraider-equipped 'Fighter' squadrons were redesignated as 514 and 516 Squadrons, based at Bien Hoa and Nha Trang, respectively. On 2 January 1963, some 26 AD-6 Skyraiders, by now fully armed with a variety of heavy ordnance, were sent against Viet-Cong bases and troop concentrations along the Cambodian border. They accounted for about 1,000 of the enemy. By 1964, a third Spad outfit had been established at Bien Hoa, the 520th Squadron, which replaced the 716th Composite Reconnaissance Squadron to give the VNAF more punch. Increasing losses and casualties among the T-28 trainer aircraft, which had been utilized in the ground-attack rôle, were alarming. Its vulnerability was making it a liability in combat with the increasing aggressive and more powerfully equipped Viet-Cong battalions, which were liberally supplied with Soviet AAA weaponry. It was decided to replace all T-28 squadrons and standardize on the Skyraider. Further extra batches were therefore requested from the USA.

This, in turn, led to a need to supply more pilots, and VA-152 was assigned to supply training detachments based at Bien Hoa to undertake conversion training for VNAF men. A nineteen-month training course and conversion programme were also established for VNAF Skyraider pilots in the USA. Entrants arrived at Randolph Air Force Base, Texas, where they underwent a 42-week course in basic flight training with the T-28.

After successfully completing this part of the course, VNAF trainees moved on to

Hurlburt Field, at Eglin Air Force Base in Florida, to take part in a further 18 weeks of air training, including between eight and 90 hours on the A-1E. To enable them to work more closely with the now fully involved USAF effort in Vietnam, pupils were also required to take part in a 15-week language course. Even veteran VNAF pilots had to take part in this; most of them, being French-trained, had little or no English.

Difficulties in transiting to the much larger and heavier Skyraider were encountered by many of the Vietnamese pilots, who were physically lighter, and used to the small T-28, with its tricycle landing gear. These problems were slowly overcome and the first Fighter Squadron to complete the course was 516.

Meanwhile, the Air Force was giving the Skyraider a detailed examination at Eglin Air Force Base, where, early in 1964, two A-1Es were put through a series of tests by the Special Air Warfare Centre. At this time, urgent consideration was being given to the arming of the VNAF with jet aircraft, and new aircraft were being designed under the Counter Insurgency (COIN) designation to take over from the Spad. The Elgin results proved to the Air Force's satisfaction that, in the words of Eugene M. Zukert, Air Force Secretary, the Skyraider's 'simplicity of operation, versatility, maintainability, minimum runway requirements and other capabilities' made it an ideal aircraft for its

tasks in South Vietnam.[85] This opinion was given powerful endorsement when Robert S. McNamara, US Secretary of Defense, declared that the new COIN designs, despite a 32-times increase in cost, actually offered little improvement over the A-1. Nor could they match the Spad's trump card – the ability to loiter over the target area for long periods as a form of 'on-call' flying artillery.

Another coup followed in September 1964. When A-1Hs flown by Colonel Ky were instrumental in saving, rather than overthrowing, the Government of President Nguyen Khanh, the Viet-Cong became bolder and struck closer and closer to the centre of South Vietnam. This new Communist boldness culminated in a daring attack on Bien Hoa itself on 1 November 1964, when six Skyraiders were among many Allied aircraft hit by mortar fire and either destroyed or damaged. In direct retaliation, heavy air strikes were made against known North Vietnamese bases all over former Indo-China. The most daring was an attack on 2 March 1965 by the full strength of all four VNAF Spad squadrons, led by Brigadier General Nguyen-cao-Ky, against the North Vietnamese Army barracks at Dong Hoi, far to the north of the DMZ. This target was well hit, but was heavily protected; a number of Spads, including Ky's, took flak hits in return, but all returned safely. A second full-strength Skyraider strike followed three days later, during which one AD was lost.

Continuing Supply and Action

By this time, American ground forces were committed to Vietnam and began to operate, at first defensively, then, increasingly, on offensive operations. There was continuous internal turmoil, as an array of shaky South Vietnamese governments succeeded each other, and added to the chaos. This was temporarily stemmed when Ky took control. A Skyraider pilot, he tended to regard the elite 86th Wing as his own particular fiefdom, and specially selected pilots, whose personal loyalty to him was not in doubt, formed a special A-1 flight at Tan Son Nhut, as much for his own government's well-being as against the VC. Ky was able to bring his powerful influence to bear, whether he was in power or not, to increase the numbers of Skyraiders serving with the VNAF, and batches of ADs continued to be readied in the USA and despatched to Vietnam.

The Skyraiders supplied to the Vietnamese Air Force had come from the US Navy's Air Storage Depot at Litchfield Park, near Phoenix, Arizona. Here, scores of operation-weary AD-4Ns had been retired, gradually replaced aboard the front-line carriers by Douglas A-4B/C Skyhawk and A-6A Intruder jets. The routine for such pensioners on arrival at the depot was a form of 'mothballing' in case of future need; few realized just how imminent that need would arise. They were stripped of much of their equipment, and

The South Vietnamese relied more and more on the Skyraider for their aerial support, and the VNAF gradually equipped its fighter squadrons with this aircraft as trained aircrew became available. These aircraft (BuNo 139629 and BuNo. 134484) are from the VNAF 1 Fighter Squadron and carry the national insignia on their tails, along with their own unique identification bands across their rear fuselage. US Air Force official photograph

Order of battle – VNAF squadrons

Squadron	Type	From	To	Base
514	A-1H	1-1-63	30-4-75	Bien Hoa
516	A-1H	1-5-64	31-5-69	Nha Trang
518	A-1H	15 -10-63	30-4-75	Bien Hoa
520	A-1E/H	16-6-64	30-8-69	Bien Hoa
522	A-1E/H	1-6-65	30-1-68	Tan Son Nhut
524	A-1E/H	15-9-65	11-1-68	Nha Trang
530	A-1R/H	1-12-70	30-4-75	Pleiku

An A1-H Skyraider (BuNo 35298) of the 522nd Fighter Squadron, Vietnamese Air Force, which normally worked out of Tan Son Nhut, seen here in November, 1966. Note the special insignia of the 83rd Special Operations group, to which they were attached, a dragon's head in white and five stars on a blue background, with the inscription Thaii Phang ('God of Wind'). The tail codes are UG, and the national flag is three red stripes on a yellow background on the upper rudder. T. Love courtesy of Robert C. Mikesh

Lieutenant-Colonel John M. Porter, USAF. They were in action the following day against VietCong targets, flying US combat missions in VNAF markings.

For three months in 1969, Commander Stephen J. Riordan, USN, was the acceptance check pilot at the Naval Air Rework Facility (NARF), Quonset Point, Rhode Island. This was a temporary appointment while his carrier, the USS *Intrepid* (CVS-11), finished her refit at the Philadelphia Navy Yard. His official title was Aircraft Inspection Officer, and he was in charge of inspecting the Skyraiders that had been reworked by NARF Quonset for the Vietnamese Air Force.

He recalled the following incident, which took place while testing one such machine:

My Pratt and Whitney 3350 went hot, dark and quiet at 10,000ft over Narragansett Bay. The Spad's gliding characteristics are better than a rock, but not as good as a brick. I elected to ride her down to a wet landing in the shallows near Quonset. The Bay area is too built up to just leave an airplane and not expect it to hit something besides empty ground, and I did not think my gliding skills were up to specifically targeting the Bachelor Officers Quarters awful kitchen.

I did receive a commendation for the ditching. Because of where I ditched, the crash crew was able to recover the Spad within twelve hours. The aircraft was emptied of several pounds of oyster shells, de-salinated, repaired and put back in service. I carried the accident report for years in my official files. Unfortunately it was deleted by some Navy personnel man who sanitized my file when I retired.[86]

Phasing out the Skyraider

The final batch of Skyraiders for the VNAF was transported across the Pacific from San Diego aboard the escort carrier *Core* (CVE-13) in January 1966.

The US Senate gradually came to accept that further modernizing the VNAF with jet aircraft was justified. The new Northrop F-5A Freedom Fighter was found to be suitable for Vietnamese pilots, and for the ground-attack rôle, and this aircraft therefore looked set to replace the Spad. A second potential newcomer was the Cessna A-37A Dragonfly, which also proved popular. A steady programme of replacement by these types saw the phasing out of the Spad but, as so often before, it took a long time to lie down and die. By the end of March 1972, the VNAF had

then coated with preservatives, which, with the dry Arizona air, ensured that they would not deteriorate too much during their stay.

With sales to Vietnam, this process had to be reversed, in a job that proved to take longer than the original storage. The preservative coating had to be stripped away, and, in most cases, up-dated equipment was fitted and all working parts were given a full-scale check before the Skyraiders were ferried out either to Quonset Point or Alameda Naval Air Stations. There, they underwent a thorough, 60-day overhaul and modification programme, which included removal of the tail hook. It absorbed 5,250 manual working hours, at a cost in 1966 of US$133,000 per aircraft. Once up to speed, each renovated

Spad had to be flight tested by the Navy before despatch to its new owners.

Later deliveries included the two-seater A-1E. This variant was introduced by the USAF after a second set of controls had been fitted, to enable them to fly two-man combat missions with a Vietnamese 'passenger'. This was a ploy to comply with the rules of combat, when it was the American technical advisor who actually carried out the mission. This aircraft did not prove so popular with the VNAF pilots, who bemoaned its poor visibility.

A few A-1Js were also shipped much later, as they too became available.

In May 1964, a group of 50 A-1Es and 25 A-1Hs were prepared at Alameda NAS. Six of these were staged to Saigon by US Air Force pilots, commanded by

taken delivery of 289 Skyraiders of all types, but had lost no less than 217 of them through accident and damage. On strength at that date were 11 A-1Es, eight A-1Gs, 52 A-1Hs and a single A-1J.[87] By the end of the war, 308 Spads had been assigned to the VNAF, including several EA-1s, which were confusingly redesignated A-1G on transfer.

For the total number and marks of the 296 Skyraiders known to have been delivered to the South Vietnamese Air Force, see the table below.[88]

Among the weaponry favoured by the VNAF Spads were Mk82 and M-117, 500lb and 250lb low-drag finned bombs, fused to detonate .025 seconds after impact; M1A2 cluster bombs, up to eight CBU-25s or CBU-55s, and 2.75 HVAR air-to-ground rockets, plus two 500-lb SUU-11 napalm tanks.

Squadrons and Operations

One of the first notable VNAF Skyraider operations took place between 27 April and the end of May 1964, when they acted in support of the Army against Viet-Cong supply dumps, and crops in the Da Nang region. The 17 Skyraiders were flown from Bien Hoa to the forward airfield, and a combat-readiness of 10 A-1Hs was maintained during the five days of intensive operations.

By October 1964, the VNAF Skyraider squadrons had reached their maximum strength of six fully operational units under the auspices of the Military Assistance Command Vietnam (MACV). As the number of A-1Hs in the VNAF grew, and the confidence and ability of the Vietnamese pilots increased, their combat sorties also became more numerous – 145 were flown in June 1964, and by December of the same

year this figure had more than doubled, to 324. The sorties also became more effective.

Night sorties by A-1Hs had at first been resisted by VNAF Skyraider commanders, but they were gradually introduced, and some units became highly proficient in this form of attack. The first real success was a night sortie mounted on 6 November 1964, when Ky led a force of 32 VNAF Spads against a Viet-Cong base camp north of Saigon. The force claimed to have killed 500 guerrillas who were caught by surprise.

On 1 April 1965, Colonel Nguyen-cao-Ky established the specially created 522 Skyraider Squadron, an elite unit with hand-picked aircrew drawn from existing Skyraider squadrons. Their high-profile rôle was to escort and support 83 Special Operations Group C-47 (and, later, Cessna 185 or U17 Skywaggon and Fairchild C-123B) aircraft in their secretive missions over North Vietnam, where they dropped sabotage and counter-insurgency agents. This CIA-funded organization, based at Nha Trang airfield between April 1961 and July 1962, was part of the VNAF but tended, by the nature of its work, to operate apart. Most of their drops were, naturally, nocturnal missions. The unit was headed up by Ky, and when, in 1964, he assumed command of the whole VNAF, he ensured that these special forces received greater status, and material. They dispensed with the national insignia on their aircraft, and carried the new disruptive-pattern, multi-coloured camouflage and their own individual insignia. The pilots were kitted out with special black flying suits and check scarves to set them apart, and each A-1H took the title Than-Phong ('God of Wind').

The combat missions of 522 Skyraider Squadron usually involved close escort of the 83 SOG transports on their flights across the DMZ deep into hostile territory. The agents would be dropped, and the transports escorted home. Often, these agents, having completed their assignments, which usually included the blowing up of strategic road and rail bridges and attacks on powerplants and oil storage installations, would make for the coast and be evacuated by sea by the Vietnamese Navy. When this occurred, 522 flew air cover for the warships back to the safety of home waters. Occasionally, the A-1Hs would sortie out on their own seek-and-destroy missions, to take out special sensitive and vital targets in the north. They also undertook close-support missions in border operations, where they often

VNAF Skyraiders listing

A-1E (57) (10)	A-1G (8)	A-1H (121)	A-1H	A-1J	A-1E (57) (10)	A-1G (8)	A-1H (121)	A-1H	A-1J
132414	132582	134454	135374	142016	132663		134609	139662	
132415	132587	134472	135376	142021	132667		134631	139664	
132425	132598	134473	135387	142028	132668		134634	139665	
132428	134042	134479	135392	142034	132669		134636	139667	
132433	134976	134482	135433	142045	132670		135206	139674	
132444	134987	134483	137493	142046	132673		135215	139685	
132445	135038	134484	137499	142054	132686		135223	139689	
132455	135047	134488	137502	142056	132860		135224	139690	
132474		134493	137505	142058	133860		135226	139703	
132482		134497	137506	142064	133861		135228	139707	
132487		134498	137519		133862		135229	139714	
132503		134499	137535		133866		135237	139718	
132524		134500	137540		133872		135243	139723	
132528		134505	137551		133875		135245	139730	
132559		134519	137554		133876		135257	139737	
132576		134526	137560		133878		135258	139744	
132602		134531	137564		133885		135281	139746	
132612		134534	137597		133891		135288	139749	
132620		134536	137609		133896		135289	139757	
132624		134550	139513		133897		135298	139769	
132628		134555	139577		133906		135308	139770	
132630		134557	139618		133914		135332	139771	
132635		134565	139622		133915		135339	139775	
132636		134569	139626		133919		135352	139778	
132643		134570	139629		133920		135355	139779	
132647		134585	139638		133922		135367	139791	
132652		134595	139643		135042		139606	139796	
132653		134600	139653				139607	139797	
132655		134605	139656				139608	139802	
132661		134607	139661				139612	139803	
							139616		

ignored the strict rules about where and when they could drop their ordnance.

The 522nd was not the only VNAF Skyraider unit regularly to attack Communist troops north of the border, in response to increasing violations of its borders from the north. With the initiation of the American 'Flaming Dart' air offensive, the VNAF mounted a heavy strike of 24 Skyraiders on 8 February 1965. Led by Air Vice Marshal Ky, they departed from a forward air base at Da Nang in six four-plane flights, with aircraft drawn from all the A-1H units and crewed by their best pilots. Their target was North Vietnamese Army units, and their supply depots in the area of Vinh Linh and Chap Le.

The Spads made a low-level outward leg out to sea to avoid radar detection. After 125 miles (205km), they turned in towards the enemy coast, before breaking up into attacking groups and then diving at their allocated targets. The strong AAA defences were ready and waiting for them. Every single AD was hit, but only one, piloted by Lieutenant-Colonel Duong-thieu-Hung, was so badly damaged that it subsequently ditched in the sea; the pilot was safely rescued by the rescue helicopter. In return, the A-1Hs hit the enemy concentrations hard, claiming 90 per cent destruction of their targets. Even allowing for exaggeration, this first mission north of the DMZ was an outstanding success and a great morale-booster. It was the first of many such sorties by VNAF Spads.

A favourite target for the AD-1Hs became the North Vietnamese radar station, established on Tiger Island just north of the DMZ, which proved a thorn in the side of the Allied forces. It was first attacked on 8 February 1965, hit again on 14 March, and visited regularly thereafter.

On 11 February, in retaliation against further Viet-Cong atrocities, VNAF Spads made a large-scale strike on the North Vietnamese Army barracks and supply depots of Chanah Hoa and Vit Thu Lu, this time acting in conjunction with American air units. Many such sorties followed, earning even hard-headed American approval – 514 Skyraider Squadron was the first Vietnamese unit to receive the United States Presidential Unit Citation, in April of that year.

In 1967, Ky became Vice-President. The neurotic President, Major General Nguyen-van-Taieu, feared that Ky (now Air Vice Marshal) might plot against him, and use the 863rd to topple him. Ky vows

he never had this in mind, but Taieu took no chances and had 83 SOG broken up; 522 was returned to normal VNAF status, transferred to Bien Hoa and placed under 23 Tactical Wing.

The 1968 Tet Offensive, which began on 30 January, proved to be a watershed. An all-out Viet-Cong assault on the south was tackled head-on, and, using correctly applied air power, totally defeated. Over a three-day period, the remaining 69 VNAF

A Vietnamese Air Force A-1H Skyraider (note chequered fuselage band) dives down in a precision attack and releases a 250lb bomb over a Viet-Cong target in South Vietnam, 27 September 1967. USAF photograph courtesy of Robert C. Mikesh

Skyraiders from the four surviving units, including those of 516 Fighter Squadron, at Bien Hoa, Binh Thuy, Da Nang and Nha Trang, contributed to the combat sorties flown by the VNAF. For the loss of five A-1s, they accounted for many of the 600 Viet-Cong guerrillas killed, and the quick defeat of the campaign.

However, this victory on the ground was, in some respects, turned into a defeat by the negative attitude of the media

reports in the West, who tended to ignore the VC atrocities and defeats. The American public, weary of a seemingly endless war, was able to pressurize the US Government into a withdrawal of American forces. A decision was made to hand the war back to the Vietnamese; by now, the VNAF had been built up to a potent force, and should be able to handle things.

At this time, the VNAF was really into its stride. Among the many successful operations in which its Skyraiders participated with their American allies was Operation Scotland, the defence, between 22 January and 31 March, by the 26th US Marine of Khe Sanh. It was a re-run of Dien Bien Phu, but with a happier outcome. In this battle, the overall mission given to Allied Air Forces, under the code-name of Operation Niagara, was the destruction of NVA forces besieging the base, the interdiction of NVA supply lines and base areas, and the provision of maximum tactical air support to friendly forces.[89]

The Marines account of this battle gives a good insight into the methods used:

Close air-support missions were utilized against pinpoint targets in proximity of friendly troops. Along with radar-controlled bombing, this type of air strike was the most responsive to the needs of the ground commanders and the most accurate. The attack pilots, however, required reasonably good weather to be able to hit their targets. There were usually fighter-bombers overhead at Khe Sanh around the clock; if not, they could be quickly scrambled from hot pads or diverted from other missions. When the pilots arrived on station, they checked in with the DASC and were handed off to a Marine or Air Force Tactical Air Controller (Airborne) who personally directed the strike.

During the day, the air around Khe Sanh was filled with the high-pitched shriek of jet engines: Marine, Navy and Air Force F-4 Phantoms; Marine and Navy A-6 Intruders, A-4 Skyhawks, and F-8 Crusaders; Air Force F-105 Thunderchiefs and F-100 Super Sabres. In addition to the jets, the South Vietnamese prop-driven A-1 Skyraider, a rugged attack aircraft of Korean War vintage, was in evidence. At times, the sky overhead resembled a giant beehive. When a flight arrived on station, the Khe Sanh DASC normally directed it into a holding pattern until a TCA(A) or a Forward Air Controller (FAC) on the ground was free to handle the strike. These patterns sometimes extended up to 35,000ft with scores of planes gradually auguring their way downward as each preceding flight unloaded its ordnance and scooted for home.

After the Paris Peace Treaty

The sole responsibility of the Vietnamese for their own defence was confirmed by the 1973 Paris Peace Treaty. The North Vietnamese regarded this as a ploy to get the Americans to stop bombing them, while they rebuilt their forces to continue the aggression, while the Americans had the face-saver the public demanded. The South Vietnamese, who all along had only wanted the tools to do the job, were now left with ample supplies, but continued support would be required to maintain them.

Their force still included the Skyraider, which continued to fight doggedly on throughout 1973. In attacks on the Communist 320 Division that year, A-1s flew numerous ground-attack missions from Pleiku. Now, the A-1 was not only vulnerable to the intensive fire from the NVA's multi-barrelled 37mm AAA weaponry and the fixed SA-7 sites, but hand-held heat-seeking missiles in the Viet-Cong and NVA armoury also posed a great threat. Between January 1973 and June 1974, five VNAF A-1Hs had fallen to these weapons. By June 1974, both 514 and 518 Fighter Squadrons were still Skyraider outfits, working as part of 23 Tactical Wing under 3 Air Division at Bien Hoa. The only other

This A-1 of the VNAF is seen at Da Nang in April 1968. It carries a modified US-type national insignia. Nick Williams

unit still flying the Spad with the VNAF was 530 Fighter Squadron was 520 Fighter Squadron, part of 72 Tactical Wing under 6 Air Division at Pleiku.

By this time, the Spads had become worn out by almost continuous operations. When France refused to sell her surplus stocks to the Americans, there was no

longer any hope of more replacements. Nor was there the political will in Washington, DC, to honour the one-for-one 'Enhance' replacement programme, which had been agreed to at the time of the ceasefire. Only 28 A-1s were ever supplied. The decision was therefore made to put the remaining A-1s (now down to 61)

Head-on view of two A-1 Skyraiders revving up on the main runway at Da Nang, Vietnam, August 1968.
Nick Williams

into 'flyable storage' and convert the final three squadrons to the A-37. Once again, and for the last time, the Spads refused to play ball! Despite the fact that their condition had placed a 3G limit on their combat operations, it was found that their ease of maintenance, at a time when all American aid had been cut off, meant that they were still the best bet operationally. A blind eye was therefore turned, and the Skyraider fought on to the bitter end.

With the final Communist offensive, airfield after airfield was abandoned as the South Vietnamese pulled back. Large numbers of aircraft were summarily abandoned, including many of the remaining ADs in their storage facilities. When the advancing enemy reached Pleiku on 14

March 1975, a complete Spad squadron was found intact; a similarly depressing scene was discovered at Da Nang.

Although the fast-dwindling numbers of Skyraiders flying with 514 Squadron did their best to stem the tide, South Vietnam was finally overrun, abandoned by her allies, and her fate ignored by the world, which looked the other way. The Skyraider had the distinction of fighting one of the last rearguard actions in defence of freedom. On 29 April, a pair of VNAF A-1 Skyraiders played a part in the defence of Tan Son Nhut airfield close to Saigon, conducting last-ditch strafing attacks against the hordes of advancing Communists. Eventually, one of the Skyraiders was destroyed by a SA-7 Strella

ground-to-air missile, and the other ran out of ammunition.

On the last day of April, President Minh was forced to surrender Saigon and South Vietnam to the enemy. In May 1975, the last eight Vietnamese Air Force A-1s fled to airfields in Thailand, being joined spasmodically by others rescued from storage, with 23 TAWs at Bien Hoa. In the end, a total of 11 A-1E and A-1Gs had found refuge there. They were claimed by the North Vietnamese as the spoils of victory, and by the United States, to whom they legally belonged under the terms of the MAD agreement. The Thais wisely denied the claims of both sides and, instead, retained the aircraft for their own use.

SKYRAIDER MEN – Air Vice Marshal Nguyen-cao-Ky, VNAF

The former Commander-in-Chief of the Vietnamese National Air Force, and one-time Prime Minister of the Republic of Vietnam, Nguyen-cao-Ky occupies a unique place in the history both of his country and of its Air Force, at one time the fourth-largest in the world. Today, living in quiet retirement in Washington State, USA, an exile from his native land, Ky still refers to himself first and foremost simply as a pilot. He was more than that – he was a Skyraider man.

Ky was born in the small township of Son Tay, 15 miles from Hanoi, on 8 September 1930. Vietnam was then under French colonial rule as part of French Indo-China, and he grew up speaking both languages. With the end of the Second World War in 1945, the Communist Guerrillas, spurred on by Stalin and aided by their Chinese counterparts, took advantage of the hiatus between the departure of the occupying Japanese, and the replacement of the collaborating Vichy-French officials by French colonial officers. The formation of the Viet-Minh and, in 1950, the start of their decade-long war against the French, their own people and, ultimately, the Americans, coincided with the young Ky reaching maturity. As an idealistic teenager, he volunteered to enlist in the army to fight against the Red insurgents.

The young Ky did well in his chosen career and rapidly rose to command his own platoon. The fighting during this early period gave him unrivalled insight into the insidious tactics of fanatical and indoctrinated guerrillas, and also into the French tactics against them, which led to their infamous defeat at Dien-Bien-Phu, in May 1954. The key element in negating the Communists' control of the jungles, and of the night, seemed to be air power, if it was correctly used. Ky volunteered to train as a pilot. His initial flight training was conducted at the Marrakech Ecole in French Morocco, some of it in the Douglas A-24 dive bomber, representing Ky's introduction to a Heinemann airplane. Subsequently, he was transferred to the Avord Ecole training school in France. For the final stage of his air training, the French Armée de l'Air sent Ky to Blida Air Base in Algeria and, in 1954, he qualified as a pilot on both the Skyraider and the C-47 transport. He

General Nguyen-cao-Ky, in a 1965 portrait.
National Archives, College Park, MD

then spent some time in Algeria to fine-tune his skills, with special emphasis on close-support operations.

With the French withdrawal from Indo-China, and the separation in July 1954 of Vietnam into a Communist dictatorship north of the 17th parallel, and a fragile democracy in the south, many Vietnamese fled to Saigon. Ky chose to serve with the South Vietnamese forces – the VNAF was formed independent of the

French on 1 July 1954, although most Vietnamese pilots were French- rather than English-speaking. On his return to Vietnam, Ky took part in a series of combat operations against the Viet-Cong, who were seeking to take over the independent state.

Ky graduated from the Thu Duc Reserve Officer's School, and then upgraded his skills at the Air Command and Staff School in the United States between 1957 and 1959. His progress continued apace until, in December 1963, at the age of just 33, he was appointed C-in-C of the VNAF. He first flew a Spad in 1965, when he 'borrowed' one from the 83rd Fighter Squadron at Son Nhut Airfield by pulling rank. He was immediately a convert. Later, he retained personal command of the 83rd, the 'Wind of God' unit, and flew combat missions, making his last A-1 flight in 1974.

Under his leadership, the VNAF mushroomed to 30 operational squadrons as the war developed. The Skyraider squadrons formed the backbone of Ky's expansion, and he became instrumental in building this force up into a formidable and wholly Vietnamese weapon.

During this troubled period, there were two coups, but Ky vehemently denies any part in them. His major concern was national unity against the ever-increasing Communist threat. He was promoted to Lieutenant-Colonel, then to full Colonel, and finally to Major General. In 1964, he received an honorary ranking of Air Vice Marshal, but continued to fly. He was directly instrumental in placing the 23rd Tactical Wing A-1H Skyraiders at Bien Hoa on full alert, thus foiling another coup by Army officers on 13/14 September 1964.

On 11 June 1965, Ky was appointed Prime Minister, a position he held until 3 September 1967. Even then, he contrived to fly when he could. He later became Vice President of Vietnam, and served the Government until the American withdrawal and the final crash of the Viet-Cong's occupation of South Vietnam in April 1975.

Ky and his family were granted asylum in America. He settled in Huntingdon Beach, California, where he helped other Vietnamese exiles with their problems, before moving north to his present home.

CHAPTER SEVENTEEN

Small Wars

The French Experience

Algeria

The French *Armée de l'Air* first requested
AD Skyraiders under the Mutual Defence
Air Programme (MDAP), commencing in
1959.[90] Although the United States had
always frowned on what it called 'colonial
wars' (despite its own commitments in the
Philippines, Panama, and elsewhere), at
this time Algeria was not considered a
colony, but an integral part of France itself.
Algerian citizens had exactly the same
rights and privileges as people living in the
rest of France.

The Soviet Union began to incite various
malcontents who, having observed events
in Indo-China, now sought independence.
An organized resistance force, the *Front de
Libération Nationale* (FLN), was established,
and terrorist murder attacks against civilian
targets soon began to spread. Starting in
1954, the confrontation had gradually escalated into an armed conflict with an increas-

ingly bitter struggle being waged against the
native guerrilla forces.

Initially, air operations were conducted
with ground-strafing Republic P-47D
Thunderbolt fighter-bombers, but these
were getting very long in the tooth, and
difficult to maintain. The French needed
an aircraft more attuned to this type of
warfare. Seeing that the US Navy was
gradually phasing out the Skyraider, the
French turned their attention to the surplus machines.

Initially, 93 ex-US Navy AD-4Ns and
five ex-US Navy AD-4Ns were obtained by
France, and these were followed by a further
20 ex-US Navy AD-4s. These Skyraiders
were refitted by the French firm SFERNA
at Mérignac airfield near Bordeaux, being
equipped with French radio and navigation
apparatus, and other internal equipment.
Various structural modifications were also
made to these aircraft, to bring them up
to AD-4NA standard and to make them

(Above) **Two French Skyraiders of the** Armée de
l'Air **practise low-level strafing runs in 1962. Such
attacks would be typical of their work during the
Algerian uprising.** SIRPA/ECPA Fort d'Ivry

Maintenance work being carried out on an Armée
de l'Air **Skyraider during operations in Algeria,
1962.** SIRPA/ECPA Fort d'Ivry

French Skyraider, BuNo 125721, of the Armée de l'Air, **preparing for engine tests on an Algerian airfield, 1962.** SIRPA/ECPA Fort d'Ivry

suitable for French service. Both bombs and T-10 air-to-ground rockets were employed by the French as standard ordnance.

The three-seat aircraft were re-converted back into single-seaters by the removal of the after cabin, along with its radar equipment and the two operator stations.

The arrestor hook was removed and the dive brakes were made non-functional. The resultant large space was not officially utilized for any other equipment, but, in practice, it came in very useful when the Skyraiders were called upon to act as supply and transport aircraft to far-flung bases.

In April 1960, the first unit, *Escuadron Ouarsenis* 2/20, based at Boufarik Air Base in Algeria, received a batch of these reconditioned AD-4s. Further squadrons followed in the same year, with AD-4Ns reaching *Escuadron Aures-Nementchas* 1/20 at Boufarik in July 1960, and Escuadron Oranie 3/20 at the same base in October.

All these units were engaged in the Algerian fighting, Ouarsenis sending detachments of AD-4Ns to other bases in the vast land, including Biskra and, later, Tebess. The squadron finally disbanded at Algiers on the last day of 1963. Aures-Nementchas also detached a flight to Bone for operations, and, in September 1962, the whole squadron moved to that airfield for operations, detaching a four-aircraft unit across the African continent to the colony of Djibouti in March 1963. In May of that year, the bulk of this unit was moved back to Boufarik again, finally disbanding at the end of September. Many of its personnel were reassigned to a new Skyraider outfit, *Escuadron d'Appui Aérien* 1/21, which was established in Djibouti on 1 October of that year, replacing the 1/20 detachment.

Meanwhile, *Escuadron Oranie* had worked out of Boufarik, sending Skyraider flights to work from Oued Zenata and also Mecheria, before being relocated itself at La Senia airfield, near Oran, in September 1962. In November 1963, the unit was redesignated as *Group de Chasse* 3.20, but

Mechanics work on a Douglas Skyraider of the 20th Escadre de Chasse **'Auers-Nementchas', while four others stand ready, at Les Salaines air base, south of Bone, Algeria, 1963.** SIRPA/ECPA Fort d'Ivry

continued to fly the AD-4N until after Algerian independence, which marked the end of the war. In March 1964, the unit was deactivated; on 30 June 1964, many of its personnel and then a number of its AD-4N and AD-4NA Spads were sent to form *Escuadron de March 2/21*, at Ivato airfield on the island of Madagascar. Redesignated as *Escuadron d'Appui Aérien 1/21*, this was the longest-serving French Skyraider squadron, being mainly based at Ivato airfield near Tananarive. It did not disband until August 1973.

Other Skyraider Locations

The last French Skyraider unit to form and be equipped with the AD-4N was Ain 1/22 in March, 1969. This flight was based at Fort Lamy airfield (now known as N'djamena) in the former French colony of Chad, to relieve a detachment of Skyraiders from 1/21, which had been sent there in August 1968. Chad was finding its new independence under constant threat from Libyan-backed guerrillas and terrorists, and even the threat of a full-scale invasion by Libyan forces. Further threats saw this squadron strengthened and enlarged to full strength, and redesignated as *Escuadron d'Appui Aérien 1/22*.

The effectiveness of the *escuadron* was limited in the war, not because of any failing of the Skyraider or of its French aircrew, but because of limitations on its active use by the authorities, who did not want to provoke the wrath of Gadaffi. Indeed, during operations at the end of the 1960s and in the early 1970s, the *escuadron* was forced to adopt ludicrous solutions in order to comply with the rules of engagement. The empty after cabins of some of the AD-4Ns were rigged up as temporary bomb bays, and thus accommodated a bombardier and a stack of his only legal ordnance – empty beer bottles! These were dropped on insurgents, in the hope that the whistling noise they made as they fell would cause panic, and that their lack of detonation would be put down to their being 'delayed-action' weapons! This was an effective enough ruse to start with, but the enemy soon became wise to it.

This *escuadron* became the last French Skyraider squadron in service and did not finally disband until it returned to Bordeaux airfield in mainland France. The final Skyraider flight was made on 21 September 1975, by AD-4N BuNo 126965, by which time the Spad had clocked up 105,000

French Skyraider at the Chateaudun Air Depot, France, 1971. Front three-quarter port view, without wheel covers fitted. SIRPA/ECPA Fort d'Ivry

flying time in French service. The *escuadron* was formally disbanded in October 1975.

As the rest of the French dependencies and colonies gained their independence, most of them initially retained strong links with France and, in many ways, continued to rely on her help with their defence. This help was given, by various methods, with that peculiarly Gallic combination of benevolence and secrecy, and it proved valuable where small nations were threatened by larger bullies, such as Libya. As part of this policy, the Skyraiders were either sent as French units to such places as French Somaliland (Territory of Afars and Issas), Madagascar, the Central African Republic (Ubangi Shari), and Chad; alternatively, those aircraft that became surplus to France's immediate needs were often passed on to

such nations to become the kernel of their own air defence.

Six of the AD-4Ns based in Chad were handed over to that country. They were flown for the *Escadrille Nationale Tchadienne* during 1976 to 1984, by mercenaries, mainly former French Air Force pilots who knew the Spad well. These Skyraiders were based at N'djamena airfield, and were flown spasmodically against Muslim rebel forces attempting to overthrow the mainly Bantu government. In a similar manner, five Skyraiders were given to Gabon, and, again, mercenary ex-French pilots, employed as part of the *Garde Présidentielle*, flew them for their new owners. Some were still operational as late as 1980.

In 1965, one final, and controversial, donation was made to a former French colony. Two batches of Skyraiders – AD-

French Skyraider squadrons

Unit	Name	Type	Tail Code	From	To
2/20	Ouarsenis	AD-4N	20-Qx	1960	1963
1/20	Aures-Nementchas	AD-4N	20-Lx	1960	1963
3/20	Oranie	AD-4N	20-Fx	1960	1964
1/21	–	AD-4N	21-Lx	1963	1972
2/21	Le Gaulois	AD-4N	U	1964	1973
		AD-4NA			
1/22	Ain	AD-4N	22-Dx	1969	1975

(Above) **Skyraider of the Gabonese Air Force revs up at Libreville airport.** SIRPA/ECPA Fort d'Ivry

Douglas Skyraider of the Armée de l'Air **landing at N'djamena airfield in the Chad Republic, 1975. The Skyraiders operated on anti-incursion patrols with French pilots during the period of the invasion threat from neighbouring Libya.** SIRPA/ECPA Fort d'Ivry

4Ns, followed by AD-4NAs, totalling 30 aircraft in all – were given to Cambodia (now known as Kampuchea). This particular deal was special, because the USA, with its ongoing commitment in Vietnam at the time, was particularly anxious to get these aircraft back from France for its own use, American stocks having been almost exhausted. France pointedly scorned this request and, despite American protests, assigned the planes to Cambodia instead. There, under the indolent rule of Prince Norodom Sihanouk, their potential was totally wasted; they contributed little to the fight against Communist Pol-Pot's infamous *Khmer-Rouge*. It was only when Sihanouk was toppled in 1970 that the Skyraiders of the *National Khmer Aviational* began to fly some anti-guerrilla missions, but with little heart or success.

Twenty former French Skyraiders survived in some form or other into the 1980s, and the majority of these are still around now (*see* the table right).

French survivors

French serial	c/n	BuNo	Type	Initial fate
11	7609	125716	AD-4N	France
14	7449	124143	AD-4N	France
19	7724	126924	AD-4NA	Gabon
21	7677	126877	AD-4NA	Scrapped
30	7462	124156	AD-4N	USA
34	7680	126880	AD-4N	Crashed Niger 1992
37	7798	126998	AD-4NA	France
38	7796	126996	AD-4NA	France
41	7712	126912	AD-4NA	Gabon
42	7722	126922	AD-4NA	Gabon
45	7756	126956	AD-4NA	Gabon
50	7759	126959	AD-4NA	Chad
53	7779	126979	AD-4NA	France
54	7765	126965	AD-4NA	Chad
61	7802	127002	AD-4NA	France
65	7803	127888	AD-4NA	USA
68	7909	127894	AD-4NA	South Africa
78	7797	126997	AD-4NA	USA
79	7770	126970	AD-4NA	Crashed USA 4/11/84
85	7682	126882	AD-4NA	Gabon

CHAPTER EIGHTEEN

End of the Line for the Spad

Accidents

The Skyraider was among the safest of US Navy warplanes ever built, with an enviable record. Even so, routine accidents took place – pilot error, fatigue of the ageing airframe, and engine failure despite the most stringent tests, all took their toll and steadily reduced the number of flyable Spads. Lieutenant-Commander L. William (Bill) Dilts was a veteran pilot who had flown Grumman F6F Hellcats, Chance-Vought F4U Corsairs and Grumman F8F Bearcats while serving with VF-93 aboard the carrier *Boxer* (CV-21) in the Second World War. Between 1952 and 1955, he was serving at Corpus Christi, Texas, NAS as an instructor teaching fresh-faced pilots in F6F-5s, North American T-28s and Beechcraft SNB-5s. While at Cabaniss Field he was appointed as the Aviation Safety Officer, and became involved in analysing all the accidents that took place at the field. As a permanent member of the Aircraft Accident Board, he investigated over a hundred incidents.

'I did not fly the AD,' said Bill Dilts [91], 'but was very familiar with it and with all the technical items connected with it. I investigated over forty Skyraider accidents, from ground incidents to fatal air crashes with the AD. The late Commander Mort Walker was my sidekick and fellow accident board member. He had flown combat tours in Korea with the AD. Both Mort and Commander Glen War were squadron mates in VF-54, which had started out as an F4U Squadron that subsequently changed over to the AD Skyraider. The Navy never did change the designation from VF [Fighter] to VA [Attack] – why not I just do not know because all the missions they flew were either bombing or rocket attacks.'

Dilts recalled one particular Skyraider accident, tragically a fatal one for the young Corpus Christi trainee, that left both the Navy and Douglas Aircraft puzzled for a considerable time:

> A student aviator was flying with seven other students on their bombing syllabus.
>
> Weather was fine, with ten-mile visibility, broken high clouds and a temperature of 70 degrees Fahrenheit. They were making bombing runs, at either glide (40 degrees) or dive (60 degrees) angles. They were naturally closely monitored by the ground crews who were able to calibrate the exact dive angles taken by the students with an instrument referred to as a 'Harp'. You could follow the dive and get the

---

SKYRAIDER MEN – Lieutenant-Commander L. William Dilts, US Navy

Bill Dilts was a Navy carrier fighter pilot from the Second World War. He never flew a Skyraider, but his job was, like that of the designers, constructors, engineers and armourers, a vital one with regard to the AD's long life. His findings in the investigation of Skyraider accidents ensured that fewer Skyraiders were lost in such incidents than other types, and saved Skyraider pilots' lives.

Dilts was born on 25 July 1925 in Dallas. After his preliminary education, he attended the Georgia Tech, and joined the Navy as a cadet aviator in December 1942. Nineteen months of intensive training followed, in which he flew a wide variety of aircraft, including Piper Cubs, N-2S Stearmans, N-2T Timms, Vultee SNVs and North American SNJ trainers. He made his first deck landings aboard the old paddle carrier *Wolverine* in the Great Lakes, was commissioned an ensign, and received his wings in June 1944.

Operational training flying the Grumman F6F-3 Hellcat fighter followed for Dilts, before he joined VF-97, a pilot pool for the East Coast. He served for a brief period aboard the escort carrier *Croatan* (CVE-25) in the North Atlantic, where his Air Group qualified for both day and night carrier landings, before being assigned to VF-93 as a fighter and photo-reconnaissance pilot for combat deployment aboard the carrier USS *Boxer* (CV-21), scheduled for the Pacific and the Japanese landings. With the early surrender of Japan, the *Boxer* Air Group saw no combat, but was in Japan in time for the surrender ceremony, and later provided air cover for the US Marine 3rd Marine Divisions landings in northern China in September and October 1945. In all, Dilts ended up with 78 carrier landings, two of them night landings, and conducted 13 missions over China, including four photo-reconnaissance sorties.

Dilts returned to the US in January 1946, and worked as a civilian for a while, as an airline pilot for TACA, a Central American outfit flying DC-3s, Avro Ansons and Lockheed 14s. Meanwhile, he continued his military flying in the Naval Air Reserve, flying Chance-Vought F4U-1D Corsairs. He married Jean Menty, the daughter of a Scottish father and an American mother, in 1948 while in British Honduras. The couple had three sons and a daughter. In June 1950, Dilts was recalled to service and assigned to a night-fighter trainer unit at Key West, Florida, completing training in F6F-5N Hellcats and

Lockheed TV-2s, the Navy version of the Shooting Star. Dilts continued flying fighters until 1956, when he was due to convert to the Douglas A-4 Skyhawk. This order was subsequently cancelled, and he was sent to a Lockheed Super Constellation school. After qualifying, he flew early warning missions in WV-2s (now called EC121J and EC121-Ks). One of the most interesting jobs he undertook was flying a special 'Super-Connie' for the US Navy's Hydrographic Office (now known as the Oceanographic Office), in Project Magnet, surveying the earth's magnetic fields (isotonic lines of force). The 26-man crew flew all over the world, including the Arctic, during 1960–61.

Bill Dilts finally retired from the service, as a Lieutenant-Commander, in June 1967. He now lives at Marietta, Georgia, where he enjoys gardening, building model aircraft and ships, hunting and fishing.

exact angle made by the pilot. Dive brakes were used on the steeper dives and the shallower glide dives were made without them. At the end of both types of dive they dropped small practice bombs that were filled with a 10-gauge shell/black powder, which made large puffs of white smoke when they exploded for easy target marking.

The student had made several normal dives without incident. On his final, fatal dive, witnesses on the ground heard a loud 'pop', followed by an abrupt and violent pitch-up of the

engine and propeller were both missing from the wreck. The prop had sheared from the engine prior to impact and a search for it was initiated. After photographs had been taken and on-scene witnesses had been interviewed, the aircraft was lifted up by the crane and placed on a flat-bed trailer. At this time, we discovered a large hole in the bottom of the fuselage, just behind the cockpit.

We found that the main-fuselage fuel tank was also missing and that the tank braces had broken away. We sent crews out in line abreast

As the aircraft started to pull up on the dive recovery a structural failure occurred at the fuel support area (main braces) and the fuel cell, with several hundred gallons in it, tore away and smashed through the belly of the plane. This caused an abrupt and radical CG [centre of gravity] change, which caused a violent pitch-up, with the engine tearing away, and probably caused a runaway prop, followed by it shearing away from the main crankshaft.

It was noted that the pilot could have had his neck broken at this time due to the violent

A three-quarter frontal port-hand view of an A-1H Skyraider, coded 001. McDonnell Douglas, Long Beach

aircraft, which then came down rapidly, but in a flat position – no oscillation was noted. The pilot did not bale out and was with the aircraft when it made contact with the ground, still in a flat attitude, the aircraft striking the earth within a few hundred yards from the ground observer crew, who had a clear view throughout.

The pilot suffered a broken neck and was apparently killed on impact. His body was removed and the accident board, together with the crash crew's 'Cherry Picker' (mobile crane), photographers and miscellaneous personnel arrived on the scene, and began the investigation. It was noted that the AD's

to comb the area to find the tank, prop and engine, which were all eventually traced. The propeller had skewed several hundred yards from where the plane had fallen; the engine was found closer in to the ground crew. The rubber fuel tank was found approximately 1,500 yards from the crash. The engine, prop, aircraft and fuel tank were then sent to the base overhaul and repair facility for more detailed investigation and an engineering report. Douglas Aircraft was advised and requested to take part in the investigation. After several months study the following summary was published.

action of his aircraft, or he may have suffered the injury as the aircraft impacted the ground.

In a Navy-side search, it was discovered that a similar accident had occurred with a Marine Corps Skyraider in Korea, prior to this one. A recommendation was made to have an engineering 'fix' to reinforce the braces that held the main fuel cell. This was done and all Skyraiders had this change installed.

So far as I know, we never had a repeat of this type of accident in the Navy or Marine Corps after the kit was installed. I investigated several other Skyraider fatal accidents, but this one was the most unusual.

(Above) **Impressive line-up of A-1s and A-4s with BuNo 137616 closest to the camera.** McDonnell Douglas, Long Beach

Douglas EA-1F Skyraider BuNo 132576, of VAW-13. Arthur Pearcy Archive, by courtesy of Audrey Pearcy

(Left) **Skyraider 516 of VA-45 makes a unique touch-down. Mishaps occur, even with the safest of aircraft. This undignified carrier deck landing fortunately led to no loss of life.** San Diego Aerospace Museum

On the side lift of the carrier USS Enterprise, **a Spad (AF 508) is brought up to the flight deck to prepare for another sortie, with an escorting destroyer in close attendance.** San Diego Aerospace Museum

Bill Dilts added the following rider to his account of this incident:

The AD Skyraider was one of the safest aircraft in the fleet.[92] These accidents were few and far between in the regular squadron operations. The Training Command, understandably, had a higher accident rate, due to inexperience and low accumulated hours of flight time.

Reserve Squadrons

The Skyraider served as one of the principal Navy and Marine Corps Reserve Squadron mounts for a number of years. The usual practice was for the same aircraft to be flown by several different outfits, both Navy and Marine, and they therefore carried the markings of both services. Commander Charles Shuford spelt out their rôle of the late 1950s and 1960s:

Reserve duty involved limited participation, usually less than most reservists preferred. Our aircraft were used three weekends each month by different squadrons. However, if an individual member [pilot] wished to schedule flights during weekdays and fourth weekends, additional flight time could be acquired. There were times fuel was not available due to Navy budget restrictions.

In addition to regular scheduled flights, there were utility flights and occasionally ferry hops to those pilots who were able to take advantage of them. Occasionally, we sent aircraft for O&R in other states (such as Providence, Rhode Island), or for long-term storage in the desert at Litchfield Park, Arizona.

Annual training periods (usually two weeks) were for the squadron members to function as a unit, away from home base, and sharpen their skills. Many of my squadron members were employed as airline pilots and therefore were racking up plenty of flight hours in multi-engine

Lieutenant-Commander Fred E. Elarbee (centre) observing the loading of practice bombs on to his VA-673 Reserve Squadron AD-5N Skyraider, BuNo 132523, with Commander Charles Shuford (right). Reserve aircraft were flown by both Navy and Marine Reserve pilots, as indicated by the dual markings on the fuselage. Charles R. Shuford

(Below) Reserve Squadron VA-673, based at NAS Atlanta on the Dobins AFB and former Lockheed Aircraft Company site, on the occasion of the 1960 Active Duty Cruise. Commanding Officer Commander John Gavin, is front left, with Executive Officer Commander Charles Shuford front right. (Gavin was of Irish extraction, and had the Shamrock stencilled on the squadron helmets.) The AD-5N has small practice bombs on most of her underwing ordnance stations. Charles R. Shuford

aircraft, both prop- and jet-driven, but not in Navy types.

Being based in Atlanta, my unit usually trained in Florida, California, Louisiana, or at bases in Texas and Pennsylvania, based on what space was available. We enjoyed having access to the military ocean restricted areas to perform our bombing and aerial gunnery on towed target sleeves.

My active and ready reserve service was a very important part of my life. I retired in 1970. Reservists are a very important and necessary part of our national defense. Retention of personnel continues to be a problem in keeping our strength up to authorized numbers.[93]

Final Navy Operations

The very last combat mission flown by the Skyraiders of the US Navy took place on 20 February 1968. This historic sortie was flown by an A-1H (BuNo 135300), which belonged to VA-25, flying from the USS *Coral Sea* (CVA-43), the carrier that had flown the first Skyraiders twenty years earlier, her pilot being Lieutenant (j.g.) Theodore F. Hill, Jr, with 79 combat missions under his belt. On 20 February 1968, in its 219th combat mission, it undertook a 4½-hour rescap flight for a helicopter attending the crash site of a USAF F-4 Phantom, which had been shot down over the target. This was followed by a call for close support from the US Marines under enemy attack along the DMZ; BuNo 135300 duly responded. The last Navy Spad mission was thus unique, in that it involved both the Air Force and the Marines. Hill landed his Skyraider back aboard *Coral Sea* at 0736; when its valiant old propeller finally stopped turning, the aircraft had completed 769.9 hours combat flight time, and 4,400 total flight hours.

When the *Coral Sea* returned Stateside, VA-25 flew their aircraft ashore to Naval Air Station LeMoore and, on 10 April 1968, a special retirement ceremony was held there to mark the passing of the Skyraider from West Coast squadrons.[94] Two rows of sideboys lined the runway and 135300 taxied through them with Lieutenant Hill at the controls. The ceremony was concluded by Chaplain John W. Berger, who gave the Spad its epitaph:

The horizon will be more empty as the familiar profile fades from view, but the deeds of man and this plane will remain on the pages of history a source of hope and courage.

The officers and men of Reserve ATTCRON 673 on the occasion of the 1961 Annual Cruise, 4–17 July, at Naval Station Mayport, Florida. Commander John Gavin, Commanding Officer, is on the right, with Executive Officer Charles Shuford at front left. Gavin went on the achieve Flag Rank in later years as an Admiral. Charles R. Shuford

CHAPTER NINETEEN

Spad Survivors

The Skyraider is still with us today in large numbers (*see* the table right), mainly owing to the fact that it served late, and survived in odd corners of the world as a fighting aircraft into the 1980s, by which time the interest in warbirds was well established. The other famous dive-bomber types are less well represented, and only a few examples remain: one American Vought SB2U Vindicator, two Curtiss SB2C Helldivers, two Japanese Aichi D3A1/2 Vals, two British Blackburn Skuas, three Soviet Petlyakov Pe-2 *Peshka*, and just five of the most famous of them all, the Junkers Ju. 87. Fortunately, more and more examples of all types are gradually coming to light. Thanks to the shallowness of the waters of Lake Michigan, the Douglas SBD Dauntless survives in good numbers, with more than 20 now saved. The Spad survivors, however, outnumber all the types in every respect – as flying aircraft, museum displays or as gate guards – although drastic cutbacks in US defence expenditure mean that the future of some of the later Skyraiders looks bleak.

Many dedicated owners in the United States and in Europe have managed to keep the Spad airborne down the decades since her final retirement: Dave Forrest from Atlanta, Georgia, Jack Spanich, Richard Bertea (who rescued the French Skyraiders), David C. Tallichet and the Yankee Air Force in California, Harry Doan in Florida, and a whole host more, have kept that familiar shape in the sky long after its day seemed to be over. Sadly, there has been a price to pay for these achievements – both Harry Doan and Jack Spanich died in a Skyraider (Doan in a ground-loop at Titusville, Florida, on 4 April 1992, and Spanich in the mountains near Culpepper, Virginia, on 4 November 1984), while a French Skyraider was lost in a sandstorm near Agades, Niger, on 1 April 1992.

Regretfully, there is not enough space to illustrate every surviving Skyraider, but the following 20 represent the more interesting of the 54 known examples around the world. The last of the dive bombers are well worth a visit!

Skyraider survivors

Type	BuNo	c/n	Civil Reg.	Known Locations as at 1998 (N.B. – checks should be made before visiting)
XAD-1	9102	1930		Oceana NAS Virginia Beach, VA, USA
XAD-1	9103	1931		Walter Soplata Collection, Newbury, OH, USA
AD-2	9257	2085	N2AD	Douglas W. Wood, Dallas, TX, USA
A-1E	122811	6933		EAA Museum, Oshkosh, WI, USA
AD-4	123827	7133	N23827	Wiley C. Sanders, Troy, AL, USA
AEW-1	124086	7392		Helston Aero Park, Cornwall, UK
AEW-1	124121	7427		FAA Museum, Yeovilton RNAS, Somerset, UK
A-1D	124143	7449	F-AZDP	Amicale J-B Salis, La Ferté, Alais, France
A-1D	124156	7462	N91935	Wiley C. Sanders, Troy, AL. USA
AD-4N	125716	7609	F-AZFN	J. J. Joyeux, Auinat, France
AD-4N	125739	7632		New England Air Museum, Windor Locks, CT, USA
A-1D	126882	7682	N91945	Sherman Aircraft, West Palm Beach, FL, USA
A-1D	126912	7712	N4277P	Erickson Air Crane, Chino, CA, USA
A-1D	126922	7722	G-RAID	The Fighter Collection, Duxford, Cambridge, UK
A-1D	126924	7724	N924JT	Vintage Wings, Anchorage, AK, USA
A-1D	126935	7735	N2088G	Richard Bertea, Corona Del Mar, CA, USA
A-1D	126956	7756	F-AZDQ	*Aero Retro*, St, Rambert-D'Albon, France
A-1D	126959	7759	N959AD	Dr Mike Schloss, CN, USA
A-1D	126965	7765	OO-FOR	Eric Vormezeele, Brasschaat, Belgium
A-1D	126979	7779		*Musée de L'Air*, Paris-Le Bourget, France
A-1D	126996	7796		Jack Spanich, Detroit, MI, USA
A-1D	126997	7797	N409Z	Cinema Air, Carlsbad, CA, USA
A-1D	126998	7798	F-AZKY	Didier Chable, Melun-Villaroche, France
A-1D	127002	7802	F-AZHK	Jean Salis Aviation, La Ferté Alais, France
AD-4N	127007	7807		USS *Yorktown* Museum, Charleston, SC, USA
AEW-1	126867	7850	N4277N	Erickson Air Crane, Medford, OR, USA
AD-4NA	127888	7903	N92034	Kalamazoo Aviation History Museum, Kalamazoo, USA
AD-4NA	127894	7909	N92072	South Africa Air Force Museum, Ysterplaat, South Africa
AEW-1	127922	7937	N5469Y	National Warplane Museum, Geneseo, New York, NY, USA
AEW-1	127949	7946	N4277L	Cham S. Grill, Chino, CA, USA
AEW-1	127945	7960		*Flygvapenmuseum*, Linkoping, Sweden
AEW-1	127947	7962		*Luftfartsmuseet*, Stockholm-Arlanda, Sweden
AEW-1	127960	7975		*Svedino's Bil Och Flymuseum*, Sloine, Sweden
AD-4B	132261	8369		United States Marine Corps Air-Sea Museum, Quantica, VA, USA
EA-1F	132532	8927		United States Naval Aviation Museum, Pensacola, FL, USA
EA-1F	132534	8929		Stored USS *Independence*, FL, USA
A-1G	132598	8993		United States Air Force Museum, Hurlburt Field, FL, USA
EA-1E	132789	9385		EAA Museum, Oshkosh, WI, USA
NA-1E	132443	9460		Texas Air Museum, Rio Hondo, TX, USA
A-1E	132463	9480		United States Air Force Museum, McClellen AFB, CA, USA

(continued overleaf)

Skyraider survivors *(continued)*

Type	BuNo	c/n	Civil Reg.	Known Locations as at 1998 (N.B. – checks should be made before visiting)
A-1E	132649	9506		United States Air Force Museum, Wright-Patterson AFB, Dayton, OH, USA
A-1E	132683	9540	N39147	United States Air Force Museum, March AFB, CA, USA
A-1H	134472	9701		Royal Thai Air Force Museum, Don Muang AB, Bangkok, Thailand
A-1H	135273	9917		Walter Soplata Collection, Newbury, OH, USA
A-1H	135300	9944		United States Naval Aviation Museum, Pensacola, FL, USA
A-1H	135332	9976	N39148	David C. Tallichet, Chino, CA, USA
EA-1F	135018	10095		United States Air Force Museum, Pima County Air Museum Tucson, AZ, USA
EA-1E	135152	10229	N65164	Avery's Antique Airplanes Inc., Morganton, NC, USA
EA-1E	135178	10255	N62466	Taylor Energy Co, New Orleans, LA, USA
EA-1A	135188	10265	N188BP	Amjet Aircraft Corp, St Paul, MN, USA
A-1H	137602	10678		United States Naval Air Station Lemoore, CA, USA
A-1H	139606	10838	N39606	Museum of Flying, Santa Monica, CA, USA
A-1H	139665	10897	N39149	David C. Tallichet, Yankee Air Force, Chino, CA, USA
A-1H	139674	10906		The War Remnants Museum, Ho Chi Minh City, Vietnam

BuNo 09102

Oddly, this most historically important preservation is hardly ever mentioned in books on the Skyraider. However, as only the third XBT2D-1, XAD-1 prototype, it deserves attention. It was retained by the Naval Historical Center, Washington Navy Yard, DC, in 1979, and stored at the United States Marine Corps MCAS Quantico, Virginia, for many years, before undergoing restoration from 1987 and being put on display at the Oceana Naval Air Station at Virginia Beach.

It initially carried the serial number F501 but this was later replaced by the current 09102/AE500.

BuNo 124086

This AEW aircraft made its maiden flight in May 1950, but only served for two years in the US Navy before being transferred to NAS Quonset Point for a major overhaul. Following this, it was transferred to NAS Norfolk for preservation treatment pending a transfer to the United Kingdom. In January 1953, it was part of a batch loaded aboard the aircraft carrier HMS *Perseus*, arriving at RNAS Abbotsinch on 20 February.

After undergoing the usual RDU procedure, the aircraft was scheduled to join the team at RNAS Culdrose, but this move was cancelled. After a year's enforced idleness, the engine was taken out and the aircraft went into storage in December 1953, where it remained until August 1955. Its next move was to RNAS Donibristle, where it arrived on 13 August 1955 for rectification and storage; another long period of enforced idleness followed.

On 13 March 1958, the aircraft was taken to RNAS Culdrose at long last, but

Starboard broadside view of the Douglas AD-1 Skyraider, 09102, of VA 176, at the Front Gate of NAS Oceana, Virginia Beach, VA. Kevin R. Smith

Royal Navy AEW-1 Skyraider WV 106 while at the Cornwall Aero Park (Flambards), 6 May, 1993.
Courtesy of Bob Turner

did not join 'D' Flight of No. 849 Squadron as 427/C until October of that year. A year later, in October 1959, it left for NARIU at Lee-on-Solent to have VHF units installed, and then returned to Cornwall, joining the 'HQ' Flight as 416.

On 23 September 1960, the aircraft returned to AHU Culdrose, was placed in long-term storage, and four years later was declared surplus to requirements and readied for total scrapping. At the last moment

it was decided to retain it on permanent display at NASU Culdrose and, it remained in store until the 1970s, being part of the display at the Cornwall Aero Park, Helston, by 1976.

On 21 March 1997, it was moved to the care of 849 NAS at Culdrose once more, to be refurbished for the fiftieth anniversary celebrations of that Naval Air Station. Parked out in the open, it suffered heavy damage from gales, and it was taken inside

for repairs to be made. In October 1998, it was due to be re-sprayed, by one of the volunteers of the Fleet Air Museum. Coincidentally, he was a former Royal Navy man, and the very same person who gave it its last service respray many years before!

BuNo 132463

This aircraft was one of 650 AD-5s built by Douglas at El Segundo, and was accepted into the US Navy in February 1954. It served aboard the aircraft carriers USS *Shangri-La*, *Franklin D. Roosevelt*, *Intrepid* and *Enterprise*, before being supplied to the VNAF, and then being taken over by the USAF and flown as 51-598 with the 1st Special Operations Wing.

After many years as an A-1E, it became part of the NASM and was stored by NAF Washington, DC, from 1974 onwards, before being packed aboard a C-5A and delivered to the McClellan Aviation Museum at McClellan Air Force Base, California, on 29 October 1985. There, the museum staff restored the aircraft, repainting it in the markings of 1 Special Operations Squadron, 14 Special Operations Wing, USAF. It was given the display serials 32463/EC and placed on display for ten years, but, with the defence cut-backs and the closure of McClellan base, the future of the Museum is currently under review.

Douglas AD-5D AIE Skyraider, BuNo 132463, EC 463, AF 32, at McClellan AFB, California. Arthur Pearcy Archive, by courtesy of Audrey Pearcy

Douglas AD-4 Skyraider (VA 125) BuNo 127888 (NX 92034) of the Kalamazoo Aviation History Museum, Michigan, seen here in a dive over the beaches of Lake Michigan. Built at El Segundo (Douglas serial 7903) under Contract Noa(SO) 51-020 she was accepted on 8 December, 1952 and delivered on 10 December, 1952. She was assigned to FASRON 691 at NAS San Diego on 30 December, 1952 and transferred to FASRON 10 at NAS Moffett Field after re-conversion from a -4N to a -4NA on 31 March 1953. She was assigned to VA-125 on 28 September, 1953 and shipped overseas with CAG-102. She returned to the US on 1 October 1954 at NAS Miramar, California and transferred to NARTU (Naval Air Reserve Training Unit) at NAS Glenview, Illinois on 28 October 1954.

On 6 May 1955 she was transferred to O&R at NAS Quonset Point, Rhode Island and then to NATC Pax River, Virginia on 9 November, 1955 before going into storage at NAF Litchfield Park, Arizona on 1 November 1957. She was reclaimed to NAS Norfolk on 10 May 1960 and sold to the French Navy on 31 May 1960, seeing limited combat action in the Algerian War before being returned to the USA from France in 1976. She was acquired by the Kalamazoo Aviation History Museum, from Mr Tom Austin in February 1983. Present paint scheme is that of VA-125 which flew from the carrier Boxer during the Korean War. There is a chronology problem with the 'B' on the tail and the yellow stripe. This aircraft was airworthy but has not been flown for a number of years because of cost of operations. Philip Makanna via Kalamazoo Aviation History Museum

Should lack of funding force the closure of the museum, plans are in hand to transfer this Skyraider to the air museum adjacent to Hill Air Force Base, close to Salt Lake City.

BuNo 127888

Ordered under Navy Contract #Noa(S) 51-020, this AD-4N, c/n 7903, was accepted into the US Navy on 8 December 1952 and delivered on 10 December 1952. It was first assigned to FASRON 691 at NAS San Diego, California, on 30 December 1952, transferring to FASRON 10 at NAS Moffett Field after being re-converted from a -4N to a -4NA on 31 March 1953.

In September 1953, it was assigned to VA-125 and was shipped overseas with Carrier Air Group 102 (CAG-102). It spent a year overseas before returning to NAS Miramar, California, on 1 October 1954. On 28 October, it was transferred to the Naval Air Reserve Training Unit (NARTU) at NAS Glenview, Illinois, but its time there was brief, and it was soon assigned to O&R with NAS Quonset Point, Rhode Island, on 6 May 1955. Its next move, in the company of many of its contemporaries, was to 'The Boneyard', the storage facility at NAF Litchfield Park, Arizona; its brief life was seemingly over.

The MDU aid to France brought a reprieve, as the aircraft was reclaimed to

NAS Norfolk for refurbishment on 10 May 1960 and formally sold to the French on 31 May of that year. Like all French Skyraiders, it retained its original BuNo with the addition of #65 and carried the code 21-ZM. It saw some limited combat in Algeria during a period of service with Armée de l'Air.

At the end of this period, the aircraft was sold to a civilian owner – Jack Spanich – and was finally returned to his home city of Detroit from Chateaudun Air Base in France on 28 May 1977. It changed hands several times subsequent to that, being operated by Preston Parish, Kalamazoo, Michigan, from 28 April 1977, and working under US Army TT contract, based

Port view of the A-1E (BuNo. 132649) Coded 2, on display at the United States Air Force Museum at Wright-Patterson Field, Ohio. This aircraft was flown by Major Bernard Fisher on 10 March 1966, when he rescued a fellow pilot shot down over South Vietnam in the midst of enemy troops, a deed for which he was awarded the Medal of Honor. This aircraft, which was later severely damaged in combat in South Vietnam, was returned in 1967 for preservation at the Air Force Museum. Courtesy of USAF Museum, Ohio

there in 1978. By August 1982, the aircraft was with the Southern Packing and Storage company at Greenville, Tennessee, before being finally acquired by the Kalamazoo Aviation History Museum, from Mr Tom Austin, in February 1983. Restored by the museum, it was repainted in the colour scheme used by VA-125 operating from the carrier USS *Boxer* during the Korean War (although there is a chronology problem with the 'B' on the tail and the yellow stripe). It carries the US Navy serial 127888/B.

BuNo 132649

This aircraft was the famous mount of Major Bernard Fisher, USAF, in which he won his Medal of Honor in Vietnam, on 10 March 1966. This A-1E, former AD-5, not only survived his daring landing under fire, but took no less than 19 hits in the process and still got off the deck again. Patched up after this episode, it suffered further heavy damage, when it was forced to make a belly landing after running out of runway while putting down with a shredded vertical stabilizer. It almost failed to make it back to the States in one piece!

Safely transported home, the aircraft arrived at the United States Air Force Museum at Wright-Patterson Air Base in 1967, where it was lovingly patched up, and put on display, in its original colours and carrying its original serial, 52-32649/IZ.

BuNo 124121

This aircraft made its maiden flight on 24 January 1951, and served with VC-11 from February of that year until August 1952, being part of Unit 'D' between August

Royal Navy AEW-1 WT121 (415/CU) at Culdrose. Arthur Pearcy Archive, by courtesy of Audrey Pearcy

1951 and May 1952. In October 1952, it was allocated as part of the first Royal Navy's AEW batch, and was sent to Quonset Point NAS to be refitted. It finally arrived at Norfolk NAS, Virginia on 16 March 1953, and had the sea-voyage preservation treatment applied on 24 April. Although originally ready for shipment by 1 May of that year, it had to undergo further modification, to Royal Navy standards and, on completion of this, was again preserved, on 3 July. On 15 September 1953, it was finally loaded aboard the American transport *Green Mountain State*, and crossed the North Atlantic, arriving at Abbotsinch RNAS on 25 September.

After going through the RDU schedule of treatment, the aircraft was delivered to Culdrose RNAS on 18 March 1954, given a Royal Navy number of 326, and assigned to 'E' Flight, which later became 'D' Flight. With this unit, it went to Malta, was based at Hal Far airfield for a period, and was then due to be shipped back to the UK as deck cargo of a freighter, and was therefore given preservation treatment. This order was rescinded and it stayed at Hal Far until 22 June 1956, when it returned home under its own power, reaching Culdrose once more on 6 July 1956.

The aircraft was renumbered as 428 and assigned to 'D' Flight, but, by May 1957, it had again been redesignated (as '428/B'), and on 13 November was temporarily assigned to 'C' Flight, before rejoining 'D' Flight on 2 December. On 30 October

1958, it was assigned to the HQ Flight; before it joined, further modernization was carried out, which was completed on 5 June 1959. It was renumbered yet again (as '415') before being transferred to NARIU at Lee-on-Solent on 22 August, where it was fitted with UHF equipment to bring it up to date. The aircraft served with HQ Flight in Cornwall between 29 September 1959 and 22 September 1960, and then was put into storage.

This aircraft was selected as one of two AEW-1s to be retained as museum exhibits and refurbished accordingly as '415/CU'. It appeared on display at 'open days' while the base remained active, being placed back into storage after each event. In 1972, it was decided finally to place it on permanent outdoor display at the Fleet Air Arm Museum. This involved a complex passage from Culdrose to Yeovilton, during which the aircraft was airlifted by a Royal Navy Sea King helicopter of 706 Squadron from Culdrose to the Royal Fleet Auxiliary ship *Engadine* in the English Channel, which then steamed up to a point off the Somerset Coast, where another Sea King from 737 Squadron carried the aircraft on a winch to HMS *Heron*.

In June 1972, the Skyraider was placed on display outside the Fleet Air Arm Museum, at RNAS Yeovilton, Somerset, as WT121/CU-415. Due to weather deterioration, it was brought inside in 1996 and stored at the back of the main hangar.

When the new hangar is constructed, funded by money from the National Lottery, this particular aircraft will be given a more prominent place of honour, as befits its long service with the Royal Navy.

BuNo 135300

Displayed in the main hangar at United States Naval Air Museum, Pensacola, Florida, since 1976, this AD-6 (A-1H) carries the paint scheme and markings of VA-25 which flew from the USS *Coral Sea* (CV-43), with tail-code NL.

This aircraft was accepted into the US Navy on 28 June 1954, serving briefly with FASRON 12 before moving to its first operational unit, VA-55, the following month. The following spring it was embarked aboard the carrier *Philippine Sea* (CVA-47) and in April sailed for the Western Pacific for a six-month cruise, returning Stateside in November. A refit at NAS Alameda, including a repaint from Midnite Blue to Light Grey, and another period with FASRON 12 followed, before 135300 was assigned to VA-155 in June 1957. Embarkation aboard the carrier *Shangri-La* (CVA-38) followed in March 1958, again for the Western Pacific.

This commission was interrupted by the war scare brought on by the shelling of Nationalist Chinese Quemoy and Matsu islands, and the threatened Communist invasion of Taiwan itself in August 1958,

Not rare at all! There are of course a large number of Douglas Skyraiders of various variants in museums and flying all over the world. This is understandable considering the success, diversity of use and ownership and longevity of this vintage dive-bomber of World War II design, but which found a useful rôle in the post-war US fleet from Korea to Vietnam, and in the air forces of many other nations in a whole variety of rôles, from Airborne Radar Warning to Anti-Submarine and Close Air Transport missions. Not a bad record for an aircraft that, legend has it, was sketched out overnight by Ed Heinemann and associates in a hotel room after the failure of the BTD!

This particular model is the pristine static display at Pensacola which carries the markings for VA-25, which served aboard the USS Coral Sea (CV-43) and was photographed at the National Museum of Naval Aviation, on 3 April 1997. Peter C. Smith

when *Shangri-La* was one of six US aircraft carriers with the Seventh Fleet that gave Beijing pause for thought. With the end of the crisis and return to San Diego, 135300 was moved into store at Litchfield Park's 'Boneyard'.

That was not the end of the aircraft's career, however. Redesignated as an A-1H, 135300 returned to active service with VA-145 aboard the new carrier USS *Constellation* (CVA-64) in February 1963, again in the Pacific, before once more being put ashore and refitted. In 1964–65, it was a reserve aircraft with VA-25, and was then assigned to VA-52. In 1966, it embarked aboard the carrier *Ticonderoga* (CVA-14), its first combat mission in 12 years of service being a rescap sortie, made on 11 November 1966. It was continually in action for the next six months, logging a total of 107 combat missions over Vietnam and Laos, including spotting for warships' heavy guns during Operation Sea Dragon.

The aircraft was recommissioned with the VA-25 aboard the carrier *Coral Sea* (CVA-43), and continued in action during 1967/68 in a wide variety of combat rôles, both north and south of the DMZ, with both 'feet wet' and 'feet dry' missions. It survived them all. By this time, the Spads were finally being withdrawn from the US Navy's front-line operations as attack aircraft. BuNo 135300 had the honour of flying the final Navy combat mission.

The aircraft arrived at Pensacola on 12 April 1968, and was placed in storage. In 1973, it was renovated, being painted in its existing livery, and put on display in the new main building.

BuNo 126935

This AD-4NA (A-1D) led an eventful life. After early service in the United States, it was assigned to the French *Armée de l'Air*, and, on arrival on 11 January 1961, received the number '56'. One of those Skyraiders that were transferred to Chad, on 7 April 1976, it was subsequently purchased as surplus to requirements by Didier Chable, in August 1988. It was transported by road from N'djamena to Niamey in Niger in September, where it underwent some restoration work. It was finally delivered to France on 7 February 1989, where it was kept at Melun-Villaroche airfield.

The aircraft received the French civil registration of F-AZFO but was then purchased by Richard Bertea, of Corona del Mar, California, who shipped it to Long Beach in September 1989. From there, it finally arrived at Chino on 9 September, received the United States registration N2088G, and now flies as 'Marines/126935/HB-14'.

The aircraft is painted Midnite Blue, and carries the colours of the US Marine Corps, with tail-coding HB, and NX 2088G, with H14 carried on her forward wheel fairings.

Frontal view of US Marines AD-4N, BuNo 126935 (coded HB) BU NX 2088G in the Aero Trader hanger on 15 March 1998. Kevin R. Smith

BuNo 132683

This aircraft is one of the ex-VNAF Skyraiders acquired by David Tallichet, shipped to Long Beach, and initially stored alongside the McDonnell Douglas Long Beach plant.

After its war service, this AD5 (A-1E) was one of the Vietnamese Spads to find sanctuary from the Communist takeover by fleeing to Thailand. In 1979, it was recovered from there by Yesterdays Air Force, who brought it back to Long Beach along with a single-seater A-1H, in January 1980. The aircraft remained at Long Beach for many years, until, in April 1983, Tallichet succeeded in making it airworthy, and it received the American Civil Registration of N39147. Apart from a period on loan to the USAF Museum at March AFB, California, it has been based at Chino Airfield, California, ever since.

Starboard quarter view of Skyraider BuNo 132683 (N39147) in natural finish on outside storage pad at the Planes of Fame Museum, Chino, 15 March 1998. Kevin R. Smith

The aircraft is currently in natural finish, with only the eye-catching propeller and the blue-tinted cockpit canopy adding any colour, but it is largely intact.

BuNo 135332

This sad Skyraider, with its outer-wing panels and much more missing, was located at the Aero Trader site, Chino Airport, California, in 1998. It is thought to be another of the David Tallichet Skyraiders, a former AD-6 (A01H) brought back from Thailand in 1982, and was stored with Yesterdays Air Force at Chino, from September of that year, with the Civilian Registration N32612. In April 1983, it was re-registered as N39148 and continued to fly for a while.

Painted overall yellow with metallic leading-edge panels, after fuselage and empennage, and stripped of its outer-wing sections, its engine and much else, the aircraft is currently stored, and no work is being done on it.

BuNo 126922

This AD-4N was supplied to the US Marine Corps, and used by them during the Korean War. It was later overhauled and then transferred to the French *Armée de l'Air* in 1960. The French used it (as No. 42) in strikes against the FNLA Guerrilla forces in Algeria and then it went to Gabon. It was handed over the Gabonese Air Force on 8 February 1976 and flew with

Starboard forward view of BuNo 135332, yellow-nosed Skyraider in storage at the Aero Trader site, Chino Airport, California, 15 March 1998. Kevin R. Smith

them as 126922/TR-K. When they had finished with it in 1985, they put it up for sale.

The aircraft was recovered by *Aero Retro*, of St Rambert-d'Albon, France, in 1985, and shipped to Le Havre, where it arrived on 17 April of that year. Registered in France as F-AZED, it was owned by Amicale Jean Baptiste Salis and Jean François Perri et Partners of Le Havre from 27 August 1986, until December 1991, when it was taken over by The Fighter Collection in England.

On arrival at their headquarters, at the Imperial War Museum airfield, Duxford, near Cambridge, on Christmas Eve 1991, the aircraft carried the registration number 26922/JS-937 until 1993. Repainted to resemble the USS *Intrepid*'s VA-176 aircraft, as 26922/AK-402, with tail-coding AK, it flies under the civilian registration G-RAID.

BuNo 122811

This Skyraider, with the tail markings 'NATTC Memphis', belongs to the Experimental Aircraft Association (EAA). It is a former AD-3 (A-1E) c/n 6933, which

The EAA Skyraider, BuNo 122811, with tail markings NATTC Memphis, seen here at Oshkosh on 29 July 1998. Frank A. Husdon

A low-level pass by this l'Armée de l'Air **Skyraider AD-4 , BuNo 125716, with French registration F-AZFN and coded 22 DG, which carries red tail and wing tips.** SIRPA/ECPA France

served with that unit before being acquired by the EAA Museum at Oshkosh in 1978, and has served as a static display aircraft there ever since.

BuNo 125716

After service in the French Air Force (as 'No. 11') this aircraft was later transferred to Chad where, on 15 February 1977, it was sold to Didier Chable, at Melun-

Villaroche. It was taken by land transporter from N'djamena air base across the Niamey, in Niger, in September 1988, for restoration, and arrived at Melun airfield in France on 9 November. Since 1993, it has been flown by J.J. Joyeux of Aulnat.

This French-owned former AD-4 Skyraider has *Armée de l'Air* colours and markings. Coded 22 DG, she carries red wing tips and rear tail tip, has the civilian registration F-AZFN, and flies as 125716/22-DC.

BuNo 126956

This is a French-owned and registered Skyraider, an AD-4NA (A-1D), which served with VMC-1 in the States before being transferred to France's *Armée de l'Air* on 4 November 1960. It served as 'No. 45' for 16 years, before being transferred to Gabon on 8 February 1976, where it flew as 126956/TR-KMP.

In 1984, it was purchased by *Aero Retro*, of St Rambert-d'Albon, took the French

Landing of US Marine Corps **Skyraider AD-4NA, BuNo 126956, formerly of VMC-1, tail coded RM, but with French registration F-AZDG.** M. Hiscock

civilian registration of F-WZDQ, and was delivered to *Amicale Jean Baptiste Salis* at La Ferté Alais airfield. On 5 September 1985, re-registered as F-AZDQ, it began flying as 126956/RM3, repainted in its former US Marine Corps livery.

BuNo 126965

This is the Skyraider of Eric Vormezeele, of Brasschaat, Belgium, which flies in French *Armée de l'Air* colours, with a unit badge proudly emblazoned on its nose, and the French civilian registration OO-FOR. It is an AD-4N (A-1D) that went to France as No. 54 and served in North Africa for many years before going to Chad, on 7 April 1976. On retirement, it was stored at Chateaudun Air Base, from 1979 to 1983, carrying the French civilian registration F-ZVMM, until it became the property of M. Vormezeele on 27 June 1985. It received its Certificate of Airworthiness on 26 November of that year, and is regularly seen at air displays all over Europe.

BuNo 139665

A former AD-6 (A-1H), this is the third of the David Tallichet Yankee Air Force Skyraiders, c/n 10897.

This was one of the VNAF Skyraiders that managed to flee to Thailand after the fall of Saigon. Confiscated by the Royal Thai Air Force, it remained in that country until 1979, when Yesterdays Air Force successfully bid for it as part of a package deal in 1979. It was brought back to the USA and, from 1980, was stored alongside the McDonnell Douglas plant at Long Beach for some time, awaiting restoration. The aircraft was transferred to Chino on April 1983, and assigned the civilian registration N39149, and has remained there ever since.

BuNo 139674

This A-1H (AD-6) aircraft is on display at the War Remnants Museum, Ho Chi Minh City. It was one of those Skyraiders belonging to the Vietnamese Air Force that was in storage, and was thus captured intact by the Communists. It has been refurbished and equipped to what is considered to be its original configuration, and has 'US Air Force' painted in white on either side of the pilot's cockpit.

BuNo 132598

This interesting machine is the gate guard at the USAF Museum at the famous conversion and training airfield of Hurlburt Field, Florida, which is home of the 'Jungle Jims'.

One of the few former AD-5Ns (A-1G) supplied to the VNAF, this aircraft was later assigned to the USAF's famous 1 Special Operations Wing, where it carried the

A former AD-6 (A-1H) this is the third of the David C. Tallichet Yankee Air Force Skyraiders, c/n 10897. She is seen here at Chino in the 1980s carrying the tail code 'NJ', nose code '263' and the markings of US Navy Squadron VA-122. Arthur Pearcy Archive, by courtesy of Audrey Pearcy

identity code of 51-598. It was brought back to the States in 1973 and has been on display there in camouflage colours as 'USAF 51-598' ever since.

BuNo 132261

On external display at Camp Barrett, close to Marine Corps Air Station Quantico, Virginia, since 1976, this AD-4B Skyraider, c/n 8369, which served with VMA-121, has suffered badly from the weather over two decades.

In July 1998, the aircraft underwent full restoration work at the US Marine Corps Air Museum at Quantico. It is still painted dark blue and carries all its original markings.

BuNo 134472

The Royal Thai Air Force Museum at Don Muang Air Base, near Bangkok, is the home of this A-1H (AD-6) Skyraider, which served with the Vietnamese Air Force as 134462 until the Communist takeover in 1972 forced it to flee. The Thai service code 14/072 and tail-code FR in black, along with the squadron badge on the tail, denote her subsequent employment.

Since 1985, the aircraft has been restored to static-display status. Its name 'Proud American' is stencilled in white, with one word on either side of the engine cowling.

BuNo 135152

This former AD-5W (EA-1E), c/n 10229, served with the NATTC at Memphis Naval Air Station, and was stored there from 1973. It was recovered in a derelict condition by Harry Doan, of New Smyrna Beach, Florida, in 1989 and restored by him between 1991 and 1992. It was bought at auction on 30 October 1992 by Richard Bertea, and was delivered to Chino, California, from Florida on 13 February 1993.

The aircraft underwent further restoration work until July of 1993 and, in April

Douglas A-1 Skyraider BuNo 139674, on display at the War Remnants Museum, Ho Chi Minh City (Saigon) on 12 November 1997. The rocket launcher pod has been mounted on the under-fuselage bomb position, where, had it been really used, would have done the prop no good at all! Stewart Lanham

Royal Thai Air Force Museum is the home of this A-1H Skyraider, BuNo 134472, which served with the Vietnamese Air Force until forced to flee on the Communist takeover. The Thai service code 14/072 and tail code FR in black along with the squadron badge on the tail denote her subsequent employment. Since 1985 she has been restored to static display status and has the 'Proud American' stencilled with one word on either side of her engine cowling in white. Simon Watson

Three-quarter starboard view of Skyraider EA1E (ex AD-5W) BuNo 135152 (N65164) at 'Sun 'n' Fun', Lakeland, Florida, on 20 April 1998. Frank A. Hudson

(Below) A nice view of 'Naked Fanny', BuNo 126959 (alter ego N959AD Skyraider AD-4NA ex) at 'Sun 'n' Fun', Lakeland, Florida, on 19 April 1998. Frank A. Hudson

1995, was being flown by Avery's Antique Airplanes, Inc., of Morganton, North Carolina, under the civilian registration N65164.

BuNo 126959

'Naked Fanny' was a former AD-4N (A-1D) Spad, with civilian registration N959AD, c/n 7759. It served in France's *Armée de l'Air* from 7 December 1960 as 'No. 50', before being transferred to Chad on 7 April 1976. In August 1988, it was part of the batch of Skyraiders purchased by Didier Chable at Melun-Villaroche, France, and was transported by low-loader from N'djamena to Naimey, Niger, in September 1988, and given the French Civilian Registration F-AZFP.

After restoration, it arrived in France on 20 March 1989, and from September of that year was owned by Chancellor Aviation of Costa Mesa, California, who shipped it to Long Beach and then to Chino. In June 1995, it became part of the collection of Warbirds Associates, Inc., of Wilmington, Delaware, and is now registered as N2088V and flown by Dr Mike Schloss.

AD-1 BuNo 09155 – Performance Data

Gross weight, lb (bomber)	16,151
Gross weight, lb (scout)	13,978
CG per cent MAC, gear extended (bomber)	21.9
CG per cent MAC, gear extended (scout)	22.8
CG per cent MAC, gear retracted (bomber)	23.0
CG per cent MAC, gear retracted (scout)	24.0
Maximum speed at normal rated power VT, knots	
Sea level	231.5
ACA, low blower (5,400ft)	244.0
ACA, high blower (16,000ft)	256.5
Maximum speed at military rated power, VT knots	
Sea level (bomber)	246.0
Sea level (scout)	272.5
ACA, low blower (4,500ft)	257.0
ACA, high blower (15,200ft)	259.0
Maximum rate of climb at normal rated power, fpm	
Sea level	2,480
ACA, low blower (3,300ft)	2,430
ACA, high blower (14,800ft)	1,740
Maximum rate of climb at military rated power, fpm	
Sea level	3,030
ACA, low blower (2,000ft)	3,000
ACA, high blower (14,300ft)	1,900
Service ceiling	
Normal rated power, ft	30,200
Military rated power, ft	31,100
Take-off data at military rated power (flap setting: full)	
True airspeed at TO, knots	71.3
Distance in zero wind, knots	725,0
Distance in 25 knot wind, ft	321.0
Calibrated airspeed at the stall, knots	
Clean condition, power on	87.2
Clean condition, power off	91.0
Landing condition, power on	72.0
Landing condition, power off	76.7

STABILITY CHARACTERISTICS

Bomber condition

Gross weight (lb)	16,151
CG per cent MAC, gear extended	21.9
CG per cent MAC, gear retracted	23.0

(Key to stability characteristics: P = Positive, PW = Positive but weak, N = Neutral, * Positive for speeds above the trim speed.)

Longitudinal

Type	Controls	NR Climb	NRP Vmax	CR	G	PA	D
Static	Free	P	P	P	P	*N	P
	Fixed	P	P	P	P	*N	P
Dynamic	Free	P	P	PW	PW	P	P
	Fixed	P	P	PW	PW	P	P

Lateral

Type	Controls	NRP Climb	CR	G	PA
Static	Free	P	P	P	PW
	Fixed	P	P	P	PW
Dynamic	Free	P	P	P	P
	Fixed	P	P	P	P

Directional

Type	Controls	NRP Climb	CR	G	PA
Static	Free	P	P	P	P
	Fixed	P	P	P	P
Dynamic	Free	P	P	P	P
	Fixed	P	P	P	P

High-Speed Longitudinal Stability Characteristics

	Dive No. 1	Dive No. 2
Loading	2,000lb bomber	2,000-lb bomber
Gross weight, lb	16,151	16,151
Altitude at start of dive		
$-H_{pi}$-ft	27,000	27,000
V_T kts	Trim for zero control	150
Force in dive		
V_iMax, kts	345	355
Altitude of V_iMax	17,500	17,000
Elv. Force, lb	35 for pull-out	80 push to hold In dive
G	2.0	–
Remarks	Acceptable	Unacceptable

*Maximum allowable push force as set forth in para D-5 of NAVER Spec SR-119A, 7 April 1945, was 60lb.

STALLING CHARACTERISTICS

Bomber condition, gross weight (lb)	16,151
CG per cent MAC, gear extended	21.9
CG per cent MAC, gear retracted	23.0

Configuration	G	CR	L	PA
rpm	600	2,170	500	2170
MAP	Power off	19in	Power off	24in
Tab – elevator	3¼ degrees NU	1½ degrees NU	5 degrees NU	3 degrees NU
Tab – aileron	3½ degrees RWD	3 degrees RWD	2 degrees RWD	10 degrees RWD
Rudder	3 degrees R	1 degree L	0	4 degrees R
Trim speed (knots, IAS)	125	125	95	95
Warning speed (knots, IAS)	93	90	78	None
Shake	Mild	Mild	None	None
Stick movement	Full aft	6in aft	7in aft	3in aft
Stalling speed (knots, CAS)	91.0	87.2	76.7	72.0
Roll	Mild	Moderate	Moderate	Moderate
Pitch	Moderate Down	Moderate Down	Moderate Down	Moderate Down
Altitude lost, ft	700	500	800	300

CARBON MONOXIDE SURVEY

Service flight configurations

	MRP level flight, mix. AR	MRP climb mix. AR	Carrier approach
Face level	.006*	.0028*	.0006 Canopy open
			0 Canopy closed
Knee level	.055*	.003*	
Oxygen regulator level	.055*	.0035*	

* Readings taken with cockpit ventilator turned 'ON', and where maximum concentrations observed.

Taxiing (canopy open)

	Wind from head-on	Wind from starboard	Wind from aft	Wind from port
Face level	.003	.0025	.003	.0025
Knee level	.003	.0025	.0035	.0025
Oxygen regulator level	.0025	.0025	.0035	.0025

TEST LOADINGS

as High-Performance Scout Plane

Main Loading Items		Main Loading Items	
Full internal fuel, lb	2,109	Full internal fuel, lb	2,109
Full oil, lb	188	Full oil, lb	188
Ammunition ballast, lb	268	Ammunition ballast, lb	268
Pilot ballast, lb	200	Pilot ballast, lb	200
Bomb installation (1-2,000lb bomb)	2,030	Airplane take-off gross weight, lb	13,978
Radar (droppable)	143	CG position, gear up, per cent MAC	24.0
Airplane take-off gross weight, lb	16,151	CG position, gear down, per cent MAC	22.8
CG position, gear up, per cent MAC	23.0		
CG position, gear down, per cent MAC	21.9		

Rescue Radio

Communications was the key to success or failure in most of the Skyraiders' missions over Vietnam. Precision and speed were vital if the Spad was to deliver her payload where it counted, and these depended on good air-to-ground and ground-to-air radio contact.

At A Shau in March 1966, one of the bravest Skyraider actions ever took place, earning Major Bernard Fisher his Medal of Honor. Just after the decision had been made to go in to rescue Myers, a C-123 crew flying in the vicinity started to tape the conversations of the mission pilots, unbeknown to the participants. While not every voice is identifiable, this transcript of the tape presents a graphic and unique insight into Skyraider action in the hell of Vietnam.[95]

Unknown voice:	He's about 20 feet.
Second unknown voice:	
	Understand he's 20 feet?
Major Fisher:	Roger.
Captain Lucas:	Which way you gonna land?
Fisher:	I'm gonna make a 180-degree, come in to the southeast.
Lucas:	OK. Well then, we'll come in behind and strafe parallel to your heading.
Fisher:	OK, I'm rolling in now.
Unknown:	Make it slow or you'll lose it.
Lucas:	I'm right behind you, Bernie. I took a hit in my pitot system, and I'm smoking a little.
Captain Hague:	OK, Luke, I'm right back at your six o'clock.
Lucas:	Do you see any smoke?
Hague:	Negative. You look pretty good.
Lucas:	OK, my air speed's gone and my hydraulic pressure's fluctuating.
Hague:	All right. You want me to stay with you?
Lucas:	OK, Bernie, you gonna land on this pass?
Unknown:	Five-two [call-sign] this is 81; over.
FAC:	Five-two [call-sign].
Unknown:	We're overhead your position for pylon turn at 1240. We're ten minutes late. We have 500 GPs [eight general-purpose bombs] and 20 mike-mike [20-mm cannon].
FAC:	All right, sir, hold high and dry. At the present time we have A-1Es working underneath. There's an aircraft down in there and we're trying to get the pilot out.
Unknown:	This is 07-1 [call-sign]. We're still orbiting up here at 20,000.
FAC:	Roger, hold high and dry now, sir.
Unknown:	Roger.
Unknown:	Now five-two, this is Crandall 56 with eight napes [napalm] and eight bombs and 20 mike-mike.
FAC:	Roger, stand by. The weather underneath is not too good for napalm at the present time.
Unknown:	Roger.
Lucas:	OK, Paco, are you in trail with us now?

[No response – Captain Vasquez was experiencing radio difficulties at this time]

Unknown:	Zero three, uh, shoe shine, zero three.
Lucas:	Roger, go ahead, Jim [fighter pilot].
Jim:	Roger, which kind of help do you need? We're three miles up the valley.

Lucas:	OK, Jim, do you read me?
Jim:	I hear ya.
Lucas:	OK, babe, come on down the valley. As you come down the valley, you run over that airstrip, pick up a heading of one five zero. You can run the napalm right down the east side of the runway.
Jim:	Understand. One-fifty down the east side of the runway. Okay, got that, Pete? [Jim's wingman].
Pete:	Roger dodger, Jim.
Lucas:	You'll see quite a bit of smoke.
Jim:	OK, I see an aircraft down there to the left. Who's that? You?
Lucas:	No, I'm coming down the east side of the runway now. Why don't you come down one time and look it over.
Unknown:	OK, this is Hobo 21. We're up here Luke.
FAC:	Hobo 21, Bird dog 52.
Unknown:	Roger 52. We're orbiting the airfield to the north at 6,000 feet.
Lucas:	OK, let's hit everything Denny, except the fort.
Hague:	Roger, I gotcha, but I'm Winchester [out of ammunition].
Lucas:	OK, so am I. Let's keep making passes through. Maybe they don't know it.
Hague:	Roger.
Lucas:	OK, Jim, the area's smokin' pretty badly, and you'll see an aircraft burning on the runway. Bernie's taking off to the north.
Jim:	OK, understand to the north. OK, I can see him. Is he rolling now?
Hague:	Roger-Roger.
Lucas:	OK, get the east side, Denny.
Hague:	Roger, Babe.
Jim:	Where do you want those trenches strafed, Jon?
Lucas:	OK, you got us in sight? We're breaking off. I'm coming left.
Jim:	Where do you want the strafe? Right on the east end of the runway?
Lucas:	Yeah, put it all down the east side of the runway, in the grass area. Put a couple of bursts in there and then get hold of Barry.
Jim:	Get hold of who?
Lucas:	Correction, it'll be Hound Dog 12 if he's still up.
Jim:	OK, right, we'll be coming right in now.
Lucas:	We already got him out.
Jim:	Roger.

All-Weather Skyraider VA(AW)-33

A selection of dates showing the detached work by this unit's Skyraiders between 1958 and 1963.

CO	VARIANT		DETACHMENT	CARRIER OR BASE	PERIOD	RÔLE
	AD-5N	AD-5Q				
Captain R.M. Bruning, USN	30	13	33	*Intrepid* (CVA-11)	1 July–22 Aug 58	
			36	*Randolph* (CVA15)	28 Jun–22 Aug 58	Active and passive electronics countermeasures
			37A	*Franklin D. Roosevelt* (CVA-42)	3 Sep–17 Oct 58	
			42	*Forrestal* (CVA-59)	16 Jul 58–12 Mar 59	Active and passive electronics countermeasures
			45	*Saratoga* (CVA-60)	30 Sep 58–1 Feb 59	
	21	20	45	*Essex* (CVA-9)	Returned 19 Oct 58	
Captain W.W. Jones, USN	9	17	33	*Intrepid* (CVA-11)	1 Jan 59–	
			43	NA Roosevelt Roads, P.A.	Feb–Mar 59	Active and passive electronics countermeasures
	7	16	7	NAS Guantanamo Bay, Cuba	26 Apr–13 Jun 59	Active and passive electronics countermeasures
				NAS Jacksonville, FLA	26–29 May 59	Active electronic countermeasures for 2nd Fleet
				NAS Oceana, VA	19–25 Jun 59	Active electronic countermeasures for 2nd Fleet
	7	17	1	NAS Oceana, VA	1–9 Jul 59	
			42	*Forrestal* (CVA-59)	13 Jul–1 Sep 59	Shakedown cruise
			43	*Saratoga* (CVA-60)	1 Aug 59–1 Mar 60	To Mediterranean
			TF-1Q	NAS Guantanamo Bay, Cuba	2 Aug–5 Sep 59	ECM duties
				NAS Oceana, VA	13 Sep–11 Oct	ECM duties
	0	14	41	*Independence* (CVA-61)	27-Oct-59	
			15	NAS Oceana, VA	13 Sep–11 Oct	ECM duties
			41	MAS Cherry Point, NC	3–7 Nov 59	ECM duties
Commander R.C. Coats, USN	0	12	42	*Forrestal* (CVA-59)	2 Jan 60–15 Feb 61	To Mediterranean
			41	*Independence* (CVA-61)	1–15 Jan 60	
			15	NAS Oceana, VA	13 Mar–1 Apr 60	
			4	MAS Cherry Point, NC	23–31 Mar 60	ECM duties
Commander H.K. Von Egger, USN	0	12	41	*Independence* (CVA-61)	1 Oct 60–1 Mar 61	Deployed to Mediterranean
		2		Sperry Corporation	6–21 Dec 60	Evaluation of MPS-21 Radar
		6		MAS Cherry Point, NC	12–19 Jan 61	ECM duties
		1		CIC School at Glynco, GA	6–20 Mar 61	Incorporation of active ECM into CIC syllabus
	AD-5W	AD-5Q				ASW function added to duties utilizing AD-5Ws
Commander H.H. Dunkim, Jr	22	13	42	*Forrestal* (CVA-59)	18 Feb–24 Aug 61	
			48	*Wasp* (CVS-18)	4 Jun–2 Sep 61	Transfer from VAW-12 to VAW-33 on 1 Aug 61
			34	*Lake Champlain* (CVS-39)	27 Jun–11 Aug 61	Transfer from VAW-12 to VAW-33 on 1 Aug 61
			45	*Essex* (CVA-9)	31 Jul–18 Aug 61	Transfer from VAW-12 to VAW-33 on 1 Aug 61
			34	*Lake Champlain* (CVS-39)	16 Aug–31 Aug	

CO	VARIANT		DETACHMENT	CARRIER OR BASE	PERIOD	RÔLE
	AD-5W	AD-5Q				
			45	*Essex* (CVA-9)	14 Sep–3 Oct	
			34	*Lake Champlain* (CVS-39)	27 Sep–13 Oct	
			41	*Independence* (CVA-61)	1 Aug 61–	
		1		NAS Jacksonville, FLA	18–21 Apr 61	OPNAV 4 evaluation
				NAS Oceana, VA	27–30 Apr 61	ECM duties 2nd Fleet
				NAS Oceana, VA	4–7 May 61	ECM duties 2nd Fleet
		4		Key West	19–27 May 61	Special ECM duties
		6		NORFOLK, VA	17–23 Jul 61	ECM duties for fleet
		4		Key West	7–14 Aug 61	Special ECM duties
				NAS Jacksonville, FLA	14–19 Aug 61	OPNAV 8 evaluation
				Charleston, SC	13–Sep 61	ECM duties for fleet
				NAS Jacksonville, FLA	17–Sep 61	OPNAV 8 evaluation
	18	12	34	*Lake Champlain* (CVS-39)	4–27 Nov 61	
			34	*Lake Champlain* (CVS-39)	8–22 Mar 62	
			41	*Independence* (CVA-61)	14–23 Mar 62	
			42	*Forrestal* (CVA-59)	5 Jan–9 Mar 62	
			43	*Saratoga* (CVA-60)	1 Nov 61–31 Mar 62	
			45	*Essex* (CVA-9)	16 Oct 61–22 Feb 62	
			48	*Wasp* (CVS-18)	20 Nov 61–31 Mar 62	
				Key West	29 Oct–4 Nov 61	Special mission ECM Key West
				Key West	26 Nov–6 Dec 61	Special mission
				Key West	26 Nov–6 Dec 61	Special mission ECM Exercise, Key West
		2		FLTRACENNPT	Various dates Dec 61	Radar service duties
		1		*Roy O. Hale*	4 Dec 61	Radar service duties
		2		*Berry*	12 Dec 61	Radar service duties
		2		*McCafferty*	13–14 Dec 61	Radar service duties
				Harwood	27 Dec 61	Services for Builders Trials Atlantic City, NJ
				FLTRACENNPT	Various dates Jan 62	Radar service duties
				McDonough	4 Jan 62	Radar service duties
				Harwood	17 Jan 62	Radar service duties
				Lawrence	25–26 Jan 62	Radar service duties
				FLTRACENNPT	Various dates Feb 62	Radar service duties
				Sampson	1–2 Feb 62	Radar services, Boston, Mass.
				DESDIV 81	6–7 Feb 62	Radar services, Charleston, NC
				Ware	12 Feb 62	Radar services
				Boxer	13 Feb 62	Radar services
				Key West	19–25 Feb 62	Special mission, ECM exercises Key West
				FLTRACENNPT	Various dates Mar 62	Radar services
				Sampson	15 Mar 62	Radar services, Boston, Mass.
				Key West	25–31 Mar 62	Special mission, ECM exercises Key West
				Warrington	30 Mar 62	Radar services
Commander J.B. Black, USN			60	*Saratoga* (CVA-60)	1 Apr–11 May 62	
			39	*Lake Champlain* (CVS-39)	5–19 Apr 62	
			11	*Intrepid* (CVA-11)	5 Apr–31 May 62	
			59	*Forrestal* (CVA-59)	8 Apr–10 May 62	
			62	*Independence* (CVA-61)	15 Apr–28 Aug 62	
			39	*Lake Champlain* (CVS-39)	26 Apr–21 May 62	
			39	*Lake Champlain* (CVS-39)	31 May–7 June 62	
			59	*Forrestal* (CVA-59)	14 Jun–13 July 62	
			11	*Intrepid* (CVA-11)	14 Jun–6 Aug 62	
			18	*Wasp* (CVS-18)	8–16 Jun 62	
			39	*Lake Champlain* (CVS-39)	25 Jun–16 July 62	
			39	*Lake Champlain* (CVS-39)	22 Jul–12 Aug 62	
			59	*Forrestal* (CVA-59)	31 Jul–30 Sep 62	
			18	*Wasp* (CVS-18)	5–22 Aug 62	
			39	*Lake Champlain* (CVS-39)	28–31 Aug 62	
			18	*Wasp* (CVS-18)	6–24 Sep 62	
			39	*Lake Champlain* (CVS-39)	24–30 Sep 62	

CO	VARIANT		DETACHMENT	CARRIER OR BASE	PERIOD	RÔLE
	AD-5W	AD-5Q				
			2	FLTRACENNPT	Various dates Apr 62	Radar services
			2	*Sampson*	7 Apr 62	Radar services
			3	*Warrington*	7 Apr 62	ECM duties
			1	Key West	12 Apr 62	Special mission, radar
				Key West	23–28 Apr 62	ECM services, Key West
			2	FLTRACENNPT	Various dates May 62	Radar services
			2	*Okinawa*	8, 29 May 62	Radar services
			2	FLTRACENNPT	Various dates June 62	Radar services
				Key West	21–26 May 62	ECM services, Key West
			1	*Bainbridge*	2, 4, 9 June 62	ECM services
			2	*Roan*	4 Jun 62	ECM services
			2	*Okinawa*	6 Jun 62	Radar services
			1	Special Exercise	11 Jun 62	ECM exercise with VF-102
			2	*Sampson*	11 Jun 62	ECM exercises
				Key West	18–23 Jun 62	Special mission, ECM exercise,Key West
			1	*Sellers*	20 Jun 62	Radar services
			2	FLTRACENNPT	Various dates Jul 62	Radar services
			3	Key West	16–21 Jul 62	Special mission, ECM exercises, Key West
			2	FLTRACENNPT	Various dates Aug 62	Radar services
			1	Special Mission	4 Aug 62	Special mission, radar services
			2	*Mitscher*	15 Aug 62	Radar services
				Tench	22 Aug 62	Radar services
			4	Key West	26–31 Aug 62	Special mission, ECM exercises, Key West
			2	*Bainbridge*	30 Aug 62	AEW/TACAN/RADAR TRACKING
			4	*Bainbridge*	1–2 Sep 62	IFF/UHF, AEW services
			2	*Essex*	4 Sep 62	Radar services
			2	Special Mission	5 Sep 62	ECM
			2	FLTRACENNPT	Various dates Sep 62	Radar services
			2	*Gearing*	12 Sep 62	ECM, radar services
			4	*Bainbridge*	18–19 Sep 62	IFF/UHF, AEW services
			3	*Becuna*	19 Sep 62	ECM services
				Key West	24–30 Sep 62	ECM services, Key West
			2	*Bainbridge*	25 Sep 62	Radar services
	EA-1E	EA-1F				
			19	10		
			59	*Forrestal* (CVA-59)	1 Oct 62–2 Mar 63	
			39	*Lake Champlain* (CVS-39)	1–11 Oct 62	
			62	*Independence* (CVA-61)	10 Oct–23 Nov 62	
			18	*Wasp* (CVS-18)	11–16 Oct 62	
			18	*Wasp* (CVS-18)	20 Oct–20 Nov 62	
			39	*Lake Champlain* (CVS-39)	24 Oct–5 Dec 62	
			60	*Saratoga* (CVA-60)	22 Nov–20 Dec 62	
			18	*Wasp* (CVS-18)	20–29 Dec 62	
			39	*Lake Champlain* (CVS-39)	28 Dec 62–10 Jan 63	
			11	*Intrepid* (CVA-11)	16 Jan–22 Mar 62	
			18	*Wasp* (CVS-18)	20 Jan–11 Feb 62	
			65	*Enterorise* (CVAN-65)	24 Jan–31 Mar 62	
			39	*Lake Champlain* (CVS-39)	8–21 Feb 62	
			18	*Wasp* (CVS-18)	4–31 Mar 62	
			39	*Lake Champlain* (CVS-39)	4–23 Mar 62	
			2	FTCNPT	Various dates Oct 62	Radar tracking
			2	*The Sullivans*	9 Oct 62	Radar tracking
			2	*Hyman, Purdy, Beatty*	12 Oct 62	Radar tracking
				Leahy	15, 17, 22–24 Oct 62	ECM and radar services
			2	*Albany*	19 Oct 62	Radar tracking
			2	*Johnston*	23 Oct 62	ECM and radar services
			2	FTCNPT	Various dates Nov 62	Radar services
			2	*Albany*	17, 28 Nov 62	Radar services
			2	*Cone*	8, 18 Dec 62	ECM and radar services
			2	*Ellison*	10–11 Dec 62	ECM and radar services
			2	*Sampson*	11 Dec 62	Radar services

CO	VARIANT		DETACHMENT	CARRIER OR BASE	PERIOD	RÔLE
	EA-1E	EA-1F				
		2		*McCard*	11 Dec 62	Radar services
		2		*Yarnell*	12 Dec 62	ECM and radar services
		2		FTCNPT	Various dates Dec 62	Radar services
		2		*Albany*	14–15 Jan 63	Radar services
		2		*Yarnell*	15 Jan 63	Radar services
		2		FTCNPT	Various dates Jan 63	Radar services
		2		*Vogelsang*	21 Jan 63	Radar services
		2		*Putnam*	26 Jan 63	ECM and radar services
		2		*Ault*	30 Jan 63	ECM and radar services
		1		Sperry Corporation	5–6 Feb 63	ECM services
		2		FTCNT	Various dates Feb 63	Radar services
		2		*Saratoga*	13–15 Feb 63	ECM service
		2		*Browns*	14 Feb 63	Radar tracking
		2		*Ault*	14 Feb 63	Radar tracking
		2		*Mills*	15 Feb 63	Radar tracking
		2		*Witek*	19, 21, 26 Feb 63	Radar tracking
		2		*Putnam*	3, 11 Mar 63	ECM and radar services
		2		FTCNPT	Various dates Mar 63	Radar services
		2		*Yarnell*	27 Mar 63	Radar services
Commander T.P. McHugh, USN	EA-1E	EA-1F				
	16	12				
	A-1E					
	1					
			65	*Enterprise* (CVAN-65)	1 Apr–3 Sep 63	
			39	*Lake Champlain* (CVS-39)	4–5 Apr 63	
			59	*Forrestal* (CVA-59)	16–22 Apr 63	
			18	*Wasp* (CVS-18)	22 Apr–19 May 63	
			11	*Intrepid* (CVS-11)	10 May–15 Jul 63	
			18	*Wasp* (CVS-18)	4 June–26 Jul 63	
			62	*Independence* (CVA-62)	27 July–30 Sep 63	
			11	*Intrepid* (CVS-11)	28 Jul–10 Sep 63	
			18	*Wasp* (CVS-18)	8–17 Aug 63	
			39	*Lake Champlain* (CVS-39)	26 Aug–30 Sep 63	
Commander R.S. Gardiner, USN	69	14	59	*Forrestal* (CVA-59)	3–20 Sep 63	
			18	*Wasp* (CVS-18)	4 Oct 65	
			66	Roosevelt Roads– *Enterprise* (CVAN-65)	6 Oct–5 Nov 65	
			18	*Wasp* (CVS-18)	20–27 Oct 65	
			18	*Wasp* (CVS-18)	30 Nov–20 Dec 65	
			66	Bermuda	14–18 Dec 65	
			42	*Franklin D. Roosevelt* (CVA-42)	24 Jan–10 Feb 66	
			6	Roosevelt Roads	24–31 Jan 66	
			18	*Wasp* (CVS-18)	24 Jan–12 Feb 66	
			6	Bermuda	4–10 Feb 66	
			18	*Wasp* (CVS-18)	14–23 Mar 66	
			18	*Wasp* (CVS-18)		
Commander C.C. Neidlinger	0	11	6	NAS Oceana, VA	2–6 Apr 66	
			2A	NAS Oceana, VA	18–20 Apr 66	
			18	*Wasp* (CVS-18)	12–19 May 66	
			3	NAS Jacksonville, FLA	21–27 May 66	
			18	*Wasp* (CVS-18)	26 May–7 Jun 66	Participation in the Gemini 9 NASA Shot
			6	NAS Roosevelt Roads, PR	12–19 Jun 66	
			21	Bermuda	5–11 Jul 66	
			3	NAS Jacksonville, FLA	28 Aug–13 Sep 66	
	0	19				
			66	*America* (CVA-66)	13–19 Nov 66	
			66	*America* (CVA-66)	27 Nov–17 Dec 66	
			66	*America* (CVA-66)	7 Jan–31 Mar 67	
			11	*Intrepid* (CVS-11)	11–25 Mar 67	

Notes

CHAPTER 1

1 *See* Peter C. Smith, *Douglas SBD Dauntless*; *Curtiss SB2C Helldiver*; *Junkers Ju. 87 Stuka* and *Aichi D3A1/2 Val* (Crowood Aviation Series), Ramsbury, 1997–99.

2 Although the Blackburn Skua *did* achieve the first British air kill of the war, when one shot down a Dornier flying boat. *See* Peter C. Smith, *Blackburn Skua* (forthcoming).

3 *See* Peter C. Smith, *North American A-36 Apache* (forthcoming).

4 *See* Peter C. Smith, *Close Air Support*, New York, and Shrewsbury, 1990.

5 *See Vengeance! The Vultee Vengeance Dive Bomber*, Shrewsbury and Washington, DC, 1986.

6 Maximum weight on take-off, according to Cayley principle.

7 The only sour note relating to this mission came from Allied left-wing politicians, in both the US Congress and the British Parliament, who repeatedly seemed to let the Communist aggressors off the hook. This approach was repeated in the Vietnam war.

8 Lee M. Parsons, *The Attack Bomber – The War Years*, *Naval Aviation Confidential Bulletin*, CinC Navaer 00-75-500, Office of the Chief of Naval Operations and Bureau of Aeronautics, Navy Department, Washington, DC, August 1951. Also Lee M. Parsons, *Development of the Attack Concept, Naval Aviation Confidential Bulletin*, CO-Navaer 00-75-500, Office of the Chief of Naval Operations and Bureau of Aeronautics, Washington, DC, August 1951.

9 Lee M. Parsons, *op cit.*

10 *See* Edward H. Heinemann and Rosario Rausa, *Combat Aircraft Designer – The Ed Heinemann Story*, Annapolis, 1980.

11 *See* Peter C. Smith, *Curtiss SB2C Helldiver, op cit.*

12 Lee M. Parsons, *op cit.*

13 *See* Peter C. Smith, *Aichi D3A1/2 Val, op cit.*

14 *See* Peter C. Smith, *The Battle of Midway*, Speldhurst, 1996.

CHAPTER 2

15 *See* Peter C. Smith, *Curtiss SB2C Helldiver, op cit.*

16 Heinemann and Rausa, *Combat Aircraft Designer, op cit.*

17 Heinemann and Rausa, *Combat Aircraft Designer, op cit.*

18 Lee M. Parsons, *op cit.*

19 Heinemann and Rausa, *Combat Aircraft Designer, op cit.*

CHAPTER 3

20 *See* Commander J.A. Thomas, USN: Navy Department, Bureau of Aeronautics, Washington, *Memorandum of a Conference, Held in Bureau of Aeronautics, 2–3 June 1944, Aer-E-12-JAT, 116715, dated 1 July 1944; General Correspondence 1943–45* (Record Group 72), National Archives, College Park, Maryland.

21 Ibid. This list is slightly different from the one in Heinemann's memoirs, for example, Fiske is not included on the Official BuAer document as being present on 3 June.

22 Ibid.

23 This section is based on Edward H. Heinemann, *Report On Trip To Pacific Combat Area*, dated 27 November 1944, Report No. ES6712, El Segundo Division, Douglas Aircraft.

24A *See* Interim Report on Project TED No. PTR R-801, Investigation of *Instrument Flight Techniques and Procedures for Naval Combat Aircraft to establish standards for use with GCA (XBT2D-1)*, 1 November, 1946 to 8 May, 1947. Report dated 10 June, 1947, NATC Report Serial No TT-122, Commander W. I. Martin, U S Navy, Directory.

CHAPTER 4

24B This chapter is mainly based upon Press Report, 12 November 1948, *Douglas Skyraider*, by E. H. Heinemann, Chief Engineer, Douglas Aircraft El Segundo Engineering, made available to the author by the Naval Historical Office, Washington, DC.

25 National Advisory Committee for Aeronautics.

26 *See* Peter C. Smith, *Junkers Ju. 87 Stuka, op cit.*

27 Lee M. Parsons, *Development of the Attack Concept, op cit.*

28 Heinemann and Rausa, *Combat Aircraft Designer, op cit.*

29 *See* Peter C. Smith, *Dive Bomber!*, Ashbourne and Annapolis, 1982.

CHAPTER 5

30 Ronald L. Gregory, *Airman* magazine, Washington, DC.

31 Heinemann and Rausa, *Combat Aircraft Designer, op cit.*

32 Charles R. Shuford to the author, 26 January 1998.

CHAPTER 6

33 Report, United States Atlantic Fleet, Attack Squadron Five Baker, *Squadron History* for Quarter Ending 30 September 1947, VA-5B/A9-3,11/JGH/JAW, Serial 220, dated 1 October 1947. National Archives, College Park, MD.

34 Report, United States Atlantic Fleet, Attack Squadron Five Baker, *Squadron History* for Quarter Ending 31 March 1948, VA-5B/A9-3, 11/JGH/ISN, Serial 47–48, dated 1 April 1948. National Archives, College Park, Maryland.

35 Reports Attack Squadron Six Baker, *Squadron History*, various dates from quarter ending 31 September 1947 to quarter ending 31 March 1948. VA6B/A9-3(S)/JMM/grp, various dates. National Archives, College Park, Maryland.

36 *See* Lieutenant-Commander Glen B. Butler, USN, *Squadron Diary* for quarter ending 31 December 1947, dated 1 January 1948. *Op cit.*

37 This section is based upon US Naval Air Test Center, Patuxent River, Maryland, *Report of the Flight Test Division on Service Acceptance and Production Inspection Trials of the Model AD-1 Airplane – Final Report*, conducted for the Board of Inspection and Survey, Project No. TED No. BIS 2191, October 29 1948; US Naval Air Test Center, Patuxent River, Report of Flight Test Division, *Temperature Survey Phase of Service Acceptance and Production Inspection Trials for the Models XBT2D-1 and AD-1 airplanes*, Final Report, Project No. TED No. BIS 2192, November 30 1948; US Naval Air Test Center, Patuxent River, Report of Electronics Test Division on *Radio Interference Tests on the Airborne Electronic Equipment installed in the XBT2D-1 Airplane – BuNo 09092*, Part 4, conducted for Board of Inspection and Survey, Project No TED No. BIS 2177, 14 November 1947; and Interim *Report on Investigation of Instrument Flight Techniques and Procedures for Naval Combat Aircraft to Establish Standards for Use with GCA*, INSURV, Naval Air Warfare Center Aircraft Division, Patuxent River.

CHAPTER 7

38 Now Kern County Airport No. 8.

39 For details of this, *see* Peter C. Smith, *Aichi D3A1/2 Val*, Crowood Aviation Series, 1999.

40 *See History of A.E.W.*, Admiralty Memorandum 1966.

41 *See USAF, Flight Manual*, Series A-1E/G/H/J Aircraft, T.O. 1A-1E-1, dated 30 April 1971, USAF, Washington, DC, 1972.

42 In the 1960s, the Royal Navy fought, and lost, exactly the same battle for its carrier. Similar battles went against the Navy in the early Thatcher years, and only the Falklands War brought belated understanding to Whitehall. Currently, new carriers of a reasonable size are due to be built again.

CHAPTER 8

43 'Striking Force' was the original term replaced by 'Fast Carrier Force' on 25 August, and later by 'Task Force 77'.

44 *See* Commander Malcolm W. Cagle, USN, & Commander Frank A. Manson, US Navy, *The Sea War in Korea*, Annapolis, 1957.

45 Ibid.

46 USS *Princeton*, (CV-37) Combat Reports, July 1951, Naval Historical Center, Washington, DC.

47 *See* Peter C. Smith, *Ship Strike*, Shrewsbury, October 1998.

48 *See* Peter C. Smith, *Pedestal; the Malta Convoy of August 1942*, Manchester, 1999.

49 USS *Boxer* (CV-21), Combat Reports, August–September 1952, Naval Historical Center, Washington, DC.

50 Ibid.

51 *See* the article *Including a Sink*, pp10 of *Naval Aviation News*, December 1952 issue.

52 *See* General Mark W. Clark, US Army, *What Kind of Air Support Does the Army Want?* Article in *Air Force Magazine*, Washington, DC, December 1950, Vol. 33, No. 3.

CHAPTER 9

53 Quoted in *Combat Forces Journal*, Washington, DC, Vol. 1, No. 12, July 1951.

53A Frank C. Kleager to the Author, 8 January 1999.

53B Master Sgt. Fred G. Braitsch, Jr. *Skyraiders* article in *Leatherneck* magazine, 1952.

CHAPTER 10

54 Admiral Sir John Treacher, KCB, RN, to the author, 19 October 1998.

55 Ibid.

56 Captain D. H. Frazer, RN, to Arthur Pearcy, RNAS Culdrose, 530/6/7A, dated 4 May 1970.

57 Lieutenant-Commander P.G.W. Morris, RN, Rtd, to the author, 6 November 1998.

58 'Bellhop' was the name given to the relay link that enabled the aircraft to pass the radar picture directly to a display in the carrier's operation room, enabling a qualified 'Direction' officer to control the fighter interception. Admiral Treacher recalled that, 'In practice it proved extremely difficult to maintain a clear link and the proven ability of the aircrew to carry out this duty resulted in little use. However, it was often of considerable help in compiling a long-range surface plot for the ship.' (Admiral Sir John Treacher to the author, 21 October 1998.)

59 For more detail of the Royal Navy's AEWs, down to itemized individual aircraft histories, *see* the thorough research of the British Aviation Research Group's Naval Aviation Research Section, which produced the Super-Monograph booklet, Mo. 2 (S) A *History of the Douglas Skyraider AEW.1* in 1974.

CHAPTER 11

60 *See Quonset Scout*, 9 March 1959.

61 'Gravel' was a particularly insidious weapon that was most effective against guerrilla forces, who generally moved around under cover of darkness. On the ground, the CBU dried out to look like small rocks or large muddy stones, which were very hard to detect.

62 *See* Report of Carrier Air Group 5, USS *Philippine Sea* (CV-45) on action of 26 July 1954, Commander George Duncan, USN.

CHAPTER 12

63 This chapter is based upon the US Navy *AD Training Manual, Ordnance Delivery section*, supplied to the author by the Naval Historical Centre, Washington Navy Yard, DC. Further reference should be made to: NAVAER 11-75-513, *Aircraft Sighting Data for AD Aircraft*; the *Delivery Handbook for AD-6 and AD-7 Aircraft* (OPDEVFOR Report); the *Final Report on Project OP/V219/X22*; and *Special Weapons Delivery Handbook* for AD-6 and AD-7 Aircraft.

64 *See Vengeance!*, op cit.

65 *See* Peter C. Smith, *Impact! The Dive Bomber Pilots Speak*, London and Annapolis, 1981.

66 Emphasis in the original syllabus.

67 A line through the bull's-eye parallel to the direction of dive.

68 Even this was exceeded in service, the record being set by Captain William Nyburg, USN. Flying an AD-4N with VC-33 from the carrier USS *Midway* (CVA-41) in the Mediterranean, he clocked up over 14 hours airborne on an exercise and landed back aboard with 26lb of fuel left.

CHAPTER 14

69 *See* VA-25 Combat Report, 20 June 1965, National Archives, College Park, MD.

70 Chuck Mullaney to the author, 21 August 1998.

71 Chuck Mullaney to the author, 18 September 1998.

72 Chuck Mullaney to the author, 21 August 1998.

73 *See* VA-176, Combat Report, dated 9 October 1966, National Archives, College Park, MD.

74 Chuck Mullaney to the author, 18 September 1998.

CHAPTER 15

75 Some stories, probably apocryphal, tell of Skyraiders that actually got airborne for a brief period with their wings still folded! One such incident is alleged to have taken place at Charlestown, Rhode Island Naval Auxiliary Station's runway 22, in 1949, when an AD-2 is reputed to have attained an altitude of 250ft in this condition, before stalling and crashing. An AD-4N belonging to VC-35 is reputed to have reached the same height from the K-18 airstrip at Kangnung, Korea. In both incidents, the aircrew survived. A third case originated from the Marines, also during the Korean War, and was reported to have taken place at the K-9 airstrip.

76 Sadly, after his early retirement from the service due to injuries, William A. Jones was killed in a plane crash at Woodbridge, Virginia, November 1969.

77 Currently known as Ho Chi Minh City.

78 *See* Kenneth Sams, *Tactical Air Support – Balancing the Scales in Vietnam*, Air Force Magazine, August 1965.

79 Ibid.

80 For more detail, *see* Earl H. Tilford, Jr, *Search and Rescue in Southeast Asia*, Chapter 5 *Son Tay to Cease Fire 1970–73*, USAF in Southeast Asia,

Centre for Air Force History Study, Washington, DC, 1992. Also Benjamin F. Schemmer, *The Raid*.

81 Some authors claim that the Skyraiders carried SMART bombs on this raid, but there is no officially released information to confirm this.

CHAPTER 16

82 For a more complete account of the VNAF, *see* Robert C. Mikesh, *Flying Dragons*; The South Vietnamese Air Force, Osceola and London, 1988.

83 Ibid. Robert Mikesh states that the original idea was for US Navy personnel to pilot these Skyraiders, unofficially, while 'on leave', in a similar manner to General Claire Chennault's much-hyped 'Flying Tigers' outfit in Burma and China in the early 1940s. However, this idea was quickly dropped.

84 Ibid.

85 *See* Eugene M. Zukert, *Air Force Magazine*, August 1946, Washington, DC.

86 Commander Stephen J. Riordan, USN, Rtd, to the author, 30 August 1998.

87 From *Journal of Military Assistance*, No. 118, 1972, Washington, DC.

88 Some sources state that the full number of Skyraiders supplied to the VNAF was 308.

89 *See* US Marine Corps, *The Battle for Khe Sanh*, official account History & Museums Divisions Headquarters, US Marine Corps, Washington, DC, 1975.

CHAPTER 17

90 France had already made widespread use of American-built dive bombers, *L'Armée de l'Air* having flown the Vultee A-35B Vengeance in North Africa 1942–1945 (*see* Peter C. Smith, *Vengeance!*, Shrewsbury and Washington, DC, 1986), and also the Douglas A-Banshee, the Army equivalent of the famous SBD, in North Africa and against German forces in northern France near the end of the Second World War. Its naval air arm the *Aéronavale* had used the Douglas SBD in a similar combat rôle in North Africa and mainland France, 1944–1945, as well as in Indo-China after the war. (*See* Peter C. Smith, *Douglas SBD Dauntless*, Ramsbury, 1996.) The French Navy had later imported batches of Curtiss SB2C Helldivers, which it flew from both carriers and land bases during the final stages of the war against the Viet-Minh, culminating in the Battle of Dien Bien Phu. The Helldivers' outstanding contribution is fully documented in Peter C. Smith, *Jungle Dive Bombers at War*, London & Washington DC, 1985, and *Curtiss SB2C Helldiver*, Ramsbury, 1997.

CHAPTER 18

91 Lt-Cdr L. William Dilts, USN, Rtd, to the author, 27 September 1998.

92 Lt-Cdr Dilts' emphasis to the author.

93 Charles R. Shuford to author, 11 November 1998.

94 On the East Coast, VA-176 still flew a few Skyraiders for several weeks longer, so, officially, these were the last Skyraiders in Navy operational service.

CHAPTER 19

95 Reproduced in *Popular Aviation*, May/June 1967 edition.

Index